CLASSICS FR

A Table in the Wilderness

Love Not the World

What Shall This Man Do?

This omnibus edition first published 2000.

ISBN 0 85476 868 8

Published by
KINGSWAY PUBLICATIONS
Lottbridge Drove, Eastbourne, BN23 6NT, England.
E-mail: books@kingsway.co.uk

Designed and produced for the publishers by
Bookprint Creative Services, P.O. Box 827, BN21 3YJ, England.
Printed in Great Britain.

Reproduced from the original typesetting
of the single-volume editions.

A Table
in the
Wilderness

Daily meditations from
the ministry of

WATCHMAN NEE

KINGSWAY PUBLICATIONS
EASTBOURNE

PREFACE

"I, JOHN, your brother and partaker with you in the tribulation and kingdom and patience which are in Jesus, was in the isle that is called Patmos, for the word of God and the testimony of Jesus. I was in the Spirit on the Lord's day, and I heard behind me a great voice, as of a trumpet saying, What thou seest write in a book." We sometimes wish God would speak thus again, perhaps through a servant of His incarcerated in some twentieth-century prison cell, to grant us, in this day of heightened spiritual conflict, some new flash of divine light upon our road ahead.

Along with many other faithful servants of Jesus Christ in modern China, Nee To-sheng, or Watchman Nee as he likes to be called, is in fact so situated. But from such as he no recent writings are of course available, and this book contains none. It is derived once again from his earlier ministry of the Word in days when God was using him widely in that land for the salvation of souls and the building and spread of His Church and Kingdom.

Yet we have no reason to believe that the author's thoughts on this theme are any different now from the day when he wrote: "John's first vision was not of events but of Jesus Christ Himself. A knowledge of coming events will only stimulate our curiosity. Even John the beloved disciple must first have a sight of his eternal Lord that shattered him to the dust. Only such a sight creates warriors. Not till we see Him thus are we equipped for conflict. For Christ is the answer to all our questions. Get clear first about Him, and we shall know all we need to know about 'things to come'. He is the risen and victorious King of kings. All the ensuing events are the outcome of His being that."

Let us follow this lead as, day by day, we share the author's meditations on the glories of Christ. If by them we can be fortified to meet the challenge of our times, then the human history which lies behind this book will not have been in vain.

In addition to much fresh material from private sources, this collection includes some extracts from earlier published books and booklets.

Unless otherwise indicated, Scripture quotations are from the English Revised Version of 1885.

ANGUS I. KINNEAR

JANUARY 1st

*Looking up to heaven, he blessed and brake the loaves; and
he gave to the disciples to set before them.* Mark 6. 41.

Surely the one fundamental need in our life and service for God is the blessing of God upon it. No other need exists. What do we mean by blessing? Blessing is the working of God where there is nothing to account for His working. For instance, you calculate that a penny should buy a pennyworth. But if you have not paid your penny, and God has given you ten thousand pennyworth, then you have no basis for your calculations. When five loaves provide food for five thousand and leave twelve baskets of fragments—when, that is to say, the fruit of our service is out of all proportion to the gifts we possess, that is blessing. Or, to be rather extreme, when, taking account of our failures and weaknesses, there should be no fruit at all from our labours, and still there is fruit—that is blessing. Blessing is fruit out of all relation to what we are, results that are not just the working of cause and effect. Blessing comes when God works wholly beyond our reckoning, for His Name's sake.

JANUARY 2nd

*O LORD, our Lord, How excellent is thy name in all the
earth!* Psalm 8. 1 and 9.

In an hour when men are blaspheming the Lord's name, the psalmist can only exclaim in wonder at its greatness. Though himself a poet, he is at a loss for words to express its worth. All he can do is cry "How excellent!" And this unspeakable excellence is "in all the earth". Here, surely is an echo of Genesis 1, where all God beheld "was very good". But having begun thus, the writer concludes his psalm with an identical tribute to the excellent Name, and this without so much as a mention of the Fall of man. Had *we* been writing, we would have felt bound to bring that in. But God is unchanging, and to the psalmist even Adam's sin could not reverse His intention that in the end *man* should "have dominion". For at this point the Lord Jesus steps in. It is Hebrews 2 that illumines Psalm 8. He is that Man, and He has already dealt with sin. In Him all God's desire is realized, and *He is related to us*. There is no deviation in the ways of God: they go straight forward. "O Lord, how excellent!"

JANUARY 3rd

Buying up the opportunity, because the days are evil.
Ephesians 5. 16 mg.

In God's appointed course for you, it may be that today was to have been the greatest day of your life; yet you would let it slip as if it were any other day. The man whose today is like his yesterday lacks a sense of God's timings. No servant of the Lord should be content with present attainment; for to be satisfied with what is, is to be a loser of opportunities.

Let us suppose that on January 3rd the Lord puts it into my heart to go and seek out a certain person who, in His providence, is destined to become five years hence a mighty instrument in His hands for the salvation of souls. To obey may be the greatest single act of service in my life. But suppose on this day I am afraid of the cold, or something equally trivial, and do not go. I have let slip an opportunity, and perhaps lost thereby a powerful instrument for God. And the trouble is, such occasions do not wait for us. They pass swiftly by. So when God moves, let us move with Him. No divinely sent opportunity must elude us.

JANUARY 4th

Working together with him we intreat also that ye receive not the grace of God in vain. 2 Corinthians 6. 1.

God has saved us for Himself. "I press on," says Paul, "if so be that I may apprehend that for which also I was apprehended of Christ Jesus." We were not apprehended for eternal salvation only, but for a quite definite purpose now: to be God's fellow-workers. What is His work today? It is to sum up all things in Christ; to leave no odds and ends of any kind in the universe out of harmony with His exalted Son. How can I cooperate with God? How can I even touch so great a work? I do not know; but with Paul, I want above all things to apprehend that.

JANUARY 5th

By the grace of God I am what I am. 1 Corinthians 15. 10.

Has the manner of God's working in relation to your own life come home to you? Have you not been arrested by the way in which He has moved, choosing you out from multitudes around you and making you His own? Oh, I think of it often. When I was saved I was a student. I had over four hundred fellow students, and out of all that number God's choice lighted on me. How could it have come about? I was one of a large clan, and out of the whole clan God chose me. How could it happen? When we think of the marvellous ways by which His grace reached us we fall down before Him in adoration and acknowledge that He is God, He alone.

You ask why He saved you? Let me tell you that He saved you because it was His delight to save you. Because He wanted you, He chose you and brought you to Himself. So there is nothing for you to say, nothing for you to do, nothing but just to worship Him.

JANUARY 6th

Thou preparest a table before me in the presence of mine enemies: thou hast anointed my head with oil; my cup runneth over. Psalm 23. 5.

Our brother Paul made a great and noble statement to the Philippians. To these who, in material things, were almost his sole supporters he dared to say: "I have all things and abound." Paul gave no hint of need, but took the position of a wealthy child of a wealthy Father, and he had no fears that by so doing he might discourage further supplies. It may be quite in order for an apostle to say to an unbeliever who is himself in distress: "Silver and gold have I none." It would never do for him to say the same thing to believers ready and eager to respond to any appeal for help. It dishonours the Lord when a representative of His discloses needs that would provoke pity on the part of his hearers. If we have a living faith in God, we shall always make our boast in Him.

JANUARY 7th

If, while we were enemies, we were reconciled to God through the death of his Son, much more, being reconciled, shall we be saved by his life. Romans 5. 10.

God makes it quite clear in His Word that to every human need He has but one answer: His Son Jesus Christ. In all His dealings with us He works by taking *us* out of the way and substituting Christ in our place. The Son of God died instead of us for our forgiveness; He lives instead of us for our deliverance. So we can speak of two substitutions: a Substitute on the Cross who secures our forgiveness and a Substitute within who secures our victory. It will help us greatly, and save us from much confusion, if we keep constantly before us this fact, that God will answer all our questions in one way only, namely, by showing us more of His Son.

JANUARY 8th

There is the sound of abundance of rain. 1 Kings 18. 41.

How utterly Elijah ventured everything on his God! For three and a half years there had been a nation-wide drought, and water was very scarce indeed. Yet he insisted it be poured lavishly on the sacrifice that was to vindicate Jehovah. "What! squander our precious reserves of water, with no rain in sight?" "Pour it on," said Elijah. "Do it a second time; do it a third!" And not content with that, he himself took a hand in filling the surrounding trench with water.

If we too are to see God vindicated, we must bring what we have and let it go to Him. "But what will happen if rain doesn't come?" you protest. "I must hold on to the water I have." God forbid! That way lies drought and barrenness. Let it go to Him! What you lose will be nothing when compared to His abundance of rain.

JANUARY 9th

Let the saints exult in glory; let them sing for joy upon their beds. Psalm 149. 5.

Here is a picture of Christians who are truly in the enjoyment of Christ's victory. They repose triumphant on their beds, joyously at rest in Him. Consider what this position signifies. Their backs are to the earth, setting the world behind them as it were, while their faces are up to heaven, keeping eternal values always in their view. Such "beds" as theirs are no mere couches of ease, but platforms of effective service. Are you perhaps forced to lie in bed? May the high praises of God still be in your mouth!

JANUARY 10th

Why do the nations rage? Psalm 2. 1.

The answer is supplied at once. It is because "the rulers take counsel together against the Lord, and against his anointed". However violent the hostility between them, world governments are at heart united on one thing: they are against the reign of Christ. We look upon the nations as some of them bad, some good; but Scripture points us to the "prince of this world" behind them all. Prompted by him, earth's rulers today seek only absolute freedom from the sanctions imposed by the law of Christ. They want no more love, no more humility, no more truth. "Let us break their bands asunder," they cry, "and cast away their cords from us."

At this point alone in all Scripture is God said to laugh. His King is already on His holy hill! The early Church was very much aware of Christ's dominion. More than ever today do we need to remember it. Soon, maybe in our lifetime, He will shepherd the nations with a rod of iron. Our task is to plead with men to "be wise"; to "put their trust in Him".

JANUARY 11th

Yet I will rejoice in the Lord, I will joy in the God of my salvation. Habakkuk 3. 18.

When the Galilean boy brought his bread to Jesus, what did Jesus do with it? He broke it. God will always break what is offered to Him. He breaks what He takes, then blesses and uses it to meet men's needs. Is not this true to your experience and mine? You give yourself to the Lord, and at once everything goes so badly wrong that you are tempted to find fault with His ways. To persist in such an attitude is to be broken, yes indeed, but to what purpose? You have gone too far for the world to use you, but you have not gone far enough for God. This is the tragedy of many a Christian. Do we want Him to use us? Then day by day let us go on giving to Him, not finding fault with His methods, but accepting His handling of us with praise and expectation.

JANUARY 12th

These were purchased from among men, to be the first fruits unto God and unto the Lamb. Revelation 14. 4.

My home province of Fukien is famous for its oranges. I would say (though doubtless I am prejudiced) that there are none like them anywhere in the world. As you look out on the hills at the beginning of the orange season, all the groves are green. But if you observe more carefully you will see, scattered here and there on the trees, golden oranges already showing up. It is a beautiful sight to see the flecks of gold dotted among the dark green trees. Later the whole crop will ripen and the groves will turn to gold, but now it is these firstfruits that are gathered. They are carefully hand-picked, and it is they that fetch the top market-prices, often as much as three times the price of the harvest.

All Christians will reach ripeness somehow, we are assured. But the Lamb seeks firstfruits for His hour of supreme demand.

JANUARY 13th

Abram said unto Lot, Let there be no strife, I pray thee, between me and thee, and between my herdmen and thy herdmen; for we are brethren. Is not the whole land before thee? Genesis 13. 8f.

To Abram, newly returned from his misguided venture to Egypt, how precious must have seemed the land which God had given him! Now however he was to learn an important new lesson, namely, not to grasp at its possession. "But surely," he might have reasoned, "so precious a gift ought to be seized and held fast at all costs!" And so do we reason when God gives us His gifts. But Abram saw that he must relinquish his grip. His nephew Lot should be given first choice of all he wanted.

This is a lesson we must all learn. Can we trust God to keep for us what He has given, never laying hold on it ourselves in our natural desire for possession? What God gives, he *gives*! We need not struggle to retain it. Indeed if we grasp it fearfully and hold on, we may risk losing it. Only what we have let go in committal to Him becomes in fact really ours.

JANUARY 14th

Joseph is a fruitful bough, a fruitful bough by a fountain; his branches run over the wall. The archers have sorely grieved him, and shot at him, and persecuted him: but his bow abode in strength. Genesis 49. 22 f.

Of the many typical servants of God in the Old Testament, Joseph is perhaps the most perfect. Yet while Scripture reveals no apparent flaw in his character, we know well that his was no easy pathway. When did his troubles begin? Surely with his dreams. They represent spiritual vision. In them he saw what God would do, and his own place in the divine plan. It was his dreams that started things off, for he saw what his brothers could not see. "This dreamer," they called him, and plotted his downfall. So he was sold for a servant and lay in chains of iron (Psalm 105. 17 f.). Yet Joseph could survive it all to become at length God's means of fulfilling a mighty purpose for His people. He stands firm to the end who can *see*.

JANUARY 15th

*Jehovah-jireh: as it is said to this day, In the mount of the
Lord it shall be provided.* Genesis 22. 14.

The only question Isaac is ever said to have asked of
his own accord was "Where is the lamb for a burnt offering?"
The answer was categorical: "God will provide." This is
typical of Isaac, whose privilege as heir was simply to receive
what was freely bestowed by his father. He did not have to dig
wells; the most required of him was to re-open those his father
had dug. Nor indeed had he any say in his own marriage; he
was not consulted about the woman, and was not expected to
make any efforts to seek her out. Even the tomb in which he
was buried had already been purchased by his father.

We too, like Isaac, have been born into a wealthy home.
What God our Father has provided for us, we are expected to
receive. The God of Isaac is our God, and is He not God the
Giver?

JANUARY 16th

*Whosoever shall call on the name of the Lord shall be
saved.* Acts 2. 21.

How is this possible? Because God has fulfilled that
other prophecy of Joel, that "I will pour forth my Spirit upon
all flesh". Because the Holy Spirit has been poured out upon
all mankind, the merest cry from the sinner to God is enough.

No preacher of the Gospel is of much use unless he believes
this. The Holy Spirit's proximity to the sinner is vital to our
preaching. God in the heavens is too far beyond man's reach.

But "Say not in thy heart, who shall ascend into heaven? that is, to bring Christ down: . . . The word is nigh thee." I always believe the Holy Spirit is upon a man when I preach Christ to him, just as He was upon the waters at the creation. He is waiting to bring Christ into his life. His ministry is like the daylight. Open the window-shutters even a little, and it floods in and illumines the whole interior. Let there be but a cry from the heart to God, and in that instant the Spirit enters and begins His transforming work of conviction, repentance and faith—the miracle of new birth.

JANUARY 17th

Repent ye, and be baptized every one of you in the name of Jesus Christ unto the remission of your sins: and ye shall receive the gift of the Holy Ghost. Acts 2. 38.

Suppose I went into a book-shop, selected a two-volume book, and having put down the price, walked out of the shop carelessly leaving one volume on the counter. When I discovered the oversight, what should I do? I should go straight back to recover the forgotten volume, but I should not dream of paying anything for it. I should simply remind the shopkeeper that both volumes were duly paid for, thank him again for the second one, and without further ado march happily out of the shop with my possession under my arm. Would you not do the same under the same circumstances?

But you *are* under the same circumstances. If you have fulfilled the conditions you are entitled to two gifts, not just one. You have already taken the remission of your sins. Why not just come, and if you have never done so, thank Him for the gift of the Holy Ghost *now*?

*It was the good pleasure of God . . . to reveal his Son in
me.* Galatians 1. 15 f.

I would not, if I could, exchange places with the
disciples, even on the Mount of Transfiguration. The Christ
with whom they lived was a Christ limited by time and space.
Was He in Galilee? Then He could not be found in Jerusalem.
Was He in Jerusalem? Then men sought Him in vain in
Galilee. But today Christ is limited neither by time nor space,
for He lives in the power of an endless life, and the Father has
been pleased to reveal Him in my heart. He was with them
sometimes; He is with me always. They knew Him then after
the flesh, saw Him, touched Him, lived with Him in the
closest contact. "Now know we him so no more", and yet I
know Him in truth, for I know Him as God is pleased He
should be known. Has He not given me the spirit of wisdom
and revelation in the knowledge of Him?

*Wherefore, O King Agrippa, I was not disobedient unto
the heavenly vision.* Acts 26. 19.

What called forth Paul's lifelong consecration of
himself was that flash of light from heaven. The obedience
sprang from the vision. For while it remains true that all self-
committal to God is precious to Him, blind self-committal
may not serve Him very far. There is, I think, a difference between the initial, pure but uninstructed consecration that

follows our conversion and that further giving of ourselves that may spring out of a seeing of the plan of God. Upon the one, based as it is on *our* salvation, He may not at once make severe demands. But when He opens His heart to reveal to us what *He* wants done, and when having asked for our willingness He receives our fresh response, then it is that His demands upon our giving intensify. We have pledged our word on the basis of a new understanding, and He takes us anew at our word. Hereafter all we have must go into it, all the way.

JANUARY 20th

When the cloud was taken up from over the tabernacle, the children of Israel went onward. Exodus 40. 36.

Just as all God's speaking to His people in those far-off days was from between the cherubim of glory, so all His leading of them onward was by means of that same glory. In the cloud by day and the fire by night the glory of God appeared, and by it they moved. For us, too, all revelation of God's will issues from His glory. See the glory of God in relation to any matter and we have discovered God's leading in regard to it. You ask me "Is this His will? Is that?" I reply by asking in turn, "Is God's glory resting there?" Discern that, and you need wait for nothing further. For the divine glory itself expresses the divine will. Guidance is thus simply a matter of correspondence to that. Where God's glory rests we need not ask the way.

JANUARY 21st

Go not up, for the Lord is not among you; that ye be not smitten down before your enemies. Numbers 14. 42.

There is always the serious possibility that God will change His mind. This fact should keep us in humble fear before Him. For if there is something in us which resists His will, God may be compelled to modify His orders to us, as He did to Israel. It is true they acknowledged they had sinned, but they were wrong in thinking they could then proceed as though nothing had altered. It had. In such a situation it is folly to hold blindly on to something the Lord gave us twenty years ago—or even last year. We must live in today, and hold on *to* God. It is the present relationship that is vital. Why, even Moses found his course redirected when he failed God. But bowing to God's present will he was blessed, whereas the Israelites who tried to ignore it met only disaster. Has something in me altered God's mind? Let me then be open to His adjustment. One day He will restore.

JANUARY 22nd

Alas, my master! how shall we do? 2 Kings 6. 15.

When God works His miracle, we have to laugh at our own foolishness. If we still persist in worrying and planning, then we are no disciples of His. Many, I fear, never see God work for them because they always have a way out— some friend perhaps, who might help a little if God does not! Most to be pitied are those who, brought to a supreme crisis, still find an avenue of escape. For necessity is the foundation for miracles. To escape the one is to miss the other. Great difficulties are meant only to force us out of ourselves into reliance on Him. When there is no way forward or back, then God is able. He has a plan. So do not fear impossibilities. They are of no account to Him. Fall at His feet and wait for Him to act. A miracle is ahead.

JANUARY 23rd

Martha, Martha, thou art anxious and troubled about many things: but one thing is needful. Luke 10. 41f.

Let us be frank: work for the Lord has its attractions. It can thrill you when crowds gather to hear you preach. If instead you are compelled to stay at home, occupied from morning to night with mundane affairs, you soon begin to think: "How meaningless life is! How grand to get out and serve the Lord! If only I were free to go round preaching!"

But that is not spirituality. It may be no more than a yielding to natural preference. Is it not possible that much of our so-called service for Him is simply the pursuit of our own inclinations? We are so restless we cannot bear to stay at home, so we run around doing God's work for our own relief. We may be doing our utmost to serve our brethren, and we may be labouring to save sinners, but one thing is needful. Are we first of all ministering to Him?

JANUARY 24th

The Lord God hath given me the tongue of them that are taught, that I should know how to speak a word in season to him that is weary. Isaiah 50. 4 mg.

Am I afraid to speak without the consciousness that what I utter has come to me here and now from God? Must I be so painfully concerned as to whether or not it is the Spirit who is moving me to say this or that? In demanding to be so conscious that what I say is indeed from God, may I merely be displaying how spiritually poor I am? A wealthy Christian speaks out of the abundance of grace in his life. Waking morning by morning to be taught in God's Word, he amasses spiritual riches on which to draw. Instead of ekeing out a hand-to-mouth existence on special dispensations of grace, he is laying up over the years a permanent overplus, out of which to bring forth things new and old. From such experience he can, if need be, speak the mind of the Spirit without the over-weening consciousness of being God's immediate oracle.

JANUARY 25th

Our God whom we serve is able to deliver us from the burning fiery furnace. Daniel 3. 17.

How does the Church reach her goal? Only by travelling the pathway from pressure to enlargement, from poverty to enrichment. You ask: What do we mean by enlargement through pressure? When three are shut into a furnace and the three become four, that is enlargement through pressure. Some find a furnace rather close quarters for three, so they seek a way of escape; others accept the limitation, and in accepting it, make room for a Fourth. Not to let difficulties shut us out from God, but to let them shut us in to Him, that is enlargement through pressure. Some, through pressure, reach God's end; others come to an end in the pressure. Some die in straitness; others, through straitness, find fulness of life. Some murmur when trials befall, finding in them only restraint, limitation and death; others praise God for the trials, and in doing so discover the pathway to enlargement, liberation and abundance of life.

JANUARY 26th

When Jesus therefore had received the vinegar, he said, It is finished. John 19. 30.

The Christian Faith begins not with a big DO but with a big DONE. Of course our reason protests at this. If we do not get moving, how can we ever reach the goal? What can we attain without effort? How can we ever achieve anything if we do not work for it? But Christianity is a queer business! It begins from rest. If at the outset we try to do anything, we get nothing; if we seek to attain, we miss it all. "It is finished," said Jesus, and Paul opens his letter to the Ephesians with the statement that God *has* blessed us with every spiritual blessing in the heavenly places in Christ. We are invited at the very outset therefore to rest and enjoy what God has done; not to try to attain it for ourselves.

JANUARY 27th

Behold I make a covenant: before all thy people I will do marvels. Exodus 34. 10.

Many of us do not differentiate clearly between the promises of God, the accomplished facts of God (His mighty works), and the covenant of God. Promises are given to encourage faith, but often we cannot rise to God's promises. At times we cannot even lay hold of divine facts; appearances seem to belie them. But when this is so we still have His covenant. And the covenant means more than the promises, more even than the mighty works. It is something God has committed Himself to do. The covenant is a handle given us by God on which faith can lay hold. Morally we have no claim on God. But He has been pleased to bind Himself to a covenant, and having thus pledged Himself to act for us, He is—and I say it reverently—bound to do so. Herein is the preciousness of the covenant. It is this that gives strength to faith when faith is at its weakest.

JANUARY 28th

Whom the Lord loveth he chasteneth, and scourgeth every son whom he receiveth. Hebrews 12. 6.

It seems clear that spiritual vision by itself is not enough to transform a life. Consider Jacob's ladder. Because of his crooked behaviour, Jacob had lost home and possessions. Yet in spite of this God favoured him at Bethel with a vision so marvellous that he was moved to exclaim, "How dreadful is this place!" The promises that accompanied it were full and unconditional. Yet contrast with them the words of his response to God: "If ... if ... if ... then I will...." Even with God he wanted to do a business deal He was the same unchanged Jacob.

Soon, however, he was to become involved with Laban, who was just such another as himself. By this and other means, God took Jacob through years of the most fruitful discipline. The spoilt son of the house became a harshly treated labourer. But His ways are always right, and it was a new Jacob who found his way back to Bethel in the end.

JANUARY 29th

I will be as the dew unto Israel. Hosea 14. 5.

These words describe the beginning of everything in the experience of God's children. Dewfall is altogether vital to the life and growth of trees and flowers; and to us the Lord Himself promises to be as the dew. Everything in our life as Christians comes down to us from Christ as source. He is made unto us wisdom, righteousness, holiness—yes, everything, and there is no human need that we shall find unmet as we receive Him, nor indeed will anything be given to us as a separate gift apart from Him.

"I will be as the dew," He affirms, and in the next half of the verse Hosea shows how life with this as its foundation takes on a mysterious dual character. In it the blossom of the lily is wonderfully linked with the roots of the cedar: frail beauty and massive strength united in a single plant. Such miracles are wrought by heaven's dewfall alone.

JANUARY 30th

He shall blossom as the lily, and cast forth his roots as Lebanon. Hosea 14. 5.

Here united in the child of God are two contrasting characters. Above ground, as it were, is the simple unsophisticated life of trust and faith represented by the lily of God's planting. That is what men see. Yet buried deep down out of sight, giving to this frail plant a wholly unsuspected strength, are the massive roots of the cedar. Here surely is the paradox of a life in which the Cross is known. Outwardly it is fragile as the lily blooming on the earth, but secretly there is a hundred times more below ground.

This is the test. How much of my life is seen? When men look on the surface, have they seen the whole, or is there something more? Have I in the unseen a secret history with God? Men take account only of the lily blooming in its weakness. God is concerned with the roots, that they shall be cedarlike in strength.

JANUARY 31st

I am as strong this day as in the day that Moses sent me; as my strength was then, even so is my strength now, for war and to go out and to come in. Joshua 14. 11.

It is a distressing fact that some of us who have proved God's saving power yet doubt His power to keep. Do we not realize that He who is the Giver of grace is the One also who maintains us in His grace? Look at Caleb. Strong as he had been in the day Moses sent him to spy out the land, he was no less strong now as he uttered these words. Moreover what had proved sufficient for the ordinary demands of daily life was equal too to the special stresses of war. Hard years had intervened; yet his vigour at eighty-five was no less than at forty. There is but one explanation of his experience, as indeed there will be of ours at the end. He had been kept by the power of God.

FEBRUARY 1st

Rejoice alway; . . . in everything give thanks. 1 Thessalonians 5. 16.

How is this possible? How can we rejoice amid difficulties? Where does that joy come from? We cannot manufacture it, for if we have not got it we just have not got it! But elsewhere Paul gives us the secret. We are to rejoice in the Lord. We are to live by the joy of Him who, where you or I would have despaired, "rejoiced in spirit" with those triumphant words: "Father . . . it was well-pleasing in thy sight!" (Luke 10. 21). His joy is yours. Learn to live by it above your troubles. When tempted to be cast down, look up and ask yourself, Has the Lord lost His joy today? Only if He has may you be content to be joyless! For it is not a question of your joy, but His. The joy of the Lord is your strength.

FEBRUARY 2nd

*Oh that thou wouldest bless me indeed, . . . and that thou
wouldest keep me from evil, that it be not to my sorrow.*
1 Chronicles 4. 10.

A life of blessing should be the normal life of a
Christian. His one concern must be in no way to obstruct that
blessing's flow. If it is withheld there is a cause, and the explanation is not to be sought in outward things. On one
occasion I observed a Christian worker at variance with another. I listened to him protesting that he had been right, and
indeed there was nothing wrong with what he said nor with
the thing he had done. But I thought to myself: Brother, you
may be perfectly correct, but if our rightness lacks the blessing
of the Lord, what does it profit?

In the work of God, all has failed when the blessing of God
has failed. If we are set on knowing God's favour, we shall find
limitations imposed on the words we utter, and on our whole
manner of life. For rightness is not our goal. The test of our
actions is not, Are they right or wrong? but always and only,
Is the divine blessing upon them?

FEBRUARY 3rd

*Was not Esau Jacob's brother? saith the Lord; yet I loved
Jacob.* Malachi 1. 2.

God has indeed said "Jacob I loved, but Esau I
hated" (Romans 9. 13), and whom He loves He blesses. This
is a very solemn matter. David failed and Abraham made
mistakes, Isaac was weak and Jacob crafty, yet the blessing of
God was with them all. You, today, may be a much better
fellow than Jacob, but without the divine favour where are

you? Learn to set high store by the blessing of God, and to view with suspicion anything that would cause you to forfeit it. Maybe you have been tempted to despise some brother less endowed with gifts than you, and yet God blesses him! And you? Again and again you have done the right thing, and yet His blessing has been withheld. Dare you say God has erred? Beware of taking offence at His choices. Envy of another man's calling can work havoc in our own. Our fruitfulness for God depends upon His blessing, but it is all too possible by our speech, our attitude, our opinions, to arrest its flow. Let us trust God so to deal with us that, without His blessing, we cannot live!

FEBRUARY 4th

The things that are despised, did God choose, yea and the things that are not. 1 Corinthians 1. 28.

The Cross is the greatest leveller in the universe. It brings every one of us to zero. It offers the whole of mankind a new beginning. The difference between a Christian who progresses fast and one who progresses slowly is in the faithfulness and obedience of the former, never in anything he possesses by nature. There are many things too strong and too imposing for God to use. Instead He not only chooses the weak things and the despised: He goes further. The apostle seems almost at a loss to know how to define the things, so weak and despicable in men's eyes, that God elects to use. In a telling phrase he sums them up as the "things which are not".

Do *you* fall in that category? Do not despair. Far from being at a disadvantage as compared with others, you may in fact have the edge over them. For at least you are already at zero, and have not a long way still to go to reach God's starting point! Simply believe Him, and obey.

FEBRUARY 5th

Abraham prayed unto God: and God healed Abimelech,
and his wife, and his maidservants; and they bare children.
Genesis 20. 17.

It is striking evidence of the spiritual life of this man
of God that he could pray for children to be granted to others
while his prayers for his own wife were still unanswered. He
interceded for Abimelech, and God heard.

It is difficult to understand Abraham's reversion to that half-
lie about Sarah being his sister, especially in view of the deep
fellowship with God which had just preceded it. But this time
he discloses that the arrangement made between them dated
right back to Mesopotamia. Some hidden root of unbelief and
fear had lingered through all these years, and now at length
had come to light. At the start of his wanderings Abraham
seems to have feared Sarah might be separated from him. Yet
surely by now he should have known God would take full
responsibility to see this did not happen.

At last, here in Gerar, the lurking fear was dragged out into
the light of day, and slain, leaving Abraham free to pray for
others. He did not pray for Sarah. Now he had no need to.
Immediately after this Isaac was born.

FEBRUARY 6th

When therefore he said unto them, I am he, they went
backward, and fell to the ground. John 18. 6.

On that last night before Calvary, everything seemed
to be going wrong. Betrayal and denial were in the air;
people were hiding, or running away naked in their eagerness

to escape. But to those who had come to take Him Jesus said so peacefully and quietly, "I am he." It was they who were nervous and who fell backward. This inward peace always marked Him. He could sleep through the storm. He could register the touch of faith amidst the jostlings of an impatient crowd, and ask who it was had touched Him. "My peace", He terms it.

This peace, He said, "I leave with you." He did not take it away, for He is here. So the martyrs of old displayed it too. They might be tortured or burnt, but they had about them a quiet dignity none could gainsay. Yes, in the world we shall have our troubles, but we shall have also His peace, which, the apostle Paul affirms, is beyond understanding.

FEBRUARY 7th

Peace I leave with you; my peace I give unto you. John 14. 27.

It is not just a question of peace but of "My peace". It is not only that God gives me peace but that "the peace of God", the deep undisturbedness of God, keeps my heart (Philippians 4. 7). We get troubled when things go wrong, but let us realize something else. God chose this world to be the arena of His plan, the centre of what He has set Himself to do. He had a definite purpose, which Satan came in and interfered with, and yet in spite of that (the implications of which we realize very little) He maintains a deep untroubled peace. He is not afraid to wait another thousand years if need be. *That* is the peace which is given to us.

Paul says the peace of God should be a garrison for my

heart. What does that mean? It means that a foe must first fight through the garrison to reach me. The garrison must be overcome before my heart can be touched. So I dare to be as peaceful as God, for the peace of God—that peace which is keeping God—is keeping me.

FEBRUARY 8th

Christ having come a high priest of the good things to come, . . . through his own blood, entered in once for all into the holy place, having obtained eternal redemption. Hebrews 9. 11 f.

If I would appreciate the value of the Blood of Christ, I must accept God's valuation of it, for the Blood is not primarily for me, but for God. Nothing illustrates this fact so clearly as the account of the Day of Atonement. In Leviticus 16 we read how on that day the blood was taken from the sin offering and brought into the Most Holy Place, and there sprinkled before the Lord seven times. The offering of course was public, in the court of the tabernacle and in full view of the people. But into the Sanctuary itself no man entered save the high priest. Alone he sprinkled the atoning blood there before God, away from the eyes of the men who were to benefit by it. We must be very clear about this. The precious Blood of Christ is in the first place for *God*, not man, to see. A holy and righteous God has accepted it and professed Himself satisfied, and our valuation of it stems from this profound fact.

FEBRUARY 9th

Grace and truth came by Jesus Christ. John 1. 17.

This statement is the key to all that follows in John's Gospel. Right through it you find the same double emphasis, upon truth on the one hand and upon grace on the other. Truth will always make demands, and grace will always be there to meet them. In the incident recorded in Chapter 8 of the woman taken in adultery, truth shines forth. The Lord did not say to her "It is all right; you have not sinned." He did not suggest to the Jews that what she had done was nothing serious, and that He was not deeply concerned about it. No, His words were: "He that is without sin among you, let him first cast a stone at her." The truth was there: she had indeed sinned, and according to the law she should be stoned; but so also was the grace, for when all had departed He turned to her with "Neither do I condemn thee". Throughout the Gospel of John you will find truth is always matched by grace in this way.

FEBRUARY 10th

When Abram was ninety years old and nine, the Lord appeared to Abram, and said unto him, I am God Almighty; walk before me, and be thou perfect. Genesis 17.1.

God did not say this to the strong Abram, he who in Ishmael could produce a son. He waited until His servant was quite incapable, even had he wanted to, of repeating the action. Then, and then only, God came to him with this new unveiling of Himself as God Almighty.

There is no sign that Abram had repented of his action. Rather does it appear that Ishmael was becoming more precious to him. Had he then not realized his error? Had he not sought after God? If indeed he had not, we might say that from a human standpoint there was not much hope for him. Hope, however, depended not so much on whether *he* wanted God but on whether *God* wanted him. And God certainly did! He was still at work in His servant. He had not let him go. "Learn that I am all-powerful," God said, "and then walk in the light of that knowledge." For "be perfect" means, among other things, "be perfect in weakness," letting God Almighty do it all.

FEBRUARY 11th

Unto him that sitteth on the throne, and unto the Lamb, be the blessing and the honour and the glory and the dominion, for ever and ever. Revelation 5. 13.

To worship the creature rather than the Creator is an inbred tendency with us. In this even John himself had to be pulled up. For all the conflict depicted in this book of Revelation turns on this issue. All the war in heaven, all the tribulation on earth, stems alike from Satan's attempt to steal to himself God's praise. But here in Revelation 5 on this great coronation day, all in heaven and earth and beneath the earth and on the sea unite to acclaim Christ as supreme. The chapter closely matches Philippians 2 with its "every knee should bow ... every tongue should confess that Jesus Christ is Lord". The death of the cross has brought this outcome; it is the newly slain Lamb who is worthy.

FEBRUARY 12th

Concerning the work of my hands, command ye me.
Isaiah 45. 11.

Here in Time, God is not free. He does not move His children about like pawns on a board, but has limited Himself to their free choice. Wittingly He has done this, knowing what it will bring Him in the end. In eternity past God was unlimited; there was no second will. Again in eternity future He will be unlimited, for love will have conquered and man's free-will will be one with His. That is His glory.

But now, in Time, God has limited Himself. Only as men of freewill are with Him today can He accomplish His purpose. And freewill means I can obey or not, as I choose. It is as though God had put at our disposal a locomotive of immense power, and we were told to lay the track. The power is there, and the destination is planned, but the engine does not control the rails. It is the rails that have power to limit the engine. "Ask whatsoever ye will, and it shall be done unto you." How great is our responsibility!

FEBRUARY 13th

What things soever ye shall bind on earth shall be bound in heaven: and what things soever ye shall loose on earth shall be loosed in heaven. Matthew 18. 18.

"What things soever": these are precious words. Here heaven is measured by earth, for there is always more power in heaven than the measure of our asking; there is always more to be loosed or bound in heaven than we ask down here. Why do we seek deliverance from sin? Why are we always crying to God for enduement with power? To pray "Thy will be done in me" is a good beginning no doubt, but we must go on to "Thy will be done *on earth*". The children of God today are taken up with far too small things, whereas their prayer is intended for the release of heaven's mighty acts. Prayer for myself or my own immediate concerns must lead on to prayer for the Kingdom. In this the Church should be heaven's outlet, the channel of release for heaven's power, the medium of accomplishment of God's purpose. Many things have accumulated in heaven because God has not yet found His outlet on earth; the Church has not yet prayed.

FEBRUARY 14th

She hath wrought a good work upon me. Matthew 26. 10.

When the Lord returns and we see Him face to face, I trust that we shall all pour out our treasures at His feet. But today—what are we doing today?

Several days after Mary broke the alabaster box and poured the ointment on Jesus' head, there were some women who went early in the morning to anoint His body. Did they do it? Did they succeed in their purpose on that first day of the week? No, He was gone! There was only one soul who in fact succeeded in anointing the body of the Lord, and it was Mary, who anointed Him beforehand. All the others were too late, for He had risen. The pressing question, then, is: What am I doing to the Lord today?

FEBRUARY 15th

Blessed be the God and Father of our Lord Jesus Christ.
1 Peter 1. 3.

This exclamation occurs in the writings of both Peter and Paul, and is one of those things which, by its spontaneity, displays the true spirit of these men. From it we get a glimpse of the man; and God allows this personal element in the message to come through, because it is never merely a question of what we say but of who we are.

It is our privilege to preach the Word, but no single one of us is God's oracle. We cannot utter His words without bringing to them something personal of our own. Many of us can preach a good message, but one spontaneous sentence of ours has the power to confirm or overthrow it all. "Out of the abundance of the heart the mouth speaketh." Humble or defiant, dealt with by the Cross or still whole and unbroken, the truth must come out, for God cannot use play-actors. Our spirit is revealed in our words.

FEBRUARY 16th

The priests that bare the ark of the covenant of the Lord stood firm on dry ground in the midst of Jordan, and all Israel . . . passed clean over Jordan. Joshua 3. 17.

We must have faith to see all God's people brought into their inheritance. That is His purpose, and it will be carried through. But as a means to realizing that purpose, God needs those willing to step right into death if need be, and to stand there steadfast until all are safely over. Because that little band of priests did so, holding firm with the ark in the place where death threatened, a whole nation passed dryshod clean through Jordan. Not one soul remained behind! Of course it was not they, but the ark of God, that opened the way into a land of promise. Never forget that. But note this too: it was they who took it there and held it there. By their act of faith in standing with the Lord amidst death, others passed into abundant life. Am I ready for this?

FEBRUARY 17th

Now he that stablisheth us with you in Christ, and anointed us, is God. 2 Corinthians 1. 21.

The Lord God Himself has put us in Christ. Our destiny is therefore bound up with His. When preaching in the villages of China one must often use very simple illustrations. I remember once I took up a small book, and into it I put a piece of paper. "Now look carefully," I said. "I take this paper. It has an identity of its own, quite separate from this book. Having no other use for it at the moment I put it into the book. Now I do something with the book. I mail it to Shanghai. I do not mail the paper, but the paper has been put into the book. Then where is the paper? Can the book go to Shanghai and the paper remain here? Can the paper have a separate destiny from the book? No, where the book goes the paper goes. If I drop the book in the river the paper goes too, and if I quickly take it out again I recover the paper also. Whatever experience the book goes through the paper goes through with it, for it is still there in the book." To be in Christ is just like that. It is to be identified with Him in all He has gone through. He was crucified. Then must I *ask* God to crucify me? Never! My Saviour's destiny is already become mine.

FEBRUARY 18th

Through love be servants one to another. Galatians 5. 13.

Legalism is bound to produce pride of heart. To live by the law I must exert my strength of will, often against my own inclinations. Such effort inevitably leads me to despise or pity those who are not trying as hard as I, or who are trying and failing. My very exertions give me a superior feeling that sours me towards them, and even though I keep my feeling to myself, I shall soon find I am too aloof even to pray with those I consider less spiritual. Living by the law leads to this. But God is too big to stereotype His saints. People are not to be conformed to me, but to His death. And that is just as well. For sourness in apples is no mark of maturity! Ripe apples are sweet. If God is really producing something in me I shall find no difficulty in going along with other saints whose history is different from mine.

FEBRUARY 19th

Bring forth quickly the best robe and put it on him. Luke 15. 22.

God is so wealthy that His chief delight is to give. His treasure-stores are so full that it is pain to Him when we refuse Him an opportunity of lavishing those treasures upon us. When the prodigal returned home the father had no word of rebuke for the waste nor of inquiry regarding the substance. He only rejoiced over the opportunity his son's return afforded him for spending more. It was the father's joy that he could find in him an applicant for the robe, the ring, the shoes and the feast; it was his sorrow that in the elder son he found no such applicant. It is a grief to the heart of God when we try to provide things for Him. He is so very, very rich. It gives Him true joy when we just let Him give and give and give again to us. He wants to be the Giver eternally, and He wants to be the Doer eternally. If only we saw how rich and how great He is!

FEBRUARY 20th

Hebron became the inheritance of Caleb, because that he wholly followed the Lord. Joshua 14. 14.

"We are well able to overcome" is the declaration of the man or woman whose confidence in the Lord is unqualified. He believes God's promises are trustworthy, and that because He is with His people, victory over every foe is assured. Do you believe this? Many do, but with a faith that vacillates. They sing their song of praise, and the words are right, but there is something hesitant about the tune. With Caleb it was otherwise. He sang the right words firmly, to the right tune. Listen to their brave, ringing tones:

> *"Let us go up at once and possess it;*
> *For we are well able to overcome."*

He had no doubts whatever about his God. But note too the urgency of that first clause: "Let us go up *at once*!" True faith brooks no delay. One who reckons God faithful to His word declares this not merely by doing His will, but by doing it instantly.

FEBRUARY 21st

We know that the law is spiritual: but I am carnal, sold under sin. Romans 7. 14.

If you have a very clumsy servant and he just sits still and does nothing, then his clumsiness does not appear. If he does nothing all day he will be of little use to you, it is true, but at least he will do no damage that way. But if you say to him: "Now come along, don't idle away your time; get up and do something!" then immediately the trouble begins. He knocks the chair over as he gets up, stumbles over a footstool a few paces further on, then smashes some precious dish as soon as he handles it. If you make no demands upon him his clumsiness is never noticed, but as soon as you ask him to do anything his awkwardness is at once apparent. As with us all, the demands were all right, but the man himself was all wrong! For we are all sinners by nature. The trouble is that without the law we do not know it. So long as God asks nothing of us, all seems to go well. It is when He demands of us something that the occasion is provided for a grand display of our sinfulness, "that through the commandment sin might become exceeding sinful".

FEBRUARY 22nd

I thank God through Jesus Christ our Lord. Romans 7. 25.

"O wretched man that I am! who shall deliver me?" had been Paul's despairing cry. Then in a flash of illumination it changed to this shout of praise.

The first words of the delivered man are most precious: "I

thank God". If someone gives you a cup of water you thank the person who gave it, not someone else. Why did Paul say "Thank God"? Because God was the One who did everything. Had it been Paul who did it, he would have said, "Thank Paul". But he saw that Paul was a "wretched man" and that God alone could meet his need; so he thanked God. God wants to do all, for He must have all the glory. God has done everything on the Cross for our forgiveness and He will do everything in us for our deliverance. In both cases He is the Doer. "It is God that worketh in you. . . ."

FEBRUARY 23rd

And David was afraid of the Lord that day. 2 Samuel 6. 9.

Probably all of us are troubled by this story of the tragic death of Uzzah. David had sinned in ignorance in using a cart to transport the ark of God "which is called by the Name". It seemed a very safe way, but man's ideas, however good, always expose their faultiness. The oxen stumbled, the ark shook, and Uzzah touched it to steady it. He did it warmheartedly, for the glory of God—and he died instantly. No wonder David was troubled!

The ark protected Israel, not Israel the ark. Who ever heard of a forest-guard protecting tigers? No, God is well able to take care of Himself. Many things which God should do, man does; many times when we should look to Him to speak, we speak; we arrange things which we should wait for God to arrange. "Why shouldn't I preach?" we protest, "I want to." This is the iniquity of our ministry. Has none of us been found out here? But praise God, if we confess our sins, He is faithful and righteous to forgive!

FEBRUARY 24th

*When he, the Spirit of truth, is come, he shall guide you
into all the truth.* John 16. 13.

One thing is certain, that revelation will always precede faith. Seeing and believing are two principles which govern Christian living. When we see something God has done in Christ, our spontaneous rejoinder is faith's "Thank You, Lord!". Revelation is always the work of the Holy Spirit, who by coming alongside and opening to us the Scriptures guides us into all the truth. Count on Him, for He is here for this very thing. And when such difficulties as lack of understanding or lack of faith confront you, always address those difficulties directly to the Lord: "Lord, open my eyes. Make this thing clear to me. Help Thou my unbelief!" He will not let such prayers go unheeded.

FEBRUARY 25th

*She opened not the gate for joy, but ran in, and told that
Peter stood before the gate. And they said unto her, Thou
art mad.* Acts 12. 14 f.

Numbers of people have come to me and told of their fears and misgivings even while they have sought to trust the Lord. They have made their requests, they have laid hold of the promises of God, and yet doubts continually arise unbidden. I love to recall that when Peter came back from prison and knocked at the door where the church was at prayer, the believers exclaimed, "It is his angel."
There are people today who claim to have greater faith than those gathered in Mary's house. They are certain God will

send an angel, and every door in the prison will swing open before him. If a gust of wind blows: "There's Peter knocking at the door!" If the rain begins to patter: "There's Peter again!" These people are too credulous, too cock-sure, Their faith is not necessarily the genuine article. For even the most devoted Christian, while exercising a faith which must surely bring an answer from God, knows what it is to have lurking just around the corner the question whether perhaps he might be mistaken.

FEBRUARY 26th

He gave him to be head over all things to the church, which is his body, the fulness of him that filleth all in all. Ephesians 1. 22 f.

Do not look at Christ in heaven as an ideal to be arrived at. See Him as God's gift to you. You feel the things of the world pulling you down, but they can no more pull you down than they can pull Him down. You are just as secure in the heavenlies as Christ is. Do you doubt this? There are some yellow flowers on my desk. I did not enter the room and repeat: "There must be some yellow flowers here, there must be some yellow flowers here," and by some kind of auto-suggestion bring them magically into being! No, they were there all the time. I just opened my eyes and looked!

Our faith is no make-believe. It is based on the eternal facts of what God has done in Christ. If we dare to venture our faith upon those facts, the Holy Spirit is here to prove them true. See ourselves there in Christ, and instead of going down, we are sustained by His power.

FEBRUARY 27th

They looked unto him, and were lightened: and their faces shall never be confounded. Psalm 34. 5.

We need to guard against being over-anxious about the subjective side of spiritual experience, and so becoming turned in on ourselves. May I illustrate this from the electric light? You are in a room and it is growing dark. You would like to have the light on in order to read. There is a reading-lamp on the table beside you. What do you do? Do you watch it intently to see if the light will come on? Do you take a cloth and polish the bulb? No, you get up and cross over to the other side of the room where the switch is on the wall, and you turn the current on. You turn your attention to the source of power, and when you have taken the necessary action there, the light comes on here. Dwell always upon what God has done in Christ, and let Him take care of what He will do in you.

FEBRUARY 28th

Rejoice in the Lord alway: again I will say, Rejoice. Philippians 4. 4.

Persecution soon compelled Paul and Barnabas to leave the group of disciples at Antioch in Pisidia and to move on (Acts 13. 50 ff.). What effect had their early departure upon the infant church? Here was a group of new believers, mere babes in Christ. Did they plead with the apostles to remain awhile and care for their spiritual welfare? "If you leave us now we shall be as sheep without a shepherd. Surely one at least of you can remain behind and look after us! The persecution is so intense, we can never get through without your help." Is this how they reasoned? No, instead of such appeals, how amazing is the Scripture record: "And the disciples were filled with joy and with the Holy Ghost"! There was no mourning when Paul and Barnabas moved on, but great gladness, surely because the apostles' departure meant an opportunity for others to hear the Gospel. But not only so. They themselves were provided for; they were filled with the Holy Ghost.

FEBRUARY 29th

I will put my spirit within you, and cause you to walk in my statutes. Ezekiel 36. 27.

Late one summer I stayed at a hill-resort in the home of a mechanic and his wife, both of whom it was my joy to lead to a simple faith in the Saviour. When the time came for me to return to Shanghai, I left with them a Bible.

During the winter the man was in the habit of taking alcohol with his meals, sometimes to excess. Soon, with the return of the cold weather, the wine reappeared on the table, and, as had now become his custom, he bowed his head to give thanks for the meal. But today no words would come! After one or two vain attempts he turned to his wife. "What is wrong?" he asked. "Why cannot we pray today?" The wife took the Bible, but turned the pages in vain, seeking light on the subject. They could find no explanation, and I was far away. "Just drink your wine," she said; but no, he knew he must give thanks, and could not. "Take it away," he exclaimed at length; and then together they asked a blessing on the meal.

When eventually the man was able to visit Shanghai he told me the story. Using an expression familiar in Chinese: "Brother Nee," he said, "Resident Boss wouldn't let me have that drink!" "Very good," I replied, "You always listen to Resident Boss!"

MARCH 1st

He grew up before him as a tender plant, and as a root out of a dry ground. Isaiah 53. 2.

Its roots are the means whereby a plant is nourished, the channel through which its life is derived. No plant can live without a root-system. Equipped with one it may survive in the most unpromising conditions. Isaiah's words suggest that Jesus Himself did not derive His life and strength from outward circumstances. Nor must we. If necessary we must be able to live without the succour of our brethren in Christ. Even with them around us, we live *with* our fellow-members, we do not live *by* them. The secret source of our life is God alone.

But to live thus "out of a dry ground" means something more. It means that nothing merely circumstantial can destroy us. No drought can wither God's tender plants. Amid barren, even hostile conditions His children are equipped to be "more than conquerors". Their life is Christ Himself.

MARCH 2nd

He is able to guard you from stumbling, and to set you before the presence of his glory in exceeding joy. Jude 24.

Here is a wonderful promise for us who have committed our lives into the hands of God. For our pathway towards "the presence of his glory" conceals many pitfalls, and He undertakes to guard us from these. When do we stumble? When, unaware of any obstruction, we strike our foot on something hidden in our path. This verse assures us that God's preserving grace will operate just there, beyond the realm of our consciousness. If we commit ourselves unreservedly to His care, we need not fear the unknown. We shall marvel to see how again and again God preserves us from dangers of which at the time we were wholly ignorant.

MARCH 3rd

The Lord said unto Abram, Get thee out of thy country . . . unto the land that I will show thee. Genesis 12. 1.

This was the second call to Abram, for the first had come when he was in Mesopotamia "before he dwelt in Haran" (Acts 7. 2). Abram had gone forward from Chaldea, but not, it seems, far enough, and it is a solemn thought that no history is recorded of all the days he spent in Haran. But God persisted with His call. We sometimes hope by procrastination to get Him to modify His demands. He will not do that, for He has never abandoned the goal He set before us years ago. If we have let it slip, God has not.

From God's point of view Haran was little advance on Mesopotamia. Abram might be satisfied that he had made a move, but God had called him *to a land*. All true calling is a high calling. Let us content ourselves with no halfway house. The question is not how far we have gone since we started, but whether our hearts are still set on God's goal.

MARCH 4th

Knowing this, that our old man was crucified with him, that the body of sin might be done away. Romans 6. 6.

For years after my conversion I had been taught to "reckon". But the more I reckoned I was dead to sin, the more alive to sin I clearly was! I simply could not believe myself dead, and I saw no way of producing death. Whenever I sought help from others I was told to read Romans 6. 11, and the more I read Romans 6. 11 and tried to reckon, the further away death was: I could not get at it. In my trouble I said to the Lord, "If I cannot be brought to see this which is so fundamental, I will not preach any more. I *must* be thoroughly clear here." For months I sought and prayed, at times with fasting, but nothing came through.

Then one morning, and it is a morning I shall never forget, as I sat with the Word open and said again, "Lord, open my eyes!" in a flash I *saw* my oneness with Christ. I saw that I was in Him, and that when He died I died. Our old man *was* crucified with Him. Oh it was so real to me! I was carried away with such joy that I longed to go through the streets of Shanghai shouting the news of my great discovery.

MARCH 5th

*Wheresoever the gospel shall be preached . . . that also
which this woman hath done shall be spoken of.*
Mark 14. 9.

Why did the Lord say this? Because the Gospel is
meant to produce this kind of action. This is what the Gospel
is for. The Gospel is not just to satisfy sinners. Praise God, the
sinner has his part. God meets his need and showers him with
blessings; but that is, we may say, a blessed by-product of the
Gospel and not its primary aim. The Gospel is preached in the
first place so that the Lord may be satisfied. But we must remember this, that He will never be satisfied without our
"wasting" ourselves upon Him. Have you ever given too
much to the Lord? May I tell you something? In divine service
the principle of waste is the principle of power. Real usefulness
in the hand of God is measured in terms of waste. Our work
for Him springs from our ministering to Him, and so do all its
fruits.

MARCH 6th

He will tell thee what thou shalt do. Ruth 3. 4.

All Israel were to preserve their family heritage from
the days of Joshua to the coming of Christ; hence the return of
alienated property in the year of Jubilee. And because con-
tinuity of possession required that the original owner have
heirs, hence too the law that if a man died leaving a widow
and no sons, a near relative must take her and preserve the
line. Naomi's case was even worse than that. Widowed, she
was now also too old to bear children. How could her late

husband's inheritance be restored? Her daughter-in-law Ruth was willing, but an alien. Only the aged Boaz was near enough of kin to help. Would he redeem a foreigner? For Ruth's need was not to be met merely by the purchase of her lands. She must be wed. She must *offer herself* to Boaz.

Without the offering up of ourselves to God, redemption is a sterile, empty thing. Boaz commended Ruth, and rightly, for turning aside from the attractions of younger men so as to fulfil God's law, and a glance at her posterity shows how greatly she was in fact rewarded. Consecration to God pays rich dividends.

MARCH 7th

I know thy tribulation, and thy poverty (but thou art rich). Revelation 2. 9.

As we look around us we cannot but sorrow over a tragic lack in the experience of so many Christians. There is so little about their lives to indicate fulness. They have scarcely sufficient for their own needs, much less anything to spare for others. Why are they so poor? Is it because they do not know what the discipline of the Spirit is designed to lead them to? The Psalmist says, "In pressure thou hast enlarged me" (Psalm 4. 1, J. N. Darby trans.). The object of temporal poverty is eternal enrichment. God never intended that pressure and poverty should issue in nothing. His purpose is that all pressure should lead to enlargement, all poverty to enrichment. God's goal for His people is neither continuous straitness nor continuous poverty. For these are never the end; they are only the means to God's end. Straitness is the pathway to expansion; poverty the pathway to wealth.

MARCH 8th

He said unto me, They are come to pass. I am the
Alpha and the Omega, the beginning and the end.
Revelation 21. 6.

"They are come to pass." At long last God's eternal
purpose has been realized. How has this happened? Why does
Scripture so confidently affirm it? Surely because He is the
Alpha and the Omega. God has begun a work, and He will
perfect it. He can do no other than finish what He has set His
hand to, for it is His very nature to do so. He is not only the
beginning, He is also the end. Hallelujah! Our God is the
Omega as well as the Alpha. This assures us that nothing He
has begun to do in us will be left unfinished. God cannot be
withstood by man's incompetence or by Satan's enmity. Sin
is too much for us, but it is not too much for Him. His Name,
which is His own nature, is our guarantee that He will see His
work in us through to its perfect completion.

MARCH 9th

I press on, if so be that I may apprehend that for which also
I was apprehended by Christ Jesus. Philippians 3. 12.

No master has so many servants as our Master; and
for each He has a suitable employment. Even the little maid
was at hand to testify to Naaman in his need. Many of us
murmur against the position God has given us. We want to
do this, but God puts us into that. We have an ambition to
serve Him here, but His plan for us lies elsewhere. When
faced by such apparent reverses, it is well to remember that

God's purpose for us goes back before our conversion, for His foreknowledge has determined our circumstances even before we were born. God never does a thing suddenly; He has always prepared long, long before. So there is nothing to murmur about, nothing to be proud of, in the calling of God. There is also no one of whom to be jealous, for other people's advantages have nothing to do with us. When we look back over life, we bow and acknowledge that all was prepared by God. So there is no need to fear we have missed something. To have this assurance is true rest.

MARCH 10th

Ye behold me: because I live, ye shall live also. John 14. 19.

John's Gospel reflects everywhere the fact that he is writing for the last days. His burden relates to the life of the eternities and to your right relationship thereto. If you go back to that, he implies, all else will follow. He is not occupied with outward and temporal things; his whole concern is that you should get behind these to the Life. Everything now is in disrepair. Go back to the Life that "came down from heaven", and when you get back there, all that threatens to be lost will be preserved. In a sense John has nothing new to offer us that the other New Testament writers have not given us already. He does not take us further, for the furthest point has already been touched by God. The object of the revelation entrusted to John is to bring people back again to that original purpose, by bringing them into a fresh touch with the risen Lord Himself.

MARCH 11th

She said, The glory is departed from Israel; for the ark of God is taken. 1 Samuel 4. 22.

The ark is taken; but the ark can defend itself, as its captors soon learn to their cost. Because it was primarily a testimony to God's own nature, the ark did something to the Philistines that unholy Israel could not do. God seeks instruments for His glory, but when He cannot find them He does the work Himself, and in so doing takes care of His own testimony. He was willing to let His ark be carried off in order to show to all the world that He will not ally Himself with the cause of His people while there is unholiness with them. God's nature and man's unholiness can never be associated, least of all in His own covenant people.

MARCH 12th

I will give unto thee the keys of the kingdom of heaven. Matthew 16.19.

What qualified Peter to become God's mouthpiece, to open the door of faith first to Jews and then to Gentiles? Surely it was that before Peter spoke he had himself been spoken to; for before he could make use of the keys of the Kingdom he must encounter the demands of that Kingdom upon himself.

What does the term "kingdom" mean? Surely it is the realm of a king, the sphere of his authority. Soon after this, in the Mount of Transfiguration, Peter made his brilliant suggestion which would have provided a place for Moses and Elijah alongside the Lord. But in the *Kingdom* you cannot do that!

You cannot have more than one authority. There can only be one Voice. It was to point this lesson that "while he yet spake" the Father broke in with a rebuke which makes it plain that in the Kingdom everything hangs upon the King Himself speaking and upon our paying heed to His words.

MARCH 13th

One is your Teacher. Matthew 23. 8.

Every Christian "disciple" is by definition a learner, and such he should remain. Set out to be a "teacher" of others and you may over-stretch yourself and create only problems in the minds of simple saints. It is such superiority, born of the overconfidence that we *know*, that effectively closes doors. You must be willing to say, "I do not know; God has not shown me." Profess great knowledge and you invite criticism. But people will not be hard on the worker who adopts the attitude: "If you have something to say to me, I am glad to listen, for I too am a disciple of the Lord." "Be not many teachers, my brethren," says James. My counsel to you therefor is that you remain very long a learner.

MARCH 14th

He is our peace, who made both one, and brake down the middle wall of partition. Ephesians 2. 14.

Like a seven-fold cord the unity of the Spirit binds all believers throughout the world. However diverse be their character or circumstances, provided they possess the vital oneness conferred by His indwelling presence, nothing can possibly separate them. Our unity is not based on our appreciation of the truth of oneness, nor is it based on our separating ourselves from all that would possibly contradict our oneness. It rests securely upon the actual fact of our union with Christ, a union wrought by His Cross and made real in our experience by His indwelling Spirit. No basis of unity could be sounder.

MARCH 15th

Hannah prayed, and said: My heart exulteth in the Lord.
1 Samuel 2. 1.

Speaking naturally, this could have been the saddest moment in Hannah's life, for she was saying goodbye to her young son. Here however we shall find no trace of sorrow or self-pity, but only the expression of a heart overflowing with that unique joy which comes to those who give their all to the Lord. With Hannah, it seems, there was a real exercise of soul in relation to the Lord's interests, and the dearest thing in her life was dedicated to those interests. Before Samuel was born she had made her vow to God. During his infancy she had waited for this day. She weaned Samuel, and now, when the moment came and he was given back to God, she found a new joy such as she had never known before, the joy of the fully committed. Her song, from which centuries later that of Mary was to find inspiration, expresses her triumphant joy.

MARCH 16th

Be it unto me according to thy word. Luke 1. 38.

How essential it was that in the virgin Mary the living Word should find a free way if God's purpose in sending it was to be fulfilled! God spoke, and because her faith responded, His miracle took place. Alas, many of us think it quite enough if we are orthodox in doctrine and give unqualified mental assent to the Word of Truth. But unless that Truth is taking effect inwardly, there may really be no great difference between assent to it and dissent from it. The difference only comes when it begins to play a vital, transforming part in a life. How tragic to have a vast knowledge of the Bible, yet little inward experience of its working. If we are to be of use to God in His great purposes it is essential that we respond not merely with our head but with our heart when His Word comes to us in a present, personal way. Can we echo Mary's prayer?

MARCH 17th

God, whose I am, whom also I serve. Acts 27. 23.

It is a great thing when I discover I am no longer my own but His. If the money in my pocket belongs to me, I have full authority over it. But if it belongs to another who has committed it to me in trust, then I cannot buy what I please with it, and I dare not lose it. How many of us dare not use our time or money or talents as we would because we realize they are the Lord's, not ours? How many of us have such a strong sense that we belong to Another that we dare not squander a dollar of our money, or an hour of our time, or any of our mental or physical powers? We are alive unto God, not unto ourselves. Real Christian life begins with knowing this.

MARCH 18th

Wherefore receive ye one another, even as Christ also received you, to the glory of God. Romans 15. 7.

This passage about differing viewpoints in church life begins with the words "God hath received him" (14. 3) and ends no less strongly with "Christ also received us" (15. 7 mg.). Here is the simple basis of all our fellowship with others. It is that they belong to the Lord and so do we. That is enough. Alas, when you and I meet we generally discuss the points on which we disagree. Instead of dwelling on the Lord whom we have in common, we turn to the negative ground of our differences and stress what is right or wrong in them. Differences abound in the passage before us, but Paul does not tell us who is right. For he is concerned with Christian fellowship, and that does not depend on whether a man's views are right or wrong. The question is not whether he believes exactly what I believe, or has had the same experience as I have had. The sole question is: Has God received him? If so, then I receive him too.

MARCH 19th

I had not known sin, except through the law: for I had not known coveting, except the law had said, Thou shalt not covet. Romans 7. 7.

God knows who I am; He knows that from head to foot I am full of sin; He knows that in the matter of pleasing Him I am weakness incarnate, that I can do nothing. The trouble is I do not know it. I admit that all men are sinners and that therefore I am a sinner, but I imagine I am not such a hopeless sinner as some. While I may agree I am weak, I do not wholly believe it, so God has to use something to convince me of the fact. That is why He gave us the Law, for the more we try to meet its demands, the more our failure becomes manifest. It was through the Law that Paul came really to understand himself—the law which begins "Thou shalt not covet". Whatever might be his experience with the rest of the Law, it was the tenth commandment, which literally translated, is "Thou shalt not desire", that found him out. It brought him face to face with a holy God.

MARCH 20th

God, sending his own Son . . . condemned sin in the flesh: that the ordinances of the law might be fulfilled in us, who walk not after the flesh but after the spirit. Romans 8. 3 f.

What does it mean to walk after the Spirit? It means two things. First, it is not a labour, it is simply a walk. Praise God, the burdensome and fruitless effort I incurred when I sought "after the flesh" to please God gives place now to a quiet and restful dependence on "his working which worketh in me mightily". That is why, in Galatians, Paul contrasts the *works* of the flesh with the *fruit* of the Spirit.

And, secondly, to "walk after" is to follow. It implies subjection, for is He not in the lead? To walk after the Spirit is to be subject to the Spirit in all things. The initiative of life must hereafter be His. There is one thing the man who walks after the Spirit cannot do, and that is run ahead of Him!

MARCH 21st

Behold we call them blessed which endured. James 5. 11.

When God takes it in hand to deal with a man, He does not leave him till He has brought him through to a clear place. In His dealings with Job, God was characteristically thorough. He first allowed all his cattle to be carried off. Then his herds were consumed by fire. Next his sons and daughters died; and he had not yet emerged from his trials when, still protesting, he lay covered with "sore boils from the sole of his foot unto his crown". But a day came when, in his utter sub-jection to God, Job's protests were silenced and God Himself was free to speak. Then at last his trials issued in final triumph. James refers to this as "the end of the Lord". Clearly therefore what matters is not the number of our trials, but that we reach God's goal through them.

MARCH 22nd

Whosoever shall compel thee to go one mile, go with him twain. Matthew 5. 41.

A brother in South China had a rice field in the middle of the hill. In time of drought he used a water-wheel, worked by a treadmill, to lift water from the irrigation stream into his field. His neighbour had two fields below his, and one night he made a breach in the dividing bank and drained off all his water. When the brother repaired the breach and pumped in more water his neighbour did the same thing again, and this happened three or four times. So he consulted his brethren. "I have tried to be patient and not to retaliate," he said, "but is it right?" After they had prayed together about it, one of them observed, "If we only try to do the right thing, surely we are very poor Christians. We have to do something more than what is right." The brother was much impressed. Next morning he pumped water for the two fields below, and in the afternoon pumped water for his own field. After that the water stayed in his field. His neighbour was so amazed at his action that he began to inquire the reason, until in due course he too found Christ.

"Right or wrong" is the principle of the Gentiles and tax-gatherers (verse 46). Not that, but conformity to Him, must govern my life.

MARCH 23rd

Whether we live, therefore, or die, we are the Lord's.
Romans 14. 8.

Never lay stress on the technical side of Christianity, but always on the fundamental fact that we are Christ's, and that all we do is unto Him. We live "unto the Lord" and we die "unto the Lord". We must never seek to persuade those who differ from us merely to think and act as we do. Our one aim must be to lead them closer to Him. For we are not working for outward correctness, or conformity to certain good things, but for a closer relationship to God Himself. Has a brother views that differ strongly from mine? Let it be my first concern that both he and I are doing what we do as unto the Lord. Where that is our goal, notwithstanding outward divergences, all is well between us. The Lordship of Jesus Christ is the central point of Christianity. If, in truth, He is your Lord and He is my Lord, then He Himself will adjust the other things.

MARCH 24th

Perplexed, yet not unto despair. 2 Corinthians. 4. 8.

From the day I was converted, my sincere ambition was to be a true Christian. Of course I had my own conception of what a Christian should be, and I tried my utmost to be that kind of Christian. A true Christian, I reasoned, should smile from morning to night! If ever he shed a tear, he had ceased to be victorious. He must, too, be unfailingly courageous. The slightest sign of fear would mean he had failed seriously to trust His Lord. He had, in fact, fallen far short of my standard.

But the Christian life, I soon learned, is very different. It is a paradox of power in weakness, joy amid pain, faith triumphing in the presence of doubt. When the Christian is strongest in the Lord he is often most conscious of inability; when he is most courageous he may be profoundly aware of fear within; and when he is most joyful a sense of distress readily breaks upon him again. It is only "the exceeding greatness of the power" that lifts him on high.

MARCH 25th

Pray to thy Father which is in secret, and thy Father which seeth in secret shall recompense thee. Matthew 6. 6.

There is no need for us to devise means to draw attention to our work. God in His sovereign providence can well bear that responsibility. We are trusting God for our living, but what need is there to make it known? I feel repelled when I hear God's servants emphasize the fact that they are living by faith. Do we really believe in God's rule and in His provision? If we do, surely we can trust Him to make our needs known to His saints, and so to order things that they can be met without our proclaiming them. Even should people conclude from our mode of living that we have a private income, and in consequence withhold their gifts, we are not to mind. I would counsel my younger brethren to keep silence not only about their personal needs but about their faith in God, so that they may the better be able to prove Him. The more faith there is, the less talk there will be about it.

MARCH 26th

Go to the sea, and cast a hook, and take up the fish that first cometh up; and when thou hast opened his mouth, thou shalt find a shekel; that take, and give unto them for me and r thee. Matthew 17. 27.

This gracious miracle must surely have been meant to speak as a parable to Peter. *For me, and for thee.* Some have remarked that this incident is the only example of the Lord performing a miracle for Himself. True, but it was only half for Himself, for half was for Peter—and you and I can add, "for me". In that single shekel, meeting by grace the temple-tribute for two men, we have wonderfully set forth the intimate union of the servant with his Lord.

And the miraculous fish? Does it not assure us that, when we are on a right basis with regard to the will of God, the expenses will be found by God Himself? Whenever love has to go further than duty, we can look to Him to meet the charges.

MARCH 27th

The house was filled with the odour of the ointment.
John 12. 3.

By the breaking of that flask for the Lord's sake, the home in Bethany was pervaded with the sweetest fragrance. Something was set free for all to appreciate, and none could be unaware of it. What is the significance of this?

Have you ever met someone who has suffered deeply, and whose experiences have compelled him to find satisfaction in the Lord alone? Then immediately you have become aware of something. Immediately your spiritual senses detect a fragrance—what Paul terms "a sweet savour of Christ". Something has been broken in that life in order to release what is there within of God Himself, and you cannot mistake it. Yes, the odour that filled the house that day in Bethany still fills the Church today. Mary's fragrance never passes.

MARCH 28th

Even though we have known Christ after the flesh, yet now we know him so no more. 2 Corinthians 5. 16.

"On the first day of the week cometh Mary Magdalene early . . . and seeth the stone taken away." But for Mary it was not enough to find the tomb empty; she wanted to see the Lord's body. "I know not where they have laid him!" she cried to the angels. Then, turning, she saw the Lord she knew so well—and she took Him for a stranger. If you doubt the need for divine revelation, consider that!

For here is an important principle. Christ "after the flesh" had been crucified. Knowing Him thus could end only in the vain search for a corpse. Mary, so engaged, saw Jesus standing there but knew Him not. Yet surely her faculties had not altered? No, it was He who had been raised with great power and restored to His glory; and because *He* had changed, the means of knowing Him had necessarily changed too. Only through His speaking to her did Mary know Him, and it is thus alone all revelation comes. This inner clarity of recognition you simply cannot explain in human terms. You just *know*, and that is enough.

Mary wept. Seeking a corpse, she mistook her Lord. Many of us have things to weep about. We reach a deadlock, with no possible way out. But then we hear close at hand a voice say "Mary"—and lo, there before us is the One we thought we had lost!

MARCH 29th

Being therefore by the right hand of God exalted . . . he hath poured forth this. Acts 2. 33.

How can I receive the power of the Spirit for service? Must I labour for it? Must I plead with God for it? Must I afflict my soul by fastings and self denials to merit it? Never! That is not the teaching of Scripture. Think again: How did we receive the forgiveness of our sins? Paul tells us it was according to the riches of His grace, and that that grace was "freely bestowed on us in the Beloved". We did nothing to deserve it. We have our redemption through His blood, that is, on the basis of what *He* has done. What then is Scripture's basis for the outpouring of the Holy Spirit? It is the exaltation of the Lord Jesus. Because Jesus died on the Cross my sins are forgiven; because He is exalted to the throne I am endued with power from on high.

MARCH 30th

It is written, He that glorieth, let him glory in the Lord.
1 Corinthians 1. 31.

Paul speaks somewhere of being "under law to Christ". For you and me this certainly does not mean striving to keep the Law, for we know all too well where that ends! It means instead that we prove His power in us to keep it, and that is something very different. But such dependence on Him can only produce in us a deep humility. Surely it is true that every grace which God produces in me will always make me humble. If I can feel some pride in an accomplishment, then I may be fairly sure that it is the result of my own efforts, for I am unlikely to have pride in what was never done by me at all! It is the one who does the work who gets the glory. God must have all the glory, so He insists on doing all the work. Mine it is to rejoice in what He is doing in me, and to be sure to give to Him the praise.

MARCH 31st

Whatsoever things were written aforetime were written for our learning. Romans 15. 4.

Christianity is built not on precepts alone but on concrete examples. One of God's methods of instruction is through history. It tells us how men knew and did His will, so that by observing their lives we may not only discover that will for ourselves, but learn also how we too may do it. His hand on their lives produced His desire in them, and He bids us take note, so that we may better understand what He designs to do in us.

Is it necessary for a child to be told explicitly how to do

everything? Must each item be specifically permitted or forbidden? Is there not much he can discover simply by watching his parents? We learn more readily by what we see than by what we hear, and the impression upon us is deeper, because of course precepts are abstract, whereas examples tangibly demonstrate their outworking. In principle the ways of God are the same today as in Bible days. He has given us so much history in the Old and New Testaments in order that through patience and comfort of the scriptures we too may have hope.

APRIL 1st

In a great house there are not only vessels of gold and silver, but also of wood and of earth; and some unto honour, and some unto dishonour. If a man therefore purge himself from these, he shall be a vessel unto honour.
2 Timothy 2. 20f.

What distinguishes between these vessels? We note at once that only their materials are specified, not their function. Clearly, in keeping with the greatness of the house, it is not relative usefulness but quality of materials that counts. Gold and silver vessels are less practically useful than wooden furniture or earthenware pots, but God is not here discussing with us what they will be used for; He is judging their value to Himself. In a day of declension God looks beyond mere usefulness to intrinsic worth, and a few ounces of gold may equal in value a whole hall full of wooden benches! In spiritual terms, two different men may utter almost identical words, but the power lies not merely in what they say but in who they are. Balaam and Isaiah both spoke of the Kingdom of Christ, but we know well to which of the two we would turn in personal need.

APRIL 2nd

*We are the circumcision, who worship by the Spirit of
God, and glory in Christ Jesus, and have no confidence in
the flesh.* Philippians 3. 3.

Circumcision was a sign that marked out the Jew
from the rest of mankind. What is the corresponding mark of
our Christian life before men? Is it charity? wisdom? sin-
cerity? zeal? Other men have these. None of them is peculiar
to the people of God; but there is one that is. It is a seemly
absence of self-confidence! What distinguishes God's own is
that their confidence in the flesh is destroyed and they are cast
back upon Him. I have known Christians who are so sure they
know the will of God that they will not for one moment consider they may be mistaken. I tell you they still lack the
supreme sign of the spiritual "circumcision", namely, *no confidence in the flesh.* The spiritual man walks humbly, always
aware he may be wrong. He assents gladly to the apocryphal
beatitude: Happy are they who realize they may be mistaken!

APRIL 3rd

*To this end Christ died, and lived again, that he might be
Lord of both the dead and the living.* Romans 14. 9.

Paul has been very strong in verse 4, demanding
"Who art thou that judgest the servant of another?" (The pro-
noun "thou" is emphatic in the Greek.) What presumption on
our part to judge the Lord's servant who is responsible to Him
alone! It is not for you or me to act as lord of the saints and to

seek to put them right, as though God could not manage His own servants without us. *We* did not die for them. *I* am lord neither of the dead nor of the living. Dare I, then, take it on myself to regulate other people's lives? Let me be patient with them, even as God has been patient with me. For after all, I trust the working of His Spirit in my own heart. Shall I not equally trust Him to work in the heart of my brother in Christ?

APRIL 4th

How good and how pleasant it is for brethren to dwell together in unity! It is like the precious oil upon the head. Psalm 133. 1 f.

Psalm 133 is a Song of Ascents, sung three times a year by those going up to worship at Jerusalem. There were all kinds of people on that road, but they had one thing in common: they were all heading for Zion, the abode of God. These men in their great variety were all brothers in unity. How? The illustration explains. It is like the oil.

There is one "holy anointing oil": the Spirit of God Himself. And the flow of oil is down (verse 2) not up! In other words, His anointing is not directly on the members, but upon Christ the Head. The Spirit finds rest and satisfaction in Christ and nowhere else. Hold fast the Head, obey Him in all things, and you will be found walking in step with all who do the same. Rules may be good in society, but the Body has one law: the law of the Spirit of life. Only disregard the anointing spirit, and all is unease; obey Him, and peace fills your heart. Here lies the simplicity of the life of God's children. There is no need for all that questioning!

APRIL 5th

Let us fetch the ark of the covenant of the Lord out of Shiloh unto us, that it may save us. 1 Samuel 4. 3.

To the Israelites the ark of the Lord was the ark of His covenant. They fancied He would fulfil that covenant therefore by protecting them from their foes, no matter how untrue to it they themselves might be. But when God's children turn from Him with a divided heart He can only hand them over to defeat. They think He must deliver them for His glory's sake, but God is more concerned to vindicate His holy character than to display an empty show of glory. When a servant of God fails badly, we feel the affair were better covered up. We pray along such lines therefore, expecting God, for His own glory, to save from open shame, even though there be secret defeat. But God's way is the very reverse of this. He *must* let His people be defeated in the world's eyes in order to dissociate Himself from their unholiness. He will never cover it up. His glory rests on moral values, and can better be maintained by their open discomfiture than by the deception of a hollow victory.

APRIL 6th

Then David arose from the earth, and washed, and anointed himself, and changed his apparel; and he came into the house of the Lord, and worshipped. 2 Samuel 12. 20.

David's son died because of David's sin. True, David had repented, and being a man of prayer had fasted and prayed earnestly for his son's life. Nevertheless the child died.

A man of less humble spirit, ignorant of divine discipline, might have been offended and have nursed a grievance against God. David did no such thing. Told of the child's death, he arose at once and worshipped. Sometimes God has to vindicate His own holiness in this way, putting his servants into the very fires of suffering. The great test in that hour is their reaction to His governmental hand. Of course David felt the sorrow keenly—he would scarcely have been human not to. But when at length he realized that this was God's way with him and there was no relenting, he bowed to it and worshipped the will of God. Should such an occasion arise, could we do this? It marked David as a man after God's own heart.

APRIL 7th

Ye shall know the truth, and the truth shall make you free.
John 8. 32.

We must avoid over-spiritualizing what we read in the Word of God. John's new heaven and new earth, for example, are as truly real as the risen Lord is real. To spiritualize away divine things is the desperate expedient of people who do not themselves know that reality. Many of us amass spiritual truth, only, I fear, to build for ourselves with it a false world. We confuse truth and doctrine, but the two are not the same. Doctrine is what is said on earth about the eternal truth. I know well that our word "truth" in the Chinese Bible is *chen-li* (roughly, "reality-doctrine"), but in fact the Greek meaning is *chen* without the *li*—"reality", and the doctrine can come afterwards. The Jesus who said "Ye shall know the truth" Himself embodies all that is true. The mark of our own spiritual maturity will always be that divine things become real to us because *He* is real to us.

APRIL 8th

*For their sakes I sanctify myself, that they themselves also
may be sanctified in truth.* John 17. 19.

One thing is certain, that while there is anything between you and your Lord you can only weaken others. You
cannot uplift them. When they are low, you will bring them
lower. When they feel heavy, your coming will only add to
their heaviness. Instead of being an asset in the fellowship of
God's people you will contribute nothing, but rather detract
from its strength.

But if all is clear between you and Him the reverse is true.
Your very presence can be a benediction, bringing freshness to
those who are jaded and adding life to the whole worship of
the saints, to their prayers and to their praises. Maintain a vital
touch with God yourself, and you may well be used to restore
that same vital touch with Him to those who may seem to
have lost it.

APRIL 9th

*By faith Abraham, being tried, offered up Isaac; yea, he
that had gladly received the promises was offering up his
only begotten son; even he of whom it was said, In Isaac
shall thy seed be called.* Hebrews 11. 17 f.

We can appreciate what Abraham might have said.
He might have argued that, whereas he could understand the
command to expel Ishmael, this new order, not merely to
expel but to slay Isaac, was quite incomprehensible. Ishmael
had been the result of his own misdirected efforts. He could

therefore respect the decision that he be turned out of the home. But Isaac! Isaac was different! He was entirely from God, given not merely to satisfy Abraham's love for a son but to be the means of fulfilling all God's pledged purposes. What could *God* do if Isaac were relinquished?

However, Abraham had learned not to reason. He made no protest at all; he did not even speak of sacrifice; he simply said he would go to Mount Moriah to worship. And true worship is just that—to let go to God all His gifts to us, all our rich experiences and all our hopes in Him, and to find unqualified joy in God Himself.

APRIL 10th

What soldier ever serveth at his own charges? who planteth a vineyard, and eateth not the fruit thereof? 1 Corinthians 9. 7.

It is upon God that our eyes are fixed, it is to Him our material needs are told, and it is He who touches the hearts of His children to meet those needs. Yes, the labourer is worthy of his hire, and the Lord ordained that they who proclaim the gospel shall live of the gospel. But we do well to ask ourselves, Whose labourers are we? If we serve men, by all means let us look to men for our support; but if we are the labourers of God, then though He may meet our needs through our fellow-men, it is to Him we must look and to no other. If the call and commission have come from Him, then the responsibility will be His for all that our obedience to Him involves, and we need never inquire how He is going to discharge it.

APRIL 11th

They have no need to go away; give ye them to eat.
Matthew 14. 16.

Spiritual poverty and spiritual straitness are two of the greatest problems in the Church. Too many Christians are so poor they have not sufficient for their own needs. Alas for any who go to them for help! But poverty is effect, not cause, and straitness is effect, not cause. The cause of poverty and of straitness is a lack of the Spirit's discipline. Those who are wealthy are they, and only they, who have known such discipline. They have a spiritual history with God, because they have suffered for the Body's sake. Their sicknesses, their domestic problems, their adversities, all were for the increase of Christ in His people. It is they who always have something to give. Those on the other hand who by-pass such discipline, choosing instead a life of ease and prosperity—they are the straitened and the poverty-stricken. The poor and needy come to them in vain for help. They have no overflow.

APRIL 12th

That through death he might bring to nought him that had the power of death, that is the devil. Hebrews 2. 14.

In the death of Jesus Christ, Satan's power of death met its match once for all. That death out-dies all other deaths. Death in Adam does not finish a man, but death in Christ does. It is a mighty death. In Christ all those who deserve to die have died, with the result that he who had the power of death no longer has dominion over them. They are dead; and ashes are something of which you can never make a fire. Christ's work was not only redemption, it was death's destruction, with all that that means. A house once burned to ashes cannot be burned a second time, for if the first fire has done its work there is nothing for the next to do. For us redeemed sinners who have already died a death in Christ, death itself is passed away. We have become possessors of His incorruptible life.

APRIL 13th

Even so reckon ye yourselves to be dead unto sin but alive unto God in Christ Jesus. Romans 6. 11.

What does reckoning mean? I assure you it is not a form of make-believe! The Greek word "reckoning" means doing accounts, book-keeping. Accounting is the one thing in the world we humans can do correctly. Can an artist paint a landscape with photographic accuracy? Can a historian vouch for the absolute correctness of any record, or the map-maker for the perfect precision of any map? They can make, at best, fair approximations. What then can a man do that is utterly reliable? Arithmetic! There is no scope for error there. One chair plus one chair equals two chairs. That is true in London or Cape Town, New York or Singapore. All the world over and for all time, one plus one equals two.

Can God's affirmations be any less true? Could He conceivably ask me to put down something false in my account book? Of course not! If then He tells us to reckon ourselves dead to sin, it is simply because, in Christ, our death to sin is a fact, one eternally to be relied on.

APRIL 14th

Bind the sacrifice with cords, even unto the horns of the altar. Psalm 118. 27.

For what purpose were burnt offerings placed on the altar of Jehovah? To be wholly consumed to God. While the animal offered might be a bullock or a sheep or a dove according to the offerer's resources, the invariable requirement was that it should be a *whole* burnt offering. For God does not accept less than an utter consecration. Today what the altar signifies is not *doing* for God, but *being* for God. He desires not our work but ourselves. Unlike the sacrifices of the Old Testament, which were immolated in one final act, the New Testament sacrifice is "a living sacrifice" (Romans 12. 1). The meaning of the altar is the offering of our lives to God to be ever consumed, yet ever living: to be ever living, yet ever consumed.

APRIL 15th

A glorious church, not having spot or wrinkle or any such thing. Ephesians 5. 27.

Divine Grace has expressed the eternal purpose of God in the statement that Christ will one day present unto Himself a glorious Church. We note that the water of life and the cleansing of the Word are needed to prepare her, marred as she now is by the Fall, to be presented to Him in glory. For today we stand within the history of fallen man's redemption, and there are defects yet to be remedied, wounds to be healed.

Yet how gracious are the words used of her: "not having spot"—the scars of sin, whose very history is now forgotten; "or wrinkle"—the marks of age and of time lost, for all is now made up and all is new; and "without blemish"—so that Satan or demons or men can find no ground for blame in her. God has leaped in thought over the whole of that history to see His Church in glory, expressing nothing of man's fall, but only the image of His glorified Son.

APRIL 16th

Seeing we have this ministry . . . we faint not. 2 Corinthians 4. 1.

In which do we discern God's highest purpose: in the ministry of gifts or in the ministry of life? For the temporary edification of the churches some may minister by miraculous gifts, but in this passage Paul points us forward to the thing most to be prized, and it is not these but the ministry of life from Christ, a life which comes through death. Not gifts, but the working of the Cross: this is the measure of a man's stature.

For the edification of young churches and the winning of souls, spiritual gifts may take on a special significance, but they are not in themselves a mark of maturity, and they are certainly never something of which to boast. Only the foolish are proud of the words God gives, for has He not shown that He will speak, if need be, through an ass!

APRIL 17th

*Be filled with the Spirit . . . singing and making melody
with your heart to the Lord.* Ephesians 5. 18 f.

Plerousthe, "be being filled", is the expression here
used in relation to the Holy Spirit. "Allow yourselves to be
continually made full." This describes, not a crisis as at Pentecost, but a condition we are to enjoy all the time. And it is not
a matter of spiritual gifts and manifestations outwardly, but
of the personal presence and activity of the Holy Spirit of God
within our spirits—the oil that guarantees the lamp shall burn
on undimmed, long after the midnight hour if need be. Moreover it is not alone a private, individual thing. It is something
we share with other Christians. Paul speaks of making melody
together. Some of us may well find it easier to sing solos than
to keep in time and harmony in a choir, or even in a duet!
Yet the fulness of the Spirit is given to us with this very object, that we shall sing *together* a new song before the throne.

APRIL 18th

*When the vessels were full . . . she said unto her son, Bring
me yet a vessel. And he said unto her, There is not a vessel
more. And the oil stayed.* 2 Kings 4. 6.

The divine almightiness is content to confine itself to
our capacity. The oil of God's Spirit flows according to the
measure man has prepared for God. Divine blessing is subject
to the limits of human channels. "Make this valley full of
ditches," said Elisha on another occasion. "For thus saith the
Lord, Ye shall not see wind, neither shall ye see rain, yet that

valley shall be filled with water. . . . And this is but a light thing in the sight of the Lord: he will also deliver the Moabites into your hand" (3. 16 ff.). Man has not the power to obtain anything more than God has given, but he has the option of taking less. "Ye will not come to me that ye may have life."

APRIL 19th

Jesus said unto him, Again it is written, Thou shalt not tempt the Lord thy God. Matthew 4. 7.

There is a world of difference between tempting God and putting Him to the test. The former is forbidden, the latter welcomed. On the surface the two things may appear the same, but they are not. What distinguishes them is a knowledge of God's will communicated through His Word. Israel and the Egyptians afford an example of this. By venturing into the Red Sea both took the same tremendous risk. It was a risk that led the Israelites to glorious salvation, the Egyptians only to death and ignominy. Why? Because, of the two, Israel alone was acting on a word from God. It was that word they put to the triumphant test.

Or again, consider Paul and his young friend Timothy. Though weak in body the apostle Paul accomplished more in his lifetime than ten strong men. Defying reason he laboured on, proving the sufficiency of God's power. Yet Timothy was not exhorted to imitate him in this. Indeed he was warned to take special care of his health. For him to have essayed what Paul did without a divine command to do so would surely have been to tempt God. But to obey such a command is only to put God's faithfulness to the proof.

APRIL 20th

Search me, O God ... and see if there be any way wickedness in me. Psalm 139. 23 f.

True self-knowledge does not come by our turning within. Introspection never leads us to clear understanding. No, it is when there is light coming from God that we see. I think it is so simple. If we want to satisfy ourselves that our face is clean, what do we do? Do we feel it carefully all over with our hands? Of course not. We find a mirror and we bring it to the light. In that light everything becomes clear.

You realize, do you not, what it means to say "Search me"? It certainly does not mean that I search myself. "Search me" means "*You* search me!" That is the way of illumination. It is for *God* to come in and search. My true knowledge of self comes not from my searching myself but from God searching me.

APRIL 21st

The law of the Spirit of life in Christ Jesus made me free from the law of sin and of death. Romans 8. 2.

A great burden to merchants in China used to be the *likin* tax, a law which none could escape, originating in the Ch'in Dynasty and operating right down to our own day. It was an inland tax on the transit of goods, applied throughout the empire, and having numerous barriers for collection and officers enjoying very large powers. But a few years ago a second law came into operation which set aside the *likin* law. Can you imagine the feelings of relief in those who had suffered under the old law? Now there was no need to worry; the new law had delivered from the old law. No longer was there need to think beforehand what one would say if one met a *likin* officer!

God delivers us from one law by introducing another. The one bound us inescapably to sin and death; the other liberates us into blessed union with the Spirit of life.

APRIL 22nd

This life is in his Son. He that hath the Son hath the life.
1 John 5. 11 f.

It is a blessed thing to discover the difference between Christian graces and Christ: to know the difference between meekness and Christ, between patience and Christ, between love and Christ. God will not give me humility or patience or holiness or love as separate gifts of His grace. He is not a retailer dispensing grace to us in packets, measuring out some patience to the impatient, some love to the unloving, some meekness to the proud, in quantities that we can take and work on as a kind of capital. He has only one gift to meet all our need: His Son Jesus Christ.

The common idea of holiness is that every item of life should be holy; but that is not holiness, it is the *fruit* of holiness. Holiness is Christ. The Lord Jesus is made over to us to *be* that. So you can put in anything there: love, humility, power, self-control. Today there is a call for patience: He is our patience! Tomorrow the call may be for purity: He is our purity. It does not matter what our personal deficiency, or whether it be a hundred and one different things, He is the answer to our every need.

APRIL 23rd

She said unto her husband, Behold now, I perceive that this is an holy man of God. 2 Kings 4. 9.

What an impression Elisha had already made on that great woman of Shunem! Yet till now he had done no miracle in her home, nor is there any record of his having brought to her some prophetic utterance from God. He had simply got into the way of looking in on them when passing, and sharing a meal. She could not know him very well; yet to her husband she said, "I can see that he is a man of God". It was not apparently what he said or did that conveyed that impression, but who he was. When he came she *sensed* God's presence with him.

What are people sensing about us? We all leave impressions of some kind. Do they register that we are clever? that we are gifted? that *we* are this or that or the other? Elisha's visits had one conscious effect: they left on that home an impression of God Himself.

APRIL 24th

I therefore, the prisoner in the Lord, beseech you to walk worthily of the calling wherewith ye were called. Ephesians 4. 1.

Has it dawned upon me yet that *the Spirit of God within me is a Person*? I am but an earthen vessel, but in that vessel I carry a treasure of unspeakable worth, even the Lord of glory. All the worry and fret of God's children would end if their eyes were opened to the wealth of resources they carry with them, resources sufficient for every demand they will ever meet. All their flippancy too would cease if they realized the greatness of the treasure hidden in their hearts. If you have only a dollar in your pocket you can march gaily along the street knowing that it matters little if you lose your money, for there is not much at stake. But if the sum you carry is five thousand dollars, the position is vastly different, and your whole demeanour will be different too. There will be great gladness in your heart, but no careless jaunting along the road; and once in a while you will slacken your pace and, slipping your hand into your pocket, you will quietly finger your treasure again, and then with joyful solemnity continue on your way. Yes, I say it with the utmost reverence: You who have been born again of the Spirit of God—you carry God in your heart!

APRIL 25th

There they dwelt with the king for his work. 1 Chronicles 4. 23.

David had many mighty men. Some were generals, others gatekeepers, according as the king assigned them their tasks. We must be willing to be either generals or gatekeepers, allocated to our parts just as God wills and not as we choose. If you are a Christian, God has marked out a pathway for you —a "course" the apostle terms it in 2 Timothy 4. 7. For not Paul's path only but the path of every child of God has been clearly marked out by Him. It is of supreme importance therefore that each should know and walk in his God-appointed course. "Lord, I give myself to Thee with this desire alone, to be led onward in the path Thou hast ordained." That is true consecration. If at the close of a life we can say with Paul: "I have finished my course," we are blessed indeed. For we have only one life to live down here, and there could be nothing more tragic than to come to its end knowing the course we had taken to have been a wrong one.

APRIL 26th

The path of the righteous is as the shining light, that shineth more and more unto the perfect day. Proverbs 4. 18.

In spite of the examples of Solomon and several other kings, we need not assume that a man's last days should be days of spiritual decline. Think of Jacob after his return to Canaan. He who had always been so restless settled down quietly in the land. There, in the sphere of his own family, he underwent many sorrows and disappointments, yet in them all he displayed a patience and a concern for others quite foreign to the selfish character of his earlier years. Or see him again in Egypt, as father of its mighty ruler Joseph. Whereas the Jacob of former days would eagerly have grasped at this new opportunity for self-advancement, the mellow old man he now was seemed quietly content to remain in the background. The mature prophetic blessings of such a man afford a fitting climax to the book of Genesis.

APRIL 27th

Here is the patience and the faith of the saints. Revelation 13. 10.

There are those who cry "How long?" who find it hard to exercise patience any more. But it is significant that right at the start of this book which deals with judgment,

John should describe himself as "your brother and partaker with you in the tribulation and kingdom and patience which are in Jesus". This book of Revelation brings us to the point where God at length sets aside patience and executes judgment. Patience is only called for while judgment lies yet in the future. Once it has begun there is no more need of patience. But that moment has not yet come, and like John we still live in the time when patience is needed. It is so easy to want to take up the sword against oppression and evil, but even the martyred saints are told to wait the completion of their number (6. 10 f.). God will never justify impatience. He Himself is long suffering. Let us display true faith in Him by availing ourselves of His patience.

APRIL 28th

Now hath God set the members each one of them in the body, even as it pleased him. 1 Corinthians 12. 18.

Tell me, which is the better member, the foot or the hand? There is, when you come to think of it, no way of comparing them. Their function in the human body is quite different, and each is equally needed there. And yet many minimize God's calling. Because they cannot be the special member they admire, they decline to take their place at all. This is exactly the situation described in Jesus' parable of the men with the talents in Matthew chapter 25. There was a servant with five talents, and another with two, but the whole emphasis of the parable is on the one-talent man. The danger is of the one-talent brother burying his talent. "Since I cannot occupy a place of prominence," he asks himself, "does it matter therefore whether I occupy any place at all?" It most certainly does! For the parable teaches that if two can grow into four, one can grow into two. It is by functioning that we discover life. The Church's life is hampered and impoverished by the holding back of the one-talent members.

APRIL 29th

My flesh and my heart faileth: but God is the strength of my heart and my portion for ever. Psalm 73. 26.

A brother I know was called to go on a preaching tour of some months. His wife, to whom he was very attached, was in poor health at the time. A friend had sent me with a last-minute letter to him, and as I came in sight of his house, unseen by him, I observed him come out, walk a little distance, then stop, and after a little hesitation begin slowly to return. I did not wait, but sensing his conflict of spirit I went ahead to the river-boat by another route. On his arrival there I handed him the letter with the words, "May the Lord bless you," and his answer revealed that he was quite at peace. When after some months he came back from the tour I alluded to the incident. "Yes," he confessed, "as I stood there, I felt I *could* not leave her and the children with no help and very little money, but as I was retracing my steps the verse came to me: 'No man, having put his hand to the plough, and looking back, is fit for the kingdom of God.' So I turned again and went down to the boat." To hold on to the plough while wiping our tears—that is Christianity.

APRIL 30th

*Fear not ye, neither be dismayed . . . for the battle is not
yours but God's.* 2 Chronicles 20. 15.

Fight to *get* the victory, and you have lost the battle
at the very outset. Your discomfiture as a Christian starts the
moment you begin to reckon that *you* must win. Suppose
Satan sets out to assault you in your home or in your business.
Difficulties mount up, misunderstandings arise, a situation you
can neither deal with nor escape threatens to overwhelm you.
You pray, you fast, you struggle and resist for days, but
nothing happens. Why? You are trying to fight *into* victory,
and in doing so are relinquishing the very ground that is
yours. For in the person of Jesus Christ God has already conquered. Victory is ours *because it is His.* He has given us His
victory to hold. Satan *is* a defeated foe. It needs but a breath
from the Lord to finish him off, and here you are trying to
raise a hurricane! What then is the secret? Simply look up and
praise Him. "Thy victory, Lord, is all-inclusive. I praise Thee
it covers this situation too!" Then be at rest in a triumph
already secured for you by God.

MAY 1st

*They presumed to go up to the top of the mountain: never-
theless the ark of the covenant of the Lord, and Moses, departed not out of the camp. Then the Amalekite came
down, and the Canaanite . . . and smote them.* Numbers
14. 44 f.

On hearing the report the ten spies brought back to
Kadesh-Barnea, Israel had rebelled and refused to enter
Canaan. Then, when condemned by God to the choice they

had made, they rebelled once more, and insisted now on going ahead in their own strength. They ignored Moses, and the ark of testimony which till now had gone before them in their journeyings. This was their undoing. Not only were they completely routed by their foes; after this incident there is no history of the ark for the 38 years that follow. How striking this is! When we wilfully go our own way, we have no testimony to the faithfulness of God's direction. By our headstrong action we have deprived ourselves of the unique privilege of being led.

MAY 2nd

So he caused the ark of the Lord to compass the city.
Joshua. 6. 11.

Mention here of the ark alone makes it appear as though the writer were ignoring the whole company of people who marched in faith round those walls. But of course it was the ark that really mattered. This stronghold of Jericho was not demolished by the march of the Israelites alone. As we know only too well, we may walk round our own Jerichos a thousand times, and still find nothing happens. Israel's strength lay in the fact that the ark of the testimony was among them. They carried with them the evidence of God's faithfulness hitherto. It was not on the basis of their present effort that they faced their foes, but on the fact of what their God had already done. For us today God's "ark of testimony" is the person of His risen Son. Make Him central, go forth proclaiming His resurrection, and God will bring down those walls.

MAY 3rd

After these things I heard as it were a great voice of a great multitude in heaven, saying, Hallelujah; Salvation, and glory, and power, belong to our God. Revelation 19. 1.

This, the first Hallelujah in the book of Revelation, is provoked by the downfall of a city which is again and again described as "great". Why does heaven so exult at the overthrow of Babylon? Because Babylon embodies the spirit of empty show and pretence. Israel's first recorded sin after entering Canaan was the taking of a Babylonish garment. Achan coveted Babylon's grand style; he wanted to look well. And the first sin recorded in the early Church was similar; an attempt on the part of Ananias and his wife Sapphira to win man's esteem by appearing more self-sacrificing than they in fact were. They too wanted to look well. How readily in the churches today do we put on an act to impress others and establish for ourselves a place of repute and acclaim! This is the principle of Babylon the whore, and it is abominable to God.

MAY 4th

If ye know these things, blessed are ye if ye do them. John 13. 17.

I knew of an old Japanese Christian woman who was disturbed by a thief who broke into her house. She saw he was desperately hungry, and in her simple but practical faith in the Lord, she cooked the man a meal; then ended by offering him her keys. He was utterly shamed by her action, and God spoke to him. Through her testimony, that man is a brother in Christ today.

Too many Christians have all the doctrine in their heads, but live lives that contradict it. They know, for example, all about Ephesians 1–3, but they neglect the practical commands of chapters 4–6: put away falsehood; be kind; forgive; subject yourselves to one another; love your wives; obey your masters; forbear threatening; pray! It were better to have no doctrine at all than to be a contradiction. Has God commanded something? Then cast yourself on Him for help— and do it!

MAY 5th

Having therefore, brethren, boldness to enter into the holy place by the blood of Jesus . . . let us draw near. Hebrews 10. 19 ff.

At my first approach to God I was made nigh by the blood of Christ, and to continue in that new relationship I come through the blood every time. It is not that I was saved on one basis and that I now maintain my fellowship with Him on another. You say, "That is very simple; it is the A.B.C. of the Gospel." Yes, but the trouble with many of us is that we have moved away from the A.B.C. We have thought we had progressed and so could dispense with it, but one can never do so.

For it is the one secure way to Him. Of course, were it conceivably possible for the precious blood to suffer any change, the basis of our approach to God might be less trustworthy. But the blood of Christ has never changed and never will. God looks upon it, and is satisfied. Our approach to Him is therefore always in boldness.

MAY 6th

If any man hath not the Spirit of Christ, he is none of his.
Romans 8. 9.

God's gift to you of the Holy Spirit depends upon the exaltation of His Son to heaven and upon this alone. Is it possible then that the Lord Jesus has been glorified and you who have believed have not received the Spirit? Yet some are confused about this. A young man I knew in Shanghai, having heard with new understanding about the glorified Christ and His outpoured Spirit, went home and began to pray earnestly: "Lord, I believe. I want Thy Holy Spirit's power. Seeing Thou, Lord, hast been glorified, pour out now Thy Spirit on me!" Then he paused, and corrected himself: "Oh no, Lord, that's all wrong!" and he began to pray again: "We are in a life-partnership, Thou, Lord Jesus, and I, and the Father has promised us two things: glory for Thee, and the Spirit for me. Thou hast received the glory; it is unthinkable, therefore, that I have not received the Spirit. Thank you, Lord, for this wonderful gift!"

MAY 7th

Joseph brought in Jacob his father, and set him before Pharaoh: and Jacob blessed Pharaoh. Genesis 47. 7.

Twice over we are told that Jacob blessed Pharaoh. How could this crippled old refugee dare to bestow a blessing on the greatest world monarch of his time? For to Jacob, such an ambition was a thing of the past. In his own eyes now he was nothing.

Yes, but God was with him! Before entering Egypt he had made sure of that. Abraham, a much greater man than he, had come down to Egypt and had sinned. So even though his own son Joseph was here, Jacob had paused at Beer-sheba to offer sacrifices to his father's God, thus putting the decision back in God's hands. And the divine re-assurance had come: "I will go down with thee." And so here he was, broken in the old strength that had grasped at blessings for himself, but mighty enough in spiritual power to bless a monarch.

MAY 8th

The Lord seeth not as man seeth; for man looketh on the outward appearance, but the Lord looketh on the heart.
1 Samuel 16. 7.

Saul was of striking stature. "From his shoulders and upward he was higher than any of the people." No wonder Israel acclaimed him: they could all see his head. Yet how often does the head of man stand in the way of the will of God! It seems David understood this—David the man after God's own heart, who time and again set human reason aside and acted instead in simple faith. Confronted with Goliath (whose head was even more prominent than Saul's) he declined helmet and mail and went out against him with but a sling. One well-aimed stone from this, lodged in the giant's brow, brought him down. That day marked David out as Israel's king.

There are Christians today who are ruled by their head. Historically our Goliath was overthrown at Calvary, but spiritually Saul lives on in us still. Yet let us not look within. Saul is not our foe; his days are numbered. But if David of the shepherd heart is to reign, it is our attitude to the uncircumcized Philistine that must be clear. What he stands for must be confronted by each of us, and it must go.

MAY 9th

For this cause shall a man leave his father and mother, and shall cleave to his wife: and the twain shall become one flesh. Matthew 19. 5.

Eve was one and alone; and she was made absolutely for Adam. This makes her unusual, even unique, among the women of the Old Testament who may be felt to be types of the Church. In each of them some aspect of the Church's redemption is depicted. We see her presented to the bridegroom (Rebekah), chosen from among the Gentiles (Asenath), passing through the wilderness (Zipporah), receiving her inheritance in the land (Achsah), altogether dependent upon her kinsman-redeemer (Ruth), and militant for her lord (Abigail). Yet none is so instructive as Eve. For they all succeed the Fall, but she, in that blessed period before sin entered, shows us the Church fulfilling all God's desire for her in union with His Son. Eve first came forth from Adam, to be then brought back to him as his help-meet. From one there became two; from those two there was again one. This is the mystery of the Church, that in her, what is altogether from Christ returns once more to Him.

MAY 10th

By faith he forsook Egypt, not fearing the wrath of the king: for he endured as seeing him who is invisible. Hebrews 11. 27.

In the preparation of His servants God is most thorough. Consider the lessons Moses learned to qualify him to lead Israel out of Egypt. He began life by being himself drawn out of the water, an experience kept always before him by his very name of Moses. This, his first exodus, was itself a triumph over death. Next he must make a deliberate choice to abandon the palace of Pharaoh, declaring thus by another exodus that the world too had no dominion over him. There followed a descent into obscurity, where for forty long years the gifted man he was remained lost to view. Only after that, at the Burning Bush, did the call come again to him to make one more exodus, now from weakness and banishment to prominence and new power as Israel's deliverer. For it was only a man so proved, in whom self, the world and death had been undone, that God could use to play the leading role in Israel's own deliverance.

MAY 11th

I am come down from heaven, not to do mine own will, but the will of him that sent me. John 6. 38.

God's will for me must not be made subject to my own temperament. When we know a man's make-up it is often all too easy to guess what "guidance" he will get, because his natural proclivities intrude so subtly upon the leading of God. Too much so-called guidance among us is little more than personal bias. A timid brother is "guided" to take a back seat. A forward brother is "guided" to take a front seat. Each claims to be led of the Lord. Is he? Or is his temperament ruling him? The pure will of God demands of me that what I am temperamentally shall be set aside. I should be so Spirit-filled that the man beside me cannot foresee, on grounds of my temperament alone, how God will lead me. Oh let me beware of slanting the will of God in the direction of my own natural leanings! Even the Lord Jesus, whose own will was surely faultless, nevertheless set it aside in favour of the Father's who sent Him. If He should do that, how much more must I!

MAY 12th

For hereunto were ye called: because Christ also suffered for you, leaving you an example, that ye should follow his steps. 1 Peter 2. 21.

How tempted we Christians are to seek spiritual experiences for their own sake! This is wrong. The Bible offers us no experience as a thing in itself apart. What God has done in His grace is to include us in Christ. In dealing with Christ He has dealt with the Christian; in dealing with the Head He has dealt with all the members. Thus we are quite wrong to think we can possess anything of the spiritual life in ourselves merely, and apart from Christ. God does not intend that we should acquire from Him something exclusively personal, and He is unwilling to effect anything of the kind in you and me. All true Christian experience is first of all true in Christ. What we call "our" experience is only our entering into His history and His experience. It is the Vine that gives character to the branches.

MAY 13th

Moses said unto the people, Fear ye not, stand still, and see the salvation of the Lord which He will work for you today. Exodus 14. 13.

It is always good to have mountains to right and left, an enemy behind and the sea in front, for then faith has its opportunity. One great hindrance to faith is lack of need. If God blesses you with need He will bless you with faith, and faith works best in really desperate need. Faith, we are told, can remove a mountain. Nothing is said about ant-hills! You will find no record in Scripture of the Lord healing a mild headache. No, He deals with the impossible cases. The trouble is that when God gives us a chance to exercise faith, you and I so often cast it aside.

There is little sense in believing if at the same time you provide yourself with an alternative way out! Faith works most convincingly when there is none. Pray boldly therefore to be shut up, as Israel was, to the Sea. Then, to unbelief's question "Can God?", you can dare to affirm as your personal confession: "He is able."

MAY 14th

Thus shall ye eat it; with your loins girded, your shoes on your feet, and your staff in your hand: and ye shall eat it in haste: it is the Lord's passover. Exodus 12. 11.

The shed blood was for God. It was sprinkled on the outside of the house where it would not even be seen by the first-born son within, he who by its virtue was being delivered. No, the blood was for God to see, and He promised that when He saw it He would pass over the house. God's need is met in the blood, but our need is provided for in the festival meal. Within the house we need to feed on the flesh of that Lamb whose blood protects us. It is by so feeding that we are strengthened for the pilgrim journey ahead. The passover meal was not for those who would settle down in Egypt, even protected there by sacrificial blood. It was for them whose manifest purpose was to move out and on with God. And so it is with us. Our needs we find met in Christ as we partake of Him. But remember, we do so always in readiness for onward movement in the will of God.

MAY 15th

*Who . . . tasted the good word of God, and the powers of
the age to come.* Hebrews 6. 5.

The kingdom of God is at once present and to come
(Matthew 6. 10 and 12. 28). As to time it lies ahead of us; as to
experience it is ours today. God intends us to enjoy foretastes
here and now of the powers of the future age. All that will be
true then universally should be the Church's experience in
some real measure now, for all is hers. What is the use of
merely knowing all about conditions in the kingdom: the rest,
the life eternal, the everlasting covenant, the overthrow of
Satan, the authority of God and of His Christ? These are not
future prospects alone, but powers to be tasted here and now.
To taste means to eat a little. It is the preliminary to a feast.
We cannot yet feast on all the good things of the kingdom,
but we should be savouring them. Where spiritual resources
are in demand, let us not live by the present alone. The powers
of the age to come are ours.

MAY 16th

*Buy the truth, and sell it not; yea wisdom and instruction
and understanding.* Proverbs 23. 23.

Lies have no price upon them. They are cheap and
they abound everywhere. But for the truth there is always a
price to pay. First there is the price of humility, for it is to the
meek that light is given from God. If we are not prepared to
buy the truth at the cost of our own humbling we shall not

receive it. Then there is the price of patience. Quick verdicts and impatient decisions have little to do with the divine light which is given to those who will wait upon God and wait for God. And supremely, there is the price of obedience. "If any man willeth to do his will, he shall know." Unquestioning obedience is essential if we would know God's will and God's ways. Is our faith the cheap, easy kind that pays no price? Or are we prepared to have it founded on the truth of God, however great to us the cost of coming by that truth?

MAY 17th

We which have believed do enter into that rest. Hebrews 4. 3.

Rest follows work. In the fullest sense, rest is only possible when the work is completed to a point of satisfaction. It is no trifling matter that God rested after those six days of creation. How, we may ask, could He—this God of purpose, this God of abounding life—come to rest? Genesis 1. 31 gives us the reason: "God saw everything that he had made, and behold, it was very good." He had accomplished something which rejoiced His heart. The good pleasure of His will had been realized, its goal attained. In resting He proclaimed His approval.

Today God invites us to share with Him His rest in Christ. Another work is accomplished, a new creation secured. His good pleasure has been realized, and no fuller realization is necessary or possible. We enter into God's rest when, ceasing from our own strivings, we find all our satisfaction in Christ.

MAY 18th

There were some that had indignation among themselves,
saying, To what purpose hath this waste of the ointment
been made? Mark 14. 4.

What is waste? Waste means, among other things,
giving more than is necessary. If a dollar will do and you give
ten, it is a waste. If fifty grammes will do and you give a kilo-
gram, it is a waste. If three days will suffice to finish a task well
enough and you lavish five days or a week on it, it is a waste.
Waste means that you give something too much for something too little. If someone is receiving more than he is considered to be worth, then that is waste. Even the twelve
thought this woman's sacrifice excessive. To Judas of course,
who had never called Jesus "Lord", everything poured out
upon Him was a waste, just as in the world's estimation today
our giving ourselves to the service of God is counted sheer
waste. But when once our eyes have been opened to the real
worth of our Lord Jesus, nothing is too good for Him.

MAY 19th

I Jesus have sent mine angel to testify unto you these things
for the churches. I am the root and the offspring of David,
the bright, the morning star. Revelation 22. 16.

The book of the Revelation is the unveiling, the
apokalupsis, of Jesus Christ. It draws aside the curtain to reveal
Him. Its object is not primarily to enlighten us regarding
coming events—the antichrist, the supposed revival of the
Roman empire, the rapture of the saints, the millennial kingdom or the final downfall of Satan. John's remedy for our ills

is not a matter of so many seals and trumpets and vials. It is not in fact designed to satisfy our intellectual curiosity at all, but to meet our spiritual need by revealing Christ Jesus Himself in fulness, that we may know Him. For Christ is the answer to all our questions. Get clear first about Him, and we shall know all we need to know about "things to come". He is the risen and victorious King of kings. All the events that follow are the outcome of His being that.

MAY 20th

Know ye not, that to whom ye present yourselves as servants unto obedience, his servants ye are whom ye obey.
Romans 6. 16.

The word here rendered "servant" really signifies a bondservant or slave. The distinction is important to us, for this word is used several times in the second half of Romans 6, where Paul writes of our usefulness to God. What is the difference between a servant and a slave? A servant may serve another, but the ownership does not pass to that other. If he likes his master he can serve him, but if he does not, he can give in his notice and seek another master. Not so is it with the slave. He is not merely another man's servant; he is his possession. How did I become the slave of the Lord? On His part He bought me at the price of His life laid down; on my part I presented myself freely and completely to Him. Let us not overlook that second statement. By right of redemption I am God's property, but if I would be useful as His slave, I must willingly give myself to Him for this. He will never compel me.

MAY 21st

To know the love of Christ which passeth knowledge, that ye may be filled unto all the fulness of God. Ephesians 3. 19.

While He was on earth Jesus was Himself the vessel of divine life. When men touched Him they touched God; when they saw Him they saw God. In Him bodily there dwelt all the fulness of the Godhead. This was the Father's pleasure (Colossians 1. 19; 2. 9).

Today what do they see? We who believe possess that life. We are said to have received of His fulness. When men meet us do they meet the surpassing love of Christ? When they touch us, do they touch something of God?

MAY 22nd

We which live are alway delivered unto death for Jesus' sake, that the life also of Jesus may be manifested in our mortal flesh. 2 Corinthians 4. 11.

What does this mean? It simply means that I will act only while leaning on God. I will find no sufficiency in myself. I will take no step just because I have inherited the power to do so. With the forbidden fruit Adam became possessed of an inherent power to act, but a power that played right into Satan's hands. You lose that power when you come to know the Lord. You live now by the life of Another, drawing everything from Him.

Oh, my friends, I think we all know ourselves in measure, but many a time we do not truly tremble at ourselves. We may say in a manner of courtesy to God, "If He does not want it, I cannot do it", but in reality we are pretty sure we can do it quite well ourselves! Too often we have been caused to decide, to act, to have power apart from Him. The Christ we manifest is too small because in ourselves we have grown too big. May God forgive us!

MAY 23rd

O the depth of the riches both of the wisdom and the know-
ledge of God! How unsearchable are his judgments, and
his ways past tracing out. Romans 11. 33.

Once and again amid the doctrinal unfoldings of God's Word we encounter sudden outbursts of worship from the full hearts of His servants. The apostle Paul displays a happy knack of doing this. In Romans 1 he breaks the flow of his grim exposure of human corruption with a cry of praise to God the Creator, "who is blessed for ever" (verse 25), adding to it his own personal "Amen". Again in Chapter 9 he interrupts his discourse on Israel's historic advantages with a closely similar cry acclaiming Christ "over all, God blessed for ever. Amen." And here at the end of Chapter 11 we find the same gay spontaneity. Speaking of God's mercy to the Gentiles and of what their response will be, he concludes: "God hath shut up all unto disobedience that He might have mercy upon all," (11. 32), and logically this is followed by Chapter 12. 1, "I beseech you therefore, brethren, by the mercies of God . . .". But once more Paul interrupts himself, and our text occupies the gap. He cannot suppress his feelings: "for of him, and through him, and unto him, are all things. To him be the glory for ever. Amen." This kind of interruption creates no problem for God!

MAY 24th

That which they have need of . . . let it be given them day by day without fail. Ezra 6. 9.

If we really trust God, we shall expect to bear unaided the spiritual burden both of our own needs and of those of the work. We must not secretly hope for support from some human source. Our faith is not to be in God plus man, but in God alone. If brethren show their love, thank God; but if they do not, let us thank Him still. For God's servant to have one eye on Him and one eye on other men is a shameful thing, unworthy of any Christian. To profess trust in God, yet to turn to the brethren for supplies, is to bring only disgrace on His name. Our living by faith must be transparently real, and never deteriorate into a living charity. Yes, in all material things we dare to be utterly independent of men, because we dare to believe utterly in God. We have cast away all other hope, because we have unbounded hope in Him.

MAY 25th

Sin shall not have dominion over you: for you are not under the law, but under grace. Romans 6. 14.

When God's light first shines into my heart my one cry is for forgiveness, for I realize I have committed sins before Him; but when once I have received forgiveness of sins I make a new discovery, namely, that I still have the nature of a sinner. There is an inward inclination to sin, a power of sin compelling me. When that power breaks out I commit sins. I may seek and receive forgiveness, but then I sin once more

So life pursues a vicious circle of sinning and being forgiven and sinning again. I appreciate the blessed fact of God's pardon, but I desperately want something more. I rejoice in the forgiveness for what I have done, but I need also deliverance from what I am. I need the Cross of Christ to strike at the root of my capacity to sin. The Blood of Christ has dealt with my sins, but only the power of His death and resurrection is sufficient to deal with me.

MAY 26th

Ye are all one man in Christ Jesus. Galatians 3. 28.

To us who believe, the Cross of Christ is central; central to all time because central to the whole work of God. We praise God for making this fact clear to our hearts. Moreover, it is central also to our lives. But we must remember that in its work for the individual sinner the Cross was, and is, a means to an end, never an end in itself. The divine end to which it leads is the one new man in Christ.

Salvation, personal holiness, victorious living, walking after the Spirit: all these most precious fruits of redemption are ours to enjoy, but they are not meant to apply to us merely as so many myriads of separate units, scattered over this earth for God. Their values are intended to go further than that. Each is ours in terms of the Body of Christ. It may be true that the children of Abraham are as the stars in multitude. Nevertheless as Christians God would have us see ourselves not as men but as a Man. The goal of the divine thought is in fact one heavenly Man, not a host of little men.

MAY 27th

*Let us hold fast the confession of our hope that it waver not;
for he is faithful that promised.* Hebrews 10. 23.

Nothing so satisfies God as our confession of Him.
Jesus often said "I am". He loves to hear us say "Thou art".
We do it far too little. When everything goes wrong and all is
confusion, don't pray! Confess "Thou art Lord!" Today,
when the world is in turmoil, stand and proclaim that Jesus is
King of kings and Lord of lords. He loves to hear us say what
we *know*.

And Satan too—he trembles when he hears the saints make
positive declarations of fact. The name of Jesus is above every
other name. Declare it! Say it to the enemy. The word of our
testimony will often prove effective where prayer fails to bring
results. We are told to speak directly to the mountain and say
"Be thou removed!"

MAY 28th

*All things whatsoever ye pray and ask for, believe that ye
have received them, and ye shall have them.* Mark 11. 24.

Faith is your acceptance of God's fact. Had you
thought of this? True faith always has its roots in the past.
What relates to the future is hope rather than faith, though of
course the two are closely interlinked. In these words of Jesus
you are assured that, if you believe you already *have received*
your requests (that is, of course, in Him), then "you shall have
them". To believe that you *may* get something, or that you
can get it, or even that you *will* get it, is not faith in the sense

meant here. This is faith: to believe that you have already got it. Such faith does not say "God can" or "God may" or "God will" or "God must". "God", it affirms, "*has done it*". The Christian life is lived progressively, as it is entered initially, by faith in divine fact.

MAY 29th

We wronged no man, we corrupted no man, we took advantage of no man. 2 Corinthians 7. 2.

The Lord's servants should be willing to be taken advantage of, but on no account should they ever take advantage of others. It is a shameful thing to profess trust in God and yet to play the role of a pauper, disclosing one's need and provoking others to pity. He who really sees the glory of God, and his own glorious position as one of His workmen, can well afford to be independent of others—independent, yes, and even liberal. It is quite in order for us to enjoy the hospitality of our brethren for a while, but we should most rigidly guard against taking liberties in such trifles as a night's lodging, an odd meal, the use of light or coal or household goods, or even a daily paper. Nothing reveals smallness of character so readily as the taking of petty advantages. Am I a beggar seeking alms? Or am I a servant of the living God?

MAY 30th

*The second time the cock crew. And Peter called to mind the
word, how that Jesus said unto him, Before the cock crow
twice, thou shalt deny me thrice. And when he thought
thereon, he wept.* Mark 14. 72.

We may think we are as good as Peter—possibly
even a little better, for he was tempted and fell. Yes, but was
he not better in his fall than many who never do so? He denied
—but he was not insensitive. He called to mind the Lord's
word; and when he thought thereon, *he wept.* The Christian
to whom God's word has no power to appeal is a poor
Christian, unworthy of the name. For His word is His instrument of cleansing and renewal. If we only realize this and let
it do its work, though we may indeed fail, we shall not long
remain unaware that we have done so.

MAY 31st

*Ye were redeemed . . . with precious blood, as of a lamb
without blemish and without spot, even the blood of Christ.*
I Peter I. 18 f.

Sin poses for God a threefold problem. Entering as
disobedience, it creates first of all an estrangement between
God and man. God can no longer have fellowship with mankind, for there is something now which hinders. Thus it is
first of all God who says, "They are all under sin" (Romans
3. 9). Then secondly, that sin in man which constitutes a
barrier to his fellowship with God gives rise in him to a sense
of guilt. Here it is the man himself who, with the help of his

awakened conscience, says "I have sinned" (Luke 15. 18). Nor is this all, for sin also provides Satan with his ground of accusation in our hearts, so that thirdly, it is the Accuser of the brethren (Revelation 12. 10) who now says, in effect, "You have sinned."

To redeem us, therefore, and to bring us back to the purpose of God, the Lord Jesus had to do something about these three questions of sin and of guilt and of Satan's charge against us. His precious Blood, shed for many, was alone sufficient to meet this problem, satisfying God, covering our sinfulness, and wholly discomfiting our great Accuser.

JUNE 1st

His branches shall spread, and his beauty shall be as the olive tree, and his smell as Lebanon. Hosea 14. 6.

Hosea surely knew something of the scent of conifers. From Lebanon he paints us a picture of what the Christian life should be in its effect on others. The impression of Christ it gives should penetrate everywhere like pine-fragrance. A man's sense of smell is the most delicate of his senses. Through it he receives impressions of what is beyond reach of touch, and even out of sight altogether. Nor need anything be said. For where there is fragrance the effect is everywhere, pervading all. You cannot hide it. So does one whose roots are in Christ shed forth, like the cedar, a sweet savour of Him who is his unseen source of life. We carry with us the unassuming beauty of the Holy Spirit, as figured in the olive, and the effect is to make people aware only of a fragrant influence of Christ. He cannot be hid.

JUNE 2nd

They that dwell under his shadow shall return; they shall
revive as the corn and blossom as the vine. Hosea 14. 7.

Who ever gave much thought to vine-blossom! It
is in fact one of the shortest-lived of flowers, scarcely noticed
before it is gone and has already turned to fruit. In nature we
may recognize three types of plants: those which flower but
bear no fruit at all; those, such as the peach, which are remarkable both for their blossom and for their fruit; and those
like the vine, whose blossoms are of small account, and which
men prize only for their fruit. Evidently God places here a
high valuation on the last of these.

How tempted we are to display what is impressive to men,
a blossom to be admired! But the Father has set us as branches
in the Vine. There, what He seeks above all is fruit-bearing.

JUNE 3rd

Every branch that beareth fruit, he cleanseth it, that it may
bear more fruit. John 15. 2.

Training of all kinds today is aimed at developing the
soul of the natural man, to make him independent, proud,
quick-witted, self-assured. This generation loves men that can
get the better of others. In thus fitting them to Satan's use it is
doing his work for him.

What God is engaged upon with you and me is the pruning
work of the vinedresser. That untimely growth in our souls
has to be checked and dealt with. God must cut it off. On the
one hand He is seeking to bring us to the place where we live

by the life of His Son, planted within us by new birth. On the other, He is doing a direct work in our hearts to weaken the fund of our natural resources which led in the first place to Adam's sin. Every day we are learning these two lessons: a rising up of the life of this One, and a checking and handing over to death of that other natural life, so that in the world's eyes we stand as weak, ignorant men who often have to admit: "I do not know—but He knows, and that is enough." May God deliver us from today's arrogance of soul!

JUNE 4th

When I am weak, then am I strong. 2 Corinthians 12. 10.

This paradox lies at the heart of true Christian experience. I came to see this in the course of a personal trial of my own, in which, like Paul with his thorn in the flesh, I had received the answer "No" to my prayer for relief. The thought came to me then of a river-boat that could not pass a deep narrows because of a boulder in the stream, jutting five feet or so up from the river bed. In my trial I had been asking the Lord to remove the boulder. Now within me the question arose: Would it be better to have the five-foot boulder out of the way, or to let Him raise the level of the water by five feet? To Paul's appeal the answer had been "My grace is sufficient." Of course it would be better to have the water-level raised! My problem was gone. For Christianity is not a matter of removing boulders, but of having deeper water!

JUNE 5th

As many as touched him were made whole. Mark 6. 56.

Recall the incident of the Pharisee and the publican at prayer in the temple. The Pharisee understood all about tithes and offerings, yet from him there was no cry of the heart to God. It was the publican who cried, "Lord have mercy upon me!" Something went out to God from that man which met with an immediate response, and Jesus singles him out as the one whom God reckoned righteous. For what is it to be reckoned righteous? It is to touch God. The great weakness of so much present preaching of the Gospel is that we try to make people understand the plan of salvation, and all too often we see little or no result. Wherein have we failed? I am sure it is in this, that our hearers do not see Him. We have not adequately presented the Person. We point them only to their sin or God's salvation, whereas their real need is to see the Saviour Himself, to meet Him and to make contact with Him.

JUNE 6th

Yea, all of you, gird yourself with humility, to serve one another. 1 Peter 5. 5.

The Body builds up itself in love. It is not that there are special apostolic workers who can stand apart from the Body as though it were a "thing", and build it up from the outside. There is a danger, to which we are all prone, of thinking of the Church of Christ as something outside of ourselves to which we are ministering. This is not possible. If we are to contribute to the life of the Body we must humbly take our place of submission within it, receiving from, as well as contributing to,

its mutual ministry of life. Do we find it easier to humble ourselves towards God than towards our fellow believers? Remember, without a continual exercise of humility, it is quite
impossible to serve one another. For better or worse we are
members of that Body, from which we cannot resign.
Offend men and we offend God. Accept help from our
brethren, and it is only that we may help others. Serve, and
we ourselves are ministered to. We are God's fellow-workers,
God's building.

JUNE 7th

Thus saith the Lord, the God of Israel, The barrel of meal
shall not waste, neither shall the cruse of oil fail. 1 Kings
17. 14.

We are God's representatives in this world, set here
to prove and to display His faithfulness. Our attitude, our
words and our actions must all declare that He alone is our
Source of supply. It is imperative, therefore, and supremely so
in financial matters, that we be in a true sense independent of
men and wholly cast upon God. If there is any weakness here,
He will be robbed of the glory that is His due. As God's servants we must show forth the abundance of His resources.
We must not be afraid to *appear* wealthy before people. I do
not suggest we should ever be untrue, but such an attitude is
perfectly consistent with honesty. Let us keep our financial
needs secret, even if our secrecy should lead men to conclude
that we are well off when in fact we have nothing at all. He
who sees in secret will take note of our needs, and He will
meet them in no stinted measure but "according to His riches
in glory by Christ Jesus". We dare to make things difficult for
God, because He requires no assistance from us to perform
His miracles.

JUNE 8th

Deep calleth unto deep. Psalm 42. 7.

Only deep can answer deep. Nothing that is merely of the shallows can respond to the depths, and only what goes deep in us can meet the deep needs of others. If we want to help those who are passing through floods, we must have been through floods ourselves. Have we a history of God's secret dealings, or does what men see represent all we have got? Many of us are shallow. We only seem to grow outwardly, with nothing in reserve. If we choose to live on the surface of things, we may be of some help to folk in need, but the happiness we bring them will pass. We shall not have been able really to meet them where they are. Paul had a secret he kept for fourteen long years, and what help has its eventual disclosure brought! When we have found God speaking to us in the depths, then it is we possess treasures of darkness to share with others in their hour of trial.

JUNE 9th

His eyes were as a flame of fire; and his feet like unto burnished brass . . . and his voice as the voice of many waters. Revelation 1. 14 f.

In the Book of Revelation God shows us an aspect of His Son not shown to us in the Gospels. In the Gospels we see Him as Saviour, in the Revelation as King. The one displays His love, the other His majesty. In the upper room Jesus girds Himself about the waist, for service; at Patmos He is discovered girt about the breasts, for war. In the Gospels His mild eyes melt Peter; in Revelation they are as a flame of fire. There His voice is gentle, calling His own sheep by name, and gracious words proceed out of His mouth; here His voice is terrible as the sound of many waters, and from His mouth a sharp two-edged sword strikes death to His foes. It is not enough that we know Jesus as Lamb of God and Saviour of the world; we must know Him also as God's King, God's Judge. When we see Him as Saviour, we exclaim "How lovable!" and lean on His bosom. When we see Him as Monarch, we cry "How terrible!" and fall prostrate at His feet.

JUNE 10th

God . . . made us to sit with him in the heavenly places, in Christ Jesus. Ephesians 2. 6.

What does it really mean to sit down? When we walk or stand we bear on our legs all the weight of our own body, whereas when we sit down our entire weight rests upon the chair or bench on which we sit. We grow weary when we walk or stand, but we feel rested when we have sat down for a while. In walking or standing we expend a great deal of energy, but when we are seated we relax at once, because the strain no longer falls upon our muscles and sinews but upon something outside ourselves. So too in spiritual things, to sit down is simply to rest our whole weight—our load, ourselves, our future, everything—upon the Lord. We let Him bear the responsibility, and cease to carry it ourselves.

JUNE 11th

*As they ministered to the Lord and fasted, the Holy Ghost
said, Separate me Barnabas and Saul for the work whereunto I have called them.* Acts 13. 2.

No one can truly work for the Lord who has not
first learned to minister to Him. It was while Barnabas and
Saul ministered to the Lord and fasted that the voice of the
Spirit was heard calling them to special service.

And it was to the divine call they responded, not to the
appeal of human need. They had heard no reports of cannibals
or head-hunting savages; their compassions had not been
stirred by doleful tales of child-marriage, foot-binding or
opium-smoking. They had heard no voice but the voice of the
Spirit; they had seen no claims but the claims of Christ. It was
the Lordship of Christ which claimed their service, and it was
on His authority alone that they went forth.

JUNE 12th

*We have no more than five loaves and two fishes; except
we should go and buy food for all this people.* Luke 9. 13.

When Jesus said "Give ye them to eat", it was not
because He expected His disciples to have a plan, but because
He wanted *them* to expect a miracle. Like us however they
chose the easier way, the way which does not require the
exercise of faith or prayer. Their solution was to "go and buy".
It was a proposal unworthy of disciples; it could as well have
been made by Pharisees or even Sadducees. It displayed no

faith, no trust in Him. As John's Gospel makes plain, their thoughts were on their pockets. They had not enough money!

We only see what *we* can do. We shut our eyes to God and His inexhaustible resources. But God is not to be measured by us. Never mind what we can or cannot do; He is waiting to show us His miracles. `

JUNE 13th

I have been crucified with Christ. Galatians 2. 20.

What does it mean for me to be "crucified"? I think the answer is best summed up in the words the crowd used of Jesus: "Away with him!" God never allows this matter of being crucified with Christ to remain for us a mere theory, though I confess that for many years it *was* no more than that to me. I myself had preached the Cross in these very terms without knowing it in my own experience—until one day I saw with dramatic suddenness that it had been I, Nee To-sheng, who died there with my Lord. "Away with him!" they had cried, and in saying it of Him they had also, un-wittingly, echoed God's verdict upon me. And that sentence of God upon me was carried out in Him. This new discovery affected me almost as greatly as did my first discovery of salvation. I tell you, it left me so humbled as to be for a while quite unable to preach at all, whereas till that day, I have to admit, preaching had been my consuming passion.

JUNE 14th

Consecrate yourselves today to the Lord . . . that he may bestow upon you a blessing. Exodus 32. 29.

Presenting myself to God "as alive from the dead" (to use Paul's words) implies a recognition that henceforth I am altogether His. This giving of myself is a definite act, just as definite as believing in Jesus Christ. There must be a day in my life when I pass out of my own hands into His, and from that day forward I belong to Him and no longer to myself. That does not mean that I consecrate myself to be a preacher or a missionary. Alas, many people are missionaries merely because they have consecrated their own natural gifts to His work. But that is not true consecration. Then to what are we to be consecrated? Not to "Christian work", but to *the will of God*, to be and do whatever He requires.

JUNE 15th

For where two or three are gathered together in my name, there am I in the midst of them. Matthew 18. 20.

The preceding verse has given a wonderful promise of answered prayer, but the promise is conditional. There must be at least two, and they in agreement. Why is their prayer answered? Because these two or three "are gathered together in my name". That is, they do not just meet; they are gathered (passive voice). We see the difference, for to be gathered is not merely to go of ourselves; it is to be moved by the Spirit of God. And they come, not on their own affairs, but having a single common concern for His. It is this that unites them in His name. And when this is so, Jesus says, "I am in the midst of them", leading, revealing, enlightening. Praise God, that is not a promise; it is a statement of fact!

JUNE 16th

The true worshippers shall worship the Father in spirit and truth: for such doth the Father seek to be his worshippers. John 4. 23.

The decalogue opens with God's claim to exclusive worship. This expression of God's will is not only His command, it is also His desire. But if the ten commandments show us what gives God joy, the temptations in the wilderness reveal what will bring joy to Satan. In both cases it is worship. So we have one thing that both God and Satan want. By it we can satisfy either heaven or hell. Worship is priceless. Satan's whole idea is to rob God of it by ensnaring His people into some kind of idolatry. Idolatry claims another, besides God, to be worthy of worship. It is our privilege to counter this by holding it exclusively for God.

JUNE 17th

This is life eternal, that they should know thee the only true God, and him whom thou didst send, even Jesus Christ. John 17. 3.

Men rejected Christ, not on the ground of what He did but of who He was, and they are invited to believe in what He is and who He is, and not, first of all, in what He has done. "He who hath the Son hath the life." The appreciation of His work must come, but the main question is whether or not you have the Son, and not, first of all, whether or not you understand the whole plan of salvation. The first condition of salvation is not knowledge, but meeting Christ.

There are people who you may feel were saved by the wrong scriptures! They were spoken to through verses that do not seem to point the way of salvation, and you almost feel they could not be saved on that basis! I used to wish that those whom I led to the Lord would be saved on the basis of a verse like John 3. 16, but I have come to see that all that is needed for the initial step is that there should be a personal touch with God. It does not matter, therefore, which scripture God elects to use for that first vital step.

JUNE 18th

One died for all, therefore all died. 2 Corinthians 5. 14.

Why does God say we are to reckon ourselves dead? Because we *are* dead. Suppose I have two dollars in my pocket, what do I enter in my account-book? Can I enter one dollar ninety-five cents or two dollars five? No, I must enter in my book what is in fact in my pocket, no more, no less. Accounting is the reckoning of facts, not fancies. God could not ask me to put down in my account-book what was not true. He could not ask me to reckon that I am dead if I am still alive. For such mental gymnastics the word "reckoning" would be quite inappropriate.

God asks us to do the account; to put down "I have died", and then to abide by it. Why? Because it is a fact. When the Lord Jesus was on the Cross, I was there in Him. Therefore I count it to be true. I count myself dead unto sin, but alive unto God in Christ Jesus.

JUNE 19th

I was in the Spirit on the Lord's day. Revelation 1. 10.

Who is qualified to study the Apocalypse? We find the answer in John's own history. His first vision was not of events but of Jesus Christ Himself. John, who had lain on Jesus' bosom, must have a sight of his eternal Lord that shattered him to the dust. Only then might he be shown "things to come". No one is qualified to study what follows who has not first seen what John saw; for not till we see Jesus thus are we equipped for conflict.

Before this John knew the love of the Lord, now he beheld His majesty. Then he knew Him as compassionate Saviour, now as glorious King. Unless we have first seen Him thus and have fallen as dead at His feet, a knowledge of coming events will only stimulate our curiosity and puff us up, producing eventual confusion or even disbelief. This book proclaims the battle of the Lord. It declares war on all that defies His kingdom. Its aim therefore is to show us Christ Jesus as King on the Throne. Only such a sight creates warriors.

JUNE 20th

There will I meet with thee, and I will commune with thee from above the mercy seat, from between the two cherubim which are upon the ark of the testimony. Exodus 25. 22.

What is the basis of our communion with God? It is His glory. At the mercy-seat with its shadowing cherubim we have fellowship with God, and they are "cherubim of glory".

It is in the place where God's glory is manifested, with its implied judgment upon man, that we find mercy—there and there alone. Cannot God, being God, show mercy where He will? No, He can only show mercy where His moral glory is also maintained. He does not divorce the mercy-seat from the cherubim.

It is the shed blood that makes communion possible for sinful man. Because of it God can show mercy without violating His glory; He can commune with man without denying Himself. Thus the blood of Christ is essential to fellowship, absolutely essential. Nevertheless it is not the basis of fellowship. When I commune with God at His mercy-seat it is not on the precious blood I gaze, but on the glory. The veil is taken away, and with unveiled face we all behold the glory of God.

JUNE 21st

Brother Saul, the Lord, even Jesus, who appeared unto thee in the way which thou camest, hath sent me. Acts 9. 17.

How often can we get help from those whom we might naturally despise! When the blinded Saul reached Damascus all he knew was that some God-sent messenger would tell him what to do. At first no man came. Only after three days of darkness did someone at length arrive, and even then he was but "a disciple". From Luke's use of this simple title we are to conclude that though devout and honourable, Ananias was just an ordinary brother, with nothing special to qualify him as helper of the destined great apostle of the Church.

And for his part too, Ananias, who knew Saul of Tarsus by repute and had every reason to fear him, must now give practical expression to a miracle of divine grace in his own heart. By his simple words of greeting he expressed his recognition of another member of Christ. So in one Spirit the two men, brethren now, gave and received counsel that was destined by God to have world-shaking repercussions.

JUNE 22nd

If any man buildeth on the foundation gold, silver, costly stones, wood, hay, stubble; each man's work shall be made manifest: for the day shall declare it, because it is revealed in fire. 1 Corinthians 3. 12 f.

It is weight that counts. Wood, hay, stubble are cheap, light, perishable. Gold, silver, precious stones are costly, weighty, eternal. Here is the key to Paul's meaning. God looks not only at the work done but at the material used, and readily distinguishes the solid from the superficial worker. The heavy metals, the gold of the divine character and glory, the silver of His redemptive work: these are the materials He prizes. Not merely what we preach, but what we are, weighs with God: not "Where is the need most evident? What ideas and resources have I got? How much can I do?" but "Where is God moving? What is there of Christ there? What is the mind of the Spirit in this?" When our work has that character we can be sure it will survive.

JUNE 23rd

*I will give thee thanks for ever, because thou hast done it:
and I will wait on thy name, for it is good.* Psalm 52. 9.

The test of time is the hardest test of all. Yet only by
learning to wait for God do we find ourselves involved in
something really done by Him. Ten years after he had believed
God for a son, Abram felt he could wait no longer. He knew
God intended him to have an heir so he sought to provide one,
and Ishmael was the result. It was not Abram's motive that
was wrong, but his starting point. He felt he could still do
something to produce a child, as indeed he could, and did.
At eighty-six he yet had that capacity.

There followed a further long wait, until at the age of a
hundred Abraham could no longer do even this; his body was
"as good as dead" (Romans 4. 19). It was to such a man,
powerless now in himself to please God, that the marvellous
gift of grace came in the person of Isaac. This was wholly
God's doing and well worth waiting for. To have God do His
own work through us, even once, is better than a lifetime of
human striving.

JUNE 24th

So mightily grew the word of the Lord and prevailed.
Acts 19. 20.

As the apostles worked, the blessing of the Lord
rested on their labours. We shall do well if we follow in their
steps, but we must understand clearly that simply to adopt

apostolic methods is not enough. Unless we have apostolic consecration, apostolic faith and apostolic power, we shall still fail to see apostolic results. I do not suggest we should underestimate the value of their methods; they are essential if we are to see equivalent results. But we must not overlook the even greater need of apostolic spirituality, nor be dismayed if along the way we encounter apostolic trials.

JUNE 25th

Know ye not that ye are a temple of God, and that the Spirit of God dwelleth in you? 1 Corinthians 3. 16.

A revelation of the indwelling Spirit was the remedy Paul offered the Corinthian Christians for their unholiness. Their need, like ours today, was to grasp the fact that God Himself had taken up His abode in them. To many of us the Holy Spirit of God is quite unreal. We regard Him as a mere influence—an influence for good, no doubt, but no more than that. In our thinking, conscience and the Spirit are more or less identified as some "thing" within us that brings us to book when we are bad and tries to show us how to be good. Like the Corinthians our trouble is not that we lack God's gift of the indwelling Spirit, but that we have not yet awakened to the reality of His presence. We fail to appreciate the essential holiness of the One who has made His abode within our hearts.

JUNE 26th

The Spirit said unto Philip, Go near, and join thyself to this chariot. Acts 8. 29.

Divine work must be divinely initiated. A worker may be called directly by the Spirit, or indirectly through the reading of the Word, through preaching, or through circumstances; but whatever the means God uses to make known His will to a man, *His* must be the Voice heard through every other voice. *He* must be the One who speaks, no matter through what instrument the call may come. Of course it is wrong to reject out of hand the opinion of fellow-workers, but it is also wrong to accept their opinions as a substitute for the direct witness of His Spirit. While it is true we must never be independent of the other members of the Body, let us never forget also that it is from the Head that all our direction comes.

JUNE 27th

The Lord of hosts is with us; the God of Jacob is our refuge. Psalm 46. 11.

How like our own is Jacob's history! Until God begins to deal with us, we are inclined to take a superior attitude to Jacob's intrigues, but as we begin to encounter the deviousness of our own thinking, we soon recognize the man's essential character in ourselves. And remember, what changed Jacob's life from vanity to profit was nothing less than the power of divine grace.

Ishmael might talk of the God of Abraham, Esau could

perhaps claim to have some dealings with the God of Abraham and of Isaac, but both of them, in doing so, could only look back. Theirs was no personal experience of Him. We read nothing of the God of Ishmael or of Esau. But for Jacob, and for us too, this is not enough. Our God is a present refuge, a present power. Like Moses at the burning bush we must hear Him say: "I am the God of Abraham, the God of Isaac, and the God of Jacob." In such a God there is hope for us all.

JUNE 28th

Having been buried with him in baptism, wherein ye were
also raised with him through faith in the working of God.
Colossians 2. 12.

Alas, some have been taught to look on burial as a means to death; they try to die by getting themselves buried! Let me say emphatically that unless our eyes have been opened by God to see that we have died in Christ and been buried with Him, we have no right to be baptized. The reason we step down into the water is that we recognize that in God's sight we have already died. It is to this that we testify. God's question is clear and simple. "Christ has died, and I have included you there. Now, what are you going to say to that?" What is my answer? "Lord, I believe you have done the crucifying. I say Yes to the death and to the burial to which You have committed me." He has consigned me to death and the grave; by my request for baptism I give public assent to that fact.

JUNE 29th

He that dwelleth in the secret place of the Most High shall abide under the shadow of the Almighty. Psalm 91. 1.

The object of temptation is always to get us to do something. During the early months of the Japanese war in China we lost a great many tanks, and so were unable to deal with the Japanese armour, until the following scheme was devised. A single shot would be fired at a Japanese tank by one of our snipers in ambush. After a considerable lapse of time the first shot would be followed by a second; then, after a further silence, by another shot; until the tank driver, eager to locate the source of the annoyance, would pop his head out to look around. The next shot, carefully aimed, would put an end to him. As long as he remained under cover he was perfectly safe. The whole scheme was devised to bring him out into the open. In the same way, Satan's temptations are designed to entice us to expose ourselves. He knows well that as soon as we step out of our Hiding Place, as soon as we move from the cover of Christ and act in self-dependence, he has scored a victory.

JUNE 30th

The flesh lusteth against the Spirit, and the Spirit against the flesh: for these are contrary the one to the other; that ye may not do the things that ye would. Galatians 5. 17.

Consider carefully what this says. "The flesh" in us is not opposed to us but to the Holy Spirit of God. It is He, not we, who meets and deals with its promptings. And with what result? "That ye may not do the things that ye would." I think we have often failed to grasp the import of that last clause. What "would we do" naturally? We would disregard the divine will and move off on some course of action dictated by our own instincts. The effect, therefore, of our refusal to come out of the cover of Christ and act of ourselves is that the Holy Spirit is free to do *His* work—free, that is, to meet and deal with the flesh in us, so that in fact we shall *not* do what we naturally would do. Instead of going off on a plan and course of our own, we shall find our joy in His perfect plan.

JULY 1st

Giving diligence to keep the unity of the Spirit in the bond of peace. There is one body, and one Spirit, even as also ye were called in one hope of your calling. Ephesians 4. 3 f.

There are several elements in that unity of the Spirit which is our common heritage. One of them is our hope. This is not just a cheerful optimism; it is the hope of our calling as Christians. What is our hope as Christians? It is to be with the Lord for ever in glory. There is not a single soul who is truly His in whose heart there is not this hope, for to have Christ in us is to have in us "the hope of glory". If anyone claims to be the Lord's and has no expectation of heaven or of glory, his is an empty profession. Furthermore, all who share this hope are one, for since we have the hope of being together for all eternity, how can we be divided in time? If we are going to share the same future, shall we not gladly share the same present?

JULY 2nd

A certain Samaritan, as he journeyed, came where he was:
and when he saw him, he was moved with compassion, and
came to him. Luke 10. 33 f.

What the helpless sinner cannot do, the Saviour is at
hand to do for him. The Lord Jesus came as a Friend of sinners,
to help sinners approach Him. Our coming to Him was made
possible by His first coming to us. By it heaven was brought
within our reach. I remember I was once sitting talking to a
brother in his home. His wife and mother were upstairs, but
his small son was in the sitting-room with us. Presently the
little fellow wanted something, and called out to his mother
for it. "It is up here," she replied. "Come up and get it." But
he cried out to her, "I can't, Mummy; it's such a long way.
Please bring it down to me." And indeed he was very small
and the stairs were steep; so down she came with it. And salvation is just like that. Only by His coming to us could our
need be met. Had He not come, we sinners could never have
approached Him; but He "came down from heaven", and we
are lifted up.

JULY 3rd

The Lord hath taken you, and brought you forth out of the
iron furnace, out of Egypt, to be unto him a people of in-
heritance. Deuteronomy 4. 20.

Nowhere in either Old or New Testament is dedication divorced from redemption. The two are intimately
linked and we never find the one without the other. The

Apostle Paul did not wait until he was a prisoner or about to be martyred before presenting himself to God. That had taken place at his conversion on the road to Damascus. Never was it God's plan that His people should wait several years, perhaps for a time of special blessing, before giving themselves wholly to Him. In His intention, when He saves a people He also gains a people. He gives me redemption; He asks for my self-dedication in return. Because of His wonderful gift to me, I give myself to God.

JULY 4th

God loveth a cheerful giver. 2 Corinthians 9. 7.

The servant of the Lord should learn to give as well as to receive. Yet how hard it often is to do so! I remember once I was setting out on a journey up river to take part in some important meetings. I had to trust the Lord for my fare, and I had only eighteen dollars in hand. The river boat would take me only so far, and I might need anything up to $300 to hire a boat for the rest of the way. Yet before I left, God told me to give away to a friend six of my sorely needed dollars. I started off, found quite unforeseen cheap travel provided from half way, enjoyed a most blessed week, and was amply provided for for my return journey. What a joy to discover when I got back that my gift of six dollars had been desperately needed!

All too often, I fear, we are bad givers. If I am only a receiver and not also a giver, I am unworthy of the God who sent me. The divine principle is not "Save and you shall grow rich." It is "Give and it shall be given unto you."

JULY 5th

Jesus therefore took the loaves. John 6. 11.

For most of His miracles God makes use of material. Here Jesus accepts five loaves and two fishes. He might have turned stones to bread, but He did not. He chose instead to work with what was offered Him. "Bring them hither to me," he said. What He does, He does through us. All miracles begin here, with my all in His hands. Keep my loaves to myself, and one man is fed. Give them up to Him, and shall I go hungry?

In a day of extreme national poverty the prophet Malachi brought to Israel God's answer to her problem. It was: Bring the whole tithe into the storehouse—and see! It takes only a tiny stopper to close a very large bottle, so withholding from us its entire contents. And heaven is like that. Often for us there is no miracle, simply because we give God nothing to work on. He asks only a very little—what we have! But He needs that.

JULY 6th

What are these among so many? John 6. 9.

The hopes of too many are still centred, not on the Lord's blessing but on the state of their treasury, the few paltry loaves in their own hands. What we have in hand is so pitifully little, and yet we keep reckoning with it; and the more we reckon the darker the prospect. My friends, miracles issue from the blessing of the Lord! Where that rests, thousands are fed; where it is lacking much more than two hundred pennyworth will never suffice. Recognize that fact, and we shall see a transformation in our work. There will be no more need to manipulate, no more need to dodge; there will be no call for human contriving nor for large, empty speeches, for we shall simply trust God and await His miracle. And where we have already made a mess of things, even there we may find that somehow all is well. A little bit of blessing can carry us over a great deal of trouble.

JULY 7th

It shall come to pass that the man whom I shall choose, his rod shall bud. Numbers 17. 5.

Aaron's priesthood had been contested. People were questioning whether he was indeed God's chosen. "Is this man ordained of God or not?" they asked. "We do not really know!" God set out therefore to prove who was His servant and who was not. How did He do so? Twelve rods were placed before Him in the sanctuary, and were left there for a night. In the morning His choice was seen in the rod which budded, blossomed and bore fruit.

New buds, flowers, ripe almonds: all these proclaim the miracle of resurrection. It is life out of death that marks divinely attested ministry—that, and that alone. Without it you have nothing. God can only use as His ministers those who, through union with Him, have come to taste the power of an endless life.

JULY 8th

*He that is entered into his rest hath himself also rested from
his works, as God did from his.* Hebrews 4. 10.

At his creation man stood in a highly significant
relation to God's rest. Adam, we are told, was created on the
sixth day. Clearly then, he had no part in God's first six days
of work, for only at their end did he exist. Thus God's
seventh day was Adam's first. Whereas God worked six days
to enjoy His sabbath rest, Adam began life with the sabbath.
God works before He rests. Man, to be in harmony with God,
must first enter into God's rest; then alone can he work. This
principle underlies all Christian service. Moreover, it was
because God's first creation was so truly complete that Adam's
life could have this satisfying starting-point. And here is the
Gospel: that for us sinners God has taken one further necessary
step, and has completed also the entire work of salvation. We
need do nothing whatsoever to merit it. At once, by an act of
simple faith, we can enter into the sabbath rest of His finished
work.

JULY 9th

*The accuser of our brethren is cast down, which accuseth
them before our God day and night.* Revelation 12. 10.

Satan is a murderer and a deceiver, he entices and he
attacks; but today he specializes in accusing. Heaven recognizes this, and so must every Christian. Night and day he
accuses us, and his charges, which are not unfounded, are
directed at our conscience—the very point where we most
lack the strength to fight him. His object is to drive us to think

in despair, "I am a hopeless failure! God can do nothing with me!" Conscience is a precious thing, but to repeat endlessly "I am no good! I am no good!" is not Christian humility. To confess our sins is wholesome, but let us never carry confession to the point where our sinfulness looms for us larger than the work of Christ. The Devil knows no weapon more effective against you and me than the creation of this illusion. What is the remedy? Plead guilty *to God*. Confess to Him "Lord, I am no good!" but then remind yourself of the precious Bloo , and looking away to His glory, add: "But Lord, I am abiding in Thee!"

JULY 10th

Be still, and know that I am God; I will be exalted. Psalm 46. 10.

If God's throne seems to rock, can our hand steady it? Some appear to think so. One such was Jacob. God had clearly stated that he should rule, and in all he did he aimed only to forward God's plans. He saw God's election and he embraced it—but then one day he learned that his father had sent Esau hunting with a view to giving him the blessing. If that happened, where was God's promise?

Something must be done! The clever, capable man was also a schemer, so he set out to do for God what it looked as though God could not do for Himself—and to achieve it he cheated his father. But of he seemed to gain from his cheating had to be abandoned, and he was forced to flee. Yes, he was God's choice, God wanted him, but as yet he knew neither his God nor himself. What in fact he received was a severe dose of the divine discipline. Clever people get a lot of that!

JULY 11th

Whatsoever a man soweth, that shall he also reap. Galatians 6. 7.

God's practical dealings with us His children follow principles peculiarly His own which faithfully express His ways. Are our sins forgiven in Christ? Then it is our privilege henceforth, to be gently handled in ways designed always to warn us when, for a moment, our course is not His. Often this means that what we are going through today is directly connected with something in our past, a reaping of what we have earlier sown. Have we been gracious? Then grace is multiplied to us. Were we critical of someone's action? Then sooner or later we discover ourselves doing that very thing—and reaping the consequences. For with what measure we mete it is meted to us again, *by God.* "If you knew what was wrong with your brother you should have known what was wrong with you!" That is the principle. His way is not harsh, for it is a way of love, so measured as to offer us all possible safeguards. Welcome it, and we shall escape many an unseen hazard.

JULY 12th

With what measure ye mete it shall be measured to you again. Luke 6. 38.

I knew a dear brother who was intensely critical. His favourite observation was: "It is the hand of God." Was someone sick? "It is the hand of God on him," he would say. Sometimes maybe he was right. But one day another brother, of whom he disapproved, lost his son, and, believe it or not, received a letter from this man saying, "It is the hand of God on you"! I saw the letter and felt highly indignant that he should thus judge another. What was my horror, then, when within two weeks his own son was taken ill and died. Then it was that temptation came to me. I took up my pen and wrote, "My dear brother, I grieve with you in your bereavement, but if that man lost his child because the hand of God was on him in judgment, then what about yourself? Are you willing to admit that God's hand is on you?" It seemed about time this was said! I finished the letter—and then God rebuked me. Was not I doing the very thing I had disapproved of? His mercy had restrained me just in time. I tore up the letter. If I too would not reap, I must not sow!

JULY 13th

We are his workmanship, created in Christ Jesus for good works, which God afore prepared that we should walk in them. Ephesians 2. 10.

The first clause could as well be rendered, "We are his masterpiece." The Church is the very best God can produce. It can never be improved on. We look around and see breakdown everywhere, and we wonder, "What is the Church coming to?" I tell you, she is not "coming to" anything; she has arrived. We do not look forward to discover her goal; we look back. God reached His end in Christ before the foundation of the world. As we move on with Him in the light of that eternal fact, we witness even now its progressive manifestation. In Romans 8. 30 Paul tells us that those God has foreordained He has both called and justified and glorified. Thus all His own have, in His intention, already been glorified. In Christ the goal is reached. The Church has already come to glory!

JULY 14th

Thou art the Christ, the Son of the living God. Matthew
16. 16.

Death is the power, the weapon, of the gates of hell.
This is still true today; yet until God has opened our eyes to
see it, we shall scarcely know the value of speaking out in confession of Him. But when suddenly, in some till now unforeseen circumstance, we find to our dismay that apparently faith
does not work, prayer does not work, our very spirits are
paralysed—then it is we shall learn the need to proclaim
Christ. In so doing we shall discover what it was God was
waiting for. "Thou art Lord. Thou art Victor. Thou art
King." The best prayer of all is not "I want" but "Thou art".
By the revelation given to us, let us speak. In prayer meetings,
at the Lord's Table, alone before the Lord, in the midst of the
thronging world, or in the dark hour of need, learn to proclaim "Thou art!"

JULY 15th

*When Abram heard that his brother was taken captive, he
led forth his trained men . . . and pursued.* Genesis
14. 14.

Lot had been quick to settle down in the land; before
long he was to lose his possessions in it. By contrast, as this
chapter reminds us, Abram was the Hebrew, the "passer-
over", the pilgrim. It is they who are content to remain in
transit in the land of promise who have real power against its
foes.

Abram had been right to leave the matter of possessions

with God, but he would have been quite wrong at the same time to have dismissed Lot from his love and concern. In this he was a true overcomer: before going out to pursue the kings he had won the victory in his own spirit. How easy to have nursed a grievance against his self-seeking kinsman! At the very least his attitude to the calamity might justly have been "I told you so!" But no, a grievance is no basis for victory. In all such circumstances we too must first win the battle in our own hearts. Is the man my brother? Then however he may have wronged or injured me, for the Lord's sake I must love him, pray for him, mobilize my forces to his aid.

JULY 16th

For of him, and through him, and unto him, are all things.
To him be the glory for ever. Romans 11. 36.

God must be the Originator of all spiritual work. His will must govern its beginnings; on this we are all agreed. Indeed we would go further and say that all is to end too with Him, so that, in Paul's words, "God may be all in all." But there is something more. He is not only the Originator and the Consummator of all things; He is the Worker too. And where His power is at work, all will issue in glory. Our trouble is that, while we know the beginning must be "of Him" and the end "unto Him", we forget the other vital fact, that all in the middle, all the great activity that lies between, must be "through Him". If He is to have glory at the last, we must be in no position to claim any. God's will governs the beginning, His glory the end, but His power must permeate the whole operation between. In practice the question of glory is settled, not at the end, but in the middle.

JULY 17th

*Grow in the grace and knowledge of our Lord and Saviour
Jesus Christ.* 2 Peter 3. 18.

We long to see men saved from perishing and won
for God's glory. But, do we stop there? When we see three or
four thousand converts—or even three or four!—all saved and
all going on fairly well with the Lord, do we feel a task has
been accomplished? Should we not regard it rather as a task
just begun? Ought we not to ask ourselves how many of them
have yet caught a glimpse of the one heavenly Man into which
God has brought them? Are they still just units, fishes in the
net, figures in a list of "campaign results", or does that supreme vision possess them? It will certainly not do so unless it
first possesses us. So I ask again, are we burdened, as were the
apostles, to see them grow up in all things into the Head, even
Christ?

JULY 18th

*Not one of them shall fall on the ground without your
Father.* Matthew 10. 29.

God is a God of purpose. Creation was no accident,
but the expression of a definite purpose on the part of God. A
great passage in Ephesians 1 speaks of His choice of us
"according to the good pleasure of his will", and tells us that
according to His purpose "we should be to the praise of his
glory, we who before hoped in Christ". When we think of
Adam's fall, and of our own sin, and of the meagreness of our

response to Him who by the grace of God tasted death for every man, we are wholly amazed at this. Can these things be? we ask ourselves. It is well, then, to be reminded that even the death of a sparrow, too trifling for us to note, is a thing of which God takes account. The Creator of the whole universe has a will regarding even one sparrow. "Fear not therefore; ye are of more value than many sparrows."

JULY 19th

My God shall fulfil every need of yours according to his riches in glory in Christ Jesus. Philippians 4. 19.

Many Christians are so poor they have not even sufficient to meet their own needs. Alas for any who go to them for help! Others are so rich you can never assess their wealth. You never seem to meet a difficulty they have not met, nor find yourself in a situation where they are unable to help. They seem to have resources enough for all who come to them in need. Many Christians do not go utterly bankrupt simply because they are being ministered to by others, who continually pour their own spiritual wealth into the Body. Such folk little know their debt to other believers, some of whom they might even be tempted to despise. It may be, when a friend comes from a journey and expects bread from us, that the Lord will permit us to turn to a neighbour for something to give him. But what if He should say to us, "Give ye them to eat"?

JULY 20th

Whom have I in heaven but thee? And there is none upon earth that I desire beside thee. Psalm 73. 25.

Our complete surrender of ourselves to the Lord often hinges upon some particular thing, and God waits for that one thing. He must have it, for He must have our all. I was greatly impressed by something a great national leader wrote in his autobiography: "I want nothing for myself; I want everything for my country." If a man can be willing that his country should have everything and he himself nothing, cannot we say to our God: "Lord, I want nothing for myself; I want all for Thee. I will be what Thou willest, and I want to have nothing outside Thy will."? Not until we take the place of a servant can He take His place as Lord. He is not calling us to devote ourselves to His cause; He is asking us to yield ourselves unconditionally to His will.

JULY 21st

Ye are the light of the world. Matthew 5. 14.

Some ask, should they preach? or should they seek employment in a profession or trade? *Are* there two roads in front of a child of God? Where in Scripture do we find such alternatives: to preach *or* find work? Is it a choice we are called upon to make? God's people are a lamp for witness. Is there then a Christian who is *not* to witness? It cannot be that a few preach, while in some mysterious sense all are the lamp. No, there is a living witness for God on earth and for that I live. This is the one road for us all and there is no other. None can be the Lord's and not testify to Him. All must preach Christ; that is the big thing. It is a secondary question whether all the time is to be given to it or some spent in breadwinning. For everything turns on where our centre is. God cannot use one who adds preaching to business; He can use one who adds business to preaching. It simply depends which side the addition is on! God, not our business, is to be the centre of our lives.

JULY 22nd

All thy estimations shall be according to the shekel of the sanctuary. Leviticus 27. 25.

Numbers opens with a census of all in Israel of an age to go forth to war. Just before it, in this last chapter of Leviticus, God provides an assessment of His children's value in terms of their self-dedication to Him. (Distinguish this carefully from the passage in Exodus 30 where the redemption price, which is identical for every soul, represented what God Himself had done for them.) Here God has a definite estimate of each one, and a quick comparison of Leviticus 27. 3 with Numbers 1. 3 makes it clear that preciousness to Him is measured in terms of readiness for war. This raises for us the question: Are we available to take our part in the age-long battle of the Lord? Jehovah is a Man of war, and energy for war is what He prizes most highly. Old or young, whatever the length of our spiritual history, the question each must ask himself today is: What, in terms of battle-preparedness, is my value to God in the sanctuary?

JULY 23rd

Let thine eyes look right on, and let thine eyelids look straight before thee. Proverbs 4. 25.

For us who are God's children the most soul-destroying thing is to turn our gaze inward. Introspection is a deadly disease. Have we realized this? Sin we readily recognize as deadly, but introspection is less obviously suspect; and it is the unsuspected disease that is more to be feared than the apparent one. If I put to you the question: "Is it wrong to be proud?" you know the answer. If I ask again: "What about envy?" you reply: "Of course it is wrong!" Yet you can turn in on yourself a score of times in a single day, imagining that in doing so you are being particularly spiritual, and be totally unaware of the evil of it.

Stop doing it! Learn to walk in the Spirit. Do you feel moved to preach Christ to a soul? Do you stay and examine yourself whether this urge is from you or from God. While you are asking your questions, the opportunity will be gone! Act, and you will be liberated.

JULY 24th

Present yourself unto God, as alive from the dead, and your members as instruments of righteousness unto God. Romans 6. 13.

Many have taken this word "present" to imply consecration, without looking carefully into its content. Of course that is what it does mean, but not in the sense in which we are inclined to understand it. It is not the consecration of our "old man" with his instincts and resources, his natural wisdom, strength and other gifts, to the Lord God for Him to use. This will be clear at once from the little clause "as alive from the dead". It defines for us the point at which consecration begins. For what is to be consecrated is not what belongs to the old creation, but only what has passed through death to resurrection. The "presenting" spoken of is the outcome of my knowing my old man to be crucified, and my reckoning myself alive unto God in Christ Jesus. Knowing, reckoning, presenting ourselves to Him: that is the divine order.

JULY 25th

And there we saw the Nephilim, the sons of Anak . . . and we were in our own sight as grasshoppers, and so we were in their sight. Numbers 13. 33.

Two thrones are at war. God claims the earth for His dominion. His arch-enemy, supported by spiritual hosts of wickedness, seeks instead to overrun it with evil, and thereby to exclude God from His own kingdom. We, God's people, are called upon to displace these mighty foes from their present realm and to make Christ head over all. What are we doing about it?

"If the Lord delight in us, then he will bring us into this land." This was the minority view of Joshua and Caleb in face of the ten spies' gloomy forecasts. *If the Lord delight in us.* One thing is certain: all talk of spiritual warfare remains but talk unless we have first learned to live a holy life. For the Nephilim *are* great, and we *are* grasshoppers; there is no disguising this. We realize it, and so do they! How do we live a life that is a delight to the Lord? Only by basing it on a true rest in Christ and in what He has done. If we lack this, Satan can afford to ignore us. With it, "their defence is removed from over them". We are more than conquerors *through Him*.

JULY 26th

So then death worketh in us, but life in you. 2 Corinthians
4. 12.

How precious is the Cross of Christ! It lies within
the scope of every single member to raise the tide of life in the
whole Body, provided only he will let the Cross deal drastically with the life of nature in him. You ask me how you can
be used to minister life to others. Not by setting out to do a lot
of things, nor yet by going into retirement and doing nothing
at all, but simply by letting the power of His death and resurrection operate in the course of your walk with God. Those
who serve only by words or works find their ministry brought
to a standstill if at any time circumstances reduce them to inactivity or silence. To be used, they must be doing or speaking.
But this should not, and need not, be so. Only let "the dying
of Jesus" work in you, and life will surely manifest itself in
others. It must be so, for it is an abiding principle of the Body
that "death worketh in us but life in you".

JULY 27th

*Five of you shall chase an hundred, and an hundred of you
shall chase ten thousand: and your enemies shall fall before
you.* Leviticus 26.8.

Here surely is a picture of our prayer. For when we
agree on earth, heaven binds ten thousand foes. How often
have the people of God, in an hour of crisis, taken these words
of Jesus at their face value and proved them! So on the night
when Peter lay in prison, the church throughout Jerusalem got
to its knees and prayed earnestly, and all Herod's authority

was as nothing before the response of heaven to that prayer. Another Kingdom had invaded his territory, and even the great prison door yielded and gave way of itself.

JULY 28th

Quench not the Spirit. 1 Thessalonians 5. 19.

Every one of us should expect to receive from God some burden to be discharged through prayer. It is as we faithfully discharge it that He entrusts to us fresh ones. The only reason we do not receive more is that we have neglected to discharge those He has already given. Unload them in prayer, and we shall find His reward is to trust us with new and weightier responsibilities.

It is vital to be sensitive in our spirits to God, for it is all too possible, by quenching the Holy Spirit, to forfeit this ministry. Should we do so, the way of recovery is to confess to Him our sin, then to respond faithfully and instantly to each new Spirit-given impression. Has He laid someone on your heart? Send up an appeal to God for him at once. Oh, my friend, if you hope to serve God usefully, recover your lost burden! Be faithful in prayer. The instant you are moved to pray, pray!

JULY 29th

The hand of the Lord was strong upon me. Ezekiel 3. 4.

All true work for God springs from a prayer burden originating with the Holy Spirit's urge upon your spirit. Try working without such a burden, and what you do is likely to prove labour in vain. But work from the knowledge of a compulsion placed upon you by God Himself, and you will find your whole being is increasingly liberated as you go forward. Moreover work so performed is sure of spiritual value. So, if you are seeking to serve God effectively, wait on Him till He communicates to you His burden and thus makes known His will. Is it a burden to speak of Christ to someone? Give expression to it first in prayer, for the ministry of prayer is indispensable to God's service. Then go out and do it.

JULY 30th

As unknown, and yet well known; as dying, and behold we live; as chastened, and not killed; as sorrowful, yet alway rejoicing; as poor, yet making many rich; as having nothing, and yet possessing all things. 2 Corinthians 6. 9 f.

To be a Christian is to be a person in whom seeming incompatibles co-exist, but in whom it is the power of God that repeatedly triumphs. A Christian is one in whose life there is inherent a mysterious paradox, and this paradox is of God. How can power be manifested to perfection in a weak man? By Christianity; for Christianity *is* that very thing. It is not the removal of weakness, nor yet is it merely the manifestation of divine power. It is the manifestation of that power in the presence of human weakness. For what God is doing in us is neither merely negative nor merely positive. It is both together. He does not eliminate our infirmity, nor does He bestow His strength just anywhere at random. No, He leaves us with the infirmity, and He bestows His strength *there*.

JULY 31st

All the saints salute you, especially they that are of Caesar's household. Philippians 4. 22.

Have you ever come across the Church that Paul describes in Ephesians 1. 18 in terms of "the riches of the glory of his inheritance in the saints"? Or that depicted in I Corinthians 6. 11 as "washed . . . sanctified . . . justified in the name of the Lord Jesus, and in the Spirit of our God"? Oh, you say, that describes the position of the Church, but look at the condition of the churches! No, I reply, it describes the reality of the Church. In addressing the Romans Paul was more daring than were some of his translators. He wrote "called saints", or "saints by calling", but they felt it was running too great a risk to translate this literally, so they safeguarded their conception of spiritual things by writing "called *to be* saints". If we are only called "to be" saints, how long shall we have to be "being" before we can actually *be*? Praise God, we *are* saints!

AUGUST 1st

The city was pure gold, like unto pure glass. Revelation 21. 18.

Gold speaks to us of something wholly of God; glass, of what is transparently pure. Might we adapt the latter simile, and suggest that *future* purity is well illustrated by glass, *present* purity by water? For water can readily become clouded with defilement, but no impurity can enter the texture of glass. Our purity today is still liable to change; our purity then will never alter. The "divine nature" imparted to us is pure gold; there is no question of that. But, alas, we contribute to it a sorry admixture of dross, so that God's chief work in us is one of subtraction. By the Cross He is seeking to eliminate the mixture, bringing to the judgment of His death all in us that is of ourselves. For the most precious thing *we* have it in our power to produce—is dross. And that must go, all of it, ere we find our place amid the pure gold of God's eternal city.

AUGUST 2nd

Father, glorify thy name. John 12. 28.

We are given a great deal of Christ's teaching, but here is one of those rare, intimate occasions when He reveals Himself. A passage of doctrine ends with verse 26, and now the Son of man Himself shines out. "What shall I say? Father, save me from this hour?" He is off His guard, as it were, exposing what He really is, but He does not speak carelessly. When speaking to His Father, no less than when preaching to men, the Cross rules Him. "For this cause came I unto this hour." I cannot say "Save me". This is what I can say: "Father, glorify thy name!"

When the heart is troubled, speak carefully. The Lord did.

AUGUST 3rd

He shall sit as a refiner and purifier of silver, and shall purify the sons of Levi, and purge them as gold and silver. Malachi 3. 3.

What do we prize in a day when values are slipping: the dross of human cleverness and worldly resources, or the gold and silver of divine origin and redemption through

Christ? Many things in Christianity have become too cheap today, but there is no easy short-cut to spiritual worth. Preaching, prayer, witness, these may not seem difficult, but to be of value they will be costly in years and blood and divine discipline. God's "vessel unto honour" is the man who has waited for the Spirit to teach him, and who has not been ashamed meanwhile to admit he does not know. For there comes a day when the true character of things is tested. Preaching, in an hour of departure and confusion, is of little value unless men see God in it. At such a time they can tell whether the speaker has really been taken by God through the things of which he speaks. What has not already touched him deeply will have little power to touch others in that day.

AUGUST 4th

We will not serve thy gods, nor worship the golden image which thou hast set up. Daniel 3. 18.

The issue which governed Israel's rise or fall was the issue of true worship or idolatry. The revival under king Hezekiah was a revival of worship first of all. So was that under Zerubbabel. The Captivity was a severe punishment, but its severity for the Israelite lay above all in its termination of their worship. For when God does not receive His portion, His people lose theirs, and the greatest of all punishments is to be forbidden to serve God.

"Our God is a consuming fire." Whatever in us can be burned, will be. I am always moved when I see our Indian brethren fall on their faces in worship. "Reverence and awe" in the presence of God are seemly in us all. Where these exist and our hearts are right with Him, we His children cannot be burned. This was the experience of Daniel's three friends.

They were clear above all on the vital issue of worship. Our God *whom we serve* is able to deliver us, they said. What was Nebuchadnezzar's paltry furnace to men who did their obeisance before the everlasting burnings? They had nothing that could be consumed.

AUGUST 5th

These are written, that ye may believe that Jesus is the Christ, the Son of God; and that believing ye may have life in his name. John 20. 31.

I was once holding meetings in a college in South China. There I found an old schoolfellow of mine was now Professor of Psychology, so before the meetings began I went to call on him, and spoke to him of Christ. After listening a while politely, he said smiling, "It's no good preaching to me. I don't believe there is a God!"

Next day to my amazement, at the end of my first meeting, who should stand up and testify that he was saved but this very professor! Afterwards I went up to him. "How did it happen?" I asked. "After you had gone," he said, "I picked up the Bible you left me and my eye caught the words in John chapter 1: 'The day after', 'the next day', 'the day after'. This writer, I thought to myself, knows what he's talking about. He *saw* it all. It is like a diary. Then I thought, What if after all there *is* a God? I should be a fool not to believe in Him. You had told me I could pray even to the God whose very existence I doubted, so I knelt and prayed. I don't know what I expected, but as I prayed I *knew* there was a God. How I knew I cannot explain; I just knew it! Then the words of that eye-witness, John, came back to me. Since there is a God, I thought, then Jesus *could* only be His Son—and I was saved!"

AUGUST 6th

The Lord that delivered me out of the paw of the lion, and
out of the paw of the bear, he will deliver me out of the hand
of this Philistine. 1 Samuel 17. 37.

David was anointed king at Bethlehem, but immediately he returned to his ordinary sphere of life to prove
the Lord there. He went back to his flock, not to some special
royal training-school. It was "with the sheep" that Saul's
messengers found him; and when his turn came to confront
Goliath, the weapons he used against him were those tested
there. Of Saul's helmet and sword and mail he said, "I have
not proved them," and he put them off him again. Instead he
chose his shepherd's sling and the stones from the brook, "that
all this assembly may know that the Lord saveth not with
sword and spear".

There is no virtue in office alone. Mere status carries with
it no spiritual power. You need to meet the enemy in secret
before you can meet him in public. You need to be in tune
with the Spirit of God at home before you can reign abroad.
But this is a training-school open to every one of us.

AUGUST 7th

The sun rose upon him as he passed over Penuel, and he
halted upon his thigh. Genesis 32. 31.

Here at Peniel, met face to face by God, Jacob received the new name of Israel. Yet the narrative continues to
call him Jacob! There is reason in this. The truth is, of course,
that nobody can completely change in one night. Jacob him-

self was not conscious of any great change. He only knew he had met God, and that now he had a permanent limp.

It is legitimate for us to use Scripture to interpret our experiences, especially when God has met us in a distinctive way. But let us beware of using it to build up false ideas of perfection. God's Word adheres firmly to hard facts, for nothing hinders spiritual growth more than pretence. For Jacob, Peniel was not the touch of perfection; it was the beginning only of a new and transforming experience of God. "The sun rose upon him."

AUGUST 8th

By faith Jacob . . . worshipped, leaning upon the top of his staff. Hebrews 11. 21.

How striking that the New Testament writer should choose this mark of apparent weakness to depict Jacob's faith. For Penuel, with its crippling divine touch, had indeed spelled an end to the supplanter with all his superabundant natural energy. In his place there stood now this gracious prince with God—and worshipped.

I was sitting one day at supper with a young brother to whom the Lord had been speaking on this very question of our natural energy. He said to me, "It is a blessed thing when you know the Lord has met you and dealt with you in a fundamental way, and that disabling touch has been received." There was a plate of biscuits between us on the table, and I picked one up and broke it in half as though to eat it. Then, fitting the two pieces together again carefully, I said, "It looks all right, but it is never quite the same again, is it? When once your back is broken, you will yield ever after to the slightest touch from God."

AUGUST 9th

The angel which hath redeemed me from all evil, bless the lads. Genesis 48. 16.

Isaac and Jacob illustrate the objective and the subjective sides of Christian experience. Isaac is a type of free grace; he received everything. Jacob on the other hand received nothing from others. His character was formed through the discipline of having to toil for it all. Both blessed their sons prophetically, but how different were their prophecies! Isaac did not understand what he was doing. The recipients of his blessing were the reverse of what he intended. But Jacob *knew.* When Joseph protested that he was making a mistake, he answered, "I know, my son, I know." He called each son by name, and he exactly understood them and their future. He had known what it was to wait for God's salvation.

AUGUST 10th

They were all together in one place. Acts 2. 1.

When at the incarnation God visited His people, but a handful of them looked for the redemption of Israel. They believed God was going to act, and through them and because of them He acted. Then in Jesus' own lifetime multitudes followed Him, but again it was a much smaller group who protested: "To whom shall we go? Thou hast the words of eternal life." And once more, before His ascension He instructed His own to await the promise of the Father. This command could well have reached over five hundred brethren who saw Him alive after His passion: yet by Pentecost only one hundred and twenty were gathered in prayer to cooperate with God in His newest move. Where were the other three hundred and eighty? No doubt they all came in later. But *now* . . .?

In practice it seems to work out that God has always to move through a faithful remnant who, within the larger number and for the sake of God's purpose in the whole, will be utter in their obedience to Him *today*.

AUGUST 11th

When they heard that the Lord had visited the children of Israel, and that he had seen their affliction, then they bowed their heads and worshipped. Exodus 4.31.

No change had actually taken place in their condition. They had only been assured by Moses and Aaron that God had not forgotten them during those four hundred and more years. This assurance was enough. They bowed in worship.

We feel unable to worship God because we think He has forgotten us in our trial and left us to our own resources. We have been sick and have longed for healing; we have been out of employment for months and still cannot find a job; our domestic difficulties seem endlessly prolonged (though scarcely yet for 430 years!); those closest to us refuse to believe in the Lord, in spite of all our prayers; the same old harassing circumstances remain. How can we worship Him? Our lips are silenced—until we see. A day comes when we understand the ways of God, and at once we *know* He has not forgotten us. In that day the silent lips are opened, the resentful heads bowed. We acknowledge God's grace in everything and we adore His ways.

AUGUST 12th

*The love of God hath been shed abroad in our hearts
through the Holy Ghost which was given unto us.*
Romans 5. 5.

Because the Lord Jesus died on the Cross I have received forgiveness of sins; because He rose from the dead I have received new life; because He has been exalted to the right hand of the Father I have received the gift of the Spirit. All is because of Him; nothing is because of me. Remission of sins is not based on my merit but on His crucifixion, regeneration is not based on my merit but on His resurrection, and the enduement with the Holy Spirit is not based on my merit but on His exaltation. The Holy Spirit has been given to you and me both to be the evidence that God's Son is in the glory, and, by the power of divine love, to lead us there. By His witness we know that Jesus of Nazareth, who was crucified by wicked men nearly two thousand years ago, did not just die a martyr's death but is exalted for us at the Father's right hand in glory. Hallelujah!

AUGUST 13th

*The word of God is living, and active, and sharper than
any two-edged sword, and piercing even to the dividing of
soul and spirit.* Hebrews 4. 12.

Some of God's children lay great emphasis on rightly dividing the word of truth. Indeed Scripture itself tells us we are to do this (2 Timothy 2. 15), but it also tells us His Word is to divide us. Where we may be wrong is in seeking to divide His Word first, before we have allowed it to do its work on us! Are we aware of this living, powerful character of God's Word? Does it deal with us like a sharp, two-edged sword? Or do we handle it as though it were just one more book to be studied and analysed?

The strange thing about Scripture is that it does not aim to make us understand doctrines in a systematic way. Perhaps we think it would have been better if Paul and the others had got together to provide a detailed handbook of Christian doctrines. But God did not permit this. How easily He could have settled some of our theological arguments, but it seems He loves to confuse those who only approach the Bible intellectually! He wants to preserve men from merely getting hold of doctrines. He wants His truth to get hold of them.

AUGUST 14th

While Peter yet spake these words, the Holy Ghost fell on all them who heard the word. Acts 10. 44.

God was always having to interrupt Peter! On the mount of transfiguration "while he was yet speaking" the Father spoke. "This is my beloved Son," He said. "Hear *him*"! Back in the house at Capernaum, when he had just committed his Lord to payment of the temple tax and was about to tell Him so, "Jesus spake first to him" to correct Peter's false ideas on the matter. And here in Caesarea, while Peter was still speaking, the Holy Spirit broke into the sermon with His mighty acts, so that Peter's six companions "were amazed", and so could be appealed to in support of his testimony on their return to Jerusalem. Father, Son and Holy Spirit each intervened to interrupt Peter. We may welcome any check upon our flow of words when it is God Himself who breaks in!

AUGUST 15th

Blessed are the pure in heart: for they shall see God. Matthew 5. 8.

Here is a heart-condition God requires for the fulfilment of His purposes of grace. Purity of heart simply means a state where there are no hindrances to seeing God. The kingdom of the heavens is here, so there is no reason why anyone should fail to see Him, *unless man himself puts up barriers.*

It is not necessary to place a dirty article in front of your eyes to prevent you seeing an object; a perfectly clean article will do just as well! The "clean heart" of the psalmist has to do with the removal of unclean things; the "pure heart" of the Sermon on the Mount has to do with the removal of all things, clean or unclean. Many have no right knowledge of God because they let their hearts run wild, so that they have numerous competing interests apart from God. Purity of heart corresponds to singleness of eye. It means that God is the exclusive object of attention. From such preoccupation there will be no loss. "Thy whole body shall be full of light."

AUGUST 16th

He shall give strength unto his king. 1 Samuel 2. 10.

The book of Judges is a record of revivals. The history of God's people is one of repeated backsliding, with God choosing one here, one there, as His instruments to bring recovery. But is this His real purpose for them? Are we today to expect another revival? Certainly our thoughts turn that way. But does God intend that, or something different?

God's eyes are towards a kingdom. He is planning for a King. The prophet Samuel becomes a link between the sorry history of the Judges and the ultimate fulness represented by David. He stands, the man of prayer, at the junction of the road to God's purpose. A great change is to take place and a kingdom be ushered in, and prayer will bridge the gap. Herein lies the wonder of Hannah's ministry. Her natural condition was no accident, but determined by God (1. 5). It brought her near to despair, yet with God in view she could not accept it as final. "O Lord of hosts!" she prayed, and in some amazing way her exercise of soul was harnessed to heaven's interests. The dearest thing in her life was dedicated in advance to those interests, and when the time came, given without regret to fulfil them.

AUGUST 17th

Seven days shalt thou tarry, till I come to thee, and shew thee what thou shalt do. 1 Samuel 10. 8.

Saul was tested on two points: faith and obedience. In a critical situation in Chapter 13 the question was, Would his faith allow him to wait for God? If you are driven into a corner and everything shouts that you should *do* something, then comes the test of whether you are carnal or spiritual. "*Till I come.*" Can the Lord count on us not to precipitate things until His hour strikes?

Again in Chapter 15 Saul was told to destroy Amalek utterly. But the bleating of sheep gave him away, for it is often the little things that betray us. Saul was attempting to judge between good and bad carnality, so as to bring something "good" in man and present it to God. That is no substitute for obedience; yet, "I have obeyed the voice of the Lord", he protested. Yes, the heart is deceitful. The Saul line of things is beyond improvement. God must have something altogether new, altogether different. He looks for one who will set his own judgment aside and be wholly governed by heaven. "But now thy kingdom shall not continue: the Lord hath sought him a man after his own heart."

AUGUST 18th

David therefore departed thence, and escaped to the cave of Adullam, ... and there were with him about four hundred men. 1 Samuel 22. 1 f.

The cave represented the answer to a spiritual need. Saul had the office of king and a great following. His was all the machinery of government, and God in sovereignty recognized him, but you will not find God with Saul. It is David who is under the Spirit's anointing, and he must go with God into the wilderness. So the cave became his headquarters. To it there found their way a band of those who were weary of existing conditions, and he became their captain. They came to Adullam in desperation, because their need was met nowhere else.

David is a type of the Lord Jesus in His present rejection. Even today, multitudes are on their way to His retreat. They crave for the reality to be found where the Spirit rules. They come to Him and He owns them as His loyal band. It is a lonely way. It is always lonely to stand against the man-made system. But that nucleus, gathered to the Lord Jesus in this day of His rejection, will be very dear to Him when He comes to the throne.

AUGUST 19th

*Praise him, O ye servants of the Lord. Ye that stand in the
house of the Lord, in the courts of the house of our God.*
Psalm 135. 1f.

What a privilege to stand in praise before the Lord!
It seems to me that today we always want to be moving on;
we cannot stand still. So many things claim our attention that
we are perpetually on the go. We cannot stop for a moment.
But he who is spiritual knows how to stand still. He can stand
before God in worship while God makes known to him His
will. He can pause and await orders.

May I ask you, dear fellow-worker, is not all your work
carried out to a schedule? And has it not to be done in great
haste? Can you be persuaded to call a halt and stand a while
before Him in praise? You will learn much that way.

AUGUST 20th

*Your fathers ... served other gods. And I took your
father Abraham from beyond the River, and led him
throughout all the land of Canaan, and multiplied his
seed.* Joshua 24. 2 f.

Abraham was called and chosen, not just for himself
but for his descendants, not merely to receive grace but to
transmit grace to others. There had been men of faith before
him, men like Abel, Enoch and Noah, who had nobly stood
out as different from their fellows; but to judge from the
record, they almost seem to have done so from birth. Abraham however was in his beginnings an idolator just like those
around him. By himself, until God called him, he could not
be ranked alongside those three.

Yet Matthew's Gospel opens with his name. Of all Old Testament names, his occurs most on the lips of Jesus. And this idolator was the man chosen to bring blessing to countless multitudes—chosen for no other reason than that God was pleased to choose him. There was nothing inherent in his character to suggest that through him such blessing should come to so many. God took him, led him and multiplied him. Cannot the same God do the same for you?

AUGUST 21st

But he, being full of the Holy Ghost, looked up steadfastly into heaven, and saw the glory of God, and Jesus standing on the right hand of God. Acts 7. 55.

Stephen's first words to the council were of God and His glory. "Brethren and fathers, hearken," he said: "The God of glory appeared unto our father Abraham. Then came he . . . and dwelt in Haran." The man who sees that glory knows he must respond. He cannot do otherwise. Abraham responded, and through all the setbacks and discouragements of his pilgrimage the vision of God's glory carried him in triumph. Stephen set out first of all to remind his hearers of this.

They heard Stephen's testimony, and rejected it, only to become suddenly aware that he himself was beholding that of which he spoke! Full of the Holy Ghost, he looked up steadfastly "and saw the glory of God". He who appeared to Abraham and He whom Stephen saw were one and the same. There is no change in Him. And that same God, His splendour still undimmed, now carried Stephen through his own terrible crisis. What matters an extra stone or two to one who beholds the glory of God!

AUGUST 22nd

*On this side of the river and on that was the tree of life,
bearing twelve manner of fruits, yielding its fruit every
month.* Revelation 22. 2.

There is one River, not four as in Genesis, where two
of them, Hiddekel and Euphrates, were one day to become
scenes of sorrow for God's people. Here one river of life, full
of water, proceeds out of the throne, to make glad the city of
God.

And there is one Tree, yielding its fruit every month. There
is no fall, no barren winter, no need to store from last month's
supply. By it we shall go on knowing Christ with ever-fresh
knowledge, for in its different fruits we shall taste Him at all
points, not just at one.

River and Tree, Christ's fulness and Christ's ever-newness:
we cannot move without them. Wherever we go we must
carry them with us now—Christ's way of life to give light and
healing to the nations.

AUGUST 23rd

*O send out thy light and thy truth; let them lead me: let
them bring me unto thy holy hill.* Psalm 43. 3.

"Thy light and thy truth": the two are connected.
The truth is complete in Christ, but the need of our hearts is to
have God's light shed on it. For while the basis of all our
certainty is the *reality* of Christ's person and of His victorious
work, we still have, with God's help, to *see* this—to know the
glorious truth that He already reigns, not that He is going to.

What God does in us today is something already *done* in Christ. Our supreme need is to be shown this fact. All spiritual experience derives from the shedding of divine light upon eternal truth. Preached without light from God, truth remains but doctrine. With that light, it will transform you and me, so that the reality, found till now in Christ alone, begins to be seen also in what God is making us to become in Him. And this pathway leads right on to God's "holy hill".

AUGUST 24th

In thy light shall we see light. Psalm 36. 9.

His light may come to us in many ways. Some of us have known saints who really knew the Lord, and through praying with them or talking with them, in the light of God radiating from them, we have seen what we never saw before. I have met one such, who is now with the Lord, and I always think of her as a "lighted" Christian. If I did but walk into her room I was brought immediately to a sense of God. In those days I was very young, and had lots of plans and schemes for the Lord to sanction. With all these I came to her to try to persuade her; to tell her this or that was the thing to do. But before I could open my mouth she would perhaps say a few words in quite an ordinary way. Light dawned! It simply put me to shame. I realized that my doing and my scheming were all so natural, so full of man. For she lived for God alone, and such a one is bathed in a light that illumines others.

AUGUST 25th

Arise, O Lord, into thy resting place; thou, and the ark of thy strength. Psalm 132. 8.

Everything in the temple of Solomon was built anew—everything, that is, except the ark. There was a new altar, a new laver or sea, new curtains, tables, candlesticks and all else. Moreover, all was on a grander scale than in the tabernacle. Lavers and candlesticks were multiplied, and the dimensions of the structure and of everything within it were greater than before. Only the ark was still the same.

The tabernacle in the wilderness typified God's presence amid His pilgrim people; the much larger temple, His presence among them in the settled kingdom. And it is certain that in the Kingdom that is to come we shall have a greater appreciation of the sacrifice of Christ than we have now, yes, and a greater apprehension too of the Spirit's fulness. Yet the changeless ark reminds us that God's testimony concerning the person of His Son is eternally the same; it can never be enlarged or elaborated. Our own grasp of Him and of His work can grow. *He changes not.*

AUGUST 26th

For I, saith the Lord, will be unto her a wall of fire round about. Zechariah 2. 5.

To describe the great city of God in the Revelation, John starts from the wall, for it is the wall that delimits all that is His own. Walls suggest security and strength. They suggest also separation. It is separation from a world out of which he has been delivered that is one distinctive mark of a Christian. Satan abhors such clear delimitation. (He much prefers walls of partition between the saints!) In Ezra's day, as later in Nehemiah's, it was the rebuilding of Jerusalem's walls which provoked such violent hostility. What comfort therefore that the Lord Himself says: "*I* will be a wall to her"!

AUGUST 27th

The natural man receiveth not the things of the spirit of God: for they are foolishness unto him. 1 Corinthians 2. 14.

It has pleased God to say many things which leave room for misunderstanding, and not to explain them. Often in the Bible there seem to be conflicting statements, or statements that seem to violate the known facts of life, and it has pleased Him to leave them there. There are many scriptures we cannot clearly explain. Had we been writing we would have put things far more plainly, so that men should have before them all the doctrine in foolproof systematic order. *But would they have had the life?*

The mighty eternal truths of God are half obscured in Scripture so that the natural man may not lay hold of them. God has hidden them from the wise to reveal them to babes, for they are spiritually discerned. His Word is not a study book. It is intended to meet us in the course of our day-to-day walk in the Spirit and to speak to us there. It is designed to give us knowledge that is experimental because related to life. If we are trying through systematic theology to know God, we are absolutely on the wrong road.

AUGUST 28th

Be ye kind one to another, tenderhearted, forgiving each other, even as God also in Christ forgave you. Ephesians 4. 32.

If you forgive a brother, the reality of your forgiveness will minister life to the Body, quite apart from any expression of it. If you truly love a brother, that love will build up the Body, even though you may never tell him how you love him. I found myself once, at short notice, taking part on the platform in a large convention meeting in England where, unknown to me, a Japanese brother was to be one of the speakers. We had not met before—and our two countries were at war. I do not know what that brother felt, and we had opportunity for but a brief conversation. I only know that while he spoke I was aware of the love and fellowship of a brother in the Lord, a love that leaped over national barriers, and that did not demand words for its expression.

AUGUST 29th

Ye search the scriptures, . . . and these are they which bear witness of me. John 5. 39.

In the Old Testament there is not only law and song and prophecy; there is Christ. But *how* is He there? We see types of Christ and prophecies of Christ and Messianic psalms; but is He merely written about there, or is there something more?

Jesus affirms that Abraham rejoiced to see His day, and saw it (John 8. 56). Moses, at a critical point of decision, rejected Egypt's wealth in favour of the reproach of Christ (Hebrews

11. 23 ff.). We read of David's sighs and desires and praises, and we say: "That's David!" No, that is Christ. For David, in describing his own experiences, "spake of the resurrection of Christ" (Acts 2. 25 ff.). And Isaiah did not just pass on information given to him; he saw His glory and he spake of Him (John 12. 41). You cannot detach God from His servants. The life of Christ in them took them through certain experiences and they recorded them. In these many persons down the centuries Christ moved to express Himself, and the sum of the records is the Word of God, "the things concerning Himself".

AUGUST 30th

And she said unto him, I am the daughter of Bethuel. . . .
And the man bowed his head and worshipped the Lord.
Genesis 24. 24 ff.

Do you see what it means to worship God? When you are faced with some difficult task about which you have sought the Lord for help, and when thereafter things fall out as you asked, do you just rejoice in the prosperity of your way? Or worse, are you inclined to attribute some of it to your own ability, or to chance? It was not so with Abraham's servant. He did not congratulate himself on the fortunate turn events had taken. He did not even stop to talk with Rebekah. Without hesitation or embarrassment he bowed his head, and his lips formed the words: "Blessed be the Lord!" His instantaneous reaction was to adore the ways of God, and at each new turn of events he saw a new opportunity to do so. To be a true worshipper is to bring glory to God by offering Him instant praise and thanksgiving for everything we meet. For God orders all our ways so that we may bring to Him the worship He desires.

AUGUST 31st

*He saith unto them, Moses for your hardness of heart
suffered you to put away your wives: but from the beginning it hath not been so.* Matthew 19. 8.

To the Pharisees there seemed to be a discrepancy
between the teaching of Jesus that what God has joined together must not be sundered and the command of Moses
concerning divorce. Superficially of course there *is* a discrepancy; but there is no change in God. It is not that what
was first forbidden became lawful in His eyes later on, and
still later was forbidden again, as though God were capricious.
No, when Jesus says "From the beginning it hath not been
so", He affirms that, despite appearances, God's will is consistent. It has never altered. Here is a most important principle.
It is not God's permissions, but His directive will we need
always to discover. We should ask ourselves what was God's
purpose from the beginning. We need to see things as they
were when they proceeded in all their purity from the mind of
God, not as they have become because of His people's hardness of heart.

SEPTEMBER 1st

*O woman, great is thy faith; be it done unto thee even as
thou wilt.* Matthew 15. 28.

In the agony of her need this Canaanite woman had
cried: "Have mercy on me, O Lord, thou son of David!"
Was she not earnest in her prayer? Truly she was. Then was it
not the kind of prayer that might be expected to receive an
immediate answer? We would think so. Yet amazingly, Jesus
"answered her not a word" To her He seemed to have

nothing to say, but to the disciples' complaints about her He replied that His mission was to "the lost sheep of the house of Israel". That answer seems to have supplied her with the clue to a right approach to Him however. For He was "son of David" only to Israel. Others had no such claim upon Him. Realizing this, she changed the ground of her appeal, addressing Him now simply as Lord.

His first response to her had *seemed* like a rebuff. But in fact He was helping her to seek Him, not on the false ground of a privilege she had no claim to, but solely on the ground of unmerited grace. Her faith now met an instant response. She had found the key.

SEPTEMBER 2nd

He said unto her, For this saying go thy way; the devil is gone out of thy daughter. Mark 7. 29.

The question is sometimes asked: Does the exercise of a ministry of prayer, so vital to the Christian, call for utterance, or is it enough if we bear our burdens silently before God? I believe the answer is that if God gives a burden of prayer, He does in fact want it to be uttered. He wants audible expression given to it, however few and disjointed the words we may use. No burden can be discharged without this expression. Even our Lord Himself in Gethsemane "offered up prayers and supplications with strong crying". It seems to me that in spiritual things there is an amazing link between faith and utterance. God not only takes account of what we believe, He takes account of what we say. The Syrophoenician woman spoke only a sentence, but as a result of this she returned to her house to find the devil gone!

SEPTEMBER 3rd

There builded he an altar unto the Lord. Genesis 12. 7.

It was where God had appeared to him that Abram built an altar. Until God appears to a man, that man does not on his own initiative offer Him his all. But the day God meets him, that day God has his life. Abram knew little of the doctrine of consecration, nor had he been urged by others to consecrate himself; which perhaps was well, for not all who preach consecration, I fear, are consecrated people, and many who understand the doctrine know little of the reality. But Abram had seen God, and so he built his altar. Catch a glimpse of Him and you are His for ever. Two thousand years of church history only go to confirm this.

SEPTEMBER 4th

Wherefore, brethren, give the more diligence to make your calling and election sure. 2 Peter 1. 10.

Spiritual wealth comes not from special gifts of grace on special occasions, but from unremitting divine activity in a human life over years of time. It is a grief to me to find brothers and sisters so dependent on special experiences that, between the periodic help these bring, they lapse into a life indistinguishable from that of the pagans around them. What a poverty-stricken state this reveals! They are laying in store no riches. Between the temporary lift they get from Christian meetings or other means of grace, they live a life of defeat. The life of the Spirit is not like that. Its wealth is not gained at the halting-places of life, but through the ceaseless operation of God's grace on the long stretch of the road between.

SEPTEMBER 5th

Flesh and blood hath not revealed it unto thee, but my
Father which is in heaven. Matthew 16. 17.

The Church's foundation is not only Christ but the
knowledge of Christ. The tragedy today is that many of us in
the churches—indeed many so-called churches—lack such
foundation. We do not know Him. To us He is a theoretical
or doctrinal Christ, not a revealed Christ. But theory will not
prevail against hell, which is what Jesus declares His Church is
to do. Have we perhaps forgotten what we are for? Visiting
Western homes I have sometimes seen a beautiful porcelain
plate, not put to use on the table, but wired and hung up to
the wall as a treasured ornament. Many, it seems to me, think
of the Church like that, as something to be admired for the
perfection of its form. But no, God's Church is for use, not
decoration. An appearance of life may seem to suffice when
conditions are favourable, but when the gates of hell come out
against us, we know well enough that what we each need
above all is a God-given vision of His Son. It is first-hand
knowledge that counts in the hour of testing.

SEPTEMBER 6th

Abide in me, and I in you. As the branch cannot bear fruit
of itself, except it abide in the vine; so neither can ye, except
ye abide in me. John 15. 4.

These familiar words remind us that it is God who
has placed us in Christ. We are there, and we are told to *stay*
there! It was God's own act, and we are to abide by it.
"Abide in me, and I in you." This is a double sentence: a

command matched by a promise. That is to say, there is an objective and a subjective side to God's working, and the subjective depends on the objective; the "I in you" is the outcome of our abiding in Him. We need to guard against being over-anxious about the subjective side of things, as though a branch of the vine should strive to produce grapes of a particular size or colour. We need to dwell upon the objective—"Abide in me"—and let God take care of the outcome. And this He has undertaken to do. The character of the fruit is always determined by the Vine.

SEPTEMBER 7th

At midnight there is a cry, Behold the bridegroom! Come ye forth to meet him. Matthew 25. 6.

It was the bridegroom's tarrying that brought to light the state of the virgins. How can I be prepared for the Lord's coming? There are some of us who would have been ready had He come five years ago, but who would not if He came today. It is good to be prepared should He come now, but it is no less important to keep prepared, should He tarry. Can we wait and still be ready? Some people can wait three days, but not three years. Some could hang on for three years at a pinch, but they may be required to watch for thirty. For consider this: if the bridegroom had come before midnight, all the virgins would have been wise! It was His delay which exposed their folly. May God preserve me from becoming foolish with the passing years! One thing only can insure me against the test of time: His Spirit's fulness. Let me but know His constant filling and there will not lack oil in my lamp when that great midnight cry goes forth.

SEPTEMBER 8th

Nay: but as captain of the host of the Lord am I now come.
Joshua 5. 14.

Faced with the task of leading Israel against this land of seven strong nations, it were little wonder if Joshua were to feel overwhelmed. But here by Jericho he was given this vision. A Man with a drawn sword stood before him. "Art thou for us, or for our adversaries?" he inquired, and the answer came back, an uncompromising "Nay". He was neither for the one side nor the other. He had come "as captain".

Praise God, this is His purpose, to take His place as Captain of His host. We want everything to circle round us and serve our interests, but God will not have it so. He does not stand in the midst of the conflict giving a little help here or there. For us the question at issue is not one of receiving help, but of accepting leadership. You do not know God if you think He can occupy a subordinate position in the battle. His place is to lead. Only then will you know what it means to have His sword drawn on your behalf.

SEPTEMBER 9th

Behold, I am with thee, . . . for I will not leave thee, until I have done that which I have spoken to thee of. Genesis 28. 15.

Here at Bethel, in spite of Jacob's spiritual state, God had no word of rebuke for him. We certainly would have berated him soundly! And God is holy; He had no liking for

Jacob's deceptions. Yet He did not reprove him. What use would it have been? Jacob could not change himself, and God did not therefore exhort him to do so. But what was impossible to Jacob God could do, and His words reveal His absolute confidence in Himself. "I will not leave thee until I have done . . ." He knew that His servant could not escape His hand, and that the Jacob who would return years later to Bethel would be a very different man. "Behold, I am with thee." This is our comfort.

SEPTEMBER 10th

By faith Noah, being warned of God concerning things not seen as yet, moved with godly fear, prepared an ark to the saving of his house; through which he condemned the world, and became heir of the righteousness which is according to faith. Hebrews 11. 7.

We cannot speak of "baptismal regeneration", but we may speak of "baptismal salvation", salvation from the *cosmos* or world-system. We are involved in Satan's world-system. To be saved is to make our exit from his world into God's. In the Cross of our Lord Jesus the world has been crucified unto us and we unto the world. This is the figure developed by Peter when he writes of the eight souls who were "saved through water" (1 Peter 3. 20). Entering into the ark, Noah and those with him stepped by faith out of that old corrupt world into a new one. It was not so much that they were personally not drowned, but that they were *out* of that corrupt system. That is salvation. When you are baptized you go down into the water and your world, in figure, goes down with you. You come up in Christ, but your world is drowned.

SEPTEMBER 11th

Look unto me, and be ye saved, all the ends of the earth.
Isaiah 45. 22.

How aptly this describes the experience of the dying thief! All history had pointed forward to the Cross of Christ. Now the event itself was being enacted before men's eyes, and this criminal was a key witness. A model sinner, he was receiving a model punishment. We must conclude therefore that his was a model conversion. Yet I ask you, did he recognize Jesus as Saviour? Consider his words: "Remember me when thou comest into thy kingdom" (Luke 23. 42). What did the Lord reply? He did not explain the atonement to this man, telling him his punishment was just, but that He, Jesus, was dying in his stead as a sacrifice for sin. To us it would have seemed an excellent opportunity to announce the truths of redemption; but no, He answered only, "Today shalt thou be with me in paradise." For the thief saw dimly who Jesus was: that through suffering unjustly, He would reign and have a kingdom. Beholding at his side the Lord of all the earth, he cried out *to Him*, and that was enough.

SEPTEMBER 12th

I had heard of thee by the hearing of the ear; but now mine eye seeth thee. Job 42. 5.

Sound doctrine can inflate us, making us proud of our knowledge or our opinions. Or we can forget the truth by having it knocked out of us by skilled argument or third-degree methods. But vision is revolutionary. Beside it everything else becomes small. Once see the Lord and we shall never forget Him. With the attacks of Satan increasing and the counsel of friends failing us, it is only the inner knowledge of God that will make us stand in the testing time.

For a year or two after my conversion I used to fear lest a modernist or an atheist should come along and prove to me that the Bible was faulty and unreliable. I thought, if he did, that would finish everything. My faith would be lost; and I *wanted* to believe. But now all is peace. If all of them came, and if they brought as many arguments against the Bible as there are bullets in the armouries of Europe, my answer would be one and the same. "There is a great deal of reason in what you say—but I know my God. That is enough."

SEPTEMBER 13th

Let us draw near with a true heart in fulness of faith, having our hearts sprinkled from an evil conscience. Hebrews 10. 22.

When we enter the Most Holy Place, on what ground dare we enter but by the precious Blood of Christ? But I have to ask myself, am I really seeking the way into the presence of God by the Blood or by something else? What do I mean when I say, "by the Blood"? Simply that I recognize my sins, that I confess that I have need of cleansing, and that I come to God on the basis of the finished work of the Lord Jesus. I approach God through His merit alone, and never on the basis of my attainment; never, for example, on the ground that I have been extra kind or patient today, or that today I have done something for the Lord.

I may be mistaken, but I fear some of us are thinking in terms such as these: "Today I have been a little more careful; today I have been doing a little better; so today I can approach God and can pray better!" No, no, *no*! A clear conscience is *never* based upon our attainment; it can only be based on the atoning work of the Lord Jesus in the shedding of His Blood.

SEPTEMBER 14th

This is nothing else save the sword of Gideon the son of Joash, a man of Israel: into his hand God hath delivered Midian, and all the host. Judges 7. 14.

It is the means it pleased God to use to reassure His servant that is so arresting. Here was this vast invading army, like locusts for multitude, and Gideon had been instructed progressively to disband his own forces. It seemed absurd to expect the three hundred that remained to overthrow this Midianite host, and Gideon seems to have had no assurance regarding the issue. It was in this state of uncertainty that he ventured into the enemy camp.

Praise God, when we have no way out it is always an easy matter for Him to open a way. That little band of men was indeed to be His instrument for the deliverance of His people, and His servant, in his own dilemma, was to hear the assuring news in the way most calculated to stir his faith, namely from the prophetic lips of one of his foes. Fear, he learned, had already struck them. No wonder he worshipped!

SEPTEMBER 15th

Ye shall not be as the hypocrites. Matthew 6.5.

Too many of us are caught *acting* as Christians. We live a "spiritual" life, talk "spiritual" language, adopt "spiritual" attitudes, but we are doing the whole thing ourselves. Perhaps indeed we are doing it fairly well, but it is the effort involved that should warn us something is wrong. We force ourselves to refrain from this, from that, from the other, and what a strain it all is! Do you ever have to talk a language not your own? If so you know what I mean. Try as you will it does not flow spontaneously. You have to force yourself to talk that way. But when it comes to speaking your own language, nothing could be easier. You speak it effortlessly, without conscious thought. Its very spontaneity reveals to everyone *what you are*.

Nothing is so hurtful to a Christian life as play-acting, nothing so blessed as when our words, our prayers, our very demeanour, all become a spontaneous expression of the life of Christ our wonderful Lord.

SEPTEMBER 16th

He hath said unto me, My grace is sufficient for thee: for my power is made perfect in weakness. 2 Corinthians 12. 9.

It is significant that Paul says very little about the nature of the "visions and revelations of the Lord" alluded to in this chapter. It would not be profitable, he says, to boast of them, and only against his desires and under strong compulsion does he mention the experiences of "fourteen years ago". Fourteen years! And yet with many of us, directly we have something from God, the whole of Shanghai knows it! To suppress it even for two years would be a feat. But Paul, even after so long, does not tell us *what* that vision was, save that it was a further seeing of Christ. He tells us however of the subsequent "thorn in the flesh" and of God's gracious answer to his prayer. It is that answer, not the visions, that has brought strength to so many.

SEPTEMBER 17th

Ye meant evil against me; but God meant it for good.
Genesis 50. 20.

God had a special work for Joseph to do: to save Israel from famine and death. His ways with His servant were most exceptional, but in the end Joseph could say to his brethren: "God sent me before you to preserve life." He understood. The question is, do we? Not only when we are consciously serving Him, but from our earliest beginnings God's hand is upon us. His foreknowledge prepared our circumstances even before we were born. He determined whose child we should be, though sometimes we may feel we have been born into the wrong family! Some of us approve of our parents but would like perhaps to change our brothers and sisters, or our other relatives! Joseph could have felt this, and with reason, for they plotted evil against him. But the whole road is prepared for us by God. He *means* it all, and He means it *for good*. If we have not seen God's hand at work in His choices, we have lost a great opportunity to bring Him praise.

SEPTEMBER 18th

The way of an eagle in the air. Proverbs 30. 19.

Consider the birds. If you could ask them whether they were not afraid of the law of gravity, how would they reply? They would say: "We never heard the name of Newton. We know nothing about his law. We fly because it is the law of our life to fly." Not only is there in them a life with the power of flight, but that life has a law which enables these living creatures quite spontaneously to overcome the law of gravity. Yet gravity remains. If you get up early one morning when the cold is intense and the snow thick on the ground, and there is a dead sparrow in the courtyard, you are reminded at once of the persistence of that law. But while birds live they overcome it, and the life within them is what dominates their consciousness. Yes, the law of the spirit of life in Christ Jesus *has* made me free from the law of sin and death!

SEPTEMBER 19th

They entered . . . into the synagogue . . . and so spake that a great multitude both of Jews and of Greeks believed. Acts 14. 1.

When we stand up and speak, folk detect at once whether we stress doctrine or life. If it is the former, we never run risks. We keep carefully within the limits of our doctrinal scheme, in order to be absolutely safe and to avoid all possible chance of misunderstanding. We present our reasons in logical

order, and by a process of induction arrive at our incontrovertible conclusions. But if it is life we are stressing, our
approach will be very different. We shall be far less concerned
with technical correctness, for we ourselves have known
conditions through which mere doctrine could never carry us.
If only we can present Christ in His living Person to our
hearers, and leave them with Him, we know our object will
be achieved.

SEPTEMBER 20th

*After these things the word of the Lord came unto Abram in
a vision, saying, Fear not, Abram: I am thy shield and thy
exceeding great reward.* Genesis 15. 1.

When God says "Fear not" it is because He detects
either fear or doubt in His servant's heart. Note the events that
have just preceded His words here. Abram, having received
from Melchizedek bread and wine, seems to have found it easy
to refuse the proffered rewards of the king of Sodom. Once
home again, however, doubts and questions may well have
crowded into his mind. Was it wise to have made so uncompromising a refusal of all help? Had his downrightness
made him new enemies?

Thank God, to every doubt there is a divine assurance.
"The word of the Lord came to Abram." As to his fears? *God*
would be to him a protecting shield. As to the future? He
offered *Himself*, no less, as Abram's superlative reward. How
Abram must have thanked God he had not after all let himself
be seduced by Sodom's pitiful substitute for this!

SEPTEMBER 21st

He that walketh in darkness, and hath no light, let him trust in the name of the Lord, and stay upon his God. Isaiah 50. 10.

When we find ourselves thrown into darkness, the one great danger is that we shall start kindling fires (verse 11), encircling ourselves with our own pale flames in the hope that they will give us light by which to walk. "I have thought things over; I have put two and two together; I feel confident that . . .; my judgment is . . .;" such thoughts and feelings as these are no source of light. They are but firebrands. Put them in the light of God and their conclusions are seen to be neither deep enough nor clear enough. In the end we shall but "lie down in sorrow". If it is confusion we want, by all means let us look to such expedients. But darkness will never be dispelled by men's fires. Light is from God alone. Look up to Him! Even when all here is darkness, there is light there. And "in thy light shall we see light".

SEPTEMBER 22nd

All the multitude sought to touch him. Luke 6. 19.

None of us can fathom the mysterious ways of God, nor prescribe for Him how He shall work. There was a Chinese boy who, when he was twelve years old, was taken by his mother to worship in a temple up in the hills. As he stood with her before the shrine, he looked at the idol, and he thought: "You are too ugly and dirty to be worshipped. I don't believe you can save me. What is the sense in worshipping you?" But out of respect for his mother he joined in the ceremony, and after it was over his mother got into her chair to be carried down the mountain. Then he slipped away to the back of the temple and found there an open space. Looking up to heaven he said, "O God, whoever You are, I do not believe You can dwell in that dirty shrine. You are too big. I do not know how to find You, but I put myself in Your hands; for sin is very strong, and the world pulls. I commit myself to You, whoever You may be." Thirty years later I met him and told him the Gospel. He said, "I have met the Lord Jesus for the first time today, but this is the second time that I have touched God. Something happened to me long ago on that mountain top."

"And as many as touched him were made perfectly whole." God does not always explain to us how.

SEPTEMBER 23rd

He put the staves into the rings on the sides of the ark, to bear the ark. Exodus 37. 5.

The ark of testimony had no fixed platform. In the entire description of the Tabernacle, no mention is made of the floor beneath it, for of course it was the same desert soil as was trodden by the feet of every Israelite. And *our* testimony as Christians is what we are proving of Christ Himself in *our* daily walk. Moreover, just as the staves ensured that the ark was ever ready to be borne forward, so our testimony can never be static, but always mobile, fresh, vital. I mean this in the sense, not of something quickly conjured up when a need arises, but rather of an always ready, always fresh evidence of what God can do. Christ, and not in the first place what we say about Him, is the testimony we bear on our pilgrimage, and every step of the journey brings us new discoveries of Him.

We, who are many, are one body in Christ and severally members one of another. Romans 12. 5.

This concept of Jesus and His people as a body and its members was bound up with the very conversion and calling of Saul of Tarsus. The Lord's first words to him, "I am Jesus whom thou persecutest," stressed the fact that in touching His own, Saul was touching Him. In a remarkable way they heralded therefore the great revelation that was to be given him of the mystery of the Church. But the Lord did not leave the matter there. He did not allow him to stay with the heavenly mystery. The command that immediately followed came right down to the practical consequences of such a revelation. "Rise, and enter into the city, and it shall be told thee what thou must do." *It shall be told thee.* He must await instructions from those he hated! Apart from the very disciples he had set himself to destroy, Saul would be helpless; he would never know.

Our citizenship is in heaven; from whence also we wait for a Saviour, the Lord Jesus Christ. Philippians 3. 20.

Though we may work our way across the Atlantic or the Pacific, we can never work our way from earth to heaven. Heaven is not a place the Church will reach at some future date. The Church *is* there. Heaven is both her origin and her abode, but not her destination. And since this is so, the question of striving to reach heaven can never arise. This statement may appear extreme, I readily admit, but it is true. Oh to see afresh the wonders of our heavenly calling! That calling does not beckon us to heaven; it makes known to us that we belong there and are there! So we Christians are not working our way heavenward. We are citizens now of heaven, with all our affections firmly set there.

SEPTEMBER 26th

Thou didst hide these things from the wise and under-standing, and didst reveal them unto babes. Matthew 11. 25.

Shortly after my conversion I went out preaching in the villages. I had had a good education and was well-versed in the Scriptures, so I considered myself thoroughly capable of instructing the village folk, among whom many were illiterate women. But after several visits I discovered that, despite their illiteracy, those women had an intimate knowledge of the Lord. I knew the Book they haltingly read; they knew the One of whom the Book spoke. I had much in myself; they had much in the Spirit. And it had not yet dawned on me that, apart from the discipline of the Cross, what I had could well prove a handicap to the Holy Spirit's working. How many Christian teachers today are teaching others, as I was then, very largely in the strength of their carnal equipment! But thank God, He reveals Himself to babes!

SEPTEMBER 27th

Sanctify in your hearts Christ as Lord. 1 Peter 3. 15.

The reason why so many Christians do not experience the power of the Spirit is that they lack reverence for Him. And they lack reverence because they have not had their eyes opened to the solemn fact of His indwelling presence. The fact is incontrovertible, but they have not seen it. Why do some of God's children live victorious lives while others are in a state of constant defeat? The difference is not accounted for by the presence or absence of the Spirit (for He dwells with every child of God) but by this, that some *know* His indwelling and others do not, and that consequently some recognize the divine ownership of their lives while others are still their own masters. Discovery of the fact that his heart is God's dwelling-place will revolutionize the life of any Christian.

SEPTEMBER 28th

While we were yet sinners, Christ died for us. Romans 5. 8.

Seeing the price of our redemption, how can we do other than give ourselves to Him? "By the mercies of God I beseech you," pleads Paul in Romans 12. Throughout the preceding eleven chapters he has recounted them, divine mercies all the way. Love led Christ to die that we might walk in newness of life. That same love of Christ draws us back to Him again. Faced by love so utterly selfless, it is harder to withhold than to offer ourselves to Him. To be for years a

Christian without total dedication to God is a wholly astounding thing; for were we not bought with a measureless price? Our willing choice therefore is to glorify God in our bodies and spirits, "which are God's" (1 Corinthians 6. 19 f.). This is His right, not a favour we are showing Him. I am not my own. Dare I purloin what is His? "Lord, all I have and am and hope for—all is Thine!"

SEPTEMBER 29th

He that cometh after me is mightier than I; . . . he shall baptize you with the Holy Ghost and with fire. Matthew 3. 11.

God only gives good gifts to His children. Unfortunately we are apt to esteem them lightly because of their sheer abundance. The Old Testament saints, who were less favoured than we are, could appreciate more readily the preciousness of this gift of the outpoured Spirit. In their day it was a gift given only to the select few, chiefly to priests, judges, kings and prophets, whereas now it is the portion of every child of God. Think! we mere nonentities who trust in Christ can have resting upon us the same Spirit who rested upon Moses the friend of God, upon David the beloved king, and upon Elijah the mighty prophet. "Among them that are born of women," said Jesus, "there hath not arisen a greater than John the Baptist: yet he that is but little in the kingdom of heaven is greater than he."

SEPTEMBER 30th

There is that scattereth, and increaseth yet more. Proverbs
11. 24.

God's principle of government in material things is
the principle of the manna, that "he that gathered much had
nothing over, and he that gathered little had no lack" (Exodus
16. 18 and 2 Corinthians 8. 14 f.). This means that if he that
has gathered little is to have no lack, anyone who has gathered
much must be willing to have nothing over. Some of us have
proved in experience the preciousness of this. When we bear
the burden for those who gather little, God sees to it that we
gather much; but if instead we think merely of our own needs,
the very utmost we can hope for is to gather little and have no
lack.

It is a privilege to be able to help our brethren in the Lord,
even to the extent of the greater part of our income. Those
who have only learned to take seldom receive; but those who
have learned to give are always receiving and have always
more to give. The more you spend on others, the more your
income will increase; the more you try to save, the more you
will be troubled by "rust" and "thieves".

OCTOBER 1st

*God remembered Abraham, and sent Lot out of the midst of
the overthrow.* Genesis 19. 29.

As soon as he understood that God was about to
execute judgment on Sodom, Abraham began to pray. It is
most instructive to see how he prayed. He did not merely
plead with God to spare the city. No, he based his appeal on
God's character. He laid hold upon the fact that He is a

righteous God. That was the secret of his prayer. In deep humility and with great earnestness he put to Him question after question. His questions were his requests, and all were based on the righteousness of God. After his final request, we are told, "the Lord went his way". Some people hold that Abraham should have continued asking. But he knew God, and above all he knew the secret of prayer. His intercession could save his kinsman because it was rightly based. When God overthrew the cities He "delivered righteous Lot" (2 Peter 2. 7).

OCTOBER 2nd

Remember Lot's wife. Whosoever shall seek to gain his life shall lose it: but whosoever shall lose his life shall preserve it. Luke 17. 32 f.

If I mistake not, this is the one passage in the New Testament that tells of our reaction to the rapture call. In that moment we shall discover our real heart's treasure. If it is the Lord Himself, there will be no backward look. It is so easy to become more attached to the gifts of God than to the Giver— and even, I may add, to the work of God than to God Himself. But he that is on the housetop is not to go back for his goods. Let me illustrate. I am engaged in writing a book. I have finished eight chapters and I have another nine to write, about which I am seriously exercised before the Lord. Now, suppose the call to "come up hither" were to come and my reaction were to be, "What about my book?" Is it not possible that that precious thing which I am doing downstairs in the house, as it were, might be enough to pin me down, a peg that could hold me to the earth? The question at issue is always, Where is my heart?

OCTOBER 3rd

It is God that worketh in you both to will and to work, for his good pleasure. Philippians 2. 13.

Now that I am in Christ, God's moral demands have not altered, but it is no longer I who meets them. Praise God, He who is the Lawgiver on the Throne is now also the Law-keeper in my heart. He who gave the Law Himself keeps it. He makes the demands, but He also meets them. While we were trying to do it all, He could do nothing. It was because we were struggling to achieve it that we failed and failed. The trouble with us was that we were weak enough not to do the will of God, but not yet weak enough to keep out of things altogether! Only utter disillusion can throw men back in despair upon the God who is ready to do it all.

OCTOBER 4th

This is the boldness which we have toward him, that, if we ask anything according to his will, he heareth us. 1 John 5. 14.

Faith only operates freely within the province of the will of God. Outside of that will we may cry, believe, act in faith, and a great deal more, without perceptible result; God is not backing us. Trying to believe along some line of our own, we shall only prove that mountains of faith cannot remove a single mustard seed of difficulty! God will not be responsible for what we undertake on the basis of our own good intentions. His power is invested in His will. Get things right there, and we may have boldness in the face of the biggest testings. For "he heareth us".

OCTOBER 5th

You . . . by the power of God are guarded through faith.
I Peter 1, 5.

There is a condition attached to God's keeping power. We are guarded *through faith*. Unless we trust Him He cannot guard us. To know His safe-keeping we must believe whole-heartedly in His promises. If we harbour doubts about our security in face of temptation, are we not discrediting His ability to keep us? For it is not we who have to grapple with Satan's enticements. Every morning when we rise, we should say to Him: "I thank Thee for guarding me yesterday. I do not know what temptations may befall me today nor how I shall overcome them, but I trust Thee again to see me through." Rely implicitly on Him, our God of power. Then, however unpredictable the evil one's fiery darts, something amazingly wards them off. It is the shield of faith.

OCTOBER 6th

The priest's lips should keep knowledge, and they should seek the law at his mouth. Malachi 2. 7.

It is possible that much so-called revival is on a wrong basis. Spiritual gifts are displayed, but without a ministration of Christ, and that is like having many utensils, but nothing to use them for. But it is worse, for without Christ, gifts are not only empty; they may also be deceptive. Some of them at least can be simulated in a way that a ministry of Christ can never be. What matters to the Lord's people is not our gifts of preaching or prayer or what-have-you, but the personal knowledge of Christ that we convey by them. In a hospital two nurses may use exactly similar spoons, but what they give in those spoons is the important thing; one may give costly and curative medicine, the other a mere palliative. It is *what* we minister that counts.

OCTOBER 7th

Ye have heard that it was said of them of old time . . . but I say unto you . . . Matthew 5. 21 f.

Bondage to law may be defined as a rigid adherence to a bygone code of life that leaves us unready to follow the Lord's speaking in the present. We see the law as a standard of living; but it is a fixed standard. When we were youngsters at school our gymnastic teacher lowered or raised the rope for the high-jump according to our age and ability. The standard was subject to adjustment, and left us scope for development. But the law's standard is rigid. It leaves no room for advance beyond a given point.

"But I say unto you . . ." These words contain a principle for all time. I have heard people dispose of an argument with "Oh, that matter was settled in Calvin's (or Wesley's, or Darby's) day!" But their days are "old time", and so are your yesterday and mine. If I do what I did a month ago because to-day the Lord leads me to do it, that is life; but if I do it because He led me to a month ago, that is law. The law can be a week old or centuries old; but the leading of the Spirit can never be twenty-four hours old. The vital question is, do we know the freshness of today's walk with Him?

OCTOBER 8th

She of her want did cast in all that she had, even all her living. Mark 12. 44.

Today we talk of "clean money" and "dirty money" but in God's sight there is only "the mammon of unrighteousness". To test this you have only to ask yourself whether money leads you to God or away from Him. You cannot serve God and mammon. How then is it possible to take this that has served the interests of Satan and use it to build up the kingdom of God? What is needed to sever the connection that binds Caesar and that which bears His image?

If your money is to come out of the world, then *you* will have to come out of the world. Merely offering money to God's treasury will not of itself change the character of what you offer. Unless your life goes out with it, your money cannot be released from Satan's kingdom to God's. Paul says of the Macedonians that "first they gave their own selves to the Lord". Today, whereas in terms of money Satan's resources are unlimited, the hard cash effectively in God's hands is limited by the number of people devoted to Him. Make sure you instantly convert every dollar you earn to the currency of the Sanctuary. See to it that it is scored off Satan's books and transferred to God's account. How? Don't send it—*bring* it to Him.

OCTOBER 9th

A friend of publicans and sinners. Luke 7. 34.

Since I saw the Saviour as Friend of sinners I have seen many unusual and difficult people brought to Him. I remember once a young woman came and attacked me, saying that she did not want to be saved. She said she was young and intended to have a good time, and had no wish to leave her ways of sin, nor the least desire for salvation. After she had more or less raved at me for a while, I said, "Shall we pray?" "What on earth should I pray?" she replied scornfully. I said, "I can't be responsible for your prayer, but I will pray first, and then you can tell the Lord Jesus all that you have been saying to me." "Oh, I couldn't do that!" she said, somewhat taken aback. "Yes, you can," I replied. "Don't you know He is the Friend of sinners?" This touched her. She did pray—a very unorthodox prayer—but from that hour the Lord began to work in her heart, for within a few days' time she was gloriously saved.

OCTOBER 10th

Cast thy burden upon the Lord, and he shall sustain thee.
Psalm 55. 22.

Many Christians cannot be used of God in a prayer ministry because they are over-burdened. They have let their burdens accumulate instead of seeking relief in prayer, and ultimately they are so crushed by the weight of them that they cannot pray at all.

Suppose you intended asking someone to help you with a certain task, but found his hands were already full. Would it not be useless to invite his aid? In the same way, if you are weighed down by the thing God has already committed to you, how can He commit to you anything further? This ministry of prayer requires a liberated spirit, or the work of God will be seriously hampered. Would you be an instrument free and ready to hand for Him to use? Seek then the spiritual emancipation that comes from casting your burden on God.

OCTOBER 11th

The eye cannot say to the hand, I have no need of thee.
1 Corinthians 12. 21.

In our early days in Shanghai I confess I was always trying to force up the level of the meetings, especially the prayer meetings, to a certain high standard. Consequently I was very dissatisfied with the way some of the brothers prayed. I felt quite bad about it, and said so. How wrong I was!

For, some time later, the Lord laid me aside and I was in real physical need. I prayed hard, but my strong, fighting prayers seemed to get me nowhere. At length the Lord seemed to say to me, "You think certain of the brothers are very weak in prayer. Invite them to come and pray for you in your need." It was a challenge. I sent for those very same brothers, and they came, knelt down, and prayed. For the first time in my life I appreciated their simple, straightforward petitions. What is more, the Lord heard them. I was raised up!

OCTOBER 12th

Thy kingdom come. Thy will be done, as in heaven, so on earth. Matthew 6. 10.

We are to pray this. "Thy kingdom come!" If His kingdom would come of itself, we should not have been given that command. But God's people are to pray, for His work is done in response to their cry. "Thy will be done!" Yes, but where? "On earth", for this is the only place where today God's will is not done. Then how can God's kingdom be brought down here? By the created will, in union with the Uncreated Will, seeking the displacement of the rebellious will of the devil. For prayer is always three-sided. It involves someone prayed to, someone prayed for, and someone prayed against; and on earth there *is* someone to pray against—a will that is opposed to God's. Against that rebellious will, God will not act alone. He awaits our prayers. The Lord's Prayer is not just a model prayer for me; it is the revelation of God's heart.

OCTOBER 13th

Shall not God avenge his elect which cry to him day and night? Luke 18. 7.

Suppose a man somehow gets into your house and occupies it without your authority. What do you do? You go to the magistrate, and, appealing to the law of the land, you get a verdict against him. You return armed with a court order, and you turn him out. He may be fortunate not to go out in chains! But the situation in this world is no different. God's "statute book" has already ruled against this world's illegal occupant. He is to go! What matters it that to Satan the law of the Kingdom of heaven is an alien law? Calvary has established the superiority of that Kingdom. At the Cross, Christ overthrew Satan's whole legal standing. Now it is the Church's task to see that other law put into effect. Crying to God like the widow in the parable, "Avenge me of my adversary!" she is to obtain the order for his eviction, and throw him out. God waits for that cry.

OCTOBER 14th

By what power, or in what name, have ye done this?
Acts 4. 7.

Our eyes must be opened to see the mighty change wrought by the ascension. The name of Jesus certainly establishes the identity of the One in the throne with the Carpenter of Nazareth, but it goes further than that. It represents the power and dominion before which every knee in heaven and earth and beneath the earth must bow. Even the Jewish leaders recognized that there could be this kind of significance in a mere name, when they asked this question of the disciples concerning the lame man's healing.

Today the name tells us that God has committed all authority to His Son, so that in the very name itself there is power. But further, not only is it His, but it is "given among men". He has placed that authority in our hands for us to use. In three passages in His last discourse the Lord Jesus repeats the words "ask in my name". What confidence He must place in us to say, "Whatsoever ye shall ask in my name, that will I do"!

OCTOBER 15th

The throne of my lord king David. 1 Kings 1. 37.

"King David" they called him with affection, for he was every inch a king. He was a king in the wilderness when as shepherd of his father's sheep he put a lion to flight in the name of the Lord. Later when Goliath threatened Israel and even Saul trembled, not to mention his people, David remained unafraid. There is no fear in the heart of a king. But above all, when as a fugitive from Saul he suddenly found his pursuer at his mercy, he resolutely refused to strike the blow that could have brought him quick relief. This was true kingship, for he who cannot control his own spirit is no king. A true king is king under all circumstances. He reigns everywhere.

OCTOBER 16th

Strengthened with all power, according to the might of his glory, unto all patience and longsuffering with joy. Colossians I. II.

Apostleship has its credentials. The signs of an apostle will never be lacking where there is a true divine commission. There was abundant evidence of the genuineness of Paul's. "In nothing am I behind the very chiefest apostles," he writes in 2 Corinthians 12. "Truly the signs of an apostle were wrought among you in all patience, in signs and wonders, and mighty deeds." From this we infer that endurance is first among the proofs of spiritual power. It is the ability to endure steadfastly under continuous pressure that tests the reality of our call as the Lord's "sent ones". Patience and longsuffering with joy are to be found only in those who know what it is to be "strengthened with all power according to the might of his glory".

OCTOBER 17th

*The men took of their provision, and asked not counsel at
the mouth of the Lord.* Joshua 9. 14.

Sin before God is of two kinds. One is the sin of re-
fusing to obey when He issues orders; the other is the sin of
going ahead when He has issued none. The one is rebellion:
not doing what the Lord has commanded. The other is presumption: doing what He has not required. How much of our
work for Him has been based on a clear command of the Lord,
and how much simply on the ground that it was a good thing
to do? We think that if only our conscience does not forbid a
thing, or if it commends itself to us as positively good, that is
reason enough to go ahead and do it. Brothers and sisters, do
you not think that any servant should await his Master's
orders before setting out to serve Him?

OCTOBER 18th

*Thou, why dost thou judge thy brother? or thou again,
why dost thou set at nought thy brother? for we shall all
stand before the judgment seat of God.* Romans 14. 10.

Two things are here forbidden to us: "judging" and
"setting at nought", an outward act and an inner attitude. I
may not yet have gone so far as openly to express a judgment
on my brother. Very good, but am I summing him up to
myself unfavourably? Do I secretly pity him because he does
not see as I see? Do I despise him in my heart as weak or
eccentric? If so I am in rare peril, for my next step is to assume

I am therefore better than he. If I despise him, then it is quite certain I think over much of myself. Let me beware of classing myself as spiritually strong, for that is only to betray to God my own carnality. Of course He would have me discern clearly between right and wrong, but I must never make others the victims of my discernment. The judgment seat is Christ's, and is still future. Who of us dare usurp its function now?

OCTOBER 19th

If because of meat thy brother is grieved, thou walkest no longer in love. Romans 14. 15.

In teaching others by example, no less than by argument, it is possible to be over-bold. Here for instance is a brother whose conscience does not allow him to eat meat. So what do I do? I sit down in his presence and eat as much meat as possible, in the vain belief that by so doing I shall show him what Christian liberty is! I do not argue with him, but I put meat here and I put meat there, all in order to demonstrate to him the nature of liberty in Christ. Am I helping him, or am I "destroying" him? For note how this verse continues. It does not say "Destroy not with your argument", but "Destroy not with your meat". So if my brother and I see differently about such a matter, I should keep that difference well in the background and not thrust it on his consciousness. God commands me to do nothing to hurt him. Why? Because this is the man for whom Christ died.

OCTOBER 20th

*The firm foundation of God standeth, having this seal, the
Lord knoweth them that are his.* 2 Timothy 2. 19.

Men may go; Phygelus and Hermogenes, Hymenaeus and Philetus, yes, all Asia too, may prove unfaithful to the Lord; and when they do we begin to look around and wonder who is to be counted upon. In an hour when many are losing their faith and lowering their standards, it is easy to become confused. If the faith of God's children can so change, we ask, is there anything that cannot? But think again: have we not all of us at some time failed the Lord? Let us beware of thinking we know human nature. Only God has that knowledge. What does the Spirit say here? The Lord knoweth them that are His. We may be mistaken; God never is. Men may disappoint; He cannot. And there is this also that is firm and unchanging: *the Lord knows.*

OCTOBER 21st

Glorify God therefore in your body. 1 Corinthians 6. 20.

Hundreds of tents made up the camp of Israel, but there was one tent quite different from all the rest. In the common tents you could do just as you pleased: eat or fast, work or rest, be joyful or sober, noisy or silent. But that other tent commanded reverence and awe. As you neared it you instinctively walked more quietly, and when you stood right before it you bowed your head in solemn silence. What was so very special about it? Outwardly it was of very ordinary material; but within was the Shekinah of the living God.

"Know ye not that your body is a temple of the Holy Ghost?" Has the solemn fact dawned on us that, at new birth, very God made our hearts His dwelling-place?

OCTOBER 22nd

The twelve gates were twelve pearls; each one of the several gates was of one pearl. Revelation 21. 21.

Pearls, unlike other jewels, are drawn from the animate creation. They are produced by life—a life which has reacted to and overcome the working of death. It is when the oyster is wounded that secretly, in the depths, it produces its pearl. It was through the wounding of Jesus for our transgressions that His life was released to us His members. By divine miracle "a glorious Church" was thereby brought into being, bearing throughout, in faultless integrity, the moral character of Christ. And Matthew 13 suggests to us how infinitely precious to the Father is that most goodly pearl.

OCTOBER 23rd

The Lord's messenger in the Lord's message. Haggai 1. 13.

To His servants God gives the gift of prophecy; to the Church He gives prophets. And a prophet is one who has a history with God, one who has experienced in his own life the formative work of the Holy Spirit. We are sometimes asked by would-be preachers how many days should be spent in preparation of a sermon. The answer is at least ten years, and probably nearer twenty! In this matter at least, the proverb is usually true that "the old is better". For the preacher matters to God at least as much as the thing preached. God chooses as His prophets those in whom He has already worked out in life the thing He intends to use as His message for today.

OCTOBER 24th

Whosoever liveth and believeth on me shall never die.
John 11. 26.

Jesus came to give men life. Look through John's writings with this thought in mind. Whosoever believes may in Him have eternal life. He is the water of life and the bread of life, come to give us life "more abundantly". Moreover, because He was first willing to die, He is also to us the resurrection and the life.

In a time of crisis and calamity it is life you cling to, because it is life that matters above all else. In the Japanese air-raids on Nanking the death and destruction seemed appalling. Where before had stood pleasant homes, now all at once there were only heaps of rubble. "Is anyone in them?" was the question in every mind. Suddenly one heap began to move. A beam was thrown aside, and a man scrambled out shaking off dust and broken tiles. He could do it, because he had life!

It is by the life of Jesus that we live, a life that has been tested by death. "I am the living one . . . I have the keys of death and Hades," He proclaims. It is safest to trust in a God who raises the dead.

OCTOBER 25th

There was nothing in the ark save the two tables which Moses put there at Horeb. 2 Chronicles 5. 10.

The law written on the two stone tablets would have been a perpetual testimony against God's people. Impotent as they were to meet its demands, they would have felt only its condemnation and judgment (compare 1 Samuel 6. 19) had those tablets not been secreted within the ark. We readily agree that this ark, with its gold and acacia wood, typifies Christ our Saviour. But not merely does He stand between us and the judgment of God; He came "to fulfil" the law for us in His person, so that what was on the tablets against us has now become what is in the Ark for us. That is why the Ark of Testimony is also the Ark of the Covenant. "One jot or one tittle shall in no wise pass away from the law, till all things be accomplished."

OCTOBER 26th

O my Father, if it be possible, let this cup pass away from me. Matthew 26. 39.

Since it was to do the will of God He came, we may feel it strange that the Lord Jesus should have prayed this prayer. Yet it brings to light an important distinction. Evidently it was possible for Him to pray that the cup might be removed from Him, while it was certainly unthinkable that He should ask to be excused from doing the Father's will. The cup is, so to say, secondary to that will. It represents the thing through which the divine will finds expression—in this case the death of the cross. The Lord Jesus was wholly taken up, not with His passion as such, but with the design it fulfilled. He drank the cup because it was His Father's will, not because it was the cup.

For Jesus "the cup" was something He shrank from; for us it more often represents something we would hold on to. Our great danger may be to hold dogmatically to some "thing" associated with the divine plan for us. Every cup, however divinely appointed, should be held to very loosely. It is not that which claims us supremely, but the present will of our Father.

OCTOBER 27th

I delight to do thy will, O my God. Psalm 40. 8.

There was one occasion when I knew without doubt God had called me to a certain task. But I had lately been ill, and was as yet too weak to undertake it. So I asked God for strength. It must, I thought, be His wish to give it to me; then I would do His will. I prayed and prayed about the matter, while three months went by. Then God seemed to say: "You have asked enough. Now drop it!" I remember I was walking along the beach with a stick at the time. Coming to a halt, I drove my stick right into the sand until it was covered, stood upon it, and proclaimed: "I have dropped here the matter of my physical need." I walked on, but had scarcely gone any distance when the reality of my continuing weakness thrust itself upon me again. *Surely*, I thought, God's purpose must be realized through a renewal of my strength, and involuntarily I began to pray once more. But I checked myself. Was I not pulling His will down to the level of my own need? Walking back to the place where my stick was buried, I pointed to it. "Lord," I said, "this is my witness that I dropped the matter here, and I refuse to take it up again. Weak or strong, I am going to do Thy will." From that day, when I abandoned my personal problem and set myself to His task, my physical need began most wonderfully to be met.

OCTOBER 28th

I beseech you therefore, brethren, by the mercies of God, to present your bodies a living sacrifice, holy, acceptable to God, which is your reasonable service. Romans 12. 1.

These words take us beyond the merely individual for they imply contribution to a whole. The "presenting" is individual but the service is corporate. There are many bodies brought to Him, but the outcome is one living sacrifice. All intelligent or reasonable service to God is like this. It is essentially one service, in which nevertheless we are each to have our personal part. None may feel that what he brings is worthless to God, for it is not counted as one more or less among many separate sacrifices. Each life yielded to Him is required, so that together they may constitute that one complete whole which, we are assured, is acceptable to God. And if God is satisfied, shall not we be?

OCTOBER 29th

That they may all be one; even as thou, Father, art in me,
and I in thee, that they also may be one in us: that the
world may believe that thou didst send me. John 17. 21.

It is "through the Church" that the wisdom of God
is manifested to spiritual powers. It is "together" that we become a habitation of God through the Spirit. Because God's
children today do not function together as the Body, they
have become as a leaking vessel. Shatter a glass tumbler and
what happens? Each piece may perhaps hold a little water, but
it is as nothing compared with what the unbroken tumbler
held. So it is in spiritual things. The individual receives in
but two dimensions, as it were; the Church in three. Ten
thousand Christians are one thing; ten thousand members of
Christ are quite another. From His fulness the Head has much
more to give; but to contain it we must return to the one
vessel, the one Body.

OCTOBER 30th

But I say unto you, Love your enemies. Matthew 5. 44.

I knew one man who hated another. The other man
had deeply sinned against him, and so great was the injury
that to have killed him would have seemed scant revenge.
The one sinned against came to know the Lord, and for years
saw nothing of the other man. Then, visiting a certain town,
he went on Sunday to join the local believers for the Communion service. Just after he was introduced, he suddenly saw
in the meeting his former enemy. He said to himself, "He is

here! I did not know he was saved. What shall I do?" During
the next prayer he got up quietly and went out. He began to
walk away and as he walked he thought on the one hand of his
salvation and on the other hand of his grievance against this
man. The further away he got the worse he felt at having left
the meeting and on the other hand the more incensed against
his enemy. Then he thought back ten years to the time when
he was saved and of how the Lord had forgiven him. Yet he
felt he *could* not forgive his enemy. But the Spirit brought to
his mind the word: "By this shall all men know that ye are my
disciples, if ye have love one to another." He stopped short.
"Lord, I forgive him!" he cried, and turning, went back to
the meeting with tears streaming down his face. When he
arrived they were just about to break the bread, so he arose
and confessed it all, telling them how God had removed the
hatred from his heart.

OCTOBER 31st

God is light, and in him is no darkness at all. 1 John 1. 5.

Whereas in John's Gospel our Lord Jesus is revealed
among men as grace and truth, here in his Epistles the same
Lord is discovered in existence with the Father as light and
love. What was truth in the Gospel is light in the Epistles;
what was grace in the Gospel is love in the Epistles. Why is
this? Because light in God, when brought to men, becomes
truth; love in God, when brought to men, becomes grace.
Truth and grace are here, light and love back there in God.
That is why it is always possible for grace to be misused, truth
mishandled. Men have misappropriated these things to themselves. But God is light and God is love, and you cannot climb

up there and touch that. It is beyond mishandling. So to re-cover what is lost, John does not offer us anything novel. He takes us back to the throne and confronts us again with the Original. For it is by returning to their source that we re-discover first things.

NOVEMBER 1st

Sarah said, God hath prepared laughter for me; every one that heareth will laugh with me. Genesis 21. 6 mg.

God had displayed complete mastery of the im-possible, and Sarah's was the laugh of grateful amazement. Earlier it had been Abraham who laughed (17. 17). But his was the laugh of incredulity—not, be it said, directed at God, before whom he was fallen low in obeisance, but surely at himself. There was no disrespect; just a sense of the utter im-possibility of it all.

Where was his faith of past years? True faith it had been, but mingled perhaps with a certain practical "realism", a touch of justifiable self-reliance. It was faith, so to say, in God–plus–Abraham. Now at length he knew that the "Abraham" con-tribution was at an end. Only God was left to believe in. But just here, that belief took on its new character; for favourable conditions do not help faith, they more often hinder it. It seems that when conditions are easy, faith is difficult; when they are more difficult faith becomes easier; and when once they are downright impossible, the faith of stark desperation, having God alone to cling to, at last gives promise of that eventual laugh of amazement.

NOVEMBER 2nd

The grace of the Lord Jesus Christ, and the love of God,
and the communion of the Holy Spirit, be with you all.
2 Corinthians 13. 14.

       Love, in the heart of God, is the source of all spiritual blessing; grace expressed in Jesus Christ has made that blessing available to us; and communion, the coming alongside of the Holy Spirit, is the means whereby it becomes ours. What the Father's heart devised concerning us the Son has accomplished for us, and now the Holy Spirit communicates it to us. When therefore we make some fresh discovery of what is ours in Christ, let us look for its outworking to the means God has provided. Walk in the Spirit. Maintain obedience to Him in all things. So doing we shall open wide the door for God to realize in us all His desire.

NOVEMBER 3rd

No wool shall come upon them, while they minister in the
gates of the inner court, and within . . . they shall not gird
themselves with anything that causeth sweat. Ezekiel
44. 17 f.

       The command is surprising, but the explanation makes sense. Those who minister in this visionary temple shall not wear wool but linen, because in these future conditions of service, no work that causes perspiration will be acceptable to the Lord. What does this tell us? The symbolism takes us back, I think, to Genesis 3 and man's fall. Because of it the curse rested on the ground, which therefore ceased to yield fruit without man's effort, and Adam was told: "In the sweat of thy face shalt thou eat bread."

The work of the Lord today is not like that, but partakes of the effortless character of the coming age. Or it should, for it should be marked by the blessing of God. Only when that is withheld does fleshly effort become necessary. Please bear with me when I say that spiritual work is God's work, and when God works, man does not need to expend so much effort that he perspires over it.

NOVEMBER 4th

David sought the face of the Lord. 2 Samuel 21. 1.

There are times when we put forth tremendous effort in prayers without getting any answer from God, yet how seldom do we seek to discover why? For how can we expect God to answer prayers that are out of harmony with His mind? In all our praying we must first find the key. It was this David sought to do at the time of prolonged famine this chapter describes.

He did not simply cry to God: "This famine has lasted three years. Have mercy on us now and grant us a rich harvest this year." No, He sought the face of the Lord. Had God something to say about it? To his direct question God gave a direct reply, and with it the key to answered prayer. Saul, it appears, by slaying some of the Gibeonites, had violated God's understanding with Israel to spare them. True, he had done it out of zeal for God; but he had sinned. God will not permit the breaking of a solemn vow. So there was something to be set right. "And after that," we read in verse 14, "God was intreated for the land." David had found the key.

NOVEMBER 5th

He that cometh to God must believe that he is, and that he is a rewarder of them that seek after him. Hebrews 11. 6.

Three facts about God underlie true faith: He is able (Matthew 9. 28), He is willing (Matthew 8. 2 f.), and the fact quoted here: He is. And mark you, by this last article of faith I do not mean some vague belief that there is a God. I mean the conviction that *God is*: living, present, active.

Let us suppose you have pointed a sinner to Christ. When you have prayed with him and he has prayed, you ask him where he stands now. If he replies that God can save him, are you satisfied? Even if he goes further and affirms that God will save him, is that enough? No, you will not be content until he has expressed the conviction that God *has* saved him, that God *is* His Saviour. We shall get nowhere with "God can" and "God will" if we stop short of "God is". For His power and His compassion by themselves may stir us only to hope. Faith rests on His activity now. Do not claim to have faith until you can say, "I am . . . and I have . . . because God is!"

NOVEMBER 6th

Put on the whole armour of God, that ye may be able to stand against the wiles of the devil. Ephesians 6. 11.

Here the verb "stand" means "hold your ground". It is not, in modern parlance, a command to march—to invade a foreign territory in order to occupy and subdue it. God has not told us to do this. "Stand" implies that the ground disputed by the enemy is really His, and therefore ours. It was the

Lord Jesus who carried the offensive into Satan's kingdom, to gain by death and resurrection a mighty victory. Today we fight only to maintain and consolidate the victory He has gained. That is perhaps why the armour described here is largely defensive. For the territory is His. We do not fight to gain a foothold on it. We only need to hold it against all challengers.

NOVEMBER 7th

In all these things we are more than conquerors through him that loved us. Romans 8. 37.

In Christ we *are already* conquerors. Is it not obvious then, since this is so, that merely to pray for victory—unless that prayer is shot through with praise—must be to court defeat by throwing away our fundamental position? Let me ask you: Has defeat been your experience? Have you found yourself hoping that one day you will be strong enough to win? Then my prayer for you can go no further than that of the apostle Paul for his Ephesian readers. It is that God may open your eyes anew to see yourself seated with Him who has Himself been made to sit "far above all rule, and authority, and power, and dominion, and every name that is named" (1. 20 f.). The difficulties around you may not alter; the lion may roar as loudly as ever; but you need no longer *hope* to overcome. In Christ Jesus you *are* victor in the field.

NOVEMBER 8th

The king's daughter within the palace is all glorious; her clothing is inwrought with gold. Psalm 45. 13.

The bride is to be led into the King's presence in a bridal dress skilfully and patiently prepared of "broidered work". There *is* a garment that is a gift outright; but the bride's attire is not merely gold, that is to say, what proceeds purely from God. It is "inwrought with gold", which surely means that gold thread is patiently woven or embroidered into the fabric itself. This suggests, does it not, the Spirit's continuous application to her experience of the realities of the cross of Calvary, in order that the glories of Christ may be displayed. Here is a divine working in which she is the willing co-operator. The Lamb's wife "hath made herself ready".

NOVEMBER 9th

The fear of the Lord is the beginning of wisdom: and the knowledge of the Holy One is understanding. Proverbs 9. 10.

Folly or wisdom? The question hinges simply on procrastination or prompt obedience. Some of us are parents and have children. How greatly those children can differ in temperament! One will obey at once; another will think that by putting it off he can avoid the need to do so. If that is indeed the case, and you are weak enough to allow him a loophole for escape, then the one who procrastinates is in fact the wise one, for he succeeds in doing nothing. But if your word holds and ultimately must be obeyed, then he is certainly the wiser who faces the issue squarely at once. Get clear about the will of God. If God's words can be discounted, then you might not be foolish to try to escape their implications; but if God is an unchanging God with an unchanging will, then be wise; act now; redeem the time.

NOVEMBER 10th

These all with one accord continued steadfastly in prayer.
Acts 1. 14.

How is God's will to be done on earth? Only by His having on his side a willing people. Only by every one of us remembering, in the solemn conditions of today, that the Church at prayer is heaven's outlet, the channel of release for heaven's power, and that this ministry is our greatest possible work. God shows what He wants, we stand and ask, and God acts from heaven: this is true prayer, and this is what we must see fully expressed in our prayer meetings. If the Church here in Shanghai, not to speak of other places, does not know this ministry of prayer, may God forgive us! Without it, all else is empty; God has no vessel here.

NOVEMBER 11th

*I will run the way of thy commandments, when thou shalt
enlarge my heart.* Psalm 119. 32.

Many of our ills today stem from the fact that we are content with a merely objective acceptance of doctrine. We seek an outward, mental light on the Scriptures, but stop short of their inward application to experience. We encounter many intellectual difficulties in the Bible; and "light", to us, is the solving of these. For many of us it is a case of feeling all is well if we are conservative or orthodox in our doctrine, and give mental assent to this and mental dissent from that. It is by this reasoning that fundamentalists consider themselves on a so much higher plane than modernists. Yet surely it must be obvious to us that we all measure up spiritually in God's eyes only in so far as we possess a true inward knowledge of His Son, and no further. We may be perfectly right, but unless we possess His life and live by that, we lack the supreme essential.

NOVEMBER 12th

Blessed are they that wash their robes, that they may have the right to come to the tree of life. Revelation 22. 14.

It was not by committing murder that Adam let sin into the world. That came later. Adam let in sin by his free choice between these two trees: the one whose name is Life, and the one that offered him the independent power to decide for himself on moral issues. By a deliberate act he turned to the latter, choosing to have his soul developed to a place where he could go on alone apart from God. When therefore God secures for His glory a race of men who will be the instrument to accomplish His purpose in the universe, they will be a people whose life—yea, whose very breath—is dependent upon Him. He will be the "tree of life" to them.

NOVEMBER 13th

*After this manner therefore pray ye: Our Father which art
in heaven, Hallowed be thy name.* Matthew 6. 9.

Our Father! The inter-dependence of God's people
is not just a comfortable thought. It is a vital factor in their
life. We cannot get on without one another. It is true that
"God hath dealt to each man a measure of faith" (Romans
12. 3), but alone in isolation man can never exercise it to the
full, as the context of that verse makes clear. It needs a complete
Body to attain to the stature of Christ and to display His glory.
That is why fellowship in prayer is so important. Trusting the
Lord by myself is good, but may not be enough. I must trust
Him also with others. I must learn to pray on the basis of one-
ness with my brethren in Christ, for only together shall we
get through in prayer to God's end. I need the help of the
Body because I need the help of the Lord, and because His life
is the life of the Body.

NOVEMBER 14th

Jesus said, Make the people sit down. John 6. 10.

Our Christian life today is a foretaste of the heavenly
banquet still to come; for God has "made us to sit down with
him" who first was seated by mighty power in the heavenly
places far above all (Ephesians 1. 20; 2. 6). This means that the
work of salvation is not ours but His. It is not that we work
for God but that He has worked for us. God *gives* us our
position of rest. He brings His Son's finished work and pre-

sents it to us, and then He says to us, "Please sit" (ch'eng tso). His offer of salvation cannot, I think, be better expressed than in the words of invitation to the great feast in the parable: "Come; for all things are now ready."

NOVEMBER 15th

Ye shall find rest unto your souls. Matthew 11. 29.

There is a rest which is given: "I will give you rest"; but there is rest also which has to be found. The first is obtained simply by coming to God and receiving His gift of life. This means something more than just believing in a well-preached evangelical gospel. It means coming as a weary, burdened sinner and making living personal contact with the Lord Jesus Christ Himself. Such contact unfailingly brings rest. Thank God for all His children who possess this fundamental gift!

But having come there, we find ourselves on the threshhold of something more. We are to learn of Him—to discover the deep satisfaction to be found in a growing knowledge of the Lord Himself. Above all, we are to learn His meekness and lowliness of heart. In doing so, He says, we shall find rest. For this rest is not a gift; it is for disciples, that is to say, learners. And learning takes time, but it is also infinitely rewarding.

NOVEMBER 16th

*Take my yoke upon you and learn of me; for I am meek
and lowly in heart.* Matthew 11. 29.

What is it to be yoked to the Lord? It implies willing,
contented cooperation with Him in the divine plan. Of course
the yoke limits the ox; it cannot wander all over the field as it
pleases, but must take a straight line forward. That way the
work gets done however. And here is the value of the lowliness of heart that does not think big, ambitious things of itself,
but is willing for any place God appoints, even though it be at
the very bottom.

In this chapter of Matthew we see the apparent frustration of
the Lord's public ministry, in that only babes had understood
and responded to it. "How undignified!" we might exclaim.
But no: "I thank thee, O Father," were His words, "for so it
was well-pleasing in thy sight." He is not aiming at anything.
He is perfectly willing for what God has ordained. And the
question is, Are we content to accept His limitations and go
along with Him? For the deepest rest is this "rest unto our
souls".

NOVEMBER 17th

*I was with you in weakness, and in fear, and in much
trembling, . . . but in demonstration of the Spirit and of
power.* 1 Corinthians 2. 3 f.

Scripture presents to us two kinds of Christian experience, both equally valid and necessary. On the one hand
there are such strong, almost boastful affirmations as: "God
. . . always leadeth us in triumph in Christ", "To me to live is

Christ" and "I can do all things in him that strengtheneth me".
Yet on the other hand the very same people, with equal truth,
have to confess: "We despaired even of life", "Christ Jesus
came into the world to save sinners; of whom I am chief", and
"We also are weak in him". This latter seems to be another
kind of Christian, faulty, frail and fearful, and alarmingly
lacking in confidence. But in fact the real life of a child of God
consists in the co-existence of these two experiences. We
would prefer of course to concentrate on the first only, to the
exclusion of the other. But to know them both is to know
Him who is the God of Israel—and the God of Jacob too!

NOVEMBER 18th

*Only rebel not against the Lord, neither fear ye the people
of the land: for they are bread for us.* Numbers 14. 9.

The trials confronting us on the way to full enjoyment of our inheritance in Christ may be quite as gigantic as
were some of the Canaanites, but God intends to use them for
our increase. Faith sees them as its food. If we but knew it, we
thrive and grow on difficulties. But the reverse is also true.
The ten spies reported in dismay that Canaan was "a land
which eateth up the inhabitants thereof" (13. 32). Abandon
your faith in God and turn away from the problem and you
put yourself in a position to be swallowed up by what was
meant for your growth. Many of us dodge difficulties. We
walk round the issue seeking an easy way out. We shelve the
question instead of confronting it squarely. We will not face
what is involved in that hazardous Jordan crossing and the
terrors we apprehend just beyond. Oh yes, we escape the
trials; but we starve!

Food is our life, but we cannot get it by a spiritual holiday. Let us miss no opportunity to prove the Lord. The foe may trouble us, but that way lies nourishment and spiritual enlargement.

NOVEMBER 19th

When the vessel that he made of the clay was marred in the hand of the potter, he made it again another vessel, as seemed good to the potter to make it. Jeremiah 18. 4.

The Potter's original design became marred by something unresponsive in the clay. Yes marred, but not destroyed, for He made it again another vessel. It is wonderful what God can still do, provided always we are prepared for His adjustments. Have we failed Him somewhere? Then it were folly to persist in what He has abandoned, falsely imagining He is compelled to go on with us in it.

Has He perchance changed His mind? Am I now ordained to be "another vessel"? If so it were death to strive to be the former one. "Cannot I do with you as this potter?" says the Lord. We cannot play with His will. Though our loving Father, He is nevertheless sovereign in His ways. Our attitude should be: "Keep me near Thee, fearing Thee, always ready for Thy best!" I find great personal comfort in the counsel of Peter: "Humble yourselves therefore under the mighty hand of God, that he may exalt you in due time" (1 Peter 5. 6).

NOVEMBER 20th

Master, we toiled all night, and took nothing. Luke 5. 5.

There are times when the efforts expended in the work of the Lord warrant our looking for certain results, but to our dismay they do not appear. "Why this vain toil?" we ask ourselves. "To think it could be possible for us to toil all night and to go unblessed!" But it is useless to argue here. The fact has simply to be faced that God has withheld His blessing. In human affairs we reason from cause to effect, but all our reasonings are irrelevant in the realm of divine favour. In that realm God is the Cause, and He alone.

"But at thy word I will let down the nets": this is the kind of faith that avails in His service. It trusts Him to bless us beyond all our deserts. Provided our expectation is in Him alone, I believe we shall see blessing on all our future way. The favour of the Lord resting on one life may mean the salvation of fifty lives; it may mean the consecration to Him of a hundred lives. God's blessing has momentous results. Let us expect the supernatural. Let us look to God for miracles.

NOVEMBER 21st

I know whom I have believed. 2 Timothy 1. 12.

If you ask a number of believers who have entered upon the fulness of life in Christ how they came by their experience, some will say in this way and some will say in that. Each stresses his own particular mode of entering in and produces Scripture to support his experience; and unhappily many Christians are using their special experiences and special Scriptures to fight other Christians. The fact of the matter is that, while Christians may enter into this fuller life by different ways, provided Christ is their centre, we need not regard their experiences or doctrines as mutually exclusive, but rather complementary. For one thing is certain: any experience of value in the sight of God must have been reached by way of a new discovery of the meaning of the person and work of the Lord Jesus. There is no other way. This is a safe test and a crucial one.

NOVEMBER 22nd

Faith is the substantiating of things hoped for. Hebrews 11. 1 (J. N. Darby Trans.).

How do we "substantiate" something? We are doing it every day. We cannot live in the world without doing it. A "substance" is an object, something before me, though it may be no more tangible than sound or colour. "Substantiating" means that I have a certain faculty of hearing or sight that makes that intangible "substance" real to me. For instance, the colour yellow is quite real; but if I shut my eyes, then to me it has lost its reality; it is simply nothing—*to me*. With my faculty of sight to substantiate it, however, yellow becomes yellow to me. Not only is the colour there; I have given it reality in my consciousness. How precious is the gift of sight!

But even more than music or colour, the "hoped for" things of Christ are eternal and therefore real; and I have been given one precious faculty that can substantiate them. Faith, the faith of the Son of God, is this faculty. It makes divine things to become real in my experience. By resting on God's faithfulness, faith substantiates *to me* the unseen things I as yet barely hope for.

NOVEMBER 23rd

*He saith unto me, See thou do it not: I am a fellow-servant
with thee . . . Worship God.* Revelation 19. 10.

What had happened? Had John lost his head, that he
should try to worship an angel? Well, he may have lost his
head, but what is quite certain is that he had been carried away
in his heart. There are those who have such good heads, they
never do stupid things. John was not of that number, for
twice he repeated this blunder (cf. 22. 8). The truth is he had a
good heart, and good hearts may sometimes become confused
and do stupid things. His heart was overwhelmed with
wonder at this glorious Church "coming down out of heaven
from God", and at the amazing fact that, in his own patience
and tribulation, he was sharing with heavenly labourers in
this the greatest divine masterpiece of all time. His act was
wrong, no doubt, but it sprang from a right attitude, and one
we might safely emulate.

NOVEMBER 24th

*A new covenant: not of the letter, but of the spirit: for the
letter killeth, but the spirit giveth life.* 2 Corinthians 3. 6.

It is wearisome to me, if not actually repulsive, to
talk with folk who aim at perfect outward correctness, while
caring little for what is vital and spiritual. "Missionary
methods", as such, do not interest me at all. In fact, it is a deep
grief to meet children of God who know practically nothing
of the hatefulness of a life lived in the energy of the natural

man, and have little vital experience of the headship of Jesus Christ, yet who all the while are scrupulously careful to arrive at absolute correctness of method in God's service. God Himself has provided for His wine the wine-skin which will best contain and mature it. It is loss, certainly, to have wine without a wine-skin, but it is worse than loss, it is death, to have a wine-skin without wine.

NOVEMBER 25th

Our old man was crucified with him . . . that so we should no longer be in bondage to sin. Romans 6. 6.

Why do you believe that the Lord Jesus died? What is your ground for that belief? Is it that you feel He has died? No, you have never felt it. You believe it because the Word of God tells you so. When the Lord was crucified, two thieves were crucified at the same time. You do not doubt that they were crucified with Him, either, because the Scripture says so quite plainly. Now, what about your own death? Your crucifixion with Christ is more intimate than theirs. They were crucified at the same time as the Lord, but on different crosses, whereas you were crucified on the self-same cross as He, for you were in Him when He died. It does not depend on your feelings. You can know it is so for the one sufficient reason that God has said it is so. That Christ has died is a fact, that the two thieves have died is a fact, and that you have died is a fact also. The self you loathe is on the cross in Christ! And "he that is dead is freed from sin"!

NOVEMBER 26th

Why stand ye here all the day idle? . . . Go ye also into the vineyard. Matthew 20. 6 f.

This word "idle", Greek *argos*, helps greatly to illumine Paul's doctrine of deliverance from sin, for it forms the root of the word he uses in Romans 6.6 when he writes of the body of sin being "done away", that is to say "made ineffective", "put out of operation", by the Cross. Sin, the old master, is still about, but in Christ the slave who served him has been put to death, and so is out of reach and his members are unemployed. The gambler's hand is unemployed, the swearer's tongue is unemployed, and these members are now available to be used instead as "instruments of righteousness unto God". To be able under these circumstances to say, in reply to the Lord's question, "Because no man hath hired us," is to invite employment by Him in the most rewarding service there is. "Go ye also into my vineyard, and whatsoever is right I will give you."

NOVEMBER 27th

As ye presented your members as servants to uncleanness and to iniquity unto iniquity, even so now present your members as servants to righteousness unto sanctification. Romans 6. 19.

Once a Chinese brother, travelling by train, found himself in a carriage together with three non-Christians. To while away the time these men wished to play cards, and lacking a fourth to complete the game, they invited him to join them. "I am sorry to disappoint you," he said, "but I cannot, for I have not brought my hands with me." "What ever do you mean?" they asked in blank astonishment. "This pair of hands does not belong to me," he said, and then there ollowed the explanation of the transfer of ownership that had taken place in his life. "Present your members," says Paul, "as instruments of righteousness unto God," and that brother regarded the members of his body therefore as belonging entirely to the Lord. This is holiness in practice.

NOVEMBER 28th

Not in wisdom of words, lest the Cross of Christ should be made void. 1 Corinthians 1. 17.

When I was younger I sought to attain to a perfect standard of presenting divine truth, determined to leave nothing that could possibly be misunderstood by the hearers. I took great care to run no risks in my preaching, but I must confess there was very little spiritual value in it. God, I soon discovered, uses the weak things as His messengers. He does not demand of us fool-proof explanations but uses fragments, a word here, a sentence there, to bring to men His flashes of light. He is not looking for perfect understanding or for fault-less teaching; indeed our very desire for perfection in these matters may itself hinder Him if it stands in the way of His first object, which is to bring life to dead souls, heavenly manna to hungry hearts. "The words that I have spoken unto you are spirit, and are life."

NOVEMBER 29th

I have seen thy face, as one seeth the face of God. Genesis
33. 10.

What does this astonishing statement mean? Jacob,
who had seen God face to face at Peniel, now describes his
meeting with Esau as if he were again seeing the face of God!
It may have been mere flattery, an evidence that Jacob still
retained something of his earlier scheming nature. It may also
have been a kind of confession that all his elaborately planned
arrangement of his family and possessions had been a waste of
time. In Esau's welcome he may have recognized that deliverance had come to him, not through his own clever artifice
but through the overruling of God. But there is one more
possible meaning, and this is a universal spiritual fact. It is that
those whom we have wronged will always represent God to
us. When we meet them, it is as though we were meeting
God. It can be in judgment. Thank God if, when this is so, our
hearts are truly humbled before Him. It can also mean mercy
and reconciliation. "First be reconciled to thy brother, and
then come and offer thy gift."

NOVEMBER 30th

I have waited for thy salvation, O Lord. Genesis 49. 18.

Genesis chapter 49 reveals Jacob as a prophet. Out of
a real understanding of God's heart he could utter its tremendous forecasts. But this verse, set right in the middle, is
not a prophecy; it is a cry of Jacob himself. For there was
sorrow and a foreboding of sin as well as joy and good in these
oracles, and he had just been compelled to paint a very dark

picture of Dan as a serpent in the pathway. Then, just here, Jacob showed himself. Lifting his eyes to heaven he revealed what he, the prophet, was. It is easy enough to preach; but when a man preaches we know at once if God has hold of him or not. The old Jacob would have begun to think up a scheme for dealing with Dan. He could always get the better of people; but not now. Now he had learned to know God. "I have waited for thy salvation, O Lord!"

DECEMBER 1st

Out of much affliction and anguish of heart I wrote unto you . . . that ye might know the love which I have more abundantly unto you. 2 Corinthians 2. 4.

A ministry that is to bring healing and life must spring essentially from experience. This fact is strikingly displayed in the apostle Paul. The ministry of 1 Corinthians, for example, is based firmly on the man revealed to us in 2 Corinthians.

In 1 Corinthians Paul writes of God's choice of "the weak things"; 2 Corinthians shows in grim reality his own experience of a divinely imposed weakness. In the first letter Paul appeals to his readers for unity; in the second he shows how, in spite of their rebuffs, he still counts himself one of them. Chapter 13 of the first letter offers his classic treatment of love; in 2 Corinthians 12. 15 he affirms, "I will most gladly spend and be spent for your souls." Finally, 1 Corinthians 15 gives us the clearest teaching anywhere in the New Testament on the subject of the resurrection; yet 2 Corinthians makes plain his own desperate need to trust from hour to hour in "God which raiseth the dead". At every point his doctrine is backed with experience. Nothing else really constitutes a basis for a ministry of Christ.

DECEMBER 2nd

Wherewithal shall a young man cleanse his way? By taking heed thereto according to thy word. Psalm 119. 9.

The Pharisees cleansed the outside of the platter, but left the inside full of impurity. Our Lord rebuked them for setting so much store on outward things and ignoring the inward, and many of us conclude from this that, provided we stress the inwardness of spiritual truth, all is well. But God demands both inward and outward purity. To have the outer without the inner is spiritual death, but to have the inner without the outer is only spiritualized life. For to by-pass things by spiritualizing them is not spirituality. "These things ye ought to have done, and not to have left the other undone" (Matthew 23. 23). No matter how trifling a divine command may seem, it is an expression of the will of God. Never dare we treat it lightly. We cannot with impunity neglect even the least of His wishes.

DECEMBER 3rd

Apart from me ye can do nothing. John 15. 5.

The temptation to try is ingrained in human nature. Let me tell you something I have seen in my own country at the salt pits. In China some coolies can carry a load of salt weighing 120 kilos; others as much as 250 kilos. Now along comes a man who can only carry 120 kilos, and here is a load of 250 kilos. He knows perfectly well it is far too heavy for him, but although he cannot possibly carry it he still tries.

As a youngster I used to amuse myself watching ten or twenty of these fellows come along and try, though every one of them knew he could not possibly manage it. In the end he must give up and make way for the man who could. How often is it only at the point of utter despair with ourselves that we remember the Lord and relinquish to Him the task He is so ready and able to perform! The sooner we do so the better, for while we monopolize it we leave little room for the Spirit's mighty working.

DECEMBER 4th

Christ Jesus, who was made unto us wisdom from God, and righteousness and sanctification, and redemption. 1 Corinthians 1. 30.

God has given us Christ. There is nothing now for us to receive outside of Him. The Holy Spirit has been sent to produce what is of Christ in us; not to produce anything that is apart from or outside of Him. *He* "was made unto us . . .". This is one of the grandest statements in Scripture. If we believe this, we can put in there anything we need, and can know that God has made it good; for, through the Holy Spirit within us, the Lord Jesus is Himself made unto us whatever we lack. We have been accustomed to look upon holiness as a virtue, upon humility as a grace, upon love as a gift to be sought from God. But the Christ of God is *Himself* everything that we shall ever need. Let us unhesitatingly draw upon Him.

DECEMBER 5th

They cast therefore, and now they were not able to draw it for the multitude of fishes. That disciple therefore whom Jesus loved saith unto Peter, It is the Lord. John 21. 6 f.

As Jesus stood there on the shore, the strange thing was that none of them knew Him; not even Peter and John who had been most intimate with Him, nor Thomas who so lately had identified Him by His wounds. The risen Lord was not to be recognized merely by human eyes, nor by hands of flesh. Even when He spoke to them of familiar things, still they did not recognize Him. But when the net was full, John suddenly knew.

Later, when on shore Jesus said "Come and break your fast," none of them, we are told, dared ask Him "Who art thou?" knowing it was the Lord. Here is a paradox. In the ordinary way, if you ask a question it implies a lack of knowledge; if you dare not ask, it suggests a fear of displaying that lack. But here we have both fear and knowledge. With the outward man they feared, but with the inward man they knew. Often you cannot explain, yet there is an inward, divinely given assurance. This is Christianity.

DECEMBER 6th

I can do all things in him that strengtheneth me. Philippians 4. 13.

In the work of God today things are often so constituted that we have no need to rely upon God. But the Lord's verdict upon all such work is uncompromising: "Apart from me ye can do nothing." For divine work can only be done with divine power, and that power is to be found only in the Lord Jesus. It is when we reach the point of saying with the prophet, "I cannot speak," that we discover God is speaking. He never asks us to do anything we can do. He asks us to live a life we can never live and to do a work we can never do. Yet by His grace we are living it and doing it. The life we live is the life of Christ lived in the power of God, and the work we do is the work of Christ carried on through us by His Spirit whom we obey.

DECEMBER 7th

He looked upon Jesus as he walked, and saith, Behold the Lamb of God! John 1. 36.

When John first announced Christ as the Lamb of God, he added: "which taketh away the sin of the world" (verse 29), thus emphasizing His redeeming work. The second time he did so, however, he simply said: "Behold the Lamb of God!" Here the accent was not so much on the work as on the Person. Real appreciation means that people are precious to us for their own sakes. We come to love them more for what they are than for what they have done. So it should be with our appreciation of Christ. We thank the Lord for His gifts, but we praise Him for His worth. Christ on the Cross calls forth from us our amazed thanksgiving; Christ on the throne our praise. We behold what He has done and we are profoundly grateful; we behold who He is and we adore.

DECEMBER 8th

Blessed is he, whosoever shall not be offended in me. Luke
7. 23. A.V.

John the Baptist did not like it. He had looked for a
new revival such as the first Elijah had witnessed, and here he
lay in prison with death imminent. If he himself must achieve
nothing, surely Jesus ought to take some action to vindicate
this second Elijah ministry.

Are we offended when God does not do what we feel he
should? We have sought to know His will and want only His
glory, and yet many of His ways we find disappointing. We
have met some impasse and found no way through; we were
ill and expected Him to heal us and we were not healed; we
are short of money and money does not come. Or far worse,
it is some matter in which God's very honour seems at stake.
He *must* come in for the sake of His name—and yet He does
not. The situation is unchanged, no prison gates open, no
hearts melt, none cry "Sirs, what must I do?"

There is a day when all will be explained. When we stand
before the judgment seat, not only shall we be judged; God
will explain things to us. In much we shall be proved wrong,
but there will be many things of which He will say: "I was
right, but you were right also."

DECEMBER 9th

Ye also ought to wash one another's feet. John 13. 14.

The washing alluded to here is for refreshment; it
does not relate to sin. Unlike sin, the dust and dirt that gather
on our feet are inevitable. To roll in the dust would be sin,

certainly, but if we touch the earth at all our feet will be dusty. A brother working long hours in an office comes back home at the end of the day, tired and out of tune with things. He finds it difficult to recover the refreshment of communion with his Lord he had in his morning quiet time. There is a coating of something upon him which makes him unable to rise up to the Lord at once.

But a friend meets him and quite spontaneously praises the Lord. At once he feels a lifting power. It is as though someone had taken a duster and wiped the film away. His feet are clean once more. To "wash one another's feet" is to return things to their former freshness in this way. It is possible to be largely unaware of the fact that we are doing it, and yet to be constantly used thus to refresh our brethren in Christ. I tell you, it is one of the greatest ministries.

DECEMBER 10th

He smote thrice, and stayed. And the man of God was wroth with him, and said, Thou shouldest have smitten five or six times. 2 Kings 13. 18 f.

We are always in danger of setting a limit to what God can do. Today God wants us to prepare for a new release in the work of the Gospel, but we set Him a target beyond which our faith is not prepared to go. We have not understood the flight of the Lord's "arrow of victory". Our gratification over the hundred souls that have come to Him may be the thing that hinders them coming in their thousands. Is it not possible that the large hall we have built for the proclamation of the Gospel may impose a limit on future growth? There is always a grave danger of circumscribing God's grace. The blessing He gives is intended to pave the way for greater blessing, never to become a barrier to it. By all means let us work to a plan, but let us shake ourselves free from all trammels of the past and live in a state of constant expectancy. Right ahead of us lies a work immensely greater than that which lies behind. God plans for us unprecedented blessings.

DECEMBER 11th

By grace have ye been saved through faith; and that not of yourselves: it is the gift of God. Ephesians 2. 8.

We rightly speak of being saved through faith, but what do we mean by it? We mean this, that we are saved by reposing in the Lord Jesus. We did nothing whatever to save ourselves; we simply laid upon Him the burden of our sin-sick souls. We began our Christian life by depending not upon our own doing but upon what He had done. Until a man does this he is no Christian; for to say, "I can do nothing to save myself, but by His grace God has done everything for me in Christ," is to take the first step in the life of faith. There is no limit to the grace God is willing to bestow upon us.

DECEMBER 12th

He is not ashamed to call them brethren. Hebrews 2. 11.

In the outset of the Fourth Gospel the Evangelist describes Jesus as "the only begotten from the Father". At the end of the same book the risen Lord says to Mary Magdalene, "Go unto my brethren, and say to them, I ascend unto my Father and your Father" (John 20. 17). Hitherto in this Gospel

Jesus had spoken of "the Father" or of "my Father". Now in resurrection He adds: ". . . and your Father". How wonderful this is, for it is the eldest Son now, "the first begotten from the dead," who is speaking. By His incarnation and Cross He has added many sons to God's family, and so in the same verse He speaks of them as "my brethren". And praise God, by His exaltation you and I have received the spirit of adoption whereby now we too cry, Abba, Father. "The Spirit himself beareth witness with our spirit, that we are children of God."

DECEMBER 13th

Nay, much rather, those members of the body which seem to be more feeble are necessary. 1 Corinthians 12. 22.

Once, years ago, I was faced with a very big problem in my life, and one to which I knew I could not find the solution alone. I was preaching the Gospel at the time in a remote region, far from other servants of God with anything approaching the knowledge of His Word that I felt was essential to help me discover the answer. Where was I to find the fellowship I needed? There were of course the few believers, country folk, among whom I was staying, but they were mere babes in Christ. How could they possibly help solve *this* problem?

However, I had reached an impasse. There was indeed nothing left but to call them in; so at my request those simple brothers came to me in my need. I told them what I could of my difficulty, and they prayed—and as they prayed, light dawned! The thing did not need explaining. It was done, and done in such a way as never to need repeating. How our God delights to display to us our dependence on His "feeble members"!

DECEMBER 14th

Not forsaking the assembling of ourselves together, as the custom of some is, but exhorting one another; and so much the more as ye see the day drawing nigh. Hebrews 10. 25.

Christ is the Head of the Church and "we, who are many, are one body in Christ, and severally members one of another". All Christian relationships therefore are of one member to another, never of a head to the members. When an apostle is preaching a grand sermon, and all the believers are nodding assent and adding their frequent and fervent "Amens", how deeply spiritual the congregation seems! But it is when they meet by themselves that their true spiritual state comes to light. The "pulpit-and-pew" principle, so vital for proclaiming the glad tidings to sinners, nevertheless tends to foster passivity in Christian life. It is by the "round table" principle of mutuality, by believers exhorting one another, that the Church lives and grows. Has our fellowship together the true stamp of "one another" upon it?

DECEMBER 15th

It is God . . . who shined in our hearts, to give the light of the knowledge of the glory of God in the face of Jesus Christ. 2 Corinthians 4. 6.

What is salvation? It is the breaking in of divine light. The veiling of that light meant perdition. But God has shined into the hearts of us who were perishing; and merely to *see* is salvation. As soon as we see the glory in the Saviour's face, in that instant we are saved. If we merely understand the doctrine and assent to it, nothing happens, for we have not *seen* Him who is the Truth. But as surely as the impression on a film follows the opening of the camera shutter, so the moment we really see Him as Saviour, in that moment the inward transformation begins, and what was to us "the heavenly vision" becomes in turn "His Son revealed *in me*" (Acts 26. 19; Galatians 1. 16). There is no need to remind ourselves of such a living experience. You can never forget it.

DECEMBER 16th

There is yet one man by whom we may inquire of the Lord, Micaiah the son of Imlah: but I hate him. 1 Kings 22. 8.

Obsession is a terrible thing. To lie is to deceive others, knowing one is lying. To be obsessed is to have deceived oneself; to lie, and not know it; to have moved beyond reach of conscience to the point where the light that is in us is darkness. It is, in short, to have shut out the truth. This state is reached by the simple choice of darkness. "Every one that doeth ill hateth the light, and cometh not to the light." "And for this cause God sendeth them a working of error, that they should believe a lie" (John 3. 19 ff.; 2 Thessalonians 2. 11). So in the end the obsessed are true; they have come to believe in what they are doing! Saul of Tarsus "verily thought . . .".

How are we delivered? By one thing only: light. "He that doeth the truth cometh to the light." God need do no further work. I am sometimes asked: "Why always speak of revelation? Why not emphasize God's work of deliverance?" I reply: Because the revelation *is* the work. By it Saul knew himself a blasphemer. By it Job was moved to say: "Now mine eye seeth thee, wherefore I abhor myself and repent." There is no second work. God makes us *see*, and that is enough.

DECEMBER 17th

O thou afflicted, tossed with the tempest, and not com-
forted, behold I will set thy stones in fair colours, and lay
thy foundations with sapphires. Isaiah 54. 11.

Along with the gold in both Eden and Paradise we
find precious stones (Genesis 2. 12; Revelation 21. 19). Gem-
stones are not produced in a day. Time is a vital factor in their
formation. They are wrought by long process in the fires of
earth, and their beauties are displayed by skilful cutting. In
spiritual terms this implies values that are inwardly wrought
by the divine patience in you and me. Such values are costly.
Those unwilling to pay will never come by them. Grace is
free; but only a high price buys precious stones. Many a time
we shall want to cry out, "This is costing too much!" Yet the
lessons we learn as we pass with Him "through fire and
water"—these are the really worth-while things. In the light
of God some things perish of themselves; there is no need to
wait for the fire. It is in what has stood God's test of time that
true worth lies.

DECEMBER 18th

In the name of Jesus Christ of Nazareth, walk. Acts 3. 6.

Consider these words of Peter to the crippled man
at the gate: *In the Name.* Clearly no other name, least of all his
own, would have brought the same dramatic result. Let me
give you a simple illustration. Some time ago my fellow-
worker sent to me for a sum of money. I read his letter, prepared what he had asked, and gave the sum to the messenger.
Was I right? Yes, certainly. The letter bore my friend's

signature, and to me that was enough. Should I instead have asked the messenger his name and age and employment and native place, and then perhaps sent him away because I objected to what he was? No, by no means, for he had come in my friend's name, and I honoured that name.

God looks at His Son in the glory; not at us here on the earth, and He honours His Son's Name. All that took place that day resulted from the impact of the Name of Jesus on the situation, and the only thing that distinguished His servants was that they were authorized to use that Name.

DECEMBER 19th

Lest any root of bitterness springing up trouble you, and thereby the many be defiled. Hebrews 12. 15.

The favour of the Lord may be likened to a wild bird that you are seeking to lure into a room. Try as you may, you cannot induce it to fly in. It must do so of its own accord; and then, if it does, you will have to be on the alert lest it fly out again. You could not persuade it to enter, but you can easily cause it to depart. Just a little carelessness on your part, and it is gone!

In blessing us, it is God who takes the initiative; no effort is called for on our side. But when His blessing has been fully bestowed, it takes but a little heedlessness on our part to lose it. The divine favour is to be found where brethren are living in harmony; never, as we well know, where there is discord among them. Do you realize how serious a thing it is to be at variance with any brother, even if a consideration of every aspect of the case proves you to be right? At all costs give heed to your words, lest you forfeit the Lord's favour, and awake to find the bird flown!

DECEMBER 20th

*Even so ye also, when ye shall have done all the things that
are commanded you, say, We are unprofitable servants;
we have done that which it was our duty to do.* Luke
17. 10.

Two kinds of work may occupy the servant in this
passage: "ploughing" or "keeping sheep", both very important occupations. Yet even when he returns from such
work, Jesus reminds us that he is expected to provide for his
master's satisfaction before sitting down to enjoy his own
meal. When we return from our toil in the field, be it preaching the Gospel to the unsaved or tending the needs of the flock,
we are apt to muse complacently on the much work we have
accomplished! But the Lord will say to us: "Gird thyself and
serve Me." Of course we ourselves must eat and drink, but
not till His thirst is quenched, His hunger satisfied. We too
shall have our enjoyment, but that can never be until His joy
is full. Let us ask ourselves often: Does our work for Him
minister first of all to our satisfaction, or to His?

DECEMBER 21st

*They shall not teach every man his fellow-citizen, and
every man his brother, saying, Know the Lord: for all
shall know me from the least to the greatest of them.*
Hebrews 8. 11.

In seeking to know God's will under the old covenant, men were, generally speaking, restricted to the law and
the prophets. But Christianity is based not on information but

on revelation. Do you have a book-knowledge of Christ? Do you know Him only by hearsay, so to speak, from some true servant of His? Or are you in direct touch with your Lord? It is one of the most precious factors in our Christian life to have friends who live close to God and who can share with us what He has shown them. Again and again we need their arresting challenge or the calm of their mature counsel. But the New Covenant affirms that "All shall know me", and the word translated "know" means "know me in themselves". We do not commit ourselves totally and exclusively to the light that comes through holy men of God, however sound it be. We are under duty bound to listen to the voice of the Lord Himself, and to follow Him.

DECEMBER 22nd

Till we all attain unto the unity of the faith, and of the knowledge of the Son of God. Ephesians 4. 13.

To have constant close association with people whose interpretation of Scripture does not tally with ours is hard for the flesh, but good for the spirit. We may have right views, but God is giving us an opportunity to display a right attitude; we may believe aright, but He is testing us to see if we love aright. It is easy to have a mind well stored with sound scriptural teaching, yet a heart devoid of true love. Oh, for Christian tolerance! Oh, for largeness of heart! Alas! that many of God's children are so zealous for the light they have that they immediately label as outsiders, and treat as such, all whose interpretation of Scripture differs from theirs. God would have us walk in love towards all who hold views contrary to those so dear to us. Nothing so tests the spirituality of a teacher as opposition to his teaching.

DECEMBER 23rd

But we have this treasure in earthen vessels, that the exceeding greatness of the power may be of God and not from ourselves. 2 Corinthians 4. 7.

Here we have possibly the clearest statement there is of the nature of practical Christianity. Christianity is not the earthen vessel, nor is it the treasure. It is the treasure in the earthen vessel. It must ever be a cause for great gratitude to God that no merely human weakness need limit divine power.

Too readily we think of power as the absence of the earthen vessel. Yet our blessed Lord Himself was for our sakes "crucified through weakness". There is nothing wrong in feeling weak. We are not meant to suppress all human emotions until we end up frigid as ice. Indeed, those who achieve this state are a constant drain on others around them, who must somehow make good their deficiency in natural affection if relationships are to remain even reasonably comfortable. No, we must rather allow God's Spirit to make His own use of our emotions. Of course He must be in command. Of course we must have the divine treasure—yes, but not in cold storage!

DECEMBER 24th

What, should I set this before an hundred men? 2 Kings 4. 43.

Faith is a most important factor in God's service, for without it there can be no truly spiritual work. But our faith requires training and strengthening, and material needs are a means God uses towards that end. It is not difficult to profess to have faith in God for a vast variety of intangible things. We may even deceive ourselves in this, simply because there is nothing concrete to demonstrate how lacking in faith we really are. But when it comes to financial needs, to food and drink and hard cash, the matter is so practical that the reality of our faith is at once put to the test. If we cannot trust God to supply the temporal needs of the work, what is the good of talking about its spiritual needs? We proclaim to others that God is the living God. Let us prove His livingness in the very practical realm of material things. Nothing will so establish in us the confidence in Him we shall certainly need to know when those other, spiritual demands come.

DECEMBER 25th

They fell down and worshipped him; and opening their treasures they offered unto him gifts, gold and frankincense and myrrh. Matthew 2. 11.

Matthew's is the Gospel of the King. "We are come to worship him," they said, and thereby at the outset established what was His right. For worship is everything. The more we worship, the more reason will God give us to do so. Before we pray let us worship; in preaching let us worship; in everything lift up adoring hearts to Him. This is the Church's work on earth today, to establish God's worship. Unless we give it to Him, God will have no worship here in this world. Of course we must not neglect other service, but let us always give to worship the first place. The wise men opened to Him their treasures. How can we hold back anything? And what we offer must be incense, not perfume:

incense that has to be wholly consumed on the altar of incense before its fragrance is released. That is true worship, and ours is the day when the Father seeks true worshippers.

DECEMBER 26th

When the fulness of the time came, God sent forth his Son, born of a woman. Galatians 4. 4.

When Jesus was born, Israel was a subject nation. The greatness of the kingdom was but a memory and the people of God paid tribute to Caesar. These were the days of Augustus, and Rome ruled the world. Yet in spite of appearances, He was born in the fulness of time. Everything was prepared. The Gospel of Christ was for all men; it could not be confined to one tiny nation. So God permitted Rome to absorb the world, and Jesus Christ was crucified in the Roman empire upon a Roman cross.

Rome's communications were good. Her roads and her ships went everywhere. Jews could come to Jerusalem at Pentecost, hear the Gospel, and carry it back home without crossing hostile national boundaries. Because Rome ruled, the apostles might travel freely from city to city within the Empire, speaking to men of the Saviour. The book of the Acts demonstrates the neutrality and the fairness of the secular authorities. Rome is likened in Scripture to a wild beast, but God who shuts lions' mouths had tamed her for His instrument. He shuts and no man opens; He opens and no man can shut.

DECEMBER 27th

There was a rainbow round about the throne. Revelation 4. 3.

The visions of Revelation chapters 4 to 11 are all related to the throne of God (4. 2); those of chapters 12 to 22 to the temple of God (11. 19). At the outset of the former ection we see a rainbow about the throne; at the outset of the latter we see the ark of the covenant in His temple. God's throne is established for the government of the universe. The full rainbow completely encircling it is His testimony to the universe that in all His administrative dealings, He that sits there will ever remain true to His covenant with mankind. God's temple is established as a habitation for Himself. The presence in it of the ark of His covenant, long since lost to unfaithful Israel as the centre of her national life, is God's testimony to Himself. It guarantees that nevertheless, true to His nature, what He has pledged Himself to do concerning His covenant people He will certainly perform. He cannot deny Himself. In Christ His faithfulness is assured—and we are in Him.

DECEMBER 28th

For this child I prayed; and the Lord hath given me my petition which I asked of him: therefore I also have granted him to the Lord. 1 Samuel 1. 27 f.

Do you notice two phrases here? To me they are exceedingly precious. Read them together: "The Lord hath given me . . . I also have granted him to the Lord." In her distress she had besought the Lord for a son, and her request had been granted. What answer to prayer surpasses this one? The sum total of her request was for this child. Yet now, when she had received all she craved, she gave all back to the Giver. And as Samuel passed out of her hands, we are told, "They worshipped the Lord there."

When the day comes for me, as it came for Hannah, that my Samuel, in whom all my hopes are centred, passes out of my hands into God's, then I shall know what it really means to worship Him. For worship follows in the wake of the Cross, where God is All and in all. When our hands are emptied of all we hold dear and the focus shifts from ourselves to God, that is worship.

DECEMBER 29th

O my dove, that art in the clefts of the rock, in the covert of the steep place, let me see thy countenance, let me hear thy voice; for sweet is thy voice and thy countenance is comely.
Song of Songs 2. 14.

How hard we often find it to drag ourselves into His presence! We shrink from the solitude, and even when we do detach ourselves physically from things outside, our thoughts still keep wandering back to them. Many of us can enjoy working among other people, but how many of us can draw near to God in the Most Holy Place? To come into His presence and kneel before Him for an hour demands all the strength we possess. We have to be violent with ourselves to do it. But every one who serves the Lord knows the preciousness of such times, the sweetness of waking at midnight and spending an hour with Him, or waking early in the morning and getting up for an hour of prayer. Let me be very frank with you. You cannot serve God from a distance. Only by learning to draw near to Him can you know what it really is to serve Him.

DECEMBER 30th

I will most gladly spend and be spent. 2 Corinthians 12. 15.

In 1929, after prolonged labours in the Gospel, I returned worn out to my home town of Foochow. One day I was walking along the street with a stick, very weak and in broken health, and I met one of my old college professors. He took me into a teashop, where we sat down. He looked me over, and then he said, "Now look here: during your college days we thought a great deal of you. We had hopes that you would achieve something great. *Do you mean to tell me that this is what you are?*" On hearing this very pointed question, I must confess my first desire was to break down and weep. My career, my health, everything had gone, and here was my old professor asking: "Are you still where you were, with no success, no progress, nothing to show?" But the very next moment I really knew what it was to have the Spirit of glory resting upon me. The thought of being able to pour out my life for my Lord literally flooded my soul with glory. I could look up silently and say, "Lord, I praise Thee! This is the best thing possible; it is the right course that I have chosen!"

DECEMBER 31st

David, after he had in his own generation served the counsel of God, fell on sleep, and was laid unto his fathers.
Acts 13. 36.

David served in one generation, his own. He could not serve in two! Where today we seek to perpetuate our work by setting up an organization or society or system, the Old Testament saints served their own day and passed on. This is an important principle of life. Wheat is sown, grows, ears, is reaped, and then the whole plant, even to the root, is ploughed out. God's work is spiritual to the point of having no earthly roots, no smell of earth on it at all. Men pass on, but the Lord remains. Everything to do with the Church must be up-to-date and living, meeting the present—one could even say the passing needs of the hour. Never must it become fixed, earth-bound, static. God Himself takes away His workers, but He gives others. Our work suffers, but His never does. Nothing touches Him. He is still God.

INDEX TO SCRIPTURES

Matthew (*contd.*):

5. 44	Oct. 30
6. 5	Sept. 15
6. 6	Mar. 25
6. 9	Nov. 13
6. 10	Oct. 12
10. 29	July 18
11. 25	Sept. 26
11. 29	Nov. 15
11. 29	Nov. 16
14. 16	Apr. 11
15. 28	Sept. 1
16. 16	July 14
16. 17	Sept. 5
16. 19	Mar. 12
17. 27	Mar. 26
18. 18	Feb. 13
18. 20	June 15
19. 5	May 9
19. 8	Aug. 31
20. 6	Nov. 26
23. 8	Mar. 13
25. 6	Sept. 7
26. 10	Feb. 14
26. 39	Oct. 26

Mark:

6. 41	Jan. 1
6. 56	June 5
7. 29	Sept. 2
11. 24	May 28
12. 44	Oct. 8
14. 4	May 18
14. 9	Mar. 5
14. 72	May 30

Luke:

1. 38	Mar. 16
5. 5	Nov. 20
6. 19	Sept. 22
6. 38	July 12
7. 23	Dec. 8
7. 34	Oct. 9
9. 13	June 12
10. 33	July 2
10. 41	Jan. 23
15. 22	Feb. 19
17. 10	Dec. 20
17. 32	Oct. 2
18. 7	Oct. 13

John:

1. 17	Feb. 9
1. 36	Dec. 7
4. 23	June 16
5. 39	Aug. 29
6. 9	July 6
6. 10	Nov. 14
6. 11	July 5
6. 38	May 11
8. 32	Apr. 7
11. 26	Oct. 24
12. 3	Mar. 27
12. 28	Aug. 2
13. 14	Dec. 9
13. 17	May 4
14. 19	Mar. 10
14. 27	Feb. 7
15. 2	June 3
15. 4	Sept. 6
15. 5	Dec. 3
16. 13	Feb. 24
17. 3	June 17
17. 19	Apr. 8
17. 21	Oct. 29
18. 6	Feb. 6
19. 30	Jan. 26
20. 31	Aug. 5
21. 6	Dec. 5

Acts:

1. 14	Nov. 10
2. 1	Aug. 10
2. 21	Jan. 16
2. 33	Mar. 29
2. 38	Jan. 17
3. 6	Dec. 18
4. 7	Oct. 14
7. 55	Aug. 21
8. 29	June 26
9. 17	June 21
10. 44	Aug. 14
12. 14	Feb. 25
13. 2	June 11
13. 36	Dec. 31
14. 1	Sept. 19
19. 20	June 24
26. 19	Jan. 19
27. 23	Mar. 17

Romans:

5. 5	Aug. 12
5. 8	Sept. 28

Romans (*contd.*):

5. 10	Jan. 7
6. 6	Mar. 4
6. 6	Nov. 25
6. 11	Apr. 13
6. 13	July 24
6. 14	May 25
6. 16	May 20
6. 19	Nov. 27
7. 7	Mar. 19
7. 14	Feb. 21
7. 25	Feb. 22
8. 2	Apr. 21
8. 3	Mar. 20
8. 9	May 6
8. 37	Nov. 7
11. 33	May 23
11. 36	July 16
12. 1	Oct. 28
12. 5	Sept. 24
14. 8	Mar. 23
14. 9	Apr. 3
14. 10	Oct. 18
14. 15	Oct. 19
15. 4	Mar. 31
15. 7	Mar. 18

1 Corinthians:

1. 17	Nov. 28
1. 28	Feb. 4
1. 30	Dec. 4
1. 31	Mar. 30
2. 3	Nov. 17
2. 14	Aug. 27
3. 12	June 22
3. 16	June 25
6. 20	Oct. 21
9. 7	Apr. 10
12. 18	Apr. 28
12. 21	Oct. 11
12. 22	Dec. 13
15. 10	Jan. 5

2 Corinthians:

1. 21	Feb. 17
2. 4	Dec. 1
3. 6	Nov. 24
4. 1	Apr. 16
4. 6	Dec. 15
4. 7	Dec. 23
4. 8	Mar. 24

2 Corinthians (*contd.*):

4. 11	May 22
4. 12	July 26
5. 14	June 18
5. 16	Mar. 28
6. 1	Jan. 4
6. 9	July 30
7. 2	May 29
9. 7	July 4
12. 9	Sept. 16
12. 10	June 4
12. 15	Dec. 30
13. 14	Nov. 2

Galatians:

1. 15	Jan. 18
2. 20	June 13
3. 28	May 26
4. 4	Dec. 26
5. 13	Feb. 18
5. 17	June 30
6. 7	July 11

Ephesians:

1. 22	Feb. 26
2. 6	June 10
2. 8	Dec. 11
2. 10	July 13
2. 14	Mar. 14
3. 19	May 21
4. 1	Apr. 24
4. 3	July 1
4. 13	Dec. 22
4. 32	Aug. 28
5. 16	Jan. 3
5. 18	Apr. 17
5. 27	Apr. 15
6. 11	Nov. 6

Philippians:

2. 13	Oct. 3
3. 3	Apr. 2
3. 12	Mar. 9
3. 20	Sept. 25
4. 4	Feb. 28
4. 13	Dec. 6
4. 19	July 19
4. 22	July 31

Colossians:

1. 11	Oct. 16
2. 12	June 28

Love Not
the World

WATCHMAN NEE

KINGSWAY PUBLICATIONS
EASTBOURNE

CONTENTS

PREFACE

THE greater part of this book derives from a series of addresses on the subject of 'the world' given by Mr. Watchman Nee (Nee To-sheng) of Foochow to Christian believers in Shanghai city in the early period of the Sino-Japanese War. They are thus coloured a little by the economic pressures of those days. To them have been added other talks on the same general theme given at various places and times during the period 1938–41. For example, Chapter Three is based on a sermon preached at a baptismal service in May 1939. I am indebted to several friends for the notes which have supplied the book's source material.

The author sees the *kosmos* as a spiritual entity behind the things seen, a force always to be reckoned with. He deals with its impact upon the Christian and his impact upon it, with the conflicting claims upon him of separation and involvement, and with the destiny of the man in Christ to 'have dominion'. As always, Mr. Nee's studies display original thinking and he is not afraid to be provocative, stirring both heart and mind to a response. It is my prayer that, despite the inevitably piecemeal construction of the book, its theme will prove to have coherence as a picture of the man of God in the world, and further, that it may challenge us all who name the name of Christ to move more courageously and positively through this earthly scene, with a thought always for our role here in God's eternal purpose concerning His beloved Son.

ANGUS I. KINNEAR

London
1968

CHAPTER ONE

THE MIND BEHIND THE SYSTEM

'Now is the judgment of this world: now shall the prince of
this world be cast out. And I, if I be lifted up from the earth, will
draw all men unto myself.' John 12. 31, 32.

Our Lord Jesus utters these words at a key point in His ministry.
He has entered Jerusalem thronged by enthusiastic crowds; but
almost at once He has spoken in veiled terms of laying down His
life, and to this heaven itself has given public approval. Now He
comes out with this great two-fold statement. What, we ask
ourselves, can it have conveyed to those who have just acclaimed
Him, going out to meet Him and accompanying Him home on
His ride? To most of them His words, if they had any meaning
at all, must have signified a complete reversal of their hopes.
Indeed the more discerning came to see in them a forecasting of
the actual circumstances of His death as a criminal (verse 33).

Yet if His utterance destroyed one set of illusions, it offered in
place of them a wonderful hope, solid and secure. For it announced a far more radical exchange of dominion than even
Jewish patriots looked for. 'And I . . .'—the expression contrasts
sharply with what precedes it, even as the One it identifies stands
in contrast with His antagonist, the prince of this world. Through
the Cross, through the obedience to death of Him who is God's
seed of wheat, this world's rule of compulsion and fear is to end
with the fall of its proud ruler. And with His springing up once
more to life there will come into being in its place a new reign
of righteousness and one that is marked by a free allegiance of
men to Him. With cords of love their hearts will be drawn away

from a world under judgment to Jesus the Son of man, who though lifted up to die, is *by that very act* lifted up to reign.

'The earth' is the scene of this crisis and its tremendous outcome, and 'this world' is, we may say, its point of collision. That point we shall make the theme of our study, and we will begin by looking at the New Testament ideas associated with the important Greek word *kosmos*. In the English versions this word is, with a single exception shortly to be noticed, invariably translated 'the world'. (The other Greek word, *aion*, also so translated, embodies the idea of time and should more aptly be rendered 'the age'.)

It is worth sparing time for a look at a New Testament Greek Lexicon such as Grimm's. This will show how wide is the range of meanings that *kosmos* has in Scripture. But first of all we glance back to its origins in Classical Greek where we find it originally implied two things: first *a harmonious order or arrangement*, and secondly *embellishment or adornment*. This latter idea appears in the New Testament verb *kosmeo*, used with the meaning 'to adorn', as of the temple with goodly stones or of a bride for her husband (Luke 21. 5; Rev. 21. 2). In 1 Peter 3. 3, the exception just alluded to, *kosmos* is itself translated 'adorning' in keeping with this same verb *kosmeo* in verse 5.

(1) When we turn from the Classics to the New Testament writers we find that their uses of *kosmos* fall into three main groups. It is used first with the sense of the *material universe, the round world, this earth*. So: Acts 17. 14, 'the God that made the world and all things therein'; Matt. 13. 35 (and elsewhere), 'the foundation of the world'; John 1. 10, 'he was in the world, and the world was made by him'; Mark 16. 15, 'Go ye into all the world.'

(2) The second usage of *kosmos* is two-fold. It is used (*a*) for *the inhabitants of the world* in such phrases as John 1. 10, 'the world knew him not'; 3. 16, 'God so loved the world'; 12. 19, 'the world is gone after Him'; 17. 21, 'that the world may believe'. (*b*) An

extension of this usage leads to the idea of *the whole race of men alienated from God and thus hostile to the cause of Christ*. So: Heb. 11. 38, 'Of whom the world was not worthy'; John 14. 17, 'whom the world cannot receive'; 14. 27, 'not as the world giveth, give I unto you'; 15. 18, 'If the world hateth you . . .'

(3) In the third place we find *kosmos* is used in Scripture for *wordly affairs: the whole circle of worldly goods, endowments, riches, advantages, pleasures, which though hollow and fleeting, stir our desire and seduce us from God, so that they are obstacles to the cause of Christ.* Examples are: 1 John 2. 15, 'the things that are in the world'; 3. 17, 'the world's goods'; Matt. 16. 26, 'if he shall gain the whole world, and forfeit his life'; 1 Cor. 7. 31, 'those that use the world, as not abusing it'. This usage of *kosmos* applies not only to material but also to abstract things which have spiritual and moral (or immoral) values. So: 1 Cor. 2. 12, 'the spirit of the world'; 3. 19, 'the wisdom of this world'; 7. 31, 'the fashion of this world'; Titus 2. 12, 'worldly (adj. *kosmikos*) lusts'; 2 Pet. 1. 4, 'the corruption that is in the world'; 2. 20, 'the defilements of the world'; 1 John 2. 16, 17, 'all that is in the world, the lust . . . the vainglory . . . passeth away'. The Christian is 'to keep himself unspotted from the world', James 1. 27.

The Bible student will soon discover that, as the above paragraph suggests, *kosmos* is a favourite word of the apostle John, and it is he, in the main, who helps us forward now to a further conclusion.

While it is true that these three definitions of 'the world', as (1) the material earth or universe, (2) the people on the earth, and (3) the things of the earth, each contribute something to the whole picture, it will already be apparent that behind them all is something more. The Classical idea of *orderly arrangement or organization* helps us to grasp what this is. Behind all that is tangible we meet something intangible, we meet a planned system; and in this system there is a harmonious functioning, a perfect order.

Concerning this system there are two things to be emphasized. First, since the day when Adam opened the door for evil to enter God's creation, *the world order has shown itself to be hostile to God.* The world 'knew not God' (1 Cor. 1. 21), 'hated' Christ (John 15. 18) and 'cannot receive' the Spirit of truth (14. 17). 'Its works are evil' (John 7. 7) and 'the friendship of the world is enmity with God' (James 4. 4). Hence Jesus says, 'My kingdom is not of this world' (John 18. 36). He has 'overcome the world' (16. 33) and 'the victory that hath overcome the world' is 'our faith' in Him (1 John 5. 4). For, as the verse of John 12 that heads this study affirms, the world is under judgment. God's attitude to it is uncompromising.

This is because, secondly, as the same verse makes clear, *there is a mind behind the system.* John writes repeatedly of 'the prince of this world' (12. 31; 14. 30; 16. 11). In his Epistle he describes him as 'he that is in the world' (1 John 4. 4) and matches against him the Spirit of truth who indwells believers. 'The whole world,' John says, 'lieth in the evil one' (5. 19). He is the rebellious *kosmokrator*, world-ruler—a word which, however, appears only once, used in the plural of his lieutenants, the 'world-rulers of this darkness' (Eph. 6. 12).

There is, then, an ordered system, 'the world', which is governed from behind the scenes by a ruler, Satan. When in John 12. 31 Jesus states that the sentence of judgment has been passed upon this world He does not mean that the material world or its inhabitants are judged. For them judgment is yet to come. What is there judged is that institution, that harmonious world-order of which Satan himself is the originator and head. And ultimately, as Jesus' words make clear, it is he, 'the prince of the world', who has been judged (16. 11) and who is to be dethroned and 'cast out' for ever.

Scripture thus gives depth to our understanding of the world around us. Indeed, unless we look at the unseen powers behind the material things we may readily be deceived.

This consideration may help us to understand better the passage in 1 Peter 3 alluded to above. There the apostle sets 'the outward adorning (*kosmos*) of plaiting the hair, and of wearing jewels of gold, or of putting on apparel' in deliberate contrast with 'the incorruptible apparel of a meek and quiet spirit, which is in the sight of God of great price'. By inference, therefore, the former are corrupt and worthless to God. We may or may not be ready at once to accept Peter's valuation, depending upon whether we see the true import of his words. Here is what he is implying. In the background behind these matters of wearing-apparel and jewellery and make-up, there is a power at work for its own ends. Do not let that power grip you.

What, we have to ask ourselves, is the motive that activates us in relation to these things? It may be nothing sensuous but altogether innocent, aiming by the use of tone and harmony and perfect matching merely to gain an effect that is aesthetically pleasing. There may be nothing intrinsically wrong in doing this; but do you and I see what we are touching here? We are touching that harmonious system behind the things seen, a system that is controlled by God's enemy. So let us be wary.

The Bible opens with God's creation of the heavens and the earth. It does not say that He created the world in the sense that we are discussing it now. Through the Bible the meaning of 'the world' undergoes a development, and it is only in the New Testament (though perhaps to a lesser extent already in the Psalms and some of the Prophets) that 'the world' comes to have its full spiritual significance. We can readily see the reason for this development. Before the Fall of man, the world existed only in the sense of the earth, the people on the earth, and the things on the earth. As yet there was no *kosmos*, no 'world', in the sense of a constituted order. With the Fall, however, Satan brought on to this earth the order which he himself had conceived, and with that began the world-system of which we are speaking. Originally our physical earth had no connection with 'the world' in this sense of a Satanic system, nor indeed had man; but Satan took advantage of man's sin, and of the door this threw open to him, to introduce into the earth the organization which he had set himself to establish. From that point of time this earth was in 'the world', and man was in 'the world'. So we may say that before the Fall there was an earth; after the Fall there was a 'world'; at the Lord's return there will be a kingdom. Just as the world belongs to Satan, so the Kingdom belongs to our Lord Jesus. Moreover it is this Kingdom that displaces and that will displace the world. When the 'Stone not made with hands' shatters man's proud image, then the kingdom of this world will 'become the kingdom of our Lord and of his Christ' (Dan. 2. 44, 45; Rev. 11. 15).

Politics, education, literature, science, art, law, commerce, music—such are the things that constitute the *kosmos*, and these are things that we meet daily. Subtract them and the world as a coherent system ceases to be. In studying the history of mankind we have to acknowledge marked progress in each of these departments. The question however is: In what direction is this 'progress' tending? What is the ultimate goal of all this development? At the end, John tells us, antichrist will arise and will set up his own kingdom in this world (1 John 2. 18, 22; 4. 3; 2 John 7; Rev. 13). *That* is the direction of this world's advance. Satan is utilizing the material world, the men of the world, the things that are in the world, to head everything up eventually in the kingdom of antichrist. At that hour the world-system will have reached its zenith; and at that hour every unit of it will be revealed to be anti-Christian.

In the book of Genesis we find in Eden no hint of technology, no mention of mechanical instruments. After the Fall, however, we read that among the sons of Cain there was a forger of cutting instruments of brass and iron. A few centuries ago it might have seemed fanciful to discern the spirit of antichrist in iron tools even though for long the sword has been in open competition with the ploughshare. But today, in the hands of man, metals have been turned to sinister and deadly uses, and as the end approaches the widespread abuse of technology and engineering will become even more apparent.

The same thing applies to music and the arts. For the pipe and the harp seem also to have originated with the family of Cain, and today in unconsecrated hands their God-defying nature becomes increasingly clear. In many parts of the world it has long been easy to trace an intimate relationship between idolatry and the arts of painting, sculpture and music. No doubt the day is coming when the nature of antichrist will be disclosed more openly than ever through song and dance and the visual and dramatic arts.

As for commerce, its connections are perhaps even more suspect. Satan was the first merchant, trading ideas with Eve for his own advantage, and in the figurative language of Ezekiel 28, which seems to reveal something of his original character, we read: 'By thy traffic thou has increased thy riches, and thine heart is lifted up' (verse 5). Perhaps this does not have to be argued, for most of us will readily admit from experience the Satanic origin and nature of commerce. We shall say more of this later.

But what of education? Surely, we protest, that must be harmless. Anyway, our children have to be taught. But education, no less than commerce or technology, is one of the things of the world. It has its roots in the tree of knowledge. How earnestly, as Christians, we seek to protect our children from the world's more obvious snares. And yet it is quite true that we *have* to provide education for them. How are we going to solve the problem of letting them touch what is essentially a thing of the world, and at the same time guarding them from the great world system and its perils?

And what of science? It, too, is one of the units that constitute the *kosmos*. It, too, is knowledge. When we venture into the further reaches of science, and begin to speculate on the nature of the physical world—and of man—the question immediately arises: Up to what point is the pursuit of scientific research and discovery legitimate? Where is the line of demarcation between what is helpful and what is hurtful in the realm of knowledge? How can we pursue after knowledge and yet avoid being caught in Satan's meshes?

These, then, are the matters at which we must look. Oh, I know I shall appear to some to be over-stating things, but this is necessary in order to drive home my point. For 'if any man love the world, the love of the Father is not in him' (1 John 2. 15). Ultimately, when we touch the things of the world, the question we must ask ourselves always is: 'How is this thing affecting my relationship with the Father?'

The time has passed when we need to go out into the world in order to make contact with it. Today the world comes and searches us out. There is a force abroad now which is captivating men. Have you ever felt the power of the world as much as to-day? Have you ever heard so much talk about money? Have you ever thought so much about food and clothing? Wherever you go, even among Christians, the things of the world are the topics of conversation. The world has advanced to the very door of the Church and is seeking to draw even the saints of God into its grasp. Never in this sphere of things have we needed to know the power of the Cross of Christ to deliver us as we do at the present time.

Formerly we spoke much of sin and of the natural life. We could readily see the spiritual issues there, but we little realized then what equally great spiritual issues are at stake when we touch the world. There is a spiritual force behind this world-scene which, by means of 'the things that are in the world', is seeking to enmesh men in its system. It is not merely against sin therefore that the saints of God need to be on their guard, but against the ruler of this world. God is building up His Church to its consummation in the universal reign of Christ. Simultaneously His rival is building up this world-system to its vain climax in the reign of antichrist. How watchful we need to be lest at any time we be found helping Satan in the construction of that ill-fated kingdom. When we are faced with alternatives and a choice of ways confronts us, the question is not: Is this good or evil? Is this helpful or hurtful? No, the question we must ask ourselves is: *Is it of this world, or of God?* For since there is only this one conflict in the universe, then whenever two conflicting courses lie open to us, the choice at issue is never a lesser one than: God . . . or Satan?

CHAPTER TWO

THE TREND AWAY FROM GOD

HAVING every one of us been in bondage to sin, we readily believe that sinful things are Satanic; but do we believe equally that the things of the world are Satanic? Many of us, I think, are still in two minds about this. Yet how clearly Scripture affirms that 'the whole world lieth in the evil one' (1 John 5. 19). Satan well knows that, generally speaking, to try to ensnare real Christians through things that are positively sinful is vain and futile. They will usually sense the danger and elude him. So he had contrived instead an enticing network, the mesh of which is so skilfully woven as to entrap the most innocent of men. We flee sinful lusts, and with good reason, but when it comes to such seemingly innocuous things as science and art and education, how readily do we lose our sense of values and fall a prey to his enticements!

Yet our Lord's sentence of judgment clearly implies that everything that constitutes 'the world' is out of line with God's purpose. His words, 'Now is the judgment of this world', clearly imply the condemnation of all that goes to make up the *kosmos*, and would never have been uttered if there were not something radically amiss with it. Further, when Jesus goes on: 'Now shall the prince of this world be cast out,' He is stressing not merely the intimate relation between Satan and the world order but the fact that its condemnation is linked with his. Do we acknowledge that Satan is today the prince of education and science and culture and the arts, and that they, with him, are doomed? Do we acknowledge that he is the effective master of all those things that together make up the world system?

When mention is made of a dance hall or a night-club, our reaction as Christians is one of instinctive disapproval. To us that is 'the world' *par excellence*. When, however, to go to the other extreme, medical science or social service are discussed, there may be no such reaction at all. These things command our tacit approval, and maybe too our enthusiastic support. And between these extremes there lie a host of other things varying widely in their influence for good or bad, between which we should probably none of us agree on where to draw an exact line. Yet let us face the fact that judgment has been pronounced by God, not upon certain selected things that belong to this world, but impartially upon them all.

Test yourself. If you venture into one of these approved fields, and then someone exclaims to you: 'You have touched the world there', will you be moved? Probably not at all. It takes someone whom you really respect to say to you very straightly and earnestly: 'Brother, you have become involved with Satan there!' before you will so much as hesitate. Is that not so? How would you feel if anyone said to you: 'You have touched education there', or 'You have touched medical science', or 'You have touched commerce'? Would you react with the same degree of caution as you would if he had said, 'You have touched the Devil there'? If we truly believed that whenever we touch any of these things that constitute the world we touch the prince of this world, then the awful seriousness of being in any wise involved in worldly things could not fail to strike home to us. 'The whole world lieth in the evil one'—not a part of it, but *the whole*. Do not let us think for a moment that Satan opposes God only by means of sin and carnality in men's hearts; he opposes God by means of every worldly thing. Oh, I agree with you that the things of the world are all in one sense material, lifeless, intrinsically without power to harm us; yet even that should itself suggest that they are resistant to the purpose of God, as indeed is everything in which there is no touch of divine life.

The recurring phrase 'after its kind' in Genesis 1 represents a law of reproduction that governs the whole realm of biological nature. It does not, however, govern the realm of the Spirit. For generation after generation, human parents can beget children after their kind; but one thing is certain: Christians cannot beget Christians! Not even where both parents are Christians will the children born to them automatically be Christians, no, not even in the first generation. It will take a fresh act of God every time.

And this principle applies no less truly in the affairs of mankind more widely. All that belongs to human nature continues spontaneously; all that belongs to God continues only for as long as God's working continues. And the world is all-inclusively that which can continue apart from divine activity, that is, which can go on by itself without the need of specific acts of God to maintain it in freshness. The world, and all that belongs to the world, does this naturally—it is its nature—and in doing so it *moves in a direction contrary to the will of God*. This statement we shall now seek to illustrate both from the Scripture and from Christian experience.

Let us take first the field of political science. The Old Testament history of Israel affords us the example of a highly privileged nation and its government. The people of Israel, we are told, wanted to be on terms with the nations around them, so they set their heart on a king. We will leave aside for the moment their election of Saul, and move on to the point where eventually, in His own time, God gave them the king of His choice who would establish the kingdom under His own direction.

Now even when this was clearly God's doing, the natural trend of the kingdom proved to be, 'like the nations', away from Him. For a kingdom is a worldly thing, and in keeping with all worldly things it tends to come into collision with the divine purpose. Wherever in the world a nation's government is left to itself, it follows its natural course which is further and further away from God. And what is true in secular national politics worked itself out equally surely even in divinely-chosen Israel. Whenever God discontinued His specific acts on their behalf, the kingdom of Israel drifted into idolatrous political alignments. There were recoveries, it is true, but every one was marked by a definite divine intervention, and without such intervention the trend was always down-hill.

It will scarcely surprise us that the same thing proves to be true in the field of commerce. I can think of no sphere where the temptation to dishonest and corrupt dealing is so great as here. We all know something of this. We all know how hard it is to remain straight and to conduct affairs honestly in the competitive world of trade. Many would say that it is impossible, and certainly to do so calls for a life that is cast upon God in an unusual way.

We recall that our Lord Jesus tells us of two contrasting men, one who gained the whole world and forfeited his life, and another, a merchant, who went and sold all that he had to buy one priceless pearl. To the latter of these Jesus likened the kingdom of heaven (Matt. 16. 26; 13. 45, 46). The Spirit of God has not infrequently moved men in business to action of a like character. There have been not a few well-known business firms whose profits have been turned over to divine ends in the spread of the Gospel and in other ways.

I think of one such enterprise that, at the outset of its history, was the creation of a God-fearing business man. Now godly fear is a quality that can only exist as it is sustained from heaven, but business acumen and the efficient organization which it creates can be self-perpetuating. In the first generation of this firm's history we find divine life being mediated through its founder sufficient to hold what was even then a worldly concern securely under the authority of God. But by the second generation that restraint was gone and, as one would expect, the business gravitated automatically into the world-system. Godly fear had drained away, but the firm itself is still flourishing.

Suppose we take now so apparently innocent a matter as agriculture. Here Genesis, written in a primitive world of flocks and husbandry, has something to tell us. After Adam's fall God was compelled to say to him, 'Cursed is the ground for thy sake; in toil shalt thou eat of it all the days of thy life; thorns also and thistles shall it bring forth to thee; and thou shalt eat the herb of the field; in the sweat of thy face shalt thou eat bread, till thou return unto the ground.' No one would suggest that in Eden, where the tree of life flourished, farming or gardening was wrong. It was God-appointed. But as soon as it was let go from under the hand of God it deteriorated. Man was condemned to an endless round of drudgery and disappointment, and an element of perversity marked the fruit of his toil. The deliverance of Noah was God's great recovery movement, in which the earth was given a fresh start. But how swift, how tragic was man's reversion to type! 'Noah began to be a husbandman, and planted a vineyard; and he drank of the wine, and was drunken; and he was uncovered within his tent.' Of course agriculture is not in itself sinful, but here already its direction is away from God. Just let it follow its natural tendency and it will contrive to take a course diametrically opposed to Him. Do we know something of this today in such physical disasters as the drying out of continents?

How different is the Church, God's husbandry! Through the grace of God and the indwelling Spirit she possesses an inherent life-power capable, if she responds to it, of keeping her constantly moving Godward, or of recalling her Godward if she strays.

When we turn to education, both the Bible and experience have something to say to us. Speaking allegorically we might say that in rejecting Saul and choosing David God was passing over a man distinguished by his head (for he was that much taller than his peers) in favour of the man after His heart! But more seriously, the men such as Joseph and Moses and Daniel of whose wisdom God made public use each received in a direct way from

God Himself the understanding they needed. They took little
account of their secular education. And the apostle Paul clearly
placed scholarship among the 'all things' that he counted to be
loss for the excellency of the knowledge of Christ Jesus his Lord
(Phil. 3. 8). He draws a clear distinction between the wisdom of
the world and the wisdom that comes from God (1 Cor. 1. 21,
30).

But it is experience that demonstrates the essential worldliness
of scholarship as such. Most of the historic University colleges of
the West were founded by Christian men with a desire to provide
their fellows with a good education under Christian influence.
During their founders' lifetimes the tone of those foundations
was high, because these men put real spiritual content into them.
When, however, the men themselves passed away the spiritual
control passed away too, and education followed its inevitable
course towards the world of materialism and away from God.
In some cases it may have taken a long time, for religious tradition dies hard; but the tendency has always been obvious, and in
most cases the destination has by now been reached. When
material things are under spiritual control they fulfil their proper
subordinate role. Released from that restraint they manifest very
quickly the power that lies behind them. The law of their nature
asserts itself, and their worldly character is proved by the course
they take.

The spread of missionary enterprise in our present era gives
us an opportunity to test this principle in the religious institutions
of our day and of our land. Over a century ago the Church set
out to establish in China schools and hospitals with a definite
spiritual tone and an evangelistic objective. In those early days
not much importance was attached to the buildings, while considerable emphasis was placed on the institutions' role in the proclamation of the Gospel. Ten or fifteen years ago you could go
over the same ground and in many places find much larger and
finer institutions on those original sites, but compared with the

earlier years, far fewer converts. And by today many of those splendid schools and colleges have become purely educational centres, lacking in any truly evangelistic motive at all, while to an almost equal extent, many of the hospitals exist now solely as places merely of physical and no longer of spiritual healing. The men who initiated them had, by their close walk with God, held those institutions steadfastly into His purpose; but when they passed away the institutions themselves quickly gravitated towards worldly standards and goals, and in doing so classified themselves as 'things of the world'. We should not be surprised that this is so.

In the early chapters of the Acts we read how a contingency arose which led the Church to institute relief for the poorer saints. That urgent institution of social service was clearly blessed of God, but it was of a temporary nature. Do you exclaim, 'How good if it had continued!'? Only one who does not know God would say that. Had those relief measures been prolonged indefinitely they would certainly have veered in the direction of the world, once the spiritual influence at work in their inception was removed. It is inevitable.

For there is a distinction between the Church of God's building, on the one hand, and on the other, those valuable social and charitable by-products that are thrown off by it from time to time through the faith and vision of its members. The latter, for all their origin in spiritual vision, possess in themselves a power of independent survival which the Church of God does not have. They are works which the faith of God's children may initiate and pioneer, but which, once the way has been shown and the professional standard set, can be readily sustained or imitated by men of the world quite apart from that faith.

The Church of God, let me repeat, never ceases to be dependent upon the life of God for its maintenance. Imagine a living church in a city today with its fellowship and prayer and Gospel witness, and its many homes and centres of spiritual activity.

Some years hence what do we find? If God's people have followed Him in faith and obedience it may be a place filled more than ever with the life and light of the Lord and the power of His Word; but if in unfaithfulness to Him they have forsaken their vision of Christ, it may equally well have become a place where people preach atheism. By then as a church it will have ceased to exist. For the Church depends for its very existence upon a ceaseless impartation of fresh life from God, and cannot survive one day without it.

But suppose alongside that church there is a school or hospital or publishing house, or other religiously founded institution, originating in the faith of the same church-members. Assuming that the need for its service continues still to exist ten years hence and has not been met by some alternative private or State enterprise, then the probability is that that work will still be operating then at a no less efficient and commendable standard of service. For given ordinary administrative know-how, a college or a hospital can continue efficiently on a purely institutional level eithout any fresh influx of divine life. The vision may have gone, but the establishment carries on indefinitely. It has become no less worldly than everything else that can be maintained apart from the life of God. And every such thing is embraced in the Lord's sentence: 'Now is the judgment of this world.'

Suppose I put to you the question, 'What work are you engaged in?' You answer, 'Medical work.' You say that without any special consciousness other than pride in the compassionate nature of your calling, and without any sense of the possible danger of your situation. But if I tell you that medical science is one more unit of a system that is Satan-controlled, what then? Assuming that as a Christian you take me seriously, then you are at once alarmed, and your reaction may even be to wonder if you had not better quit your profession. No, do not cease being a doctor! But walk softly, for you are upon territory that is governed by God's enemy, and unless you are on the watch you are as liable as anyone else to fall a prey to his devices.

Or suppose you are engineering, or farming, or publishing. Take heed, for these too are things of the world, just as much as running a place of entertainment or a haunt of vice. Unless you tread softly you will be caught up somewhere in Satan's snares and will lose the liberty that is yours as a child of God.

How then, you ask, are we to be delivered from his entanglements? Many think that to escape the world is a matter of consecration, of dedicating themselves anew and more wholeheartedly to the things of God. No, it is a matter of salvation. By nature we are all entrapped in that Satanic system, and we have no escape apart from the mercy of the Lord. All our consecration is powerless to deliver us; we are dependent upon His compassion and upon His redemptive work alone to save us out of it. He is well able to do so, and the means whereby He does it will be the theme of our next chapter. God can set us upon a rock and keep our feet from slipping. Helped by Him we may turn our trade or profession to the service of His will for as long as He desires it.

But let me repeat again that the natural trend of all the 'things that are in the world' is towards Satan and away from God. Some of them may have been set going by men of the Spirit with a goal that is Godward, but as soon as the restraint of the divine life is removed from them, they automatically swerve around and take that other direction. No wonder then that Satan's eyes are ever on the world's end, and on the prospect that at that time all the things of the world will revert to him. Even now, and all the time, they are moving in his direction, and at the end time they may be expected to have reached their goal. As we touch any one of the units of his system, this thought should give us pause, lest we be found inadvertently helping to construct his kingdom.

CHAPTER THREE

A WORLD UNDER WATER

'Go ye into all the world, and preach the gospel to the whole creation. He that believeth and is baptized shall be saved; but he that disbelieveth shall be condemned.' (Mark 16. 15, 16.)

To many of us the form of that second sentence comes as a surprise. Jesus did not say that he who believes and is saved shall be baptized. No, He put it the other way round. He who believes and is baptized, He said, shall be saved. It is only at our peril that we change something that the Lord has said into something that He did not say. Everything He says matters, and He means every word of it. But if this is so, then it must be a fact that only by having faith in Him and being baptized are we saved. Some will be puzzled at this. What do you mean? they will protest. But do not puzzle; and do not blame me! *I* did not say that; my Lord said it. He it was who laid down the order: faith, then baptism, then salvation. We must not reverse it to faith, salvation, baptism, however much we might prefer it that way. What the Lord said must stand, and it is for us only to pay heed to it.

(I make no apology for taking these words of Mark 16. 16 as authentic words of Jesus, though I am aware that there are critics who question them. Once in a country village I came across a tailor named Chen. He had picked up a Gospel of Mark, and when he reached this passage which the critics all affirm does not belong to that Gospel at all, he believed and trusted in the Lord. There were no other Christians in the place and so no one to baptize him. What should he do? Then he read verse 20. God

Himself would confirm to him His word: that was sufficient. So in his simplicity he decided to test out one of the promises in verse 18. Accordingly he visited several neighbours who were sick. After prayer, he laid hands on them in Jesus' name and then returned home. In due course and without exception, he told me, they recovered. That satisfied him. With his faith confirmed he carried quietly on with his tailoring, where, when I came across him, he was faithfully witnessing to his Lord. If *he* could take God's word seriously, must not I?)

So I repeat, 'He that believeth and is baptized shall be saved.' Do you mean to tell me, you will now exclaim, that you believe in baptismal regeneration? No indeed I do not! The Lord did not say, 'Believe and be baptized and thou shalt be born again'; and since He did not say that, I have no need to believe in that. His words are: 'He that believeth and is baptized *shall be saved.*' What therefore I do believe in is baptismal salvation.

So the question naturally arises: What does this statement *mean*? And what does it mean when Luke tells us that, in response to Peter's exhortation to '*save yourselves* from this crooked generation', then they that receive his word *were baptized*?

To answer this we must ask ourselves first what we mean by the word 'saved'. I am afraid we have a very wrong idea of salvation. All that most of us know about salvation is that we shall be saved from hell and into heaven; or alternatively, that we are saved from our sins to live henceforth a holy life. But we are wrong. In Scripture we find that salvation goes further than that. For it is concerned not so much with sin and hell, or holiness and heaven, but with something else.

We know that every good gift that God offers to us is given to meet and counter a contrasting evil. He gives us justification because there is condemnation. He gives us eternal life because there is death. He offers us forgiveness because there are sins. He brings us salvation—because of what? Justification is in terms of condemnation, heaven is in terms of hell, forgiveness is in relation to sins. Then to what is salvation related? Salvation, we shall see, is related to the *kosmos*, the world.

Satan is the personal enemy of Christ. He works through the flesh of man to produce this pattern of things on the earth in which we have all become involved; not one of us is exempt. And this whole cosmic pattern is peculiarly at odds with God the Father. I think we all know how the three dark forces, the world, the flesh and the devil, stand in opposition to the three divine persons. The flesh is ranged against the Holy Spirit as Paraclete, Satan himself against Christ Jesus as Lord, and the world against the Father as Creator.

What we are speaking of as the *kosmos* always stands opposed to God as Father and Originator. His was the eternal plan in creation hinted at in the words 'It was very good', a plan towards which He has not ceased to work. From before the foundation of the world He had purposed in His heart to have on earth an order of which mankind would be the pinnacle and which should freely display the character of His Son. But Satan intervened. Using this earth as his springboard and man as his tool, he usurped God's creation to make of it instead something centred in himself and reflecting his own image. Thus this alien system of things was a direct challenge to the divine plan.

So today we are confronted by two worlds, two spheres of authority, having two totally different and opposed characters. For me now it is no mere matter of a future heaven and hell; it is a question of these two worlds today, and of whether I belong to an order of things of which Christ is sovereign Lord, or to an opposed order of things having Satan as its effective head.

Thus salvation is not so much a personal question of sins forgiven or of hell avoided. It is to be seen rather in terms of a system from which we come out. When I am saved, I make my exodus out of one whole world and my entry into another. I am saved *now* out of that whole organized realm which Satan has constructed in defiance of the purpose of God.

That realm, that all-embracing *kosmos*, has many strange facets.
Sin of course has its prior place there, and worldly lusts; but no
less part of it are our more estimable human standards and ways
of doing things. The human mind, its culture and its philo-
sophies, all are included, together with all the very best of
humanity's social and political ideologies. Alongside these too
we should doubtless place the world's religions, and among
them those speckled birds, worldly Christianity and its 'world
Church'. Wherever the power of natural man dominates, there
you have an element in that system which is under the direct
inspiration of Satan.

If that is the world, what then is salvation? Salvation means
that I escape from that. I go out, I make an exit from that all-
embracing *kosmos*. I belong no more to Satan's pattern of things.
I set my heart on that upon which God's heart is set. I take as
my goal His eternal purpose in Christ, and I step into that and
am delivered from this.

He that believeth and is baptized shall be saved. What Jesus
said He plainly means. I take that step of faith: I believe and
am baptized, and I come out a saved man. *That* is salvation. So
never let us regard baptism as of small concern. Tremendous
things hang upon it. It is no less a question than of two violently
opposing worlds and of our translation from the one into the
other.

There is in Scripture another passage which brings baptism
and salvation together to illustrate this theme. I allude to Chapter
3 of 1 Peter. There the apostle tells us how 'the longsuffering of
God waited in the days of Noah, while the ark was a preparing,
wherein few, that is, eight souls, were saved through water'
(verse 20). The water, he says, is a figure or likeness, or (as the
R.V. margin reads) an antitype, of something else. 'Which also
in the antitype doth now save you, even baptism.' So baptism,
he reasons, saves us *now*. Clearly Peter believed in our salvation
through baptism as firmly as he believed in Noah's salvation

through water. Please remember, I am not saying regeneration, and I am not saying deliverance from hell or from sin. Understand clearly that we are talking here about salvation. It is not just a question of terms; it concerns our being fundamentally severed from today's world-system.

To understand better what Peter means we should turn back to his source in Chapters 6 to 8 of Genesis. The picture is instructive. There in Noah's day we find a wholly corrupt world. Created first by God, the earth had become corrupted by man's act on that day when he placed himself under Satan. Sin, once introduced, had developed and run riot, until even God's Holy Spirit cried Enough! Things had reached a state where they could never be remedied; they could only be judged and removed.

So God commanded Noah to build an Ark, and to bring his family and the creatures into it, and then the flood came. By it they were 'lifted up above the earth' upon waters that covered 'all the high mountains that were under the whole heaven'. Every living thing, both man and beast, perished and those only who rode the waters in the ark were saved. The significant thing here is not just that they escaped death by drowning. That is not the point. The real point for us is that they were the only people to come out from that corrupt system of things, that world under water. Personal life is the inevitable consequence of coming out, personal perdition of staying in, but salvation is the coming out itself, not the effect of it. Note this difference for it is a great one. Salvation is essentially a present exit from a doomed order which is Satan's.

Praise God, they came out! How? Through the waters. So today when believers are baptized they go symbolically through water, just as Noah passed in the ark through the waters of the flood. And this passage through water signifies their escape from the world, their exodus from the system of things that, with its prince, is under the divine sentence. May I say this especially to those who are being baptized today.[1] Please remember, you are not the only one who is in the water. As you step down into the water, a whole world goes down with you. When you come up, you come up in Christ, in the ark that rides the waves, but your world stays behind. For you, that world is submerged, drowned like Noah's, put to death in the death of Christ and never to be revived. It is by baptism that you declare this. 'Lord, I leave my world behind. Thy Cross separates me from it for ever!'

Speaking figuratively, therefore, when you go through the waters of baptism everything belonging to the former system of things is cut off by those waters never to return. You alone emerge. For you it is a passage into another world, a world where you will find a dove and the fresh leaves of olive trees. You go out of the world that is under judgment, into a world that is marked by newness of divine life.

I want to emphasize again that you were not the only one that went down into the water; your world went down with you. And there it stayed. From the standpoint of your new situation you will find that the water always covers the world to which you belonged before. The same flood which saved Noah and his family drowned the world in which they had once lived their lives—the very same flood. So the same water on the one hand puts you and me on salvation ground in Christ, and on the other hand buries Satan's whole system of things. Not only does your own history as a child of Adam end in your baptism; your world also ends there. In both cases it is a death and a burial with nothing resurrected. It is an end of everything.

This means that you cannot carry over anything from that former world into the new one. What belonged to that former realm of things in Adam stays there and may never be recalled. Formerly perhaps you were an employee in a shop, or a servant in a house. Or perhaps you were the master, or the manager or

[1] The occasion of this address was a baptismal service in London in the month of May 1939.

director of a business. Still today you may be a master, or still a servant, but you will find that when coming to divine things, when coming to the Church of God and the service of God, there is neither bond nor free, neither employer nor employee. Again you may be a Jew or a Gentile, or any of a hundred-and-one things that were of repute—or of disrepute—in Adam. When you pass through this water, all that system of things goes, never to return. Instead you see yourself in Christ, where there is neither Jew nor Greek, barbarian nor Scythian nor anything else, but one new man. You have entered an order of things characterized by olive trees and olive leaves, whose secret is divine life. The expression 'through the resurrection of Jesus Christ' colours the whole future (1 Pet. 3. 21). It implies that you have passed into something altogether new which God is creating. According to commentators (Robert Young *Analytical Concordance of the Holy Bible*), the very name Ararat means 'Holy Ground'. Be that as it may, we praise God that the ark which rested on that renewed earth was filled with creatures, typifying a new creation. Out of the death of Christ God brings into being an entire new creation, and in union with Christ risen He is introducing man into that. In Christ, you and I are there!

You ask me now whether it matters if we are not baptized. My only answer is that the Lord Himself commanded it (Matt. 28. 19). And it was a step from which He Himself refused to be dissuaded (Matt. 3. 13-15). Peter describes baptism as the appeal, or testimony, of a good conscience towards God (verse 21). A testimony is a declaration. So through this act you say something, you declare where you stand, perhaps without using words but certainly by what you do. Passing through the water you proclaim to the whole universe that you have left your world behind and have entered into something utterly new. That is salvation. You take a public stand where God has placed you in Christ.

This helps to explain why in Scripture we find passages con-

cerning salvation which are hard to interpret if we relate salvation
only to hell or to sin. It illumines, for instance, the apparently
difficult words of Paul and Silas to the jailor at Philippi. The man
asked, 'What must I do to be saved?' What will your answer be?
If you are a sound evangelical preacher in the present day, you
will say with assurance, 'Believe on the Lord Jesus Christ, and
thou shalt be saved.' But Paul in fact added: 'thou and thy house'.
Do you really mean to say, I can hear you exclaim, that if I believe
on the Lord Jesus, both I and my family will be saved? Now
once again we must be careful. Paul did not say, Believe on the
Lord Jesus and thou and thy house will have eternal life. He said,
'Believe on the Lord Jesus Christ, and thou shalt *be saved*, thou
and thy house.' Remember, he is concerned with a system of
things, and with the jailor's repudiation of and exit from that
system. When, as head of his family, that man makes the declaration that from that day forward he and his house are going
to serve the Lord, and when that declaration becomes publicly
known, even people passing through the street will point in the
door and say, 'They are Christian folk.'

That is what it means to be saved. You declare that you belong
to another system of things. People point to you and say, 'Oh
yes, that is a Christian family; they belong to the Lord!' That is
the salvation which the Lord desires for you, that by your public
testimony you declare before God, 'My world has gone; I
am entering into another.' May the Lord give us that kind
of salvation, to find ourselves uprooted entire out of the old,
doomed order of things and firmly planted in the new, divine
one.

For, praise God, there is a glorious positive side to all this. We
are saved 'through the resurrection of Jesus Christ, who', Peter
goes on to say, 'is on the right hand of God, having gone into
heaven, angels and authorities and powers being made subject
unto him' (verse 22). God has set His Son supreme above everything, and made all authorities His subjects. A God who can do

this is well able to bring me, body and soul, into that other realm.

So, to recapitulate, we have here two worlds. On the one hand there is the world in Adam, held fast in bondage to Satan; on the other hand there is the new creation in Christ, the sphere of activity of God's Holy Spirit. How do you and I get out of the one sphere, Adam, into the other sphere, Christ? If you are uncertain how to answer that question, may I ask you another? How did you get *into* Adam in the first place? For the way of entry indicates the way out. You entered the sphere of Adam by being born into Adam's race. How then do you get out? Obviously by death. And how, in turn, do you enter the sphere of Christ? The answer is the same: by birth. The way of entry into the family of God is by new birth to a living hope, through the resurrection of Jesus Christ from the dead (1 Pet. 1. 3). Having become united with Him by the likeness of His death, you are united with Him also by the likeness of His resurrection (Rom. 6. 5). Death puts an end to your relationship with the old world, and resurrection brings you into living touch with this new one.

Finally, what occupies the gap? What is the stepping-stone between those two worlds? Is it not burial? 'We were buried therefore with him through baptism into death' (Rom. 6. 4). From one point of view there is a grim finality about those words 'buried into death'. My history in Adam has already been concluded in the death of Christ, so that when I walk away from that burial I can say I am a 'finished' man. But I can say more, for, praise God, it is no less true that there is the other side. Since 'Christ was raised from the dead', when I come out of the water and walk away, I may walk 'in newness of life' (6. 4).

This double outcome of the Cross is implied too in the preceding words of Romans 6. 3. 'Are ye ignorant that all we who were baptized into Christ Jesus were baptized into his death?' Here in a single sentence the two aspects of baptism are again hinted at. It is baptism into two things. First, we who believe were 'baptized *into his death*'. This is a tremendous fact, but is it all? Not by any means, for in the second place the same verse says that we were 'baptized *into Christ Jesus*'. A baptism into the death of Christ ends my relation with this world, but a baptism into Christ Jesus as a living Person, Head of a new race, opens up for me a new world of things altogether. Going into the water I simply act the whole thing out, affirming publicly that the 'judgment of this world' became real to me from the day when the 'lifted up' Son of man drew me to Himself.

What a Gospel to preach to the whole creation!

CHAPTER FOUR

CRUCIFIED UNTO ME

SEPARATION to God, separation from the world, is the first principle of Christian living. John, in his revelation of Jesus Christ, was shown two irreconcilable extremes, two worlds that morally were poles apart. He was first carried away in the Spirit into a wilderness to see Babylon, mother of the harlots and of the abominations of the earth (17. 3). Then he was carried in the same Spirit to a great and high mountain, from whence to view Jerusalem, the bride, the Lamb's wife (21. 10). The contrast is clear and could hardly be more explicitly stated.

Whether we be a Moses or a Balaam, in order to have God's view of things we must be taken like John to a mountain-top. Many cannot see God's eternal plan, or if they see it they understand it only as dry-as-dust doctrine, because they are content to stay on the plains. For understanding never moves us; only revelation does that. From the wilderness we may see something of Babylon, but we need spiritual revelation to see God's new Jerusalem. Once see it, and we shall never be the same again. As Christians therefore we bank everything on that opening of the eyes, but to experience it we must be prepared to forsake the common levels and climb.

The harlot Babylon is always 'the great city' (16. 19, etc.) with the emphasis on her attainment of greatness. The bride Jerusalem is by contrast 'the holy city' (21. 2, 10) with the accent correspondingly on her separation to God. She is 'from God', and is prepared 'for her husband'. For this reason she possesses the glory of God. This is a matter of experience for us all. Holiness

in us is what is of God, what is wholly set apart to Christ. It
follows the rule that only what originated in heaven returns
there; for nothing else is holy. Let go this principle of holiness
and we are instantly in Babylon.

Thus it comes about that the wall is the first feature John mentions in his description of the city itself. There are gates, making
provision for the goings of God, but the wall takes precedence.
For, I repeat, separation is the first principle of Christian living.
If God wants His city with its measurements and its glory in that
day, then we must build that wall in human hearts now. This
means in practice that we must guard as precious all that is of God
and refuse and reject all that is of Babylon. I do not imply by
this a separation between Christians. We dare not exclude our
brethren themselves, even when we cannot take part in some of
the things they do. No, we must love and receive our fellow
Christians, but be uncompromising in our separation from the
world in principle.

Nehemiah in his day succeeded in rebuilding the wall of Jerusalem, but only in the face of great opposition. For Satan hates
distinctiveness. Separation of men to God he cannot abide.
Nehemiah and his colleagues armed themselves therefore, and
thus equipped for war they laid stone to stone. This is the price
of holiness we must be prepared for.

For build we certainly must. Eden was a garden without
artificial wall to keep foes out; so that Satan had entry. God intended that Adam and Eve should 'guard it' (Gen. 2. 15) by
themselves constituting a moral barrier to him. Today, through
Christ, God plans in the heart of His redeemed people an Eden
to which, in triumphant fact, Satan will at last have no moral
access whatever. 'There shall in no wise enter into it anything
unclean, or he that maketh an abomination and a lie; but only
they which are in the Lamb's book of life.'

Most of us would agree that to the apostle Paul was given a
special revelation of the Church of God. In a similar way we

feel that God gave to John a special understanding of the nature of the world. *Kosmos* is in fact peculiarly John's word. The other Gospels use it only fifteen times (Matthew nine, Mark and Luke three each) while Paul has it forty-seven times in eight letters. But John uses it 105 times in all, seventy-eight in his Gospel, twenty-four in his epistles and a further three in the Revelation.

In his first epistle John writes: 'All that is in the world, the lust of the flesh, and the lust of the eyes, and the vainglory of life, is not of the Father, but is of the world' (2. 16). In these words that so clearly reflect the temptation of Eve (Gen. 3. 6) John defines the things of the world. All that can be included under lust or primitive desire, all that excites greedy ambition, and all that arouses in us the pride or glamour of life, all such things are part of the Satanic system. Perhaps we scarcely need stay here to consider further the first two of these, but let us look for a moment at the third. Everything that stirs pride in us is of the world. Prominence, wealth, achievement, these the world acclaim. Men are justly proud of success. Yet John labels all that brings this sense of success as 'of the world'.

Every success therefore that we experience (and I am not suggesting that we should be failures!) calls in us for an instant, humble confession of its inherent sinfulness, for whenever we meet success we have in some degree touched the world-system. Whenever we sense complacency over some achievement we may know at once that we have touched the world. We may know, too, that we have brought ourselves under the judgment of God, for have we not already agreed that the whole world is under judgment? Now (and let us try to grasp this fact) those who realize this and confess their need are thereby safeguarded.

But the trouble is, how many of us are aware of it? Even those of us who live our lives in the seclusion of our own private homes are just as prone to fall a prey to the pride of life as those who have great public successes. A woman in a humble kitchen

can touch the world and its complacency even while cooking the
daily meal or entertaining guests. Every glory that is not glory
to God is vainglory, and it is amazing what paltry successes
can produce vainglory. Wherever we meet pride we meet the
world, and there is an immediate leakage in our fellowship with
God. Oh that God would open our eyes to see clearly what the
world is! Not only evil things, but all those things that draw us
ever so gently away from God, are units of that system that is
antagonistic to Him. Satisfaction in the achievement of some
legitimate piece of work has the power to come instantly between us and God Himself. For if it is the pride of life and not
the praise of God that it awakens in us, we can know for certain
that we have touched the world. There is thus a constant need
for us to watch and pray if we are to maintain our communion
with God unsullied.

What then is the way of escape from this snare which the
Devil has set to catch God's people. First let me say emphatically
that it is not to be found by our running away. Many think we
can escape the world by seeking to abstain from the things of the
world. That is folly. How could we ever escape the world-
system by using what, after all, are little more than worldly
methods? Let me remind you of Jesus' words in Matt. 11. 18, 19.
'John came neither eating nor drinking, and they say, He hath a
devil. The Son of man came eating and drinking, and they say,
Behold, a gluttonous man, and a winebibber, a friend of publicans and sinners!' Some think that John the Baptist here offers us
a recipe for escape from the world, but 'neither eating nor
drinking' is not Christianity. Christ came both eating and drinking, and that *is* Christianity! The apostle Paul speaks of 'the
elements of the world', and he defines these as, 'handle not, nor
taste, nor touch' (Col. 2. 20, 21). So abstinence is merely worldly
and no more, and what hope is there, by using worldly elements,
of escaping the world system? Yet how many earnest Christians
are forsaking all sorts of worldly pleasures in the hope thereby of

being delivered out of the world! You can build yourself a hermit's hut in some remote spot and think to escape the world by retiring there, but the world will follow you even as far as that. It will dog your footsteps and find you out no matter where you hide.

Our deliverance from the world begins, not with our giving up this or that but with our seeing, as with God's eyes, that it is a world under sentence of death. In the figure with which we opened this chapter, 'Fallen, fallen is Babylon the great!' (Rev. 18. 2). Now a sentence of death is always passed, not on the dead but on the living. And in one sense the world is a living force today, relentlessly pursuing and seeking out its subjects. But while it is true that when sentence is pronounced death lies still in the future, it is nevertheless certain. A person under sentence of death *has* no future beyond the confines of a condemned cell. Likewise the world, being under sentence, has no future. The world-system has not yet been 'wound up', as we say, and terminated by God, but the winding-up is a settled matter. It makes all the difference to us that we *see* this. Some folk seek deliverance from the world in asceticism, and like the Baptist, neither eat nor drink. That today is Buddhism, not Christianity. As Christians we both eat and drink, but we do so in the realization that eating and drinking belong to the world and, with it, are under the death sentence, so they have no grip upon us.

Let us suppose that the municipal authorities of Shanghai should decree that the school where you are employed must be closed. As soon as you hear this news you realize there is no future for you in that school. You go on working there for a period, but you do not build up anything for the future there. Your attitude to the school changes the instant you hear it must close down. Or to use another illustration, suppose the government decides to close a certain bank. Will you hasten to deposit in it a large sum of money in order to save the bank from collapse? No, not a cent more do you pay into it once you hear it has no future. You put nothing in because you expect nothing from it.

And we may justly say of the world that it is under a decree of closure. Babylon fell when her champions made war with the Lamb, and when by His death and resurrection He overcame them who is Lord of lords and King of kings (Rev. 17. 14). There is no future for her.

A revelation of the Cross of Christ involves for us the discovery of this fact, that through it everything belonging to the world is under sentence of death. We still go on living in the world and using the things of the world, but we can build no future with them, for the Cross has shattered all our hope in them. The Cross of our Lord Jesus, we may truly say, has ruined our prospects in the world; we have nothing to live for there.

There is no true way of salvation from the world that does not start from such a revelation. We need only try to escape the world by running away from it to discover how much we love it, and how much it loves us. We may flee where we will to avoid it, but it will assuredly track us down. But we inevitably lose all interest in the world, and it loses its grip on us, as soon as it dawns upon us that the world is doomed. To see that is to be automatically severed from Satan's entire economy.

At the end of his letter to the Galatians Paul states this very clearly. 'Far be it from me to glory, save in the cross of our Lord Jesus Christ, through which the world hath been crucified unto me, and I unto the world' (6. 14). Have you noticed something striking about this verse? In relation to the world it speaks of the two aspects of the work of the Cross already hinted at in our last chapter. 'I have been crucified unto the world' is a statement which we find fairly easy to fit into our understanding of being crucified with Christ as defined in such passages as Romans 6. But here it specifically says too that 'the world has been crucified to me'. When God comes to you and me with the revelation of the finished work of Christ, He not only shows us ourselves there on the Cross. He shows us our world there too. If you and I cannot escape the judgment of the Cross, then neither can the world escape the judgment of the Cross. Have I really seen this? That is the question. When I see it, then I do not try to repudiate a world I love; I see that the Cross *has* repudiated it. I do not try to escape a world that clings to me; I see that by the Cross I *have* escaped.

Like so much else in the Christian life, the way of deliverance out of the world comes as a surprise to most of us, for it is so at odds with all man's natural concepts. Man seeks to solve the problem of the world by removing himself physically from what he regards as the danger zone. But physical separation does not bring about spiritual separation; and the reverse is also true, that physical contact with the world does not necessitate spiritual capture by the world. Spiritual bondage to the world is a fruit of spiritual blindness, and deliverance is the outcome of having our eyes opened. However close our touch with the world may be outwardly, we are released from its power when we truly see its nature. The essential character of the world is Satanic; it is at enmity with God. To see this is to find deliverance.

Let me ask you: What is your occupation? A merchant? A doctor? Do not run away from these callings. Simply write down: Trade is under the sentence of death. Write: Medicine is under the sentence of death. If you do that in truth, life will be changed for you hereafter. In the midst of a world under judgment for its hostility to God you will know what it is to live as one who truly loves and fears Him.

CHAPTER FIVE

DISTINCTIVENESS

MAY I now invite your attention to words Jesus addressed to the Jews in John 8. 23. 'Ye are from beneath; I am from above: ye are of this world; I am not of this world.' I wish us to note especially here the use of the words 'from' and 'of'. The Greek word in each case is *ek*, which means 'out of' and implies origin. *Ek tou kosmos* is the expression used: 'from, *or* of, *or* out of, this world.' So the sense of the passage is: 'Your place of origin is beneath; my place of origin is above. Your place of origin is this world; my place of origin is not this world'. The question is not: Are you a good or a bad person? but, What is your place of origin? We do not ask, Is this thing right? or, Is that thing wrong? but, Where did it originate? It is origin that determines everything. 'That which is born of the flesh is flesh: that which is born of the Spirit is spirit' (John 3. 6).

So when Jesus turns to His disciples He can say, using the same Greek preposition, 'If ye were of the world (*ek tou kosmos*), the world would love its own: but because ye are not of the world, but I chose you out of the world, therefore the world hateth you' (John 15. 19). Here we have the same expression, 'not of the world', but in addition we have another and more forceful expression, 'I chose you out of the world'. In this latter instance there is a double emphasis. As before there is an *ek*, 'out of', but in addition to this the verb 'to choose', *eklego*, itself contains another *ek*. Jesus is saying that His disciples have been 'chosen-out, out of the world'.

There is this double *ek* in the life of every believer. Out of that vast organization called the *kosmos*, out of all the great mass of individuals belonging to it and involved in it, out, clean out of all of that, God has called us. Thence comes the title 'Church', *ekklesia*, God's 'called-out ones'. From the midst of the great *kosmos* God calls one here and one there; and all whom He calls He calls out. There is no such thing as a call from God that is not a call 'out of' the world. The church is *ekklesia*. In the divine intention there is no *klesia* which lacks that *ek*.

If you are a called one, then you are a called-out one. If God has called you at all then He has called you to live in spirit outside the world system. Originally we were in that Satanic system with no way of escape; but we were called, and that calling brought us out. True, that statement is a negative one, but there is a positive side also to our constitution; for as the people of God we have two titles, each of them significant according to the way we view ourselves. If we look back at our past history we are *ekklesia*, the Church; but if we look to our present life in God we are the Body of Christ, the expression on earth of Him who is in heaven. From the standpoint of God's choice of us we are 'out of' the world; but from the standpoint of our new life we are not of the world at all, but from above. On the one hand we are a chosen people, called and delivered out of the world system. On the other we are a regenerate people, utterly unrelated to that system because by the Spirit we are born from above. So John sees the holy city coming down 'out of heaven from God' (Rev. 21. 10). As the people of God, heaven is not only our destiny but our origin.

This is an amazing thing, that in you and me there is an element that is essentially other-worldly. So other-worldly is it indeed that, no matter how this world may progress, it can never advance one step in likeness to that. The life we have as God's gift came from heaven and never was in the world at all. It has no correspondence with the world but is in perfect correspondence with heaven; and though we must mingle with the world daily, it will never let us settle down and feel at home there.

Let us consider for a moment this divine gift, this life of Christ
indwelling the heart of regenerate man. The apostle Paul has a
great deal to say about this. In an illuminating passage in 1
Corinthians he makes a striking two-fold statement: (a) that God
Himself has placed us in Christ, and (b) that Christ has been 'made
unto us wisdom from God: righteousness and sanctification and
redemption' (1. 30). Here are examples of the whole range of
human need that God has met in His Son. We have shown elsewhere[1] how God does not distribute to us these qualities of
righteousness, holiness and so on in instalments 'to be taken as
required'. What He does is to give us Christ as the inclusive
answer to all our needs. He makes His Son to be my righteousness and my holiness, and everything else I lack, on the ground
that He has already placed me in Christ crucified and risen.

Now I would draw your attention to the last word, 'redemption'. For redemption has a great deal to do with the world. The
Israelites, you will recall, were 'redeemed' out of Egypt, which
at that time was all the world they knew, and which is for us a
figure of this world under Satanic rule. 'I am Jehovah,' God said
to Israel, 'and I will redeem you with a stretched out arm.' So
God brought them out, setting a barrier of judgment between
them and Pharoah's pursuing host, so that Moses could sing of
Israel as 'the people which thou has redeemed' (Exod. 6. 6; 15.
13).

In the light of this, let us now take Paul's double statement. If
(a) *God has placed us in Christ*, then since Christ is altogether out
of the world, we too are altogether out of the world. He is now
our sphere, and being in Him, we are by definition out of that
other sphere. The Father 'delivered us out of the power of darkness, and translated us into the kingdom of his dear Son; *in whom
we have our redemption*' (Col. 1. 13, 14, A.V.). This transfer was
the subject of our last two chapters.

Furthermore, if also (b) *Christ is 'made unto us redemption*'—if

[1] *The Normal Christian Life*, London, 1961, pp. 127 f.

that is to say, He is given to us to be that—then that means that *within us* God has set Christ Himself as the barrier to resist the world. I have met many young Christians trying to resist the world, trying in one way or another to live an un-worldly life. They found it very hard and, moreover, such effort is of course wholly unnecessary. For by His own essential 'otherness' Christ is our barrier to the world, and we need nothing more. It is not that we must do anything in relation to our redemption, any more than the people of Israel did anything in relation to theirs. They simply trusted in God's redeeming arm out-stretched on their behalf. And Christ *is made* to us redemption. In my heart there is a barrier set up between me and the world, the barrier of another kind of life, namely that of my Lord Himself, and God has set that barrier there. And because of Christ, the world cannot reach me.

What need therefore have I to try either to resist or to escape the system of things? If I look within myself for something with which to meet and overcome the world, I instantly find everything within me crying out *for* that world, while if I struggle to detach myself from it I simply become more and more involved. But let the day once come when I recognize that within me Christ is my redemption, and that in Him I *am* altogether 'out'. That day will see the end of struggling. I shall simply tell Him that I can do nothing at all about this 'world' business, but thank Him with all my heart that He is my Redeemer.

At risk of monotony let me say again: the character of the world is morally different from the Spirit-imparted life we have received from God. Fundamentally it is because we possess this new life of God's gift that the world hates us, for it has no hatred for its own kind. This radical difference leaves us indeed with no way of making the world love us. 'If ye were of the world, the world would love its own: but because ye are not of the world, but I chose you out of the world, therefore the world hateth you.'

When the world meets in us a natural human honesty and decency, it appreciates this, and is ready to pay us due respect and place in us its confidence. But as soon as it meets that in us which is not of ourselves, namely the divine nature of which we have been made partakers, its hostility is at once aroused. Show the world the fruits of Christianity and it will applaud; show it Christianity and it will oppose it vigorously. For let the world evolve as it will, it can never produce one Christian. It can imitate Christian honesty, Christian courtesy, Christian charity, yes, but to produce one single Christian it can never aspire. A so-called Christian civilization gains the recognition and respect of the world. The world can tolerate that; it can even assimilate and utilize that. But Christian life—the life of Christ in the Christian believer: that it hates, and wherever it meets it it will assuredly oppose it to the death.

Christian civilization is the outcome of an attempt to reconcile the world and Christ. In Old Testament figure we see that represented by Moab and Ammon, the fruit indirectly of Lot's involvement and compromise with Sodom; and neither Moab nor Ammon proved any less hostile to Israel than were the heathen nations. Christian civilization proves that it can mix with the world, and may even be found taking the world's side in a crisis. There is one thing, however, that is eternally apart from the world and can never mix with it, and that is the life of Christ. Their natures are mutually antagonistic and cannot be reconciled. Between the finest specimen of human nature the world can produce and the most insignificant Christian there is no common ground, and thus no basis of comparison. For natural goodness is something we had by natural birth and can by our own resources naturally develop; but spiritual goodness is, in John's words, 'begotten of God' (1 John 5. 4).

God has established in the world a universal Church; and in one place and another He has planted many local churches. God, I say, has done this. It would be unreasonable therefore to expect that His way of deliverance from the world would be by physical separation from it. But as a consequence many sincere Christians are greatly perplexed by the problem of absorption. If God plants a local church here, will it, they ask, one day be reabsorbed by the world?

That in fact presents no problem to the living God. Inasmuch as its origin is not of the world, there is in the family of God no correspondence whatever with the world and thus no possibility of the world absorbing it. This is of course no credit to us, His children. It is not because we earnestly desire to be heavenly that the Church is heavenly, but because we are born out of heaven. And if, by our heavenly origin, we are absolved from trying to work our way thither, we are absolved also thereby from studying to keep ourselves physically clear of this world.

How can the world possibly mix with what is other-worldly? For all that is of the world is empty dust, whereas all that is of God has the miraculous quality of divine life. Some of our brothers in Nanking were once assisting in relief work after the bombing of the city by Japanese planes. Suddenly, as they stood before a shattered house wondering where to begin, there was a violent upheaval of bricks and timbers, and a man emerged. Shaking the dust and rubble from him he rose and struggled to his feet. The fallen beams and rafters fell back into place behind him and the dust settled again, but out he walked alive! While there is life what fear is there of mixture?

The prayer of Jesus to His Father which John records in Chapter 17 contains a plea that is most arresting. Having repeated the statement that 'the world hated them, because they are not of the world, even as I am not of the world', Jesus continues: 'I pray not that thou shouldest take them from (*ek*) the world, but that thou shouldest keep them from (*ek*) the evil one' (verses 14, 15).

Here we have an important principle which will occupy our next chapter. Christians have a vital place in the world. Though saved from the evil one and his system they have not yet been removed from his territory. They have a part to play there for which they are indispensable. Religious people, as we saw, attempt to overcome the world by getting out of it. As Christians, that is not our attitude at all. Right here is the place where we are called to overcome. Created distinct from the world, we accept with joy the fact that God has placed us in it. That distinctiveness, our gift from God in Christ, is all the safeguard we need.

LIGHTS IN THE WORLD

WITHOUT fear of challenge Jesus could say: 'I am the light of the world' (John 8. 12). His claim does not surprise us in the least. What *is* surprising, however, is that He should then say to His disciples, and so by implication to us: '*Ye* are the light of the world' (Matt. 5. 14). For He does not exhort us to be that light; He plainly says that we *are* the world's light, whether we bring our illumination out into places where men can see it, or hide it away from them. The divine life planted in us, which itself is so utterly foreign to the world all around it, is a light-source designed to illumine to mankind the world's true character by emphasizing through contrast its inherent darkness. Accordingly Jesus goes on: 'Even so let your light shine before men, that they may see your good works, and glorify your Father which is in heaven.' From this it is clear that to separate ourselves from the world today, and thus deprive it of its only light, in no way glorifies God. It merely thwarts His purpose in us and in mankind.

It is true that, as we saw earlier, the career of John the Baptist was rather different. He did in fact withdraw from the world to live austerely in desert places apart, subsisting, we are told, on locusts and wild honey. Men went out there to seek him, for even there he was a burning and a shining light. Yet we are reminded that 'he was not that Light'. He came only to bear witness to it. His testimony was the last and greatest of an old prophetic order, but it was so because it pointed forward to Jesus. Jesus alone was 'the true Light which lighteth every man, coming into the world'; and He certainly 'was in the world', not outside of it. (John 1. 9, 10.) Christianity derives from Him. God can use a John crying in the wilderness, but He never intended His Church to be a select company living by the principle of abstinence.

Earlier we saw how abstinence—'handle not, nor taste, nor touch'—was merely one more element in the world system, and as such was itself suspect (Col. 2. 21). But we must go a stage further than this, and once again the apostle Paul comes to our help. In Romans 14. 17 he shows how the Christian life is something removed altogether from controversy about what we do and what we don't do. 'The kingdom of God is not eating and drinking'—not, that is to say, to be conceived in those terms at all—'but righteousness and peace and joy in the Holy Ghost,' which are in a realm wholly different. The Christian lives, and is guided, not by rules specifying just how far he may mix with men, but by these inward qualities which are mediated to him by God's Holy Spirit.

Righteousness and peace and joy in the Holy Ghost. It may be good for a moment to direct our attention to the second of these. For peace, we find, is a potent element in God's answer to His Son's prayer that He would keep us from the evil one (John 17. 15).

In God Himself there is a peace, a profound undisturbedness of spirit, which keeps Him untroubled and undistressed in the face of unspeakable conflict and contradiction. 'In the world ye have tribulation', Jesus says, but 'in me ye may have peace' (John 16. 33). How easily we get troubled as soon as something goes wrong! But do we ever pause to consider what went wrong with the great purpose upon which God had set his heart? God, who is light, had an eternal plan. Causing light to shine out of darkness He designed this world to be the arena of that plan. Then Satan, as we know, stepped in to thwart God, so that men came to love darkness rather than light. Yet in spite of that setback, the implications of which we appreciate all too little, God preserves in Himself a quite undisturbed peace. It is that peace of God which, Paul tells us, is to garrison our hearts and thoughts in Christ Jesus. (Phil. 4. 7.)

What does 'garrison' really mean? It means that my foe has to fight through the armed guard at the gates before he can reach me. Before I can be touched, the garrison itself has first to be overcome. So I dare to be as peaceful as God, for the peace that is keeping God is keeping me. This is something that the world knows nothing about. 'Peace I leave with you; my peace I give unto you: not as the world giveth, give I unto you.' (John 14. 27.)

How utterly men failed to understand Jesus! Whatever He did was wrong in their eyes, for the light that was in them was darkness. They even dared to identify the Spirit that was in Him with Beelzebub the prince of devils. Yet when they accused Him of gluttony and drunkenness, what was His response? 'Father, I thank thee!' (Matt. 11. 19, 25). He was unmoved, because in Spirit He abode in the peace of God.

Or recall that last night before His passion. Everything seemed to be going wrong: a friend going out into the night to betray Him, another drawing a sword in anger, people going into hiding, or running away naked in their eagerness to escape. In the midst of it all Jesus said to those who had come to take Him, 'I am He', so peacefully and so quietly that instead of Him being nervous it was they who trembled and fell backwards. This was an experience that has been repeated in the martyrs of every age. They could be tortured or burned, but because they possessed His peace, the onlookers could only wonder at their dignity and composure. It is no surprise to us therefore that Paul describes this peace as beyond understanding.

How striking is the contrast Jesus draws between 'in the world' where we are to have tribulation, and 'in me' where we may have peace. If God has placed us in the one, to be thronged by its pressures and claims and needs, He has placed us also in the Other, to be held by Him undisturbed amid it all. Jesus Himself once asked, 'Who touched me?' The believing touch of one in that Capernaum multitude registered with Him. It matched His own heart of compassion, whereas the pressure of the rest crowding upon Him had no such effect. All their impatient jostling did not touch Him in the least, for there was little in common between them and Him. 'Not as the world giveth, give I unto you.' If our life is the life of men, we are swayed by the world. If it is the life of the Spirit it is unmoved by worldly pressures.

'Righteousness and peace and joy': with such things is the kingdom of God concerned. Never let us be drawn away, therefore, into the old realm of 'eating and drinking', for it is neither the prescription of these things nor their prohibition that concerns us, but another world altogether. So we who are of the kingdom need not abstain. We overcome the world not by giving up the world's things but by being other-worldly in a positive way: by possessing, that is, a love and a joy and a peace that the world cannot give and that men sorely need.

Far from seeking to avoid the world we need to see how privileged we are to have been placed there by God. 'As thou didst send me into the world, even so send I them into the world.' What a statement! The Church is Jesus' successor, a divine settlement planted here right in the midst of Satan's territory. It is something that Satan cannot abide, any more than he could abide Jesus Himself, and yet it is something that he cannot by any means rid himself of. It is a colony of heaven, an alien intrusion on his territory, and one against which he is utterly powerless. 'Children of God', Paul calls us, 'in the midst of a crooked and perverse generation, among whom ye are seen as lights in the world' (Phil. 2. 15). God has deliberately placed us in the *kosmos* to show it up for what it is. We are to expose to the divine light, for all men to see them, its God-defying rebelliousness on the one hand and its hollowness and emptiness on the other.

And our task does not stop there. We are to proclaim to men

the good news that, if they will turn to it, that light of God in the face of Jesus Christ will set them free from the world's vain emptiness into the fulness that is His. It is this two-fold mission of the Church that accounts for Satan's hatred. There is nothing that goads him so much as the Church's presence in the world. Nothing would please him more than to see its tell-tale light removed. The Church is a thorn in the side of God's adversary, a constant source of irritation and annoyance to him. We make a heap of trouble for Satan simply by *being* in the world. So why leave it?

'Go ye into all the world and preach the gospel' (Mark 16. 15). This is the Christian's privilege. It is also his duty. Those who try to opt out of the world only demonstrate that they are still in some degree in bondage to its ways of thinking. We who are 'not of it' have no reason at all to try to leave it, for *it is where we should be*.

So there is no need for us to give up our secular employments. Far from it, for they are our mission-field. In this matter there are no secular considerations, only spiritual ones. We do not live our lives in separate compartments, as Christians in the Church and as secular beings the rest of the time. There is not a thing in our profession or in our employment that God intends should be dissociated from our life as His children. Everything we do, be it in field or highway, in shop, factory, kitchen, hospital or school, has spiritual value in terms of the kingdom of Christ. Everything is to be claimed for Him. Satan would much prefer to have no Christians in any of these places, for they are decidedly in his way there. He tries therefore to frighten us out of the world, and if he cannot do that, to get us involved in his world-system, thinking in its terms, regulating our behaviour by its standards. Either would be a triumph for him. But for us to be in the world, yet with all our hopes, all our interests and all our prospects out of the world, that is Satan's defeat and God's glory.

Of Jesus' presence in the world it is written that 'the darkness overcame it not' (John 1. 5 mg.). Nowhere in Scripture does it tell us of sin that we are to 'overcome' it, but it distinctly says we are to overcome the world. In relation to sin God's word speaks only of deliverance; it is in relation to the world that it speaks of victory.

We need deliverance from sin, because God never intended we should have any touch with it; but we do not need, nor should we seek, deliverance from the world, for it is in the purpose of God that we touch it. We are not delivered out of world, but, being born from above, we have victory over it. And we have that victory in the same sense, and with the same unfailing certainty, that light overcame darkness.

'This is the victory that hath overcome the world, even our faith. And who is he that overcometh the world, but he that believeth that Jesus is the Son of God?' (1 John 5. 4, 5). The key to victory is always our faith-relationship with the victorious Son. 'Be of good cheer,' He said. 'I have overcome the world' (John 16. 33). Only Jesus could make such a claim; and He could do so because He could earlier affirm: 'The prince of the world ... hath nothing in me' (John 14. 30). It was the first time that anyone on earth had said such a thing. He said it, and He overcame. And through His overcoming the prince of the world was cast out and Jesus began to draw men to Himself.

And because He said it, we now dare say it too. Because of my new birth, because 'whatsoever is begotten of God overcometh the world', I can be in the same world as my Lord was in, and in the same sense as He was I can be utterly apart from it, a lamp set on a lampstand, giving light to all who enter the house. 'As he is, so are we in this world' (1 John 4. 17). The Church glorifies God, not by getting out of the world but by radiating His light in it. Heaven is not the place to glorify God; it will be the place to praise Him. The place to glorify Him is here.

CHAPTER SEVEN

DETACHMENT

WE have seen the Church as a thorn in Satan's side, causing him acute discomfort and reducing his freedom of movement. Though in the world, the Church not only refuses to aid in the world's construction but persists in pronouncing judgment upon it. But if this is true, if the Church is always a source of irritation to the world, then equally the world is a source of constant grief to the Church. And because the world is always developing, its power to distress God's people is ever expanding; in fact the Church has to meet a force in the world today with which in the early days she was not confronted at all. Then the children of God met open persecution in the shape of outward physical assault upon their persons. (Acts 12; 2 Corinthians 11.) They were always coming into collision with material, tangible things. Now the chief trouble they meet in the world is more subtle, an intangible force behind its material things, that is not holy but spiritually evil. The impact of that spiritual force today is far greater than it was then. And not only is it greater; there is an element present now that was not there formerly.

In Revelation 9 we read of a development which, to the author of that book, lay far in the future. 'The fifth angel sounded, and I saw a star from heaven fallen unto the earth: and there was given to him the key of the pit of the abyss. And he opened the pit of the abyss; and there went up a smoke out of the pit, as the smoke of a great furnace. . . . And out of the smoke came forth locusts upon the earth; and power was given them, as the scorpions of the earth have power. And it was said unto them that they should not hurt the grass of the earth, neither any green thing, neither any tree, but only such men as have not the seal of God on their foreheads' (verses 1-4). This is figurative language, but the star falling from heaven obviously refers to Satan, and we know that the bottomless pit is his domain—his storehouse, we might say. Thus it appears that the end-time is to be marked by a special release of his forces, and men will find themselves up against a spiritual power with which they had not before to contend.

Surely this accords with conditions in our day. While it is true that sin and violence will be greater than ever at the close of this age, it is apparent from God's Word that it is not specifically these with which the Church will have to grapple then, but with the spiritual appeal of far more every-day things. 'As it came to pass in the days of Noah, even so shall it be also in the days of the Son of man. They ate, they drank, they married, they were given in marriage, until the day that Noah entered into the ark, and the flood came and destroyed them all. Likewise even as it came to pass in the days of Lot; they ate, they drank, they bought, they sold, they planted, they builded; but in the day that Lot went out from Sodom it rained fire and brimstone from heaven, and destroyed them all' (Luke 17. 26-29). The point being made here by Jesus is not that these things—food, marriage, trade, agriculture, engineering—were outstanding characteristics of Lot's and Noah's day, but that they will in a special way characterize the last days. 'After the same manner shall it be in the day that the Son of man is revealed' (verse 30): that is the point. For these things are not inherently sinful; they are simply things of the world. Have you ever in all your days paid such attention to the good life as now? Food and raiment are becoming the special burden of God's children today. What shall we eat? What shall we drink? Wherewithal shall be clothed? For many these are almost the sole topics of conversation. There is a power that forces you to consider these matters; your very existence demands that you pay attention to them.

And yet Scripture warns us that 'the kingdom of God is not eating and drinking, but righteousness' and so on. It bids us first of all seek the kingdom of God and His righteousness, and assures us that as we do so, all these things will be added to us. It bids us be carefree regarding matters of food and clothing, for if God cares for the flowers of the field and the birds of the air, will He not much rather care for us, His own? Yet to judge by our anxieties it would almost seem that they are cared for, but not we!

Now here is the point that needs special emphasis. This condition of things is abnormal. The undue attention to eating and drinking, whether at the extremes of subsistence or luxury, that characterizes so many Christians these days is far from normal; it is supernatural. For it is not just a question of food and drink that we are meeting here; we are meeting demons. Satan conceived and now controls the world order, and is prepared to use demonic power through the things of the world to lure us into it. The present state of affairs cannot be accounted for apart from this. Oh that the children of God might awaken to this fact! In past days God's saints met all sorts of difficulties; yet, in the midst of pressure, they could look up and trust God. In the pressures of today, however, they are so confused and bewildered that they seem unable to trust Him. Oh, let us realize the Satanic origin of all this pressure and confusion!

The same is true in matrimonial affairs. Never have we met so many problems in this field as today. There is confusion abroad as young people break with old traditions but lack the guidance of any new ones to replace them. This fact is not to be accounted for naturally, but supernaturally. Marrying and giving in marriage are wholesome and normal in any age, but today there is an element breaking into these things that is unnatural.

So it is with planting and building, and so too with buying and selling. All these things can be perfectly legitimate and beneficial, but today the power behind them presses upon men until they are bewildered and lose their balance. The evil force that energizes the world system has precipitated a condition today where we see two extremes; the one extreme of utter inability to make ends meet, and the other extreme of unusual opportunity to amass wealth. On the one hand many Christians find themselves in unprecedented economic difficulties: on the other hand many are faced with no less unprecedented opportunities of enriching themselves. Both of these conditions are abnormal.

Enter any home these days and listen in on the conversation. You will hear remarks such as these: 'Last week I bought such-and-such goods at such-and-such a figure, and I have thereby saved so much.' 'Happily I purchased that a year ago, otherwise I would have lost badly.' 'If you want to sell, sell now while the market is good.' Have you not noticed the way people are rushing hither and thither, feverishly making business deals? Doctors are stocking up with flour, cloth-manufacturers are selling paper, men and women who have never touched such things before are being swept off their feet by the current of speculation. They are caught up in a marketing maelstrom that is whirling them madly around. Do you not realize that this state of affairs is not natural? Do you not see that there is a power here which is captivating men? People are not acting sanely; they are beside themselves. Today's buying and selling spree is not just a question of making a little money—or losing it. It is a question of touching a Satanic system. We are living in the end-time, a time when a special power has been let loose which is driving men on, whether they will or no.

So the question today is not so much one of sinfulness as of worldliness. Who would dare to say you do wrong to eat and drink? Who would dare to disapprove of marrying and giving in marriage? Who would question your right to buy and sell? These things are not in themselves wrong; the wrong lies in the spiritual force behind them, which, through their medium, presses relentlessly upon us. Oh that we might awake to the fact that, whereas these things are so common and so simple, they are yet being used by Satan to ensnare God's children into the great net of his world order.

'Take heed to yourselves, lest haply your hearts be over-charged with surfeiting, and drunkenness, and cares of this life, and that day come on you suddenly as a snare' (Luke 21. 34). Note the term 'life' in Jesus' words. In the Greek New Testament three words are commonly used for life: *zoe*, spiritual life; *psuche*, psychological life; and *bios*, biological life. The last is the word used here, appearing in its adjectival form, *biotikos*, 'of this life'. The Lord is warning us to beware lest we be unduly pressed with this life's cares, that is to day, with anxieties regarding quite ordinary matters such as food and dress which belong to our present existence on the earth. It was over just such a simple thing that Adam and Eve fell, and it will be due to just such simple matters that some Christians may overlook the heaven-ward call of God. For it is always a matter of where the heart is. We are exhorted not to let our hearts be 'overcharged' or 'laden' with these things to our loss. That is to say, we are not to carry a burden regarding them that would weigh us down. We are to be in a true sense detached in spirit from our goods in the house or in the field (Luke 17. 31).

For let us realize who we are! We are the Church, the light of the world shining amid the darkness. As such let us live our lives down here.

There was a time when the Church rejected the world's ways. Now she not only uses them; she abuses them. Of course we must use the world, because we need it; but let us not want it, let us not desire it. So Jesus continues, 'Watch ye at every season, making supplication, that ye may prevail to escape all these things that shall come to pass and to stand (literally 'be set') before the Son of man' (Luke 21. 36). Would God urge us to watch and pray were there not a spiritual force to guard against? We dare not take our destiny as a matter of course, but must be constantly on the alert that we be truly disentangled in spirit from the elements of this world. There are things of the world that are essential to our very existence. To be concerned with them is legitimate, but to be weighed down by them is illegitimate and may cause us to forfeit God's best.

The book of Revelation suggests that Satan will set up his kingdom of antichrist in the political world (Ch. 13), in the religious world (Ch. 17), and in the commercial world (Ch. 18). On this three-fold basis of politics, religion and commerce, his reign will find its last violent expression. In the latter two chapters this kingdom appears under the figure of Babylon, the special instrument of Satan. Babylon seems to represent corrupted Christianity—Rome perhaps, but bigger and more insidious than Rome—and it is on the ground of her commerce that she is judged. The whole record of Chapter 18 revolves around merchants and merchandise. Those who bemoan the great city's fall, from the king right down to the ships' helmsmen, all bewail the thought that her flourishing trade has suddenly ceased. Evidently it is neither religion nor politics but trade that causes the spirit of Babylon to flourish again, and that is bewailed in her downfall. We dare not emphatically state that pure commerce is wrong, but this we do say on the ground of God's own Word, that its beginning is connected with Satan (Ezek. 28) and its end with Babylon (Rev. 18). And this we add from hard-earned experience, that commerce is the field in which, more than in any other, 'the corruption that is in the world through lust' relentlessly pursues even the most high-principled of Christians, and apart from the grace of God, will all too easily overtake them to their undoing.

Are we sensitive to Babylon? The merchants wept, but heaven cried Hallelujah! (19. 1). These (verses 1–6) are the only Hallelujahs recorded in the New Testament. Do we re-echo them?

For we are in a perilous realm when we touch commerce. If by reason of our calling we engage in pure trade, and if we do so ın fear and trembling, we may with God's help escape the snare of the Devil. But if we are over-confident, then there is no hope of escape from the unscrupulous self-seeking that such business engenders. So the problem that confronts us these days is not how to refrain from buying and selling, from eating and drinking, marrying and giving in marriage; the problem now is to avoid the power behind these things, for we dare not let that power triumph over us.

What, then, is the secret of holding our material things in the will of God? Surely it is to hold them *for God*, that is to say, to know we are not hoarding useless valuables, or amassing vast bank deposits, but laying up treasures to His account. You and I must be perfectly willing to part with anything at any moment. It matters not whether I leave two thousand dollars or merely two. What matters is whether I can leave whatever I have without a twinge of regret.

I am not suggesting by this that we must try to dispose of everything; that is not the point. The point is that as God's children you and I may not accumulate things for ourselves. If I keep something it is because God has spoke to my heart; if I part with it it is for the same reason. I hold *myself* in the will of God and am not afraid to give if God asks me to give. I keep nothing because I love it, but let it go without regret when the call comes to leave it behind. That is what it means to be detached, free, separated to God.

CHAPTER EIGHT

MUTUAL REFRESHING

IN John's Gospel there is recorded an event which only he has preserved for us. It is an event full of divine meaning and one which greatly helps to illumine for us this problem of living in the world. I refer to the incident in Chapter 13 in which our Lord Jesus girds Himself with a towel, and taking a basin, washes His disciples' feet. This action of Jesus has lessons to teach us which I do not propose to go into fully here. Instead I want us to look in particular at His command which follows it. 'Ye also ought to wash one another's feet. For I have given you an example, that ye should also do as I have done to you. . . . If ye know these things, blessed are ye if ye do them' (verses 14–17). What is this mutual feet-washing? What does it mean that I should wash my brother's feet and that my feet should be washed by my brother?

The aspect of truth specially emphasized here is refreshment. As we shall shortly see, it is something very dear to the Lord that we as His children should learn to minister refreshment to our brethren, and that they in turn should be a means of refreshment to our spirits.

Let me say at once that this passage does not concern sins. Whether I go barefoot or wearing sandals, or even shoes, the dust that gathers on my feet is something inevitable. I cannot avoid it. But for me to have a fall, and having fallen to roll in the dust so that it collects on my body and on my clothes—that is not inevitable; it is altogether wrong! I have to walk from one place to another, but it is quite unnecessary for me to roll along

the street in order to get there. I can do so without floundering in
the mud!

Equally in the Christian life, to stumble and fall and then to
flounder in the dust is sin, certainly. It calls for repentance and
it needs God's forgiveness. For it is not necessary for me to walk
with the Lord like that, hiding behind the excuse that 'I must
fall once in a while; it is inevitable!' That, we all agree, is wrong.

But the point about the dust on our feet is this, that in walking
through the world, no matter who we are or how careful we
may be, it is inevitable that our feet will collect something. Of
course if we do not touch the earth at all, we certainly pick up
nothing, but to achieve this we should have to be carried around.
If we do touch the ground—and who seriously expects not
to?—we are certain to pick up what is there. Even our Lord
Jesus rebuked His host with the words: 'Thou gavest me no
water for my feet' (Luke 7. 44). So please remember that the
mutual washing in John 13 is not concerned with sins committed,
for which there is always forgiveness through the Blood, but
from which anyway God intends that we should be delivered.
No, it is concerned rather with our daily walk through the world,
during which it is unavoidable that we shall contract something.
'Ye are clean,' Jesus says. The precious Blood sees to that. 'He
that is bathed needeth not . . .' and as far as sin is concerned the
sentence might end there. But move about in Satan's kingdom
and something certainly clings to us. Like a film upon us it
comes between us and our Lord. This is inescapable, simply
because we are touching the world's things all the time, its business and its pleasures, its corrupt scale of values and its whole
ungodly outlook. Hence the words with which Jesus concludes:
'. . . save *to wash his feet*'.

So let us come now to the practical outworking of this. Some
of you brothers and sisters in Christ have to go our to work in
offices or shops for, say, seven or eight hours a day. It is not
wrong that you do so. It is not sin to work in a shop or a factory.

But when you come home from your place of employment, do you not find yourself tired and dispirited and out of tune with things? You meet a brother, but you cannot slip easily and directly into speaking with him of divine things. It is as though there were a coating of something contaminating you. I repeat: that is not necessarily sin at all; it is just that your contact with the world has deposited upon you that film of tarnish. You cannot help feeling it, for there seems to be an inability to rise up to the Lord at once. The luminous touch which you had with Him in the morning seems to have been darkened; its freshness has gone from you. We all know that experience.

Or again, some of our sisters have to attend to domestic duties. Let us suppose a young mother is preparing dinner and has something cooking on the stove. All at once the baby cries, the door bell rings, the milk boils over—everything comes upon her together in a rush. She runs to one and misses the other! After everything is eventually settled she sits down, and it seems as if she needs a power to lift her up to God again. She is conscious of something there—not sin, but as it were a deposit of dust over everything. It clings like a film, coming between her and her Lord, and she feels tarnished, soiled. There is not that clear way which takes her through to God at once. This I think illustrates for us the need of feet-washing.

Many a time we are tired and jaded by our secular duties. When we get down to pray, we find we have to wait for a while. It seems to take us ten or twenty minutes to come back to that place where we can really get through to God. Or if we sit down to read the Word, we find it requires a determined effort to restore again that openness to His speaking. But how good it is if on the road home we meet a brother with an over-flowing heart, fresh from communion with God! Without meaning to do anything he just spontaneously shakes our hand and says, 'Brother, praise the Lord!' He may not know it, but somehow it is as if he has come with a duster and wiped everything clean. Immediately we feel that our touch with God has been restored.

Sometimes you may come into a prayer meeting with a heavy spirit, through the effect of your work during the day. Someone may pray, and you still feel the same; and another prays, and there is no difference. But then another brother or sister prays, and somehow you immediately feel the lifting power. You are refreshed; your feet have been washed. What, then, does washing mean? It means to restore to the original freshness. It means to bring things back to a point of such clearness that it is once again as though they came out of God's immediate presence, new from His hand.

I do not know how many times I personally have felt low like that, when it was not exactly sin that was troubling, but that feeling of a coating of the world's dust; and then I have met a brother or a sister, one who may have known nothing at all of my condition, but who has just passed on a remark that has brightened everything. When this happens you simply feel all the darkness gone, the film swept away. Praise God, you are refreshed and put back at once into the condition where you can directly enjoy touch with Him again. That is feet-washing—to refresh my brethren in Christ; to bring a brother again to the place where it is as though he had just come out from the very presence of God. It is this ministry to one another that the Lord desires to see among His children.

If we are walking with God there is not a day when we may not, if we wish, be a refreshment to our brethren. This is one of the greatest ministries. It may be no more than a handshake. It may be a word of encouragement almost casually spoken. It may be just the light of heaven on our faces. But if the Lord has got His way with us and we are in the state of having no cloud between ourselves and Him, we shall find that we are quietly being used. We may not know it, for it is better not to seek to know it—indeed it may be better *never* to know it. But whether we know it or not, we are constantly being used to refresh our brother. When he is low and in darkness, when he has a burden on his heart or a film before his eyes, when he has been tarnished and stained, then to us he will come. He may not stay long, perhaps only for a few minutes. Seek for that ministry. Find grace from God to help him. Often we think it would be good if we could give long sermons that command a wide hearing, but few have that gift, and many are not reached by those few who have. To refresh the hearts of the saints is the kind of ministry which everyone can fulfil and which can reach everywhere. In the valuation of God it is without price.

But to serve others in this way we must fulfil the conditions. If we are really going on with the Lord there is of course no question that we shall be used, for there are no limitations with Him. If we ourselves are untarnished, with hearts brimming with His joy and peace, there is bound to be an overflow. So the simple question I put to you is this: Is there any point of controversy between you and God? I refer of course to real, known issues. If there is nothing special, then there is no need for you to search around to find something; the Lord Himself will always discover it. When *He* wants to bring to light something you are overlooking, He will always point His finger there, and you will know it. There is no need for you to turn your eyes within and by checking up and analysing every feeling to try to dig it out. Just praise Him! It is the Lord's business, not yours, to shine into your heart and show you when you are astray from Him.

But one thing is certain. If you do have a controversy with God, you can only tarnish others. You can never wash their feet. When they are low, you will bring them lower. When they feel heavy, you will come to them and make them heavier still. Instead of refreshing them and restoring to them the newness that comes out from God, you can only plunge them into deeper gloom. To be at odds with God is the sure way to be a drain upon the life of His Church, whereas the greatest manifestation of power is, I believe, to be able constantly to refresh others. It is a priceless thing, that touch of heaven that lifts, cleanses, renews.

'Ye also ought to wash one another's feet.' Of all His commandments to His disciples this is—and I use the expression in its purest sense—the most dramatic. To impress on them its importance He Himself acted it out before them. It was an expression of His love for 'his own which were in the world' (verse 1). He set Himself to show His disciples what He meant by ministry. It is not platform work. It is serving one another with a basin and a towel. There will always be a need of restoring people who have fallen, of bringing back to repentance the weak ones who have sinned; but the greatest need of the saints today is of refreshment, by which I mean recalling them afresh to what is original and of God. That is power. Jesus Himself 'came forth from God' (verse 3) to do this. I do not know how it strikes you, but I think there is no greater power for God than to be fresh from Him before the world. Do you not find it to be the greatest manifestation of the power of divine life? In a world-system darkened with the smoke of the pit, how we rejoice to meet saints who are fresh with the clean air of heaven. Such freshness brings anew to you and me the divine breath of life.

I thank the Lord that in my younger days I had the great privilege of knowing one of the rarest of saints. I knew her for many years, and found her to have many spiritual qualities; but I think the thing that impressed me above them all was the sense of God. You could not for long sit in her presence, or even walk into her room and have a hand-shake, without feeling a sense of God coming over you. You did not know why, but you felt it. I was not the only one who felt this. Everyone who had touch with her gave the same testimony. I have to confess that in those days many a time I was feeling downhearted, and it seemed as though everything had gone wrong. I walked into her room, and immediately I felt rebuked. Immediately I felt I was face to face with God, I was refreshed.

Why should this thing happen, this immediate restoration? Surely not because it is just the ministry of a privileged few. The Lord would like every single one of us to be like that, to impart that power to brighten our brothers and sisters when they have become tarnished. Please remember—dare I say this?—that sometimes being tarnished does more to hurt the impact of the Christian's life upon the world than do his actual, conscious sins. Once in a while we may sin, any of us, but because we are sensitive to that, we know at once that we have done so and will seek and find forgiveness. But many a time we have been tarnished for hours with the world's tarnish, and because it is not actual sin we remain unconcerned. Then it is that our impact for God upon the world becomes blunted. How good it is at such a time to have around a brother or sister through whom we are lifted once more to a renewed communion with God!

What, then, are the rules? They are two. First, as we have seen, there must be no known discord between me and my Lord that is not at once cleared up; for if there is, that effectively puts me out of this ministry altogether. Whatever the matter be, it is to be settled at once or I am useless. Far from being an asset to the Church of God I have become only a burden. I can contribute nothing; I can only add to the debit side of the life of His children. In order to be a contributor, there must be a transparent clearness between me and God on every conscious issue. Then, free of such disharmony, I too may be the means of lifting my brethren back to their place of power against the world.

Secondly—and to avoid misunderstanding this needs stating plainly: please remember that this refreshing is mutual. 'Wash one another's feet,' Jesus said. The refresher must expect also to be refreshed by others. Many a time the Lord may use you, but equally, many a time He may use someone else to refresh you. There exist no chosen few set apart for a spiritual task as 'refreshers', just as none of us are absolved from walking through this world and needing therefore to be refreshed. As with Peter, no single one of us is entitled to say of himself: 'I have gone beyond that stage. I am now in such touch with God that I am above tarnish, and can pray or preach without the need of such a ministry. Thou shalt never wash my feet!'

No superior class of brothers exists in the Church that has no need to be refreshed. It is something every servant of God depends on. Employed in a workshop or a kitchen all day, you may well need brightening up; but some of us have been working all day in churches, and we too need to be brightened! Our need of restoration is often just as great, though we may well be lulled into overlooking that fact. Whether we work in any obviously secular sphere or are engaged in so-called spiritual things, the world is all around us, closing in. Ever and anon therefore we need the help of some brother or sister to lift us again to that fresh touch of God, that renewal of divine power.

Thus the principle of the Body is, quite simply, refreshing and being refreshed. The more we go on with the Lord the more we need the brethren. For in this ministry not one of us is insignificant, and not one of us ever reaches the point where he has no need to be ministered to by another. My prayer for myself is that God may once in a while use me to refresh someone else's spirit when it is jaded, and that likewise He may once in a while use someone else to touch my flagging spirit and refresh me. If by that brother the tarnish of the world is wiped off me, so that coming weary I go away renewed, then his has been a ministry of Christ to me.

What I have thus sought to describe in simple terms amounts to a united front against the world. This is no small thing. If we will believe it enough to practise it, it possesses, I am convinced, the power to make Satan's mightiest strongholds tremble. In Jesus' words: 'If ye know these things, blessed are ye if ye do them.'

CHAPTER NINE

MY LAWS IN THEIR HEARTS

IN earlier chapters we have been building up a picture of this world, not just as a location, nor as a race of people, nor indeed as anything merely material, but rather as a spiritual system at the head of which is God's enemy. 'The world' is Satan's masterpiece, and we have thought of him as directing all his strength and ingenuity into causing it to flourish. To what end? Surely to capture men's allegiance and draw them to himself. He has one object: to establish his own dominion in human hearts world-wide. Even though he must be aware that that dominion may last only briefly, that, without question, is his goal. And as the end of the age approaches and his efforts increase, so does the distress of God's people intensify. For as aliens and sojourners their position, in the world and yet not of it, is an uncomfortable one. They would fain seek relief from the spiritual tension in physical distance. How good it would be to escape from this world completely and be for ever with the Lord!

But clearly that is not His will. As we saw, He prayed the Father not to take His own out of the world but to preserve them there from the evil one. And Paul takes a similar line. Having in a particular instance exhorted the Corinthian believers not to have fellowship with a certain class of sinner, he immediately takes steps to guard against possible misunderstanding. They are not to isolate themselves. They are not to sever connections with all sinners in the world, nor even with those in the category described, for to do so would involve their leaving the world altogether. 'I wrote unto you in my epistle to have no company with fornicators; not altogether (*i.e.* not at all meaning) with the fornicators of this world, or with the covetous and extortioners, or with idolators; for then must ye needs go out of the world' (1 Cor. 5. 9, 10).

It is clear from Paul's words therefore that we may, and indeed must, associated with the world to a certain extent, for it is not the world that God so loved? But here is the question: To what extent? How far may we go? All of us agree that we are obliged at some points to touch the things of the world. But presumably there is a limit somewhere. Keep within that limit and we are safe; exceed it and we risk becoming implicated by Satan.

I do not think we can exaggerate this problem, for it is an acute one and the dangers are real. If the time should come when you are acutely ill and in great pain, and the doctor should prescribe for you heroin or morphine, you would instantly be alive to the danger of developing a craving for the drug. You would obey him and take the treatment, but you would take it fearfully and prayerfully, for you know there is a power in it, and you know you are liable to come under that power. This would be especially so if the treatment had to be prolonged.

Every time you and I touch the world through the things of the world—and we must do so repeatedly—we should feel much as we would feel about taking morphine, for there are demons at the back of everything that belongs to the world. Just as I may, if seriously ill, be prescribed opium as a treatment, so also, because I am still in the world, I have to do business with the world, follow some trade or employment, earn my livelihood. But how much treatment with dangerous drugs I can safely take without falling a prey to the opium-craving I do not know; and how many things I can buy, or how much money I can make, or how close can be my business or professional associations, without my becoming hooked, I likewise do not know. All I know is that there is a Satanic power behind every worldly thing. How vital therefore for every Christian to have a clear revelation of the spirit of the world in order to appreciate how real is the danger to which he is continually exposed!

Perhaps you think I am going too far. Perhaps you say: Oh yes, that may be a good sermon-illustration, but I find it hard not to feel you are overstating the case. But when you *see*, then you will say of the world, as you say of opium, that there is a sinister power behind it, a power designed to seduce and to captivate men. Those whose eyes have been really opened to this world's true character find they must touch everything in it with fear and trembling, looking continually to the Lord. They know that at any moment they are liable to be caught in Satan's entanglements. Just as the drug which, in the first instance, is welcomed to relieve sickness may ultimately become itself a cause of sickness, so equally the things of the world which we can legitimately use under the Lord's authority may, if we are heedless, become a cause of our downfall. Only fools can be careless in circumstances like these.

No wonder we look with envy upon John the Baptist! How easy, we feel, if like him we could simply withdraw into a safe place apart! But we are *not* like him. Our Lord had sent us into the world in His own footsteps, 'both eating and drinking'. Since God so loved, His command to us is to go 'into all the world' and and proclaim His good news; and surely that 'all' includes the the folk with whom we must rub shoulders daily!

So a serious problem faces us here. As we have said, presumably there must be a limit. Presumably God has drawn somewhere a line of demarcation. Stay within the bounds of that line and we will be safe; cross it and grave danger threatens. But where does it lie? We have to eat and drink, to marry and bring up children, to trade and to toil. How do we do so and yet remain uncontaminated? How do we mingle freely with the men and women whom God so loved as to give His Son for them, and still keep ourselves unspotted from the world?

If our Lord had limited our buying and selling to so much a

month, how simple that would be! The rules would be plain for any to follow. All who spent more than a certain amount per month would be worldly Christians, and all who spent less than that amount would be unworldly.

But since our Lord has stipulated no figure, we are cast on Him unceasingly. For what? I think the answer is very wonderful. Not to be tied by the rules, but that we may remain all the time within bounds of another kind: the bounds of His life. If our Lord had given us a set of rules and regulations to observe, then we could take great care to abide by these. In fact however our task is something far more simple and straightforward, namely, to abide in the Lord Himself. Then we could keep the law. Now we need only keep in fellowship with Him. And the joy of it is that, provided we live in close touch with God, His Holy Spirit within our hearts will always tell us when we reach the limit!

We spoke earlier of the kingdom of antichrist, soon to be revealed. John, in his epistle, writing to his 'little children' about the world and the things of the world (1 John 2. 15) goes on to warn them: 'As ye heard that antichrist cometh, even now have there arisen many antichrists' (verse 18). Faced with these, and with that even more insidious 'spirit of the antichrist, whereof ye have heard that it cometh; and now it is in the world already' (4. 3), what are they to do? How are they in their simplicity to know what is true and what is false? How are they possibly to tell which ground is treacherous to walk upon and which is safe?

The answer John gives them is so simple that today we are afraid to believe it. 'Ye have an anointing from the Holy One, and ye know all things. . . . The anointing which ye received of him abideth in you, and ye need not that anyone teach you: but as his anointing teacheth you concerning all things, and is true, and is no lie, and even as it taught you, ye abide in him' (2. 20, 27). This is certainly an allusion to the Spirit of truth, who, Jesus promised His disciples, would both convict the world and guide them into all the truth. (John 16. 8. 13.)

In any given instance there must be safe limits known to God beyond which we should not go. They are not marked out on the ground for us to see, but one thing is certain: He who is the Comforter will surely know them, even if perhaps Satan knows them too. Can we not trust Him? If at some point we are about to overstep them, can we not depend on Him at once to make us inwardly aware of the fact?

In 1 Corinthians 7 the apostle Paul offers us some further guidance on the same theme. 'This I say, brethren, the time is shortened, that henceforth both those that have wives may be as though they had none; and those that weep, as though they wept not; and those that rejoice, as though they rejoiced not; and those that buy, as though they possessed not; and those that use the world, as not abusing it; for the fashion of this world passeth away. I would have you to be free from cares' (verses 29–32). Here several matters are in turn touched upon, but the governing factor in them all is clearly this, that 'the time is shortened', or, as some translators render it, 'straitened'. We are living, the apostle says, in days of peculiar pressure, and the principle that must guide us for such days is this, 'that they who have . . . be as not having'.

Does Paul, we wonder, contradict himself? In Ephesians 5 he enjoins husbands to love their wives with as perfect a love as that with which Christ loved the Church—no less. Yet here he tells them to live as though not having wives at all! Does he honestly, we exclaim in dismay, expect us at one and the same time to reconcile such complete opposites?

Here at once it must be said that such a paradoxical life is a life that none but Christians *can* live. Perhaps the expression 'as not having' affords us a clue. It reveals that the matter is an inner matter, a question of the heart's loyalty. In Christ there is an inner liberation to God, not merely an outward change of conduct. They have, and having, they rejoice in Ephesians 5; but they are not bound by what they possess, so that having not, they equally rejoice in 1 Corinthians 7. Notwithstanding all they 'have' they are so truly delivered in spirit from the world's possessiveness that they can live 'as not having'.

The natural man lives at one extreme or the other—either having, and being wholly taken up with what he has, or if he is religious, putting away what he has so that he no longer has it, and so being no longer concerned with it at all. But the Christian way is utterly different from the natural way. The Christian way to solve the problem is not by removing the thing, but by delivering the heart from the grip of that thing. The wife is not removed, nor the affection for the wife, but both wife and husband are freed from the overweening dominance of that affection. So, too, the trouble that caused weeping is not re-moved, but the life is no longer controlled by that trouble. The cause of joy still remains, but there is an inner check against vain abandon to the thing that caused it. Buying and selling go on as before, but an inward deliverance has loosened the personal grip upon them. We have them all, but we have them 'as not having'.

We talk sometimes about our desire to maintain, like John, the testimony of Jesus in the earth. Let us remember that that testimony is based, not on what *we* can say about this or that, but on what Satan can say *about us*. God has put us in the world, and often he locates us in some specially difficult places, where we are tempted to feel that worldlings have a much easier time than do Christians. That is because Christians are indeed aliens, living here in an element that is not naturally theirs. A swimmer may dive deep into the sea, but without special clothing and an air-line to the atmosphere that is his own, he cannot stay there. The pressure is too great and he must breathe the air of the world to which he belongs. He stays deep as long as there is a task to do and as long as he is supplied with the power to overcome the element around him, but he does not belong to the element and *it has no part in him*.

Thus it is that the problem of our touch with the world is not solved by any change of outward action. Some think that, at a time like this in which we are living, it is a sign of spirituality to make no provision for the coming days. That is not spirituality, it is folly. What we may *do* with the provision we make is a question we shall consider in our final chapter, but God's word makes it plain that we are to use the world. We are to eat and drink, to trade merchandise and grow crops, to rejoice, yes and if need be to weep, and yet not to use any of these things to the full. We have learned what is at stake in all our relationships with the world. It is no wonder therefore that we have learned also to tread softly, heedful all the while of the Comforter's gentle constraining.

Jesus came 'from above'. He could claim without fear of challenge: 'The prince of this world cometh and hath nothing in me.' The line of demarcation was drawn, not on the ground at His feet but in His own heart. But just as truly, everything in this world that is 'from above' is as safe as He is. God is at the head of the air-line working the pumps, as it were. A life that belongs above is being sustained and provided for down here *by Him*. Thus it comes about that if a thing is spiritual and 'of God', we need not worry about it nor contend for its preservation. 'My kingdom is not of this world, else would my servants fight.' They have no need to.

God does not worry about us, simply because He has no anxiety about His Holy Spirit. There is a sense in which poor-quality spiritual life is impossible, because spiritual life is God's life; and just as truly, spiritual life can only be overwhelmed if God Himself can be overwhelmed. God does not argue about this fact. He is content to leave it to the Comforter to make it real in us. 'Ye are of God, my little children, and have overcome them; because greater is he that is in you than he that is in the world' (1 John 4. 4).

Again, the same verse which tells us that the whole world lies in the lap of the evil one—yes, the very same verse!—assures us once more that 'we are of God' (1 John 5. 19). *We are of God!* Could we possibly discover a more blessed fact to balance against that other ugly fact and to outweigh it? We who believe on Jesus' name 'were born, not of blood, nor of the will of the flesh, nor of the will of man, but of God' (John 1. 13). And praise Him, because we are begotten of God, the evil one cannot touch us. (1 John 5. 18.)

Put very simply, Satan's power in the world is everywhere. Yet wherever men and women walk in the Spirit, sensitive to the anointing they have from God, that power of his just evaporates. There *is* a line drawn by God, a boundary where by virtue of His own very presence Satan's writ does not run. Let God but occupy all the space Himself, and what room is left for the evil one?

Are we thus utterly for God? Can Satan testify of you and me: 'I cannot entrap that man!'?

CHAPTER TEN

THE POWERS OF THE AGE TO COME

WHAT does the writer to the Hebrews mean when he says of Christians that they have 'tasted . . . the powers of the age to come' (Heb. 6. 5)? We would all readily agree that there is a splendid future age to which we look forward. In it the kingdom that is now 'in the midst' of us in terms of the mighty acts of the Spirit of God (Matt. 12. 28) will then become universally visible and unchallenged. The kingdom of the world will have become the kingdom of our God and of His Christ (Rev. 11. 15). But what, we may wonder, are these 'powers' that now we only taste but cannot as yet feast upon? Clearly they are to be received and enjoyed, for the word 'taste' implies not merely a doctrine to be thought about and analysed, but something subjectively experienced and made our own. These powers are the preliminaries of a feast of which there is much more to follow but of which we already eat just a little.

We could list a number of such things to which Scripture looks forward. There is a salvation to be revealed in the last time (1 Pet. 1. 5). There is a fresh aspect of eternal life in the age to come (Luke 18. 30). There is a rest remaining to the people of God (Heb. 4. 9). There will be the raising and renewal of our mortal bodies (Rom. 8. 23; 1 Cor. 15. 14). There will be a day when everything that stumbles men will be removed (Jer. 31. 9; Isa. 57. 14; 62. 10). There will be a time when all shall know the Lord from the least to the greatest (Jer. 31. 34; Heb. 8. 11) and indeed when the earth shall be filled with the knowledge of the glory of the Lord as the waters cover the sea (Isa. 11. 9; Hab. 2. 14). Of all these things we have now a real foretaste in Christ, but we do not yet see them in completeness.

More directly related to our present study are the following considerations. The Epistle to the Hebrews applies to our Lord Jesus the words from Psalm 8: 'Thou didst put all things in subjection under his feet', and then goes on quite frankly to express what experience generally must compel us to admit, namely, that 'we see not yet all things subjected to him' (Heb. 2. 8). But alongside these two contrasting statements we must place also that of Jesus in Luke 10. 19, where He already gives to His disciples 'authority . . . over all the power of the enemy'. Surely this promises to us a *present* foretaste of that future day that we do not yet see.

Again, in the same Gospel passage, Jesus is recorded as saying, 'I beheld Satan fallen as lightning from heaven' (10. 18). This event John, in Revelation 12. 9, seems to place far in the future. Yet clearly Jesus implies that from the standpoint of the witnessing Church it is already in some sense a present fact. Furthermore, in a later chapter of Revelation John is shown a day when Satan is to be bound with a chain for a thousand years (20. 1-4). Yet Jesus speaks of 'the strong man' as already bound, so that we may even now break into his house and despoil it (Matt. 12. 29).

These are significant statements; for surely if we possess salvation and eternal life in the present, as we most certainly do, then we should also be knowing some foretastes today of the rest of these future 'powers'. For though not yet manifest universally, they are quite evidently fruits of the Cross and resurrection of Christ that must be, at least in principle, the Church's present possession.

God's eternal purpose is bound up with man. 'Let us make man in our image, after our likeness,' He said, 'and let them have dominion.' God intended man to wield power, to reign and rule, to control other created things. We cannot say that redemption was God's design—or even a part of it—for man was never intended to fall, still less to perish. Genesis 3 represents man's history, not God's purpose for him. A workman may fall from the fifth story of a building under construction, but that was never in the architect's plan!

No, God's plan is concerned with man's dominion, and it is well to note the special sphere of this, namely, 'all the earth' (Gen. 1. 26). Heaven has no problem; the problem is on earth. Man is told to 'subdue it' (verse 28) and we ask ourselves why. If there were no forces to be subdued, why this need? Furthermore we are told that the Lord God took the man and put him into the Garden of Eden to dress it and 'to keep it' (2. 15). This is more than the usual Hebrew word for 'to keep'. Adam is to *guard* God's Paradise, and again this implies the proximity of an enemy to be kept at bay.

It is interesting to note the wording of Genesis 1. 26. Man is to have dominion 'over all the earth', and the clause is expanded to cover, among other things, 'every creeping thing that creepeth upon the earth'. But in the event the first thing that man failed to control was a creeping thing, a worm. And by man's failure Satan obtained, in a new way in man himself, legal rights on the earth. True, the dust of the earth was the lowly sphere appointed to him. 'Upon thy belly shalt thou go, and dust shalt thou eat' (3. 14). But what is dust? It is the substance of which Adam was made! Thus man in the flesh is now morally subject to Satan. God's foe has secured a clear title to all that by natural birth man is and has. Natural human life is the foothold here on earth of Satan's activity. Satan's world springs from and finds its strength in his rights in man, and even God does not dispute these rights. He has acquired by Adam's default a full title to all that is of the old creation.

If Satan is to cease to act in us, then his ground in us must be taken from him. So God meets the situation in redemption, not by dealing with Satan directly but, as we have seen, by taking the whole of the old creation—the man himself, his world, everything—clean out of the way, and thus removing from Satan his legal stand. Satan's overthrow is compassed not by a direct blow aimed at him, but indirectly by the removal from him in the death of Christ of all that gives him the moral right of control. 'Our old man was crucified with him, that the body of sin might be done away, that so we should no longer be in bondage to sin' (Rom. 6. 6).

Praise God, Satan has therefore no longer any rights in us. But that is a merely negative fact. There is a positive one also. God has not only removed all that was in the way of His eternal purpose by removing the old creation; He has also secured all that is necessary to realize that purpose by bringing in a new creation—His new Man. 'Christ being raised from the dead dieth no more; death no more hath dominion over him' (verse 9). The purpose revealed in Genesis 1 and lost in Genesis 3 is not lost for good. What God could not secure in the first man He obtained in the second; and that second Man is on the throne. No wonder the New Testament writer dares to reapply the psalmist's words: 'What is man, that thou art mindful of him? Or the son of man, that thou visitest him? Thou crownest him with glory and honour.' Thus he quotes the psalm, and then he exclaims: 'We behold him . . . even Jesus . . . crowned!' (Psalm 8. 4–6; Heb. 2. 6–9). If the creation of mankind was intended to meet the need of God, that need has now at last been met. God has got His Man.

Genesis 1, Psalm 8 and Hebrews 2 are thus uniquely linked. Psalm 8 is of course poetry and sings of God's plan for mankind, but the significant thing is that in spite of the Fall the singer does not deviate. He only reaffirms the original plan of Genesis 1: 'Thou madest him to have dominion.' It has not changed. Moreover, he not only begins but ends his chant with the exclamation of praise: 'How excellent is thy name in all the earth!'

The enemy has done his worst; man has been trapped into blaspheming God, and if you or I had composed this Psalm we

would surely have followed the eighth verse with a cry of distress: 'But alas, man has fallen; all is lost!' Not so the psalmist.
It is as though he had forgotten the Fall completely, for he does
not even allude to it. He leaps in thought across the whole history
of redemption, and cries again, 'How excellent!' Adam and Eve
could fall, but they could not alter God's purpose that man
should eventually overthrow Satan's power. His purpose stands
unaltered and this excellence is to be known—where? In all the
earth.

Nor is it in the Son of man merely that this purpose is realized,
but in the sons of men—those 'many sons' whom God is bringing to glory. The psalmist is at pains to underline this fact.
Though the enemy do his worst, the rights he has gained through
the Fall have not proved inalienable. Still among men there are
those he cannot touch. 'Out of the mouths of babes and sucklings
hast thou established strength, because of thine adversaries, that
thou mightest still the enemy and the avenger' (verse 2). God
does not depend on great military leaders. Little children, yea,
very babes, are sufficient to quell the hosts of His foes.

As we saw, Hebrews 2 draws its inspiration from this Psalm.
Yet it goes a step further. While reaffirming God's purpose in
creation and the goal to which it points, it does more than this.
Looking back realistically over the course of fallen man's dark
history it establishes now that God's purpose in redemption and
recovery is directed to the identical end. In all the new circumstances that redemption has called into being, the plan is still
unchanged. God has not abandoned His goal. Moreover, from
the writer's viewpoint beyond the triumph of the Cross he can
confidently reaffirm the psalmist's affirmation of faith. So, far
from all being lost, it is true to say that in Christ the end *has been*
secured.

Oh yes, it is still the same plan: 'He left nothing that is not
subject to him' (verse 8). Appearances would tend to deny this,
so that 'we see not yet all things subjected to him'. Yet true as this

is, the writer disregards it and at once proceeds triumphantly: 'But we behold him who hath been made a little lower than the angels, even Jesus, because of the suffering of death, crowned with glory and honour, that by the grace of God he should taste death for every man' (verse 9). And then, almost defiantly he adds: 'that he might bring to nought . . . the devil' (verse 14).

What man was to do on earth for God, and failed to do, our Lord Jesus has accomplished. He 'tasted death for everything' (as the original Greek implies—not just 'for every man'). That is to say, it was not for man's redemption alone that He died but for that of the whole creation, and, going back further, for the recovery of the Father's purpose in the complete oversetting of the Satanic world order.

Thus it comes about that today the Church has a definite responsibility before God to register the victory of Christ in the devil's territory. If there is to be a testimony to the principalities and powers, if the impact of Christ's sovereignty through His Cross is to be registered in the spiritual realm, it can only be as the judicial foothold in our hearts of the 'pretender' in the race is met and, by the same Cross, removed and repudiated. For God's object is still that man should 'have dominion'. Our work for Him does not stop with proclaiming a Gospel that was designed merely to undo the effect of Genesis 3, marvellous as was that undoing. God wants also to take us back further to Genesis 1 itself. He wants us in Christ to regain the moral dominion over His foe that was there in view, and thus effectively to restore the earth to Him. This is surely why, as Paul tells us, 'the earnest expectation of the creation waiteth for the revealing of the sons of God' (Romans 8. 19).

The Gospel of salvation is necessary and vital in order to meet man's need. But if as God's servants we are only labouring for others we are missing God's first aim in creation, which was to supply not merely man's need but His own. For as we have said already, the creation of man was to meet the need of God. Thus if today we are going to meet God's need we must go a step further and deal with Satan himself. We must steal back from him his power, evict him from his territory, spoil him of his goods and set free his captives—for God. The question is not merely, Of what account are we in the winning of souls? Rather is it, Of what account are we in the realm of principalities and powers? And for that there is a price to pay.

It is often possible to move men when it is quite impossible to move Satan. The plain fact is that it costs much more to deal with Satan than to win souls. It demands an utterness of spirit Godward that in itself effectually deprives Satan of any moral ground in us he may claim to possess. This is the costly thing. God in His merciful love for the lost can often bypass and over-look in His servants what one might justly feel to be appalling weakness and even failure. But while He may do this for the soul-winner, when it comes to our dealing with the devil it is another matter.

Evil spirits can see right through the witness of man. They can tell when it is compromised by being half-hearted or in-sincere. They are aware when we are holding back a part of the price. Looking at us they are under no illusions as to whom they can safely defy or ignore; and conversely, they know perfectly well against whom they are powerless. 'Jesus I know, and Paul I know; but who are ye?' (Acts 19. 15). Because they believe, they know when to tremble. And let me say this: since our most important task is their overthrow, it is better always that we should have the witness of evil powers than the praise of men.

But the price of this witness to the principalities and power is, I repeat, an utterness of allegiance to God that is unqualified. To entertain our own opinions or desires, or to prefer our own variant and contrary choices, is simply to present the enemy with his advantage. It is, in short, to throw the game away. In any other sphere there may perhaps—I do not know—be room among our motives for something of self-interest, without appreciable loss. But never, and I repeat never, in this. Without such utterness for God nothing can be achieved, for without it we make even God powerless against His enemy.

So I say it once again: the demand is very high. Are you and I here on earth, utterly committed, utterly given to God Himself? And because this is so, are we tasting even now the powers of that future glorious age? Are we reclaiming territory from the prince of this world for the One whose alone it rightly is?

CHAPTER ELEVEN

ROBBING THE USURPER

'CHRIST JESUS came into the world to save sinners.' Since in the eternal purpose of God it is man (and not some other being) who is to have dominion, it is natural and right that our compassion should be drawn out to those sinners. Notwithstanding anything said hitherto, we might well feel that in this brief day of grace the winning of souls to the Saviour of the world is perhaps the supreme means available to us of robbing Satan of his spoils. Certainly were 'man' himself our theme, we should give a big place at this point to the subject of soul-winning.

But we have dealt with evangelism already elsewhere.[1] Instead, therefore, I propose in closing these studies of 'the world' to take another and more materialistic area of Satan's dominion by way of practical illustrations of the art of 'despoiling the strong man'. I refer to the field of finance.

Money is opposed to God. The Word of God speaks of it as the mammon of unrighteousness (Luke 16. 9). Since Jesus says, 'Make to yourselves friends by means of the mammon of unrighteousness', He clearly cannot mean to describe it as the mammon that you have obtained through unrighteous dealings. He is therefore saying that the mammon itself is unrighteous. What is being brought before us here is not the unrighteous means by which money is procured, nor the unrighteous use to which money is put, but *the unrighteous character of money*. Money in its essential character is evil. We talk of 'clean money' and 'dirty money', but in God's sight there is only dirty money. The

[1] *What Shall This Man Do?* London, 1961, Chapter 3.

man who knows God knows the character of money. He knows that money in itself is evil.

If you would test the character of anything, you only need to enquire whether that thing leads you to God or away from God. Money invariably leads away from God. Jesus lays down clearly in verse 13 the principle that it is impossible to serve God and mammon, though I think that even without His statement, most of us would be convinced that this is so. For experience tells us that God and mammon are never on the same side; mammon is always set over against God.

Of course it would be possible to interpret Jesus' words more widely, and to see 'mammon' as representing everything in general that opposes itself to God. But the apostle Paul helps us to pin-point money as the means the world uses most successfully to draw us away from God. 'They that desire to be rich,' he says, 'fall into a temptation and a snare and many foolish and hurtful lusts, such as drown men in destruction and perdition. For the love of money is the root of all kinds of evil: which some reaching after have been led astray from the faith, and have pierced themselves through with many sorrows' (I Tim. 6. 9, 10). In other words, if anything can lead us astray from God, money will.

The essence of the world is money. Whenever you touch money you touch the world. The question arises, How can we take a thing which we know assuredly to be of the world, and yet not become involved with the world system? How can we handle and do business with money, that most worldly of worldly things, and not, in doing so, become implicated with Satan? Still more to the point, since nothing can be done today without paying for it, how is it possible for us to take money, that thing which is a supreme factor in building up the kingdom of antichrist, and use it to build up the kingdom of Christ?

The widow who dropped her mite into the temple treasury did something so acceptable to the Lord that she received from

Him special commendation. What in fact she did was just this: she took something out of the kingdom of Satan and contributed it to the kingdom of God. And Jesus approved. So how, let us ask ourselves, is such a transfer made? How is it possible to take money, which in its character is essentially unrighteous, and with it build up the kingdom of God? How can you make sure that all connection between the world and the money in your pocket has been severed? Do you dare to say that none of the money in your possession figures in Satan's books?

On every Roman *denarius* there was an image of Caesar. In Jesus' words, all such coins 'are Caesar's'. How could the connection between Caesar and that coin be severed? Money is a thing of the world. It is an essential part of the world system. How then can it be taken out of the world that claims it and devoted to God for His use?

In Old Testament times a rigid principle was laid down. 'No devoted thing, that a man shall devote unto the Lord of all that he hath, whether of man or beast, or of the field of his possession, shall be sold or redeemed: every devoted thing is most holy unto the Lord' (Lev. 27. 28). In other words, there is no true devotion without destruction. If in those days a sheep was devoted to God, it was not placed before Him to remain there a living sheep and to bring forth lambs; it was placed before Him to be sacrificed. 'It shall certainly be put to death' (verse 29). Its destruction was the sign of its acceptance.

All money that is truly devoted to God must come under the principle of destruction; that is to say, it must cease to exist as far as the world is concerned, and it must cease to exist also as far as I am concerned. When our Lord commended the widow for putting her two coins into the treasury, He observed that she had put in her *bios*, that is, her life. 'She of her want did cast in all that she had, even all her living' (Mark 12. 44). Many people just put money into the treasury of the Lord; she put her life in with her money. In other words, when that money went out of

ROBBING THE USURPER 91

her possession, her life went out with it. In giving her two coins she gave her all.

If your money is to come out of the world, then your life will have to come out of the world. You cannot keep your self back and contribute anything significant to God. You cannot *send* your money out of the world at all: you can only *bring* it out of the world!

Thus it is no easy matter to transfer money from the realm of Satan to the realm of God; it involves travail. To convert souls from Satan to God is in fact easier than to convert money from Satan to God. By the grace of God men and women may be won to Him whether or not we ourselves are devoted in any utter sense; but this is not so with money. It takes great spiritual power to convert our shekels, which in their character are evil, into shekels of the sanctuary. Money needs converting as truly as men need converting; and money can, I believe, be made anew (if in a rather different sense) as truly as souls can be made anew. But your bringing of an offering of money to the treasury will not in itself change the character of the money you offer. Unless your life goes out with your money it cannot be released from the kingdom of Satan and transferred to the kingdom of God. The spiritual value of your work for God will largely depend on whether or not the money you handle has been delivered from the world system. I ask you, Has it? Can you claim that there is no money in your hand that belongs to the world? Are you able to say now that your money is no longer a part of the *kosmos*, for it has all been converted? Are you willing to tell God: 'I will convert all the money I earn by labour, and all the money I receive by gifts, that it all may be Thine?'

To Paul the principle was very plain: We want you, not yours. Of the Macedonian saints, who out of their poverty contributed so liberally, he said that 'first they gave their own selves to the Lord', then they gave their money (2 Cor. 8. 5). Paul had his training in the Old Testament, where the consecration of material gifts was always connected with the consecration of those who brought the gifts. His reasoning may have had its roots there.

For it may sound startling, but it is true, that God has a limited supply of money, whereas Satan's supply is unlimited. You wonder perhaps how this statement can be reconciled with that other one, that all the silver and the gold are His. Yet our Lord Jesus Himself says that there is that which belongs to God and that which belongs to Caesar. Ultimately no doubt all material things belong to God as Creator, but the amount of money in God's treasury today is limited by the number of people who are devoted to Him.

If I had lived in Old Testament times I could have calculated immediately the amount of money in the sanctuary. I should have enquired the total number of the children of Israel and reckoned half a shekel of silver for the redemption of each of them (Exod. 30. 11–16). To that I should have added five shekels per head for the redemption of each of the firstborn of Israel in excess of the Levites (Num. 3. 39–51). And then to these two amounts I should have added the valuation, according to the shekel of the sanctuary, put upon each individual who of his free will devoted himself to the Lord (Lev. 27. 1–8). Yes, it is the number of God's people that determine the amount of God's money. The margin of wealth in God's treasury is based on the number of people devoted to Him.

Here, then, is a vital question for each one of us to answer: Does the money I am touching today represent shekels of the sanctuary or the mammon of unrighteousness? Whenever I receive a dollar, or whenever I earn a dollar, let me make sure that that dollar is instantly converted from world currency into the currency of the sanctuary. Money can be our destruction, but money can also be our protection. Do not despise money; its value is too real for that. It can be of great account to the Lord. If you yourself come heart and soul out of the world, then you can, if God so wills it, bring many precious things out of the world with you. When the Israelites came out of Egypt they brought away much treasure with them. They spoiled the Egyptians, and the spoil they carried away with them went to construct the Tabernacle. Some too, we recall, went to construct a golden calf and was lost to God. But when God's people left Egypt the Tabernacle, at least in its materials, left Egypt with them. Egyptian gold, silver, copper, linen—all was converted and contributed to the sanctuary of God.

If you can find that reality in Old Testament times, how much higher still must be the standard set in the New! The New Testament key to all finance is that we hold nothing to ourselves. 'Give, and it shall be given unto you', those were our Lord's words (Luke 6. 38) and not, 'Save and ye shall grow rich'! That is to say, the principle of divine increase is giving, not storage. God requires of every one of us proportionate and not just random giving. He desires, that is to say, giving that is not subject merely to the whim of the moment but that is the fruit of a definite covenant reached with Him about the matter—and stuck to.

This is because the real secret of spoiling Satan is, as we saw, personal dedication. For us to be redeemed from the world and not as a consequence offer ourselves to God is an utterly impossible thing. 'Ye are not your own; for ye were bought with a price' (1 Cor. 6. 19, 20). It matters not whether we follow a profession or trade that brings us an income from the world, or occupy ourselves solely in preaching the Word and depend for our sustenance upon the gifts of God's people, there is only one road before us, not two. We are all equally dedicated to God and we are all His witnesses. It is simply not true that preaching the Gospel in itself is clean and business unclean, so that those who engage in the latter must become so tainted as to be of less account to God. What matters is simply that God, and not our business, must be the centre of our lives.

'Love not the world, neither the things that are in the world.'

You have an anointing from the Holy One: live by it! Give
yourself to God; live for Him wholly and utterly; see to it that,
where you personally are concerned, the things of this world
are scored off Satan's books and transferred to God's account.
For 'the world passeth away, and the lust thereof: but he that
doeth the will of God abideth for ever.'

What Shall This Man Do?

WATCHMAN NEE

KINGSWAY PUBLICATIONS
EASTBOURNE

CONTENTS

PREFACE

THIS digest of the spoken ministry of Mr. Watchman Nee (Nee To-sheng) of Foochow is compiled, as were two earlier books, from notes and translations for which I am once again indebted to a number of friends who heard him. The addresses were originally given at various times and in widely different circumstances in China and the West over the five-year period from 1938 to 1942, a period of, for those days, severe testing for the Church in China.

In publishing these messages in their present form, I think it well to introduce a word of caution. The matter, some of it fragmentary, that I have brought together in this collection was not all in this proximity originally, nor can it be regarded as in any sense complete. While I have used prayerfully what is available to me without conscious bias, the arrangement of the material is in part my own, and the book may of necessity omit some aspects of the themes treated that the author, were he accessible, would wish to provide. Moreover the unavoidable effect of editing is to make the studies appear more systematic than they were ever intended to be, and this in itself could be misleading. For, notwithstanding the appearance of design given to them, they remain essentially talks, and reflect the preacher's need to emphasize, and even sometimes to seem to overstate, his points in order to bring them home to his hearers.

On the subject of 'system' in Christian teaching, the author may perhaps be allowed to express himself. Discussing, twenty years ago, one of his early writings in Chinese, Mr. Nee said: 'Some years back I was very ill, and the doctors said I could only live a few months. In the face of this I felt burdened to write down in book form what the Lord had shown me on the subject of "the spiritual man", and thus to share with others the light I had been given. I did so and it was published, and the edition is now exhausted. It will not be reprinted. It was not that what I wrote was wrong, for as I read it now I can endorse it all. It was a very clear and complete setting forth of the truth. But just there lies its weakness. It is *too* good, and it is the illusion of perfectness about it that troubles me. The headings, the orderliness, the systematic way in which the subject is worked out, the logic of the argument—all are too perfect to be spiritual. They lend themselves too easily to a merely mental apprehension. When a man has read the book he ought not to have any questions left; they ought all to be answered!

'But God, I have discovered, does not do things that way, and much less does He let *us* do them. We human beings are not to produce "perfect" books. The danger of such perfection is that a man can understand without the help of the Holy Spirit. But if God gives us books they will ever be broken fragments, not always clear or consistent or logical, lacking conclusions, and yet coming to us in life and ministering life to us. We cannot dissect divine facts and outline and systematize them. It is only the immature Christian who demands always to have intellectually satisfying conclusions. The Word of God itself has this fundamental character, that it speaks always and essentially to our spirit and to our life.'

It will help readers of the following pages if they bear the above remarks in mind. To some this book may appear to attempt too much, and to raise more questions than it answers. May some part at least of its message nevertheless have this power to speak, as from God, to any of us whose ambition is to become more effectual servants of Jesus Christ.

ANGUS I. KINNEAR

London
1961

CHAPTER ONE

GOD'S SKILLED CRAFTSMEN

THE calling of God is a distinctive calling. In some degree at least, this statement is true of all whom He calls. Their commissioning is always personal; it never stops at being general—to all men. 'It was the good pleasure of God,' says Paul, 'to reveal His Son in *me*.'

Moreover its object is always precise; never merely haphazard or undefined. By this I mean that, when God commits to you or me a ministry, He does so not merely to occupy us in His service, but always to accomplish through each of us something definite towards the attaining of His goal. It is of course true that there is a general commission to His Church to make disciples of all the nations'; but to any one of us, God's charge represents, and must always represent, a personal trust. He calls us to serve Him in the sphere of His choice, whether to confront His people with some special aspect of the fulness of Christ, or in some other particular relation to the divine plan. To some degree at least, every ministry should be in that sense a specific ministry.

It follows from this that, since God does not call each of His servants to precisely identical tasks, neither does He use precisely identical means for their preparation. As the Lord of all operations, God retains the right to use particular forms of discipline or training, and often, too, the added test of suffering, as means to His end. For His goal is a ministry that is not merely common or general, but rather, one specially designed for the service of His people in a given hour. To the servant himself, such a ministry must become peculiarly his own—something to be specially expressed because specially experienced. It is personal because it is first-hand; and it cannot be escaped because, in so far as it directly relates to the purpose of God, that purpose itself demands that it be fulfilled.

9

Every Spirit-taught reader of the New Testament will have noticed something of this. In its pages we can, I think, recognize at least three such distinctive emphases in ministry, represented by the particular historic contributions of three leading apostles. These three men, while certainly having very much in common, nevertheless display, at certain points in the record, differences of emphasis sufficiently striking to suggest that something quite original was being committed by God to each of them. I allude of course, to the special contributions of Peter, Paul and John. In the New Testament it is, I suggest, possible to trace three lines of thought, expressed no doubt in varying measure by all the apostles, but specially defined and illustrated by the unique contributions of these three in particular.

It will be seen that the distinctiveness of their three ministries is in part chronological, each apostle bringing, in the course of the history, his own fresh and timely emphasis to the fore. Moreover, it is certainly never such as to set the three men apart from or in conflict with one another, for what each one has is not something opposed, but rather, complementary to what the others have got. And perhaps, too, the difference between them lies less in their ministry as a whole than in what is recorded of it for our instruction. Yet I think it can be shown that the Petrine, the Pauline and the Johannine strands or themes running through the Scriptures indicate three main historic emphases given by God to His people for all time. All the many and diverse ministries of the New Testament—those for example of Philip and Barnabas, Silas and Apollos, Timothy and James—together with the countless more that should follow in history, contain in differing proportions the distinctive elements of these three. It will be well, therefore, if we seek to understand what God is saying to us through the experiences of these three typical men and this will be the aim of our present study.

'CASTING A NET INTO THE SEA'

We begin with Peter. It is generally held that Mark, in writing his Gospel, was placing on record what were in fact

Peter's recollections of his Lord. Added to these we have Peter's own Epistles, and of course the incidents of his life recorded by the other evangelists in the four Gospels and the book of the Acts. These together form the special contribution of Peter. What, then, was his ministry? Well, his Epistles certainly indicate to us how widely representative it was of all that made up the work of an apostle; but in the narrative passages one thing perhaps stands out above others. It is the thing to which I think the Lord drew special attention when, in calling him to follow, He used the term 'fishers of men'. That was to be Peter's distinctive task, and the one that fell first to him. He was to bring men, urgently and in great numbers, into the Kingdom. Further on in the story Jesus reaffirmed this, when, at Cæsarea Philippi, Peter had confessed Him to be the Christ of God. The Lord would build His Church, and Peter might later be called to a pastoral ministry of 'feeding His sheep' therein; but, in relation to that Church, Jesus' first words to him are: 'I will give unto thee the keys of the kingdom of heaven'.

A key implies, among other things, an entry, a beginning. You come in by a door, and you use a key for opening it, or for letting others in. In the outcome, Peter's ministry often issued in such a beginning of things, and his was in fact the first to do so. The Church in Jerusalem began when three thousand souls received his word, and the church in Cæsarea began when, in his presence, the Holy Spirit fell on Cornelius and his household. Thus we may say that, when Peter stood up with the eleven, he opened the door to the Jews, and when later he preached Christ in that Roman home, he opened it again to the Gentiles. So although on neither occasion Peter was alone, for the commission extends always to others beside him, and although later on we find that Paul too was a man chosen of God to have a still wider ministry of the Gospel among the Gentiles, yet in a true sense Peter was the pioneer. Historically he held the key and he opened the door. His task was to initiate something. He was ordained by God to make the beginnings.

The burden of Peter's message was salvation—a salvation not for its own sake, but always with a view to the Kingdom in fulness, and in relation to Jesus, its exalted King. Yet when first he preached the Kingdom it was inevitably to lay stress, not upon its other aspects, but upon the beginning. It was to emphasize the keys, and their function of introducing the Kingdom to men. It may be more than a coincidence that this was, as we have said, in keeping with the details of his own call. For Peter was called under circumstances quite different from Paul, and even, as we shall see, from John. Since those circumstances are recorded for us in Scripture, we should not discount them as fortuitous. They are worthy of notice.

Peter, we are told, was called while engaged in the main skill of his trade, namely, 'casting a net into the sea'. That occupation seems (speaking figuratively) to have given character to his ministry throughout his life. He was to be first and foremost an evangelist: one who starts something by 'taking men alive'. By casting a net you draw in fish—all sorts of fish. That is Peter; and without for one moment forgetting the wider range of what he did and wrote, it is nevertheless true to say that the main emphasis of what is recorded of his active ministry is placed there.

'THEY WERE TENT-MAKERS'

We come next to Paul. He is a servant of the Lord, but he is a different one. No one would suggest that Paul did not preach the Gospel. Of course he did. To have done otherwise would have been to repudiate the pioneer work of Peter and throw away the ground gained by him. Do not let us make the mistake of thinking there was some basic conflict between the ministries of these two men, or that the ministries of God's servants should ever be in conflict. Paul makes it clear, in writing to the Galatians, that such differences as there were related to geography and race, and that in essence their tasks were complementary, not only by mutual consent, but in their value to and attestation by God (Gal. 2. 7–12).

But the point is that there came a day when Paul was required to go further. Whereas Peter initiated things, Paul's task was to construct. God entrusted to him in a special way

the work of building His Church, or in other words, the task
of presenting Christ in His fulness to men, and of bringing
those men *as one* into all that God had in His mind for them in
Christ. Paul had glimpsed that heavenly reality in all its greatness, and his commission was to build together the gathered
people of God, according to that reality.

Let me illustrate. You recall the vision that was granted to
Peter before he set out to go to the Gentiles in Cæsarea. He
saw a sheet coming down out of heaven, held by the four
corners and containing every kind of beast, clean and unclean.
That vision signified the inclusive and universal intention of
the Gospel. It is directed *to every creature*. And that, again, is
Peter first and foremost. His ministry is a ministry with a sheet
—or a net, if you like—putting something of everything into
it. It is God-ordained, for it comes to him 'out of heaven'. His
commission from God, renewed and interpreted here at Joppa,
was to bring as many as possible of every kind to the Saviour.

But our brother Paul is different in this, that he is not a man
holding a sheet; he is a tent-maker. The sheet of Peter's vision
—again I speak figuratively—becomes in Paul's hand a tent.
What do I mean? I mean this, that a sheet is something as yet
without form; it is not yet 'made up' into anything. But now
Paul comes onto the scene as a tent-maker, and under the
direction of the Spirit of God—under the constraint of a vision
that, equally with Peter's, came to him out of heaven (2 Cor.
12. 2–4; Eph. 3. 2–10)—he gives that formless 'sheet' a form
and a meaning. He becomes, by God's sovereign grace, a
builder of the House of God.

With Paul, it is not now a question merely of so many souls
saved, but of something taking a definite form. It is probable
that Paul never experienced anything like three thousand souls
believing in one day. That was Peter's privilege; but the
special ministry of Paul was to build believing souls together
according to the heavenly vision which God had given him.
God is not satisfied for His people merely to become converts,
'going to church', sitting and hearing well-composed sermons,
and feeling content that as a result they are good Christians.
He is not even greatly interested in their special experiences of

'second blessing', 'sanctification', 'deliverance' (or whatever terms they use)—*as experiences*. There is something more in the mind of God for His children even than these—something in terms of a 'new Man' from heaven. God has in view, as His goal and object in redemption, the union of Christ the Head and the Church His Body, so that the whole, Christ *and* His Church, make up together His one new Man—'the Christ'.

It is good to look through the Scriptures to find '*the* Christ'. How blessed it is that the one thought in the mind of God is His Son, Jesus Christ! Many times in Scripture it is 'Jesus the Christ', and many times again it is simply 'the Christ'. But look carefully and you will find that, not only is the term used of the Son of God personally, but it is used too so as to embrace others with Him. (See especially 1 Cor. 12. 12.) What measureless grace! God is securing for Himself many redeemed sons, not just as individuals but as one gathered people. And with what object? To make of them, in the Son and with Him, one new Man—one united whole wherein is expressed, through all those human lives, the heavenliness and the life and the glory of the blessed Sons of God.

That is God's tremendous object; and Paul was one called of God in a special way to be the steward of that mystery, both to set it forth and to bring His people into it. In saying this we do not mean in the least to belittle the ministry of Peter. We do not imply that evangelism should ever have less than its full place. But what we all need to see is this, that the special ministry of Paul is the necessary complement of that of Peter. Paul goes beyond Peter, but not to Peter's destruction or discredit. Even brother Peter, with all his own growing understanding of God's 'spiritual house' (1 Peter 2. 1-9), recognized that in some degree Paul had out-distanced him in this. It is very good to read the closing verses of his last Epistle, in which he refers to 'the wisdom' given to Paul, and then goes on to class Paul's writings along with 'the other scriptures'. It may have needed grace to do that; but Peter had come to the place where he saw that, in the plan of God, the teaching of Paul had been truly complementary to his own.

'Woe is me', said Paul, 'if I preach not the gospel'; and he sought the help of God to carry it to the farthest limits of the Roman world. But wherever he preached, it was not to stop with the first effect of the preaching but always to follow it through to its further purpose in the saints. For he was essentially a builder. Indeed, as he himself put it, he was a 'master-builder' (1 Cor. 3. 10). He laid the foundation—yes, the foundation of Jesus Christ—and then he went further and built on that foundation. To attempt to build on any other foundation would, he insisted, totally disqualify him. But even with that settled, he saw that the character of the building matters too. It matters greatly how you build, and with what materials. There can be no shoddy workmanship in God's house, no substitutes. God would have His people bonded together in love, framed and builded into a holy temple in the Lord and fitted to reveal and display the glories of His Son. That was the goal which Paul, by his ministry, set before us all. All the lessons of his eventful life, and all the rich contribution of his many writings, covering as they do so wide a range of time and space and action, have this one end in view: that Christ might have for Himself the glorious Church for which He died.

'MENDING THEIR NETS'

But at the last there came set-backs and disappointments. In his letter to the Philippians, Paul tells us why. 'All seek their own', he says, 'not the things of Jesus Christ' (Phil. 2. 21). Writing a little later to Timothy, he says of the saints in one Roman province that 'all they of Asia' have turned away. Who are these Asian believers? Some of those, surely, whom the Lord Himself challenges in His Apocalypse. Seven representative churches in the province of Asia are there addressed, because in their spiritual state they are typical, we believe, of the churches throughout the whole of this age (Rev. 1. 11). For already, in the eyes of God, all the churches of that first new Testament period seem to have departed from His standard and missed something of the divine purpose.

At this point God calls in John. Till now, so far at least as the written New Testament record goes, he has remained in the background. But with Paul gone, the Lord now brings to light His further vessel of ministry, and with him a fresh distinctive emphasis to meet a new need.

The ministry of John is quite different from that of Peter. John was not personally or uniquely commissioned, as was Peter, to originate something. So far as our record tells us, the Lord only used him at the beginning *alongside* Peter. Nor is he shown to have been entrusted in any distinctive way with the task of making known the mystery of the Church. No doubt he was as concerned as were the other apostles in its foundation (Eph. 2. 20), but in this too his calling was in no sense unique. Doctrinally he has nothing to add to the revelation given through Paul. In Paul's ministry the things of God reach a climax, an absolute, and you cannot improve on that. Paul's concern is with the full realization of divine counsels that had been formed in the Godhead before the foundation of the world. Those counsels in His Son—that plan for man's redemption and glory—God had caused to be unfolded age by age, glimpse by glimpse, until at last, in this special age of grace, it was made fully manifest in the birth and death, resurrection and exaltation, of His Christ. The presentation of that plan in its wholeness, and the bringing of it to full realization in the people of God, was Paul's special burden. His task was to express, for the benefit of us all, something coming out of the very heart of God—something from the eternities, now brought to light in time. To improve, therefore, on what God entrusted to Paul, you would have to improve on God, and that is inconceivable. The divine plan is absolute.

Then why to Paul add John? What need is there for this further ministry? The answer is that, at the end of the New Testament period, the enemy of souls found entry into the house of God, and caused God's own people, the very heirs of redemption themselves, to turn aside from His ways. Even those entrusted with the 'Ephesian' vision failed and fell away, and indeed the church in Ephesus was foremost in that failure. If you compare the first epistle to the Ephesians with the second epistle to the Ephesians—that of Paul with that of Jesus through John (Rev. 2. 1–7)—the two letters show you where these

people are. Something terrible has happened; and now John
is brought in and commissioned—for what? Not to lead further, but to restore. You will find that, throughout the New
Testament, the ministry of John is always restorative. He does
not say anything startlingly new and original. He does not
introduce anything further, (though it is true that in the
Apocalypse he carries what has already been given to its consummation.) What distinguishes John, whether in Gospel,
Epistles or Revelation, is his concern to bring the people of
God back to a position they have lost.

Once more, this is in keeping with the circumstances of
John's call to be a disciple. Peter was called to follow when he
was casting a net into the sea; Paul was (presumably) already
by trade a tent-maker when God named him a 'chosen vessel
unto me'; and John was called quite differently again. Like
Peter, John was a fisherman, but unlike him he was not in the
boat but on the shore of the lake at the moment of his call, and
we are told that he and his brother were 'mending their nets'.
When you set yourself to mend something, you seek to bring
it back to its original condition. Something has been damaged
or lost, and your task is to repair and recover it; and that is the
special ministry of John. He is always bringing us back to
God's original.

Perhaps that statement may seem to call for fuller explanation, but we will leave that to come in its place. And lest we
be thought to make too much of the coincidence of the secular
occupations of these three apostles, let it be said at once that we
regard these details, providentially recorded as they doubtless
are, purely as convenient pegs on which to hang our thoughts,
and to help fix in our minds the infinitely greater things for
which each of them stood as a servant of God.

So we have before us these three representative men. We
have Peter, concerned first with the ingathering of souls; we
have Paul, the wise master-builder, building according to the
heavenly vision given to him; and then, when failure threatens, we have John introduced to re-affirm that there is an original purpose still in view, and one that, in the mind of God, has
never been abandoned. There is still something which He

intends to fulfil, and from that intention He will never be deflected.

The practical point of what we have been saying is this, that it takes these three complementary and inter-related ministries to make the Church perfect. It takes the ministry of Peter to initiate things in any given situation; it takes the ministry of Paul to build upon that beginning; and it takes the ministry of John to bring things back, where that has become necessary, into line with God's original intention. Few will deny that the need of each of these three ministries is with us to-day, or that the third, that of recovery, is perhaps the greatest need of all in this closing period of the age. It will help us therefore to look at some of the key points of each of them in more practical detail, and to give special attention to the present implications of the last of the three.

Accordingly, in the chapters that follow we shall consider in turn Peter, Paul and John—first the men themselves, and then their characteristic ministries of initiation, construction and recovery. Let us, as we do so, allow the Spirit of God to speak through them His own personal challenge to each of our hearts.

CHAPTER TWO

PETER—AND THE WAY

ONE of the features that strike most forcibly any reader of
the opening chapters of the book of Acts is the unquestioned authority with which the apostle Peter proclaims the
Gospel of salvation through Jesus Christ. He is the first great
example of an effective evangelist. Listen to him as he points
men to God: 'Ye men of Judæa, and all ye that dwell at Jerusalem, . . . give ear unto my words. . . . Repent ye, and be baptized every one of you. . . . Save yourselves from this crooked
generation' (Acts 2. 14, 38, 40). 'Ye rulers of the people, and
elders, . . . be it known unto you all, . . . In none other is there
salvation. . . . We cannot but speak the things which we saw
and heard' (Acts 4. 8, 10, 12, 20). In such striking phrases as
these we hear Peter speak as a herald of the Kingdom proclaiming to men the way of life; and we see God authenticating
his utterances by the manifest presence with him of the Holy
Spirit, and by the deep and lasting work of conviction
wrought in his hearers.

It is important, therefore, that we should understand first of
all what it was that qualified Peter to become God's mouthpiece. For before Peter could speak he had to be spoken to;
before he could serve as custodian of 'the keys of the kingdom
of heaven', he had to encounter the demands of that Kingdom
upon himself.

What is the meaning of the term 'kingdom'? Surely it is the
realm of a king. It is the sphere of his authority, his reign. So
when Jesus comes into His Kingdom, He comes into the place
of power. Wherever the sovereignty of the Lord Jesus is recognized, there His Kingdom is; and wherever that sovereignty is
not recognized, there His Kingdom has not yet come. If the
Kingdom of God is to be established on earth, then men must

be brought under the unquestioned rule of God. Man must bow to the absolute authority, dominion and sovereign rule of Jesus Christ. It is *His Kingdom* that is to come.

It is therefore most helpful to notice what followed in the Gospel narrative upon that promise to Peter about the keys of the Kingdom. First there intervened a set-back, in which Peter clearly demonstrated that he was certainly not yet a consistent subject of the Kingdom, but rather a stumbling-block to his Lord. There followed some very striking words, addressed by Jesus to the whole group of His disciples, about the Son of man 'coming in his kingdom'. And then, only a few days later, these very words found visible expression on the mount of transfiguration, when Peter in particular came in a special way to feel their force.

We know the incident well. Jesus was transfigured before them, presenting to their view in those moments the Kingdom in its nature and essence—though not yet, of course, in its full scope —in the person of the King. Immediately Peter burst out with his spontaneous response. 'Not knowing what he said', yet ever ready to say something, he proposed that they should build three tabernacles, one each for Jesus, Moses and Elijah.

THE FATHER INTERVENES

Three tabernacles—not one! Do you see the import of Peter's brilliant suggestion? There were two very great men there with Jesus in the mount—great not alone for their own sakes but because of what they represented. There was Moses standing for the law, and there was Elijah for the prophets, and, in proposing to prolong the mountain-top experience, Peter would make provision for these two alongside the Lord. They would, of course, be in a subordinate position, but nevertheless they would have some standing beside Him and a position of authority to be reckoned with.

But in the *Kingdom* you cannot do that! You cannot have more than one authority. You cannot have a multitude of voices. There can be only one Voice. It was to point this lesson that, 'while he yet spake', the Father broke in with what

amounted to a rebuke. Interrupting Peter, as though to say:
'This is not the time for you to speak but to listen,' He directed
him to the One who alone has a right to speak in the Kingdom.
'This is my beloved Son, . . . hear ye him.' In other words:
'Everything in the Kingdom hangs upon Jesus Christ speaking
and upon your paying heed to His words.'

We said that Moses and Elijah represent the law and the
prophets. God's word makes it clear that now, with the coming of the Kingdom, these were to give way before it. 'The
law and the prophets were until John: from that time the gospel of the kingdom of God is preached, and every man entereth
violently into it' (Luke 16. 16). In its very nature the Kingdom
supersedes them both. If there is still law, there is no Kingdom;
if there are still prophets there is no Kingdom. The law and
the prophets must yield to the Kingdom of Jesus Christ; they
cannot claim equal place with it. They must not usurp its
authority. That is why Peter's speech was brought to a sudden
conclusion by the intervention of God. His suggestion was set
aside by a definite and deliberate utterance from heaven itself,
for the whole basis of the Kingdom was at stake, the very
foundation of Christianity was involved. If the Kingdom is to
come, then Moses must give place to it, and so must Elijah. If
you hold on to the law and the prophets you forfeit the Kingdom, and if you have the Kingdom you must let go the law
and the prophets.

Let us think about this a little further, for we want to be
quite practical, and at the same time we need to be careful to
make no mistake. What is law? And what are the prophets?
Well of course in the Jewish usage these terms stood together
for the whole of the Old Testament Scriptures, and we must be
be clear first of all that the Lord Jesus never for one moment
proposed that these be wholly cast aside. (See for example:
Matthew 5. 17, 18; Luke 24. 27, 32, 44.) No, I think we must
look a little deeper for the principles envisaged here.

The law is the written word which expresses the will of God;
the prophets are the living men who also express that will. In
Old Testament days God usually expressed His will to ordinary Israelites by one or other of these means. For God dwelt

not in man's heart but in an unapproachable Holy of Holies. How then could man inquire of Him? First he could do so by reference to the law. Suppose he desired to know the appropriate procedure for dealing with leprosy or defilement with a dead body, or whether or not he might use a particular species of animal or bird for food, he would go with his question to the Book of the law. By careful searching he would find the answer there, and he might do so without direct personal reference to God Himself. But suppose instead he wished to know whether or not he should go on a particular journey to a particular place. He might read the Book from beginning to end and nowhere discover even a mention of that place's name. What would he do then? He would turn to a prophet and say, 'Kindly enquire of the Lord for me whether I should make this journey or not.' But here again the answer came to him second-hand, as it were. He had no authority to go to God direct. Whether through law or prophets, his knowledge of God always came to him indirectly, through a book or through a man; never by direct revelation from God Himself.

But that is not Christianity. Christianity always involves a personal knowledge of God through His Spirit, and not merely the knowing of His will through the medium of a man or a book. Many Christians to-day have a book-knowledge of Christ; they know Him indeed through God's own Book, but they have no vital relationship with Him. Worse still, many know Him only 'by hearsay', from their pastor or from some other man, but they are not in direct communication with Him. Their knowledge is outward, not inward; and let me affirm that anything short of a personal, inward revelation of the Lord is not Christianity. In seeking to know God's will under the old covenant, men were restricted to the law and the prophets, but under the New Covenant God has promised that 'they shall not teach each his fellow-citizen, and each his brother, saying, Know the Lord; because all shall know me in themselves, from the little one unto the great among them' (Heb. 8. 11.[1]). 'You shall know Him *in yourselves*', and know-

[1] J. N. Darby, *New Translation*.

ing Him thus it will be unnecessary to refer either to a 'brother'
or a 'neighbour' for information concerning the Lord. Christianity is based not on information but on revelation. That is
where the Lord began with Peter in the very passage before us:
'Blessed art thou, Simon, . . . for flesh and blood hath not revealed it unto thee, but my Father which is in heaven.' The
Kingdom of God is founded on a personal knowledge of the
Lord which comes through a direct speaking by Him and a
direct hearing by you and me.

Thus, in practical terms to-day, we have the written Scriptures, represented by Moses, and we have the living human
messenger, represented by Elijah who never tasted death.
These two God-given gifts to every believer are among the
most precious factors that contribute to our Christian life: the
Book of God in our hand to instruct us, and the friend who
lives close to the Lord and who can often make known to us
what the Lord has shewn him. The Book is always right; the
counsel of a friend so often is. We need God's Book and we
need God's prophets. He would not have us discard either.
But the lesson of this incident on the mount of transfiguration
is surely that neither of these can take the place of the living
voice of God to our hearts.

We dare not despise God's messengers. We need again and
again the arresting challenge of a truly prophetic spoken word
or the calm of mature spiritual instruction. But we do not
commit ourselves totally and exclusively to the revelation
which comes through holy men of God, however sound it be.
We are under duty bound to listen to the voice of the Lord and
to follow Him.

Still less dare we despise God's written Word. The inspired
Scriptures of truth are vital to our life and progress, and we
would not—we dare not—be without them. Nevertheless
there are those of us who may be in danger of looking to the
letter of the Word even more than to Jesus Christ Himself as
our final authority. What the Bible says we set ourselves to
carry out, religiously and in detail, and God may honour us
for that. Yet if, in doing so, we go further, and exalt the
Bible to a position where our use of it challenges even the very

lordship of Christ Himself, we may run the risk of remaining tragically out of touch with *Him*.

For the Kingdom is more than these. It involves on the positive side a recognition of the absolute authority of Christ, and on the negative side a repudiation of every authority but His as final. It demands a personal, first-hand intelligence of the will of God, that embraces these other God-given aids but that does not end with them. Christianity is a revealed religion, and revelation is always inward, direct and personal. That was the lesson Peter had to learn. In the Kingdom there is only one Voice to be heard, through whatever medium it speaks. I still have the written Scriptures and I still have my brother's 'prophetic' word (for Moses and Elijah *were* there on the mount!). Christianity is not independent of men and books—far from it. But the way of the Kingdom is that the 'beloved Son' speaks to me personally and directly, and that personally and directly I *hear Him*.

THE SON INTERVENES

We have dealt at some length with what I feel to be a fundamental lesson in the training of Peter as a servant of God. We must now notice two instances in which that lesson is further applied, first to the practical question of personal contact with men, and then to the communication to them of the Gospel.

It has always seemed to me that Peter was a man with whom it was easy to talk. It was only too easy to draw him into conversations in which he himself became trapped, as the maid proved later in the courtyard of the high priest's house. Now, only a short time after the events we have discussed, someone approached him with a question about Jesus to which he at once responded with a ready answer (Matt. 17. 24). 'Doth not your master pay the half-shekel?' 'Yes,' replied Peter, as though to say: 'Of course! Naturally He does. Why not?' And having said this, we are told, he went in to Jesus in the house.

Now I want you to notice carefully what it says next. Mat-

thew tells us that 'Jesus spake first to him'. Peter was apparently on the point of opening his mouth to say something like:
'Master, they have come about the temple tax. We *do* pay it,
don't we?' He was in fact, we might almost feel, about to tell
the Lord what He should do!

But Jesus anticipated Peter with a statement of His own true
position. Is this payment indeed required of Him? No, certainly not! The sons of the Kingdom are free. There is of
course no obligation laid upon them to pay the half shekel.
Ah, but wait a minute! That does not mean that in this instance it will go unpaid. What Peter has impetuously committed Him to, Jesus will most certainly pay in full, meeting
with a gracious miracle the situation created by His disciple's
impulsiveness. But let Peter be clear about this one thing, that
Jesus does so, not on the basis of moral necessity, but of free
grace.

Here, then is the new principle with which the Lord confronts His servant, a principle touching directly upon the
matter of our contact with men as yet outside the Kingdom.
What is it that should govern our relations with them in order
that they might be won for the Lord? As in this instance, so
always, it is not the will of God as it may have been revealed
to us in its ultimate intention, but rather, that will *as it is expressed first of all in terms of the Cross of Christ*. God had never
laid it down that His Son must pay the temple tax, and as Son
of God there was no necessity for Him to do anything whatever about it. Indeed we might feel that for Him to do so
would be to put Himself in the wrong position of the 'stranger'. Then why did He do it? '*Lest we cause them to stumble.*'
Has it occurred to you that the very Son of God Himself
uttered these words? There could of course be no question at
any time of His evading a duty; but that was not the point at
issue here. Indeed the situation was quite different: it was a
question rather of His discarding a privilege. This is the way of
the Cross; and the principle involved is a significant and searching one.

Think again. Here are two demands upon us which, superficially at least, may appear to be in conflict. On the one hand

it is perfectly clear from the Lord's words that the will of God
for us as sons is that we should be free. Let us call this 'God's
will A'. On the other hand we are presented with a different
expression of His will in the Cross of Christ, and one requiring
that, to our own loss if need be, we forego what we might
enjoy, in order that others be not offended. Call this 'God's
will B'.[2] How do we reconcile these two conflicting principles, A and B, exemption from duty and the sacrifice of
privilege?

First, let me make it clear that in this we are not making provision for the fear of man. The fear of man is a snare, and we
must be delivered from it. With regard to duty the fear of
man has no place, but only the fear of God. With regard however to privilege, we may legitimately fear lest, in asserting our
rights, we become guilty of causing men to stumble. There
are many things which God shows us personally that come
under the head of will A—things that, as children of God, we
should expect to be free to do (or to be exempt from doing).
If however we try to pursue them, we come up against difficulties with our parents or our family, our employers or perhaps other servants of God, and we are compelled to take into
account will B. We have a right to be exempt, but God also
tells us something about not giving offence. Which principle
are we going to follow?

In His Word God has spoken to us, on the one hand, of 'forsaking all and following Him', and yet, on the other, of obedience to parents and to husbands, of consideration for wives and
children, of subjection to one another in love; and dare we
ignore these latter commands? It would almost seem as
though God's will comes into conflict with itself here, but that
cannot ultimately be the case. We ourselves of course, if once
we have set ourselves to serve God as the Son served the

---

[2] Put differently, the distinction I am seeking to draw is between, in the first
case, a matter that is between the Lord and ourselves—will A—and, in the
second, a matter between the Lord, ourselves, *and other people*—will B. The one
is straightforward, between God and me; the other is complicated by the need,
imposed upon me by God, to consider also a third party. Such a consideration
must have in view *their* relation, or potential relation, to God, no less than
mine.

Father, instinctively prefer will A to will B, because the latter brings in a human element which conflicts with our conception of that service, and we do not like it. We would rather hang on to will A—no tribute money—at any cost. Yet what we shrink from is not in fact merely a human element, for, I repeat, it is *God* who has imposed will B. And I want to suggest that, wherever in God's Word provision is made under the heading of will B, the divine principle is that we should do will B *before* will A, doing it in the faith that the Lord Himself will eventually bring will A to pass. It is not an abandonment of will A, but a surrendering of it *to Him*. Because the Son Himself acted thus, so must we.

Often our hearts are so taken up with will A—the liberty and calling of sons—that we feel that we must push through at any cost, and so we find ourselves kicking against everything and everyone in the way, and as a consequence we very soon forfeit our rest and the blessing of God. God's cure for this is, as always, to remind us once again of the action of His Son. The Lord Jesus had absolutely no need to forego the high place that was His *by the will of God*—and yet He 'emptied Himself'. In sheer grace He let go His own preferences, and yielded His soul to the very death of the Cross for our sakes. Recall His words at the great crisis in the garden: 'O my Father, if it be possible, let this cup pass away from me; nevertheless, not as I will, but as thou wilt.' They reveal what it was that, as Son, He would naturally prefer, but that, as Saviour, He would forego. Whatever the cost to Himself, *it was impossible for Him not to do the will of God.*

For the will of God is never really in conflict with itself. It goes behind 'A or B' just as it goes behind 'the cup'. If we are taken up with 'the cup'—with the pros and cons, the effects and contingencies, involved in obeying the Lord—we shall run a grave risk of missing that will. If, on the other hand, we try to push things through in our own way, we get away from the pathway of the Cross. Our attitude should be: God showed me that thing, but I am perfectly prepared to be contradicted, limited, checked if need be, and *to abide God's time.* I must submit myself to His will B, and I have to trust Him to bring His will A to pass through it all. It is not necessary for *me* to force the issue. I can safely entrust it to Him. This, I say, is 'bearing the cross'.

For there are two sides to cross-bearing. The first and obvious one is that the Cross of Christ 'crosses out' our own will. We recognize that and assent to it, and thereafter are resolved to serve Him and Him only. But when that has been settled in principle, we encounter something else. One day it may seem unmistakeably clear that it is the will of God for us to do a certain thing, and our heart responds to that and we seize upon it. We have no difficulty, for we truly *want* the will of God. But alas, a little later we find the very thing revealed to be His will is frustrated by events, or, as all too often happens, by others, and with it of course *our* perfectly sincere and devoted will has to be crossed also—and that is something we do not like at all! This is a second, and often inevitable, effect of bearing the cross.

Let me illustrate. When I was a young man at college in Foochow, God showed me I was to go in my vacation to an island which was infested with pirates, to preach the Gospel. It was a step of faith, and it required quite a struggle for me to be willing to do so. I visited the island and found the people willing, and after much difficulty I rented a house, got it repaired and had everything ready. One hundred of the brethren were praying for me, and many had also given money towards the expenses. All this time my parents had said nothing, and then, five days before I was to go and when I was already packed up, they suddenly stepped in and forbade it! The house was ready, the money was spent, the will of God was burning in my heart; what was I to do? My parents, God-fearing folk, said 'No'; I was still a student; and God said 'Honour thy father and thy mother.' I sought light from God, and God said to me, 'Yes, that plan is indeed My will, but it is never My intention that you should bring that will to pass by violence. Wait, and *I* will work out My will. It is right for you to submit to your parents.' I had no liberty to explain to others the reason for my change of plan—that it was my parents who had stopped me—and all, I fear, misunderstood me. It wounded me deeply when the one whose opinion I valued most said, 'It will be difficult to trust you in future.'

In God's time the way to that island *was* opened, and His will that souls should be won there came wonderfully to pass. But this experience had taught me an important lesson. I already *liked* that will! Not going was difficult. It cut me; which showed that this particular expression of God's will was in fact now in danger of becoming *my* will in a possessive way; *I* had entered into it too much. I had made up *my* mind to go. If I had had a pure desire for God's will alone to be done, the set-back would not have touched me in the way it did. There would have been a detachment of spirit. So God had to allow the disappointment, with its attendant misunderstanding, in order to teach me this valuable lesson.

If a thing is revealed in the Word of God, we dare not cast it aside; we have to submit. If the written Word of God— 'honour thy father and thy mother'—cuts across will A, we must wait for Him to bring will A to pass. He needs no help to do so. God is seeking to show us that we do not need to push. Self so easily steps in to do the will of God; but God has His time, and He will accomplish it in His own way. Self is fed and nourished because we say 'I am doing God's will'. In our eagerness we think nothing on earth should cross that—and then God himself lays something across our path in order to counter this attitude. The most difficult and painful thing for the Cross to do is to cut across our zeal for the will of God and our love for His work. We have to learn that, for the Lord Jesus Himself, the Cross was will B—something that, though it cut across His path, was revealed in the Scriptures to be in fact the divinely chosen way to the fulfilment of will A (see Luke 18. 31–33). Alone He might have by-passed the Cross, but if others were to have a part with Him in the Kingdom, that Cross was necessary. That surely is the meaning of His words in John 17. 19: 'For their sakes I sanctify myself'. The Kingdom and the throne represented will A for Him, but the Cross was the way to it. You and I may be one hundred per cent sure of will A for our lives, but we shall often encounter will B on the road thither. And because of the carnality of our

nature, in one way or another the Cross has always to intervene and deal with what is of ourselves, in order that the outcome may be all of God.

In what we have been saying, our eyes have been on the
Lord Jesus, not on Peter. Peter himself can have grasped little
of this principle, though the day would come when he understood it. One day he would not only see the necessity of the
death of the Lord Jesus on his behalf, but would come to be
personally identified with that death and ready to face its practical implications in his own experience. 'When thou wast
young thou girdedst thyself, and walkedst whither thou
wouldest: but when thou shalt be old, thou shalt stretch forth
thy hands, and another shall gird thee, and carry thee whither
thou wouldest not' (John 21. 18.) To give in *to others* is what
we find so hard.

But the Lord Jesus does not press the issue any further with
Peter at this time. Instead he performs a gracious miracle, and
one which must surely also have been meant to speak as a
parable to him. 'Go to the sea, and cast a hook, and take up
the fish that first cometh up; and when thou hast opened his
mouth, thou shalt find a shekel: that take, and give unto them
for me and for thee.' Yes, *for Me and for thee.* Some have remarked that this incident is the only example of the Lord performing a miracle for Himself. True, but it was only half for
Himself, for half was for Peter—and you and I can add, 'for
me'. In that single shekel, meeting by grace the temple-tribute
for two men, we have wonderfully set forth the intimate
union of the servant with His Lord in one Church, one Body.

And the miraculous fish? Does it not assure us that, when
we are on a right basis with regard to the will of God, the expenses will be found by God Himself? Whenever love has to
go further than duty, we can look to the Lord to meet the
charges.

THE SPIRIT INTERVENES

But we have not finished with Peter and the interruptions
that he suffered so profitably at the hand of God. We have
heard the voice of the Father intervene on the mountain-top,

and the Son 'speak first' in the house. We move on now briefly to Acts chapter 10 and the account of Peter's visit to the house of Cornelius. By now he is in the full stream of his life's ministry as an evangelist. He has witnessed the outpouring of the Spirit at Jerusalem as multitudes were swept into the Kingdom. Overcoming any natural hesitation he might have had, he has been present to witness too the outpouring of the same Spirit upon the Samaritans. Now, quite lately, he has come to Joppa and has been given the strange vision of the 'great sheet' coming down from heaven, a vision consistent in some ways with his calling and yet having new and startling implications. 'What God hath cleansed, make not thou common.' Impelled by these words, he sets out for Cæsarea, but it is difficult to avoid the impression of caution, and even of reluctance, that the narrative of his visit creates.

Peter was still a Jew at heart. Even after the vision of the sheet, he went unwillingly and as by compulsion to this Gentile household. He went as a disciplined, if somewhat puzzled, servant of God, but inwardly he seems to have stood, as it were, aloof. He was not yet wholly committed, and could very easily, even now, have stood in God's way.

Then, too, there were those brothers with him—good men from Joppa, but of course lacking the striking personal vision he had thrice received on the housetop. How would they react? And not only they but his own more orthodox fellow apostles and elders in Jerusalem? It would not be surprising if his mind held some real anxiety about their possible reactions, once they came to hear of his visit.

So he opened his mouth and began his sermon. There is nothing lacking in the message he gave. Luke's summary of it reveals a well-constructed setting forth of the essentials of the Gospel. What Peter makes clear however is that he never even got half way through! By his own estimate he had barely 'begun to speak' (Acts 11. 15) when the Holy Spirit Himself intervened and brought him to a full stop.

Notice that Peter had not reached the point of mentioning the Spirit. (Would he have done so had he been allowed to go on?) He got as far as the Cross and remission of sins, and then, while he 'yet spake these words, the Holy Spirit fell'. The Lord Himself assumed command, and Peter had learned enough by now to know that this was the time to stand back. Indeed, there was nothing more to be said. When God acts directly on the audience, the preacher's task is ended.

How gracious it was of God to intervene in this way! Had He waited for Peter to do something—perhaps to baptize or lay hands upon these men (compare Acts 8. 17; 19. 5-6)—how would Peter have answered the brethren when he got back to Jerusalem? 'This is all your fault, Peter', they would have said. 'You started it all. If you had not laid hands on the Gentiles nothing would have happened!' But to the brothers with him at Cæsarea Peter had been able to appeal on the ground of God's *fait accompli* 'Can any man forbid the water?' So now to these others in Jerusalem, he can say: 'Who was I, that I could withstand God?'

How vividly this illustrates the words of Jesus in Luke: 'The gospel of the kingdom is preached, and every man'—Jew, Samaritan and Gentile—'entereth violently into it'. The sovereign Lord Himself had, as it were, turned the key and opened the door. There can be no questioning the authority of the King. The way to the kingdom lies open at His command. As Peter had said, but with perhaps greater truth than he as yet knew, 'He is Lord of all'.

With this principle established in the servant, we can turn in the next chapter to look at the needs of the sinner.

CHAPTER THREE

CATCHING MEN

How do men press into the Kingdom? We have considered at some length how a preacher of the Gospel needs to be personally prepared in spirit for his task. But what of the hearers? What is the minimum requirement in the sinner if he is to find the Lord and be saved? This question now claims our attention, for it is as important for the preacher to know what he is attempting to do as it is for him to be prepared in spirit to do it.

In the discussion which follows we can only deal with a single point in the preaching of the Gospel. I take it for granted that the servant of the Lord knows the facts of redemption through the atoning death of Christ, and that he himself is born of the Spirit. I assume also that he knows how to present those facts clearly and with power. I am concerned here not with the substance of his preaching, but rather with the principles that should guide in the actual task of leading the individual soul to Christ.

What is necessary for a man to be saved? How can he be prevailed upon to come to the door of the Kingdom and enter? How do we bring men who have only the absolute minimum of knowledge or desire for God into a living touch with Him? These are our questions, and I am going to lay down four guiding principles that will, I hope, be found to go a long way towards answering them.

God has made, from His side, a threefold provision for every man in his hour of crisis. Firstly, Jesus has come as the Friend of sinners; secondly, it is He personally (and no intermediary) whom men are called to meet; and thirdly, the Holy Spirit has been poured out upon all flesh, to bring to pass in man the initial work of conviction of sin, repentance and faith, and, of course, all that follows. Then, finally, from the side of the sinner, one condition and one only is demanded. He is not required—*in the first place*—to believe, or to repent, or to be conscious of sin, or even to know that Christ died. He is required only to approach the Lord with an honest heart.

This last statement may at first startle you, but as we go on, I think you will see how helpful it is. We will, however, take these points in order, beginning from the side of God's provision.

THE SINNER'S FRIEND

In the Gospels the Lord Jesus is presented as the Friend of sinners, for historically He was found, first of all, moving among men as their Friend before He became their Saviour. But do you realize that to-day He is still in the first place our Friend, in order that He may become our Saviour? Before we have reached the point where we are willing—or indeed able —to receive Him as Saviour, He comes to us as a Friend, so that personal encounter is not debarred to us and the door is held open for us to receive Him as Saviour. This is a precious discovery.

Since I saw the Saviour as the Friend of sinners I have seen many unusual and difficult people brought to the Lord. I remember how in one place a young woman came and attacked me, saying that she did not *want* to be saved. She said that she was young and intended to have a good time, and did not want to have to leave her ways and become sedate and sober, for then there would be no joy in life. She said she had no intention of forsaking her sins and had not the least desire for salvation! It transpired that she knew quite a lot about the Gospel, for she had been brought up in a Mission School, and this was her reaction against it. After she had more or less raved at me for a while, I said, 'Shall we pray?' 'What should *I* pray?' she replied scornfully. I said, 'I can't be responsible for your prayer, but I will pray first, and then you can tell the Lord all that you have been saying to me.' 'Oh, I couldn't do that!' she said, somewhat taken aback. 'Yes, you can', I replied. 'Don't you know that He is the Friend of sinners?' This touched her. She did pray—a very unorthodox prayer—but from that hour the Lord worked in her heart, for in a couple of days' time she was saved.

It is clear from the New Testament that the Lord Jesus came as a Friend, *in order to help sinners to come to Him*. Our coming to Him was made possible by His first coming to us. He came to bring heaven down within our reach. I remember that I was once sitting talking to a brother in his home. His wife and mother were upstairs, but his small son was in the sitting-room with us. Presently the little fellow wanted something, and called out to his mother for it. 'It is up here', she replied; 'come up and get it.' But he cried out to her, 'I can't, Mummy, it's such a long way. *Please* bring it down to me.' And indeed he was very small; so she brought it down. And salvation is just like that. Only by His coming right down to us could our need be met. Had He not come, sinners could not have approached Him; but He came down in order to lift them up.

At the hour of crisis there are many practical difficulties that face the sinner. For example, in the Scriptures we are often told to believe. The Word lays much stress on the necessity of faith. But you say, 'I have not got faith'. A girl once said to me, 'I can't believe. I would like to believe but I can't! My parents keep on saying to me 'You *must* believe', but it is no good; I haven't got it in me. The desire is there, but I find faith lacking. It is *impossible* to believe.' 'That is all right', I I said. 'You can't believe. But you can ask the Lord to *give* you faith. He is prepared to help you to that extent. You pray: "Lord, help Thou my unbelief!"'

Or again, the Word tells us that we are to repent. What if we have no desire whatever to repent? I met a student once who said it was too early for him to come to the Lord. He wanted more time in which to taste the pleasures of sin and to enjoy himself. He said to me, 'The thief on the cross was saved, but he had had his fling, and it was high time that he repented. But I—I am young.' 'Well, what do you want to do?' I asked him. He replied, 'I want to wait for another forty years and have a good time, and then I will repent.' So I said, 'Let us pray'. 'Oh, I can't pray', he answered. 'Yes, you can,'

I said. 'You can tell the Lord all you have told me. He is the Friend of unrepentant sinners like you.' 'Oh, I couldn't say *that* to Him'. 'Why not?' 'Oh, but I could not.' 'Well, be quite honest. Whatever is in your heart, you tell it to Him. He will help you.' Finally he prayed, and told the Lord that he did not want to repent and be saved, but that he knew he needed a Saviour; and he just cried to Him for help. The Lord worked repentance in him and he got up a saved man.

In England in the early 19th century there was a woman who had Christian parents and who for years had longed to be saved. She went to hear this and that preacher and visited churches and chapels in her search for salvation, but all in vain. One day she wandered into a little chapel with no real expectation in her heart, for she was almost in despair. She sat down at the back. The speaker was an elderly man. Suddenly in the middle of his address he stopped and pointing his finger at her said: 'You Miss, sitting there at the back, you can be saved *now*. You don't need to *do* anything!' Light flashed into her heart, and with it peace and joy. Charlotte Elliott went home and wrote her well-known hymn: 'Just as I am, without one plea . . . O Lamb of God I come.' Those words have pointed to countless sinners the way of humble access to God through the blood of Christ. Yes, we dare to say to-day, to every one of the inhabitants of Shanghai or of any other city, that they can come to Him and be saved *just as they are*.

I repeat these incidents just to emphasize that what the sinner cannot do the Saviour is at hand to do for him. It is for this reason that we can tell people that they need not wait for anything, but can come to Him immediately. Whatever their state, whatever their problem, let them bring it and tell it to the Friend of sinners.

FIRST CONTACT WITH THE LORD

What is salvation? Many think that to be saved we must first believe that the Lord Jesus died for us, but it is a strange fact that nowhere in the New Testament does it say precisely that. Of course the whole message of the New Testament is that Jesus died and rose again that we might be saved. But read through your New Testament carefully and tell me where you can find one verse that says that the condition for being saved is to *believe* that Christ died for our sins? You cannot find it anywhere. We are told to believe *in* Jesus, or to believe *on* Him; not to believe *that He died* for us. 'Believe on the Lord Jesus Christ and thou shalt be saved' were Paul's words. We are to believe first of all in *Him;* not specifically in what He has done.

In John 3. 16 we are told that 'whosoever believeth on him' shall have everlasting life. Earlier in his Gospel John says that 'He came unto his own, and they that were his own received him not.' At the end of the same Gospel John states that he wrote it 'that ye may believe that Jesus is the Christ, the Son of God; and that believing ye may have life in his name.' Men rejected Him, not on the ground of what He did but of who He was, and they are invited to believe in what He is and who He is, and not, first of all, in what He has done. John 3. 16 does not say: 'Whosoever believeth that Christ died for him and bore his sins on the Cross hath everlasting life'. Its message is that God gave His Son, and it is He Himself in person upon whom we are to believe. 'He that hath the Son hath the life.'

Of course I do not want you to think me a modernist, who would dare to belittle the Cross or give a lower place to the substitutionary work of Christ. I *do* believe in the necessity of His atonement, and so I am sure do you. I trust you will not misunderstand me therefore when I say that the appreciation of that work may not be the *first* step in the sinner's initial contact with the Lord. That appreciation must follow, but the main question is whether or not we have the Son, and not, first of all, whether or not we understand the whole plan of salvation. The first condition of salvation is not knowledge, but *meeting Christ.*

There are many people of whom you may feel that they were saved by the wrong scriptures! They were spoken to through verses that do not seem to point the way of salvation, and you almost feel they cannot be saved on that basis! You feel that there must be a weakness somewhere, and yet you have to recognize that God is often pleased to work in that way. I used to wish that those whom I led to the Lord would be saved on the basis of John 3. 16 or 5. 24 or 6. 40. But I have come to see that all that is needed for the *initial* step is that there should be a personal touch with God, and when that is so the rest will surely follow. It does not matter, therefore, which verses God elects to use for that first step. After all, we do not need to study the theory of electricity and to understand it thoroughly before we can turn on the electric light. The light does not say, 'I am not going to shine for you, for you know nothing of the principle on which I work'. And God does not set understanding as the condition of our approach to Him. 'This is life eternal, that they should know thee, the only true God, and Jesus Christ whom thou hast sent'.

Let us take three examples from the Gospels. Which was the first outstanding conversion recorded in the New Testament? Surely that of the thief on the cross. Up till then everything had been pointing forward to the Cross of Christ. Now it was being enacted before men's eyes, and the thief was a witness. This man was a model sinner and was receiving a model punishment, and his was, we may say, a model conversion. Yet did he recognize the Lord as Saviour? What were his words? 'Remember me when thou comest in thy kingdom' (Luke 23. 42). What did the Lord reply? He did not remind him of his evil life, or tell him that he was suffering justly and *ought* to die, and that instead He, Jesus, was suffering on the cross for him and dying for his sins. It seems to us that it would have been an excellent opportunity to announce the plan of redemption—but no, the Lord only answered: 'To-day shalt thou be with me in paradise'. For the thief *recognized who Jesus was*—that though suffering unjustly He was going to reign and would have a Kingdom—and he believed *in the Lord*, and that was enough.

Consider next the woman with an issue. In Mark 5. 24 we are told that the multitude 'thronged' Jesus. There were many among the crowd who were touching and even pressing upon Him, but only one among them was healed. She was healed because with a special intention she 'touched' Him. And it only required a touch; for in her it represented a reaching out in spirit to God for help in her deep need.

Or recall the incident of the Pharisee and the publican at prayer in the temple. The Pharisee understood all about offerings and sacrifices and tithes, but there was from him no cry of the heart to God. But the publican cried, 'Lord have mercy upon me!' Something went out from him to God which met with an immediate response, and the Lord Jesus singles him out as the one whom God reckoned righteous. For what is it to be reckoned righteous? It is *to touch God*.

The Epistle to the Romans tells us in much detail about sin and about the way of salvation, and from a study of it we can learn a great deal about the doctrine of redemption; and yet it was written for the saved. John's Gospel, on the other hand, gives no doctrine in any systematic form; in fact there seems to be little or no plan to the book at all; and yet it was written for the world (John 20. 31). We would have arranged things the other way round, I am sure; and we should have been wrong! For consider: if your house is on fire and there is no way of escape for those on the top storey, and if the firemen come and set up a ladder to save you, what will you do? Will you say, 'Not so fast! Tell me first why your ladder sticks up without any support. Ordinary ladders have to lean against something. And what material are your clothes made of? Why do they not catch fire?'—and so on? No, you will allow yourself to be saved, and afterwards you may inquire all about the fire escape and the firemen's uniforms and everything else that interests you.

After I was saved I used to feel very dissatisfied with Peter's sermon on the day of Pentecost. Indeed I thought it was in some respects, a very poor one, for it seemed so inadequate for its purpose. It did not, I thought, make things clear at all, for there is nothing in it about the plan of redemption. What does Peter say? 'Jesus of Nazareth, a man approved of God unto you by mighty works and wonders and signs, which God did by him in the midst of you, even as ye yourselves know; him, being delivered up by the determinate counsel and foreknowledge of God, ye by the hand of lawless men did crucify and slay: whom God raised up . . .' Surely, I felt, here was the golden opportunity Peter needed to press the point home. Surely here was the time to introduce some reference to Isaiah 53, or otherwise to explain the doctrine of the atonement. But no, he let the opportunity pass, and went on: 'Let all the house of Israel therefore know assuredly, that God hath made him both Lord and Christ, this Jesus whom ye crucified'. How strange that Peter did not even use the title 'Saviour'! But nevertheless, what was the result? The people, we are told, were pricked in their heart, and cried, 'What shall we do?'

Later on Peter went to Gentiles who had a different religious background altogether. There surely, you feel, the Gospel would be plainly preached. Yet to Cornelius Peter only spoke about who Christ was, and though he certainly mentioned the remission of sins he gave no explanation of the meaning of His death—yet even so, the Holy Spirit fell upon them all.

Surely it becomes clear from this that salvation is not initially a question of knowledge but of 'touch'. All who touch the Lord receive life. We might say that, judged by his sermons in the Acts, even Paul was not clear in his Gospel. Those many years ago the Gospel was not preached as it is now! There was not the same clear presentation of truth! But *is* it the truth which is the most important? The great weakness of the present preaching of the Gospel is that we try to make people *understand* the plan of salvation, or we try to drive people to the Lord through the fear of sin and its consequences. Wherein have we failed? I am sure it is in this, that our hearers do not see *Him*, for we do not adequately present the Person. They only see 'sin' or 'salvation', whereas their need is to see the Lord Jesus Himself, and to meet Him and 'touch' Him.

Too often those who have been saved merely through knowledge develop big heads. They progress without seeming to feel much need of God. They *know* it all and they even feel qualified to criticize the preacher's presentation of facts. But when it comes to a crisis in which they lose their known bearings and have to trust the Lord over something, they cannot do so. They are not in living touch with Him. Yet there are others, who may know very little but have come out of themselves, and have touched the living God, who develop and grow in faith even through the severest trial. That is why our first object must be to lead people to meet Him.

None of us can fathom the mysterious ways of God. None of us dare prescribe for Him how He should work. There was a Chinese boy who, when he was twelve years old, was taken by his mother up to a temple in the hills. As he was worshipping before the shrine with his mother, he looked at the idol and thought, 'You are too ugly and too dirty to be worshipped. I don't believe you can save me. What is the sense of worshipping you?' But out of respect for his mother he joined in the ceremony, and after it was over his mother got into her chair to go down the mountain. But he slipped away to the back of the temple and found an open space where he stood and looked up to heaven and said, 'O God, whoever You are, I do not believe that You can dwell in that shrine. You are too big, and it is too small and dirty for You. You surely must dwell right up there in the heavens. I do not know how to find You, but I put myself in Your hands; for sin is very strong, and the world pulls. I commit myself to You, wherever You may be.' Thirty years later I met him and told him the Gospel. He said, 'I have met the Lord Jesus for the first time to-day, but this is the second time that I have touched God. Something happened to me that day thirty years ago on the mountain top.'

It is the living Lord who becomes our Saviour. Jesus is no longer the crucified but the reigning One, and to-day therefore we go for salvation not to the foot of the Cross but to the Throne, to believe in Him as Lord. Perhaps we need to see more clearly the difference between redemption and salvation. Redemption was secured by the Lord Jesus on the Cross two thousand years ago. Our salvation rests to-day upon that redemption, accomplished once for all in time. Nevertheless it is equally true that you may have been 'saved' ten, twenty or thirty years ago and I quite recently, because for each of us salvation is a personal matter—a personal partaking, as it were, of Christ. There is surely a parallel here with the Israelites of old in Egypt. The redeemed firstborn was to partake of the Pass-over sacrifice *by eating the meal*, and not merely to observe the shed blood of his redemption upon the door posts, where God had caused it to be placed for His own purposes of atonement.

It comes to this, that salvation, which is a personal and a sub-jective experience, may be said to rest rather upon the Lord's resurrection than upon His death. The death of Christ was necessary for atonement objectively before God. But for sal-vation the New Testament lays emphasis upon our faith in His resurrection, for that resurrection is the proof that His death has been accepted. We believe *in the Lord Jesus Christ*, per-sonally risen and ascended to glory, and we seek to bring sin-ners *now* into immediate contact with Him.

AN HONEST HEART TOWARDS GOD

Before we come to the third provision that God has made for the crisis of salvation in a man's life, I am going to digress, and to deal first with what seems to me to be the single require-ment demanded from man himself.

When you have preached the Gospel of repentance and of faith through Jesus Christ for the remission of sins, you en-counter various difficulties in your hearers which may bring you up short, One man, having heard you tell all about sin and its punishment, says quite frankly, 'Yes, I know it all, but I *like* sinning.' What will you do? As we have suggested, the Friend of sinners is the One to help him here. Another man listens to you and assents to everything, and yet does not seem to be able to take it in. You meet him next day, and he says, 'I have forgotten the third point. What was it?' Salvation is not a question of 'points'! Salvation is not even a question of understanding or of will. It is, as we have seen, a question of meeting God—of men coming into first-hand contact with Christ the Saviour. So what, you ask me, is the minimum re-quirement in a man to make that contact possible?

For my reply I would turn you to the parable of the sower. It seems to me that here we are plainly told the one thing that God does demand. 'That in the good ground, these are such as in an honest and good heart, having heard the word, hold it fast, and bring forth fruit with patience' (Luke 8. 15). What God demands of man is 'an honest and good heart'—good, because honest. It does not matter if a man wants or does not want to be saved, it does not matter if he understands or does not understand; provided that he is prepared to be honest with God about it, God is prepared to meet him.

The question has been raised: How do you reconcile God's requirements of 'an honest and good heart' with the statement that 'the heart is deceitful above all things' (Jer. 17. 9)? But the point in the parable of the sower is not that the man who receives the Word is a perfectly honest man in God's eyes, but that he is honest *towards* God. Whatever is in his heart, he is prepared to come to God frankly and openly with it. Of course, it is a fact, and it remains a fact, that the heart of man is 'deceitful above all things', but it is still possible for a man with a deceitful nature to turn honestly to God. A dishonest man can come to God and say honestly to Him, 'I am a sinner; have mercy on me!' In the realm of desire towards God he can be true. This is what God seeks in men, and something of this meaning is contained in the word which says: 'The eyes of the Lord run to and fro throughout the whole earth, to show himself strong in the behalf of them whose heart is perfect toward him' (2 Chron. 16. 9).

The basic condition of a sinner's salvation is not belief or repentance, but just this honesty of heart towards God. God requires nothing of him but that he come in that attitude. Into that spot of straightforwardness that lies in the midst of much deceitfulness, the good seed falls and brings forth fruit. Of the two thoroughly dishonest thieves crucified with the Lord, there was in the one a little bit of honest desire. The publican who prayed in the temple was a crooked man, but in him too there was that honesty to acknowledge his sinfulness and cry to God for mercy. And what of Saul of Tarsus? He certainly lacked even the desire for salvation through Jesus Christ, but the Lord saw in him on the Damascus road an honest heart Godward, and that was the starting-point of his history with the Lord. He honestly touched the Lord when he said 'Lord,

what wilt thou have me to do?' and that 'touch' was enough
to save him instantly. For it is the *fact* of the Gospel, making
possible the initial touch with Jesus Christ, that saves the sinner,
and not the sinner's understanding of it.

As several of the incidents recounted earlier have indicated,
we should encourage every sinner to kneel down with an
honest heart and pray, telling the Lord frankly where he stands.
As Christians we are told that we must pray in the name of the
Lord Jesus (John 14. 14; 15. 16; 16. 23, 24), by which, of
course, we understand not a mere formula of words but an act
of faith in Him. But with sinners it is different, for there are
prayers which God will hear that are not uttered in the name
of Jesus. In Acts 10. 4 the angel says to Cornelius: 'Thy prayers and thine alms are gone up for a memorial before God.'
If there is a sincere cry from the heart, God hears. A sinner's
heart can touch God.

A striking example of one who came to God without even
wanting to be saved is afforded by the experience of an English lady of the last century. One of a wealthy family of good
social position, she was well educated, a good musician and an
accomplished dancer, and she was both young and beautiful.
One night there was a ball to which she was invited. She had
a wonderful ball dress specially made for the occasion, and that
night she was the one who compelled most attention and was
most sought after by all. It was, one might say, a great
triumph for her.

After the ball was over she went home, took off her ball
dress and cast it aside. She flung herself down and said, 'O
God, I have everything I want, wealth, popularity, beauty,
youth—and yet I am absolutely miserable and unsatisfied.
Christians would tell me that this is a proof that the world is
empty and hollow, and that Jesus could save me and give me
peace and joy and satisfaction. But I don't want the satisfaction that He could give. I don't want to be saved. I hate You
and I hate Your peace and joy. But, O God, give me what I
don't want, and if You can, make me happy!' It is recorded
that she got up from her knees a saved woman, and became
one who knew the Lord in a deep way.

I affirm once again: all that is needed is an honest heart. If you *want* God there is no difficulty. But praise God, even if you do *not* want Him. He will still hear you if you will come to Him and be honest about it.

THE HELPER NEAR AT HAND

We have said that a cry to God from the heart is sufficient. In the words of Joel, quoted by Peter: 'Whosoever shall call on the name of the Lord shall be saved.' How is this possible? Because God has fulfilled the other promise (quoted by Peter from the same prophecy) that: 'I will pour forth of my Spirit upon all flesh' (Acts 2. 17, 21). Because the Holy Spirit has been poured out upon all mankind, a cry is enough.

No preacher of the Gospel is of much use unless he believes this. The presence of the Holy Spirit, and His proximity to the sinner, is vital to our preaching. God in the heavens is too far away; He is, as it were, out of reach of man. But to the Romans Paul writes: 'Say not in thy heart, who shall ascend into heaven? (that is, to bring Christ down:) ... The word is *nigh* thee. ... For whosoever shall call upon the name of the Lord shall be saved.' (Rom. 10. 6, 8, 13).

I always believe that the Holy Spirit is *upon* a man when I preach to him. I do not mean to say that the Spirit is *within* the hearts of unbelievers, but that He is outside. What is He doing? He is waiting, waiting to bring Christ into their hearts. The Holy Spirit is waiting to enter the heart of the hearer of the Gospel. He is like the light. Open the window-shutters even a little, and it will flood in and illumine the interior. Let there be but a cry from the heart to God, and *at that moment* the Spirit will enter and begin His transforming work of conviction and repentance and faith—the miracle of new birth.

Not only had Peter observed the miraculous intervention of the Holy Spirit upon his hearers as he preached to them in the home of Cornelius; he had also, of course, his personal experience of the Spirit's work in his own heart. 'As I began to speak,' he reports, 'the Holy Ghost fell on them, *even as on us at the beginning*' (Acts 11. 15). Perhaps the biggest condition of success in bringing men to Christ is to remember that the same Holy Spirit, who came to our help in the hour of darkness, is at hand waiting to enter and illumine their hearts also, and to make good the work of salvation to which, in crying to God, they have opened the door.

I had a friend who was preaching in a certain city. A woman sought him out and he talked to her and preached Christ to her. He spoke of her sin, and of the punishment for sin, and of the Lord who came to save. But the woman said to him, 'I don't think you know how nice sin is; you have never tasted its delights. I *like* to sin. Life would be empty otherwise.' After a while my friend suggested that they pray. The woman said, 'What could one so sinful as I say to your God? I cannot find repentance in my heart. I have nothing I could say that would be acceptable to Him.' But my friend replied: 'My God understands. He is *near* to you and He can hear *any* prayer; so you say to Him just what you have said to me.' She was amazed, for till now she had only heard the kind of formal prayer where you have to say what you do not believe, for politeness' sake! Then he showed her the verse in Acts II where it says of the Gentiles on whom the Holy Ghost fell that God 'granted' them repentance unto life. So she prayed, and told it all to the God who understands sinners. 'Though I do not want to repent', she pleaded, 'O God, help me and grant me repentance.' And He did! She had opened to His Spirit's illumination the windows of her heart, and she arose from her knees a saved woman.

Here then is a principle, that because Jesus is the Friend of sinners, and because the Holy Spirit undertakes to do what men themselves cannot do, therefore sinners can come to God just as they are. *They do not need to change at all*, and it is not necessary for them to find *in themselves* the ability to do anything. If a man asks you to tell him the Gospel of salvation and afterwards he says to you, 'Sir, I want to be saved,' and on your telling him to believe, he replies, 'I can't believe', what will you do? Will you say, 'I am afraid you are no good. You go away, and come back when you *can* believe'? Are you not thereby asking him to do something towards his salvation?

Another man says to you, 'I don't *want* to be saved.' What will you do then? Will you send him off to wait until some difficulty or sorrow drives him to God? May you not thereby be closing the door to him? Why need we lay down so many conditions for sinners before they can be saved? Surely if Jesus is the Friend of sinners all men can come as they are, and because His Spirit is at hand to work, we can count on Him to do in them what they themselves can never do.

During the twenty years that I have preached the Gospel in China, many of course *have* initially understood the way of salvation, many *have* first of all been convicted of sin, *have* repented, *have* believed—and they have come to Christ on that basis and been saved. But, praise God, there have also been many others who, though they did not in the first place repent or believe, or even consciously desire to be saved, yet were persuaded to come honestly to the Lord and make personal contact with Him; and in many of these, too, understanding, conviction, repentance and faith have followed, and they have, as a result, been gloriously saved. This gives me the confidence to state unequivocally that *there is not one other condition necessary to being saved except that of being a sinner and being honest enough to say so to the Lord.* That condition is enough to allow the Holy Spirit to begin His convicting and transforming work.

We have spoken of those who won't repent, and of those who cannot believe; we have spoken of those who have no desire for salvation, and of those who think they are too bad to be saved; we have spoken of those who are confused and cannot understand the Gospel, and of those who understand but will not acknowledge the claim of God upon them. May I tell you that it is yet possible for any of these to be saved? I have met all of these six types of people and *many* of them have been saved on the spot; and in addition I have met a seventh type—those who do not believe there is a God at all—and I have dared to say even to them that they do not need first to substitute theism for atheism. They can be saved *as they are*, even without any belief in God at all, if they will be honest about it.

Some will at once rejoin: 'But what about Hebrews 11. 6?
Surely that verse demands faith in God's existence at least.'
Well, there was a time when I should certainly have said so;
but one day I learned afresh how infinitely far God is prepared
to go to meet the son returning from the far country. It happened in the following way.

I was once holding evangelistic meetings in a college in
South China. There I met an old friend, in fact an old schoolfellow. He had been in America and was now in this college
as Professor of Psychology. He had made up his mind about
religion and had been in the habit of telling his students that he
could explain all so-called conversions on purely psychological
grounds. Before the meetings began I went to call on him,
and preached to him Christ. Out of politeness he had to listen
for a while, but finally he smiled and said, 'It is no good
preaching to me. I don't believe there *is* a God'. I said, perhaps a little rashly, 'Even if you do not believe in a God, just
pray. You will discover something.' He laughed. 'Pray,
when I don't even believe in a God!' he exclaimed; 'how
could I?' Then I said, 'Though you cannot find a ladder up to
God it does not alter the fact that He has come down to find
you. You pray!' He laughed again; but I still urged him to do
so. I said, 'I have a prayer that even you can pray. Say this:
"O God, if there is no God, then my prayer is useless and I
have prayed in vain; but if there is a God, then somehow make
me know it."' He replied, 'But what has this hypothetical
God got to do with Jesus Christ? Where does Christianity
come in?' I told him just to add a sentence to his prayer asking
God to show him this also. I explained that I was not asking
him to admit there was a God; I was not asking him to admit
anything; but that there was one thing and one thing only that
I asked of him, and that was that he must be honest. His heart
must be in his prayer. It must not just be an empty repeating
of words. I was not sure that I had accomplished anything;
but when I went away I left with him a Bible.

The next day, at the end of the first meeting of my campaign, I asked any who had been saved to stand up, and the
first one to do so was this professor. I went up to him after-

wards and asked him, 'Has anything happened?' He replied, 'Much. I am saved.' 'How did it happen?' I asked. He replied, 'After you went I picked up the Bible and opened it at John's Gospel. My eye caught the words: 'The day after', 'the next day', 'the day after', and I thought to myself, this man knows what he is talking about. He *saw* it all. It is like a diary. After that, I thought about what you had said to me, and I tried to see if there was any catch in it—if you were getting at me in any way. I went over it point by point and could see no flaw in it. It all seemed perfectly sound. Why should I not pray as you suggested? But suddenly the thought came to me: What if there *is* in fact a God? Where do I stand then? Having told my students that there is nothing in religion at all, and that psychology accounts for everything, am I willing to admit to them that I have been wrong all the time? I weighed this up carefully, but nevertheless I felt I had to be honest about it. For if, after all, there really was a God, I would be a fool not to believe in Him!

'So I knelt down and prayed; and as I prayed I just *knew* there was a God. How I knew, I cannot explain, but I just knew it! Then I remembered the Gospel of John that I had read, and how it seemed to be written by an eye-witness, and I knew that if that was so, then Jesus was the Son of God—and I was saved!'

Oh, it is wonderful what our God can do! When you go out preaching the Gospel, never lose sight of the fact that He is *a living God*, ready to act in mercy. Even if men could be a little better than they are it would not help matters, and if they were much worse it would not hinder. All He looks for is 'an honest and good heart'. And never forget that the Holy Spirit is present in power to move men's hearts to God. Have faith in Him in respect of every soul with whom you have to deal. Alone you may not be much of a fisherman, but co-operating with the Spirit of God, you may have confidence enough to land the biggest fish.

CHAPTER FOUR

PAUL—AND THE LIFE

As we move on now to consider the special contribution in the New Testament of the ministry of the apostle Paul, we shall once again be compelled to take a great deal for granted. For I must repeat that it will be his 'specific' ministry that we shall have in mind here, namely, that represented in our analogy by the figure of a 'tent'. But in dealing thus especially with the collective or corporate theme in his ministry we do not overlook the very wide range of spiritual revelation given to Paul on other matters, such as the divine plan of redemption and the individual believer's growth in Christ.

The letter to the Romans was written, as we have seen, not to show sinners how to enter the door of the Kingdom, but to show us as Christians how God made it possible for us to do so, and what are the consequences of our entry. With this as his object, Paul enlarges in that letter on the great themes of justification and sanctification, of deliverance from sin and from the law, of eternal life in Christ and the walk in the Spirit, and of sonship and the purpose of God. We have dealt at length with some of these matters elsewhere,[1] and have shown that the key to faith and experience in relation to all these things is the opening of our eyes to the great historic fact of Jesus Christ, crucified, risen and exalted, and with it, to the further fact of our death, resurrection and exaltation with Him. God has judged our sins and passed upon our fallen nature the sentence of death, and that sentence has been carried out upon us *in Christ*. We are received into His Kingdom on the basis, not of our somehow escaping judgment, but of our *having* judged in Him, and of our *having been* raised in Him to newness

[1] *The Normal Christian Life*, Bombay and London, 1958.

of life. The Cross of Christ is for us the gateway to everything.

With this principle established, Paul next sets before us, in a remarkably vivid chapter (Romans 7), first of all his total failure *as a believer* to live the Christian life in his own natural strength, and then his glorious discovery (expanded in Chapter 8) that nevertheless this *is* possible 'through Jesus Christ our Lord'. The power of Christ indwelling—'the law of the Spirit of life in Christ Jesus'—is superior to the law of sin and death in his members. In the words of Philippians 4. 13, 'I can do all things in him that strengtheneth me'.

Thus for Paul, the Christian life was a continual miracle—a paradox in which the divine life planted within by new birth shone forth through the 'mortal body' of one who consciously walked after the Spirit. 'If Christ is in you, the body is dead because of sin; but the spirit is life because of righteousness' (Rom. 8. 10). Before we proceed to consider Paul as 'tent-maker', and his understanding of the House of God (to which the Epistle to the Romans itself inevitably leads), we will pause to look at the man himself, and to learn a lesson from this personal paradox, so strikingly exemplified in him, of the 'earthly house of our tabernacle' and the 'earnest of the Spirit' enshrined within it (2 Cor. 5. 1-5).

In considering the apostle Paul, I wish to direct your attention to his Second Epistle to the Corinthians, and to ask you first of all to note its special character. The peculiarity of this letter lies in its expression of Paul's inner life and experience. It is the most personal of his letters—indeed of all the New Testament epistles —and without it we should know far less than we do of the man himself. Paul did not want to write the letter, but because of the attitude of the Corinthians God permitted it to be written, and in doing so He allows us to see something which the other epistles partly conceal. *They* are full of teaching; this lifts the curtain briefly on the man behind the teaching. *They* present the revelation of God to us; this letter shows us the kind of man to whom God entrusts that revelation.

A few minutes' thought will, I think, suffice to confirm this. In 1 Corinthians 1 Paul writes of God's choice of 'the weak things'; 2 Corinthians shows us the grim reality, in Paul himself, of a divinely imposed weakness. In 1 Corinthians 3 Paul is appealing for unity; 2 Corinthians 1 reveals that, for all their rebuffs, he who so strongly exhorted them against factions still counted himself one of them. Further on in 1 Corinthians, after some exceedingly firm dealing with the irregularities at Corinth, Paul follows in chapter 13 with his classic treatment of love; but in 2 Corinthians 2 he explains, concerning the apparent harshness of that earlier letter, how 'out of much affliction and anguish of heart I wrote unto you with many tears; not that ye should be made sorry, but that ye might know the love which I have more abundantly unto you.' Later still, in 1 Corinthians 16, Paul has to exhort his readers to a practical care for the needs of others; while 2 Corinthians 11 lets us into the secret of how he himself acted in money matters. For it is a principle that there never was a man not clear in respect of money who could really serve God; he who is wrong there is wrong everywhere. Finally, and most relevant to our present purpose, 1 Corinthians 15 gives us the clearest teaching in the New Testament on the subject of the resurrection; but already 2 Corinthians 1 finds Paul himself despairing even of life, 'that we should not trust in ourselves, but in God which raiseth the dead'.

For Paul, doctrine is everywhere backed by experience. Nothing else constitutes any basis for ministry, whatever men may think about it to-day. A ministry that is built upon mere theory leads only to impoverishment; a ministry of life springs essentially from experience. 1 Corinthians is concerned with gifts and preaching, 2 Corinthians with life. Because the death of Christ works in him, Paul has life; and because he has life, others have life. The ministry of 1 Corinthians, and indeed of all his epistles, is based on the man of 2 Corinthians.

THE TREASURE IN THE EARTHEN VESSEL

Now let us go further, and turn our attention to something that arises out of all this, namely the element, already alluded to, of seeming contradiction in Paul.

As we read 2 Corinthians carefully we seem to meet two persons: Paul in himself, and Paul in Christ. Those who observed him found him an anomaly. Lowly and weak in bodily presence, unskilled and of no account in speech, yet somehow he was confident and of good courage, rich in knowledge and strong and weighty in his letters (see 10, 1, 10; 11. 6), and his dealings with men were always marked by consistency, a fact made possible by his steadfast resolve to know them no longer 'after the flesh' but always only in Christ (1. 17; 5. 16). Inwardly, too, there was the same seeming contradiction in his make-up, as becomes abundantly clear in several passages where he uses the significant words, 'but', 'yet', 'nevertheless'. 'We despaired', he writes; 'we that are in this tabernacle do groan; we were afflicted; without were fightings, within were fears; *nevertheless* God comforted us—God who raiseth the dead.' (See 1. 8, 9; 5. 4; 7. 5, 6.)

And not only was this dual consciousness a present experience with him at the time he wrote 2 Corinthians, but there are two great passages which show that it was a usual experience. (See 4. 8–10; 6. 8–10.) Indeed almost everything Paul speaks of, from the opening chapter of the Epistle to its conclusion, is in this one strain. There is one governing principle throughout, which we may best summarize in his own words: 'We have this treasure in earthen vessels, that the exceeding greatness of the power may be of God, and not from ourselves' (4. 7). In the very first chapter we see 'this treasure' in an earthen vessel, and right to the last chapter we keep meeting the earthen vessel—but we keep meeting the treasure also.

'We have this treasure in earthen vessels.' This is possibly the clearest statement there is of the nature of practical Christianity. Christianity is not the earthen vessel, nor is it the treasure, but it is *the treasure in the earthen vessel*.

All people, whether Christians or not, have their ideal man. All have their own particular conceptions of what constitutes a good man. They think that if a man does such-and-such things, or behaves in some particular way, or if he *is* a certain kind of person, that man is good. We have each a set standard in our minds, and if a man measures up to that we call him a 'good' man. Before we were saved we had a certain standard, but of course after our salvation we came to see that many whom we admired before were not really to be admired. We judge them now by our new-found light, and we see that they come short. Our scale of measurement has altered.

We even had our ideas about Christ. Before we were saved we had certain opinions about Him, but after our salvation those opinions were all thrown out of gear as the Holy Spirit opened our eyes to something of His true nature. As a result, we now have a new standard of Christian living, and we make that on the one hand the goal towards which we ourselves strive and on the other hand the measure by which we judge others. So far so good; but when all this has been said, I want to suggest to you that God's thoughts as to what constitutes a true Christian may even yet take more into account than ours do, and that as a consequence He may require us still further to adjust our thinking regarding ourselves and others.

What is our conception of holiness? Too readily we think of it as the absence of the earthen vessel. We imagine that if we can reach a stage where we have, ourselves, so controlled our affections and emotions that there is virtually no more trace of them, then we have attained to holiness. We fancy that to suppress our feelings, so as to be insensible to suffering or untouched by natural relationships, is a proof of spirituality. In effect, we think that to become spiritual is to cease to be human, and many of us are engaged in covering over the earthen vessel in the mistaken idea that, if it can no longer be seen, that is holiness.

You can tell at once when someone is doing this because he is so unnatural. He dare not let himself go. He dare not speak or act freely, lest the earthen vessel be disclosed. But such a man does not know what true Christianity is. He is artificial, and he uses his artificiality to conceal his actual condition. He schools himself so that the earthen vessel shall not appear. And alas, many think that if only they can get to the state where they do not care what is done or said in their presence, they have indeed attained to Christian holiness.

When I first became a Christian, I too had my own conception of what a Christian was, and I tried my utmost to be that kind of Christian. I thought that if only I could attain to the standard I had conceived, I should have achieved my object. To be a true Christian was my sincere ambition, but of course I had my own mentality as to what that meant. I thought a true Christian should smile from morning to night! If at any time he shed a tear, he had ceased to be victorious. I thought, too, that a true Christian must be an unfailingly courageous person. If under any circumstances he showed the slightest sign of fear, I reasoned that he failed seriously, in that he lacked the faith to trust the Lord. He had in fact fallen short of my standard.

I retained these clearly defined ideas as to what a Christian should be until, one day, I read 2 Corinthians and came to the passage where Paul said he was sad. 'As sorrowful . . .', I read (6. 10), and I was arrested. 'Paul sorrowful!' I thought. Then I read that he shed 'many tears' (2. 4), and I wondered, 'Can it actually be that Paul wept?' I read that he was 'perplexed' (4. 8), and I thought 'Was Paul *really* perplexed?' And I read this: 'We were weighed down exceedingly, beyond our power, so that we despaired even of life' (1. 8); and I asked myself, amazed, 'Is it possible that Paul even *despaired*?' It had never occurred to me that a person like Paul could have such experiences as these; but as I read on I gradually awakened to the fact that Christians are not another order of angelic beings, incapable of human feeling, and I saw that, after all, Paul was not so very remote from us. In fact I discovered that Paul was *a man*, and the very sort of man I knew.

Numbers of people have their own conceptions of a Christian, but these conceptions are one-sided, because they are just a creation of the human mind; they are not a creation of God. In Paul I meet 'this treasure', but, praise God, I also meet 'an earthen vessel'! And this, I repeat, is the distinctive feature of Christianity, that 'we have this treasure in earthen vessels'. Here is a man who is afraid and yet determined; he is encompassed by foes and yet he is not bound; he seems about to be overcome and yet he is not destroyed. It is plain enough that he is weak, and yet he declares that just when he is weak he is strong. You can see that he bears in his body the dying of Jesus and yet he regards this as the very ground for the manifesting of the life of Jesus in his mortal body.

For appearances are not the whole story. Behind the man himself, and giving the lie to those appearances, there is the exceeding greatness of the power which is of God. Men may behold him 'as deceiver, as unknown, as sorrowful, as poor, as having nothing, yes, as dying' even—and notwithstanding all this, God will support his bold assertion: '. . . and yet true, well-known, always rejoicing, making many rich, possessing all things: Behold we live!' (See 2 Cor. 6. 8–10.)

POWER IN WEAKNESS

Do you begin now to understand what it means to be a Christian? To be a Christian is to be a person in whom seeming incompatibles exist together, but in whom it is the power of God that repeatedly triumphs. A Christian is one in whose life there is inherent a mysterious paradox; and this paradox is of God. Some people conceive of Christianity as being all treasure and no vessel. If sometimes the earthen vessel is evident in a servant of God, they feel he is a hopeless case, whereas God's conception is that, in that very vessel, His treasure should be found.

At this point we must distinguish carefully between man, and 'the flesh' in man—between the limitation that is inherent in our being human at all, and the carnal nature of man with its inveterate tendency to sin, a tendency that leaves us (apart from the help of the Holy Spirit) totally powerless to please God. This distinction is the more important because of the ease with which, even in a child of God, the one leads over into the other, and human nature in us gives way to carnal nature. Let it be quite clear, therefore, that I certainly do not mean in this chapter to excuse or condone sin or carnality. The flesh is to be withstood and given over to death—the death of the cross. (I have developed this theme at greater length elsewhere.[2]) But weakness, in this other sense, is to remain. Our

---

[2] *The Normal Christian Life*, Chapters 9 and 10.

blessed Lord Himself was for our sakes 'crucified through weakness', yet lives through the power of God (2 Cor. 13. 4); and as for ourselves, it is in our very weakness that *His* power is to be made perfect. There is therefore an 'infirmity' in which it is possible to glory (12. 9).

So Paul tells us that he had 'a thorn in the flesh'. What it was I do not know, but I do know that it greatly weakened him, and that three times he prayed for its removal. But for answer, God only assured him: 'My grace is sufficient for thee'. Only that—but that was enough.

How can the Lord's power be manifested to perfection in a weak man? By Christianity; for Christianity *is* that very thing. Christianity is not the removal of weakness, nor is it merely the manifestation of divine power. It is the manifestation of divine power *in the presence of* human weakness. Let us be clear on this point. What the Lord is doing is no merely negative thing—that is to say, the elimination of our infirmity. Nor, for that matter, is it merely positive—the bestowal of strength anywhere at random. No, He leaves us with the infirmity, and he bestows the strength *there*. He is bestowing His strength upon men, but that strength is manifested *in* their weakness. All the treasure He gives is placed in earthen vessels.

FAITH IN THE PRESENCE OF DOUBT

What we have just said is strikingly true of faith. Numbers of people have come to me and told of their fears and misgivings even whilst they have sought to trust the Lord. They have made their requests, they have laid hold of the promises of God, and yet doubts continually arise unbidden. Let me tell you, the treasure of true faith appears in a vessel that may be sorely assailed by doubt, and the earthen vessel, by its presence, does not nullify the treasure; rather does the treasure in such an environment shine forth with enhanced beauty. Do not misunderstand me, I am not encouraging doubt. Doubt is a mark of deficiency in a Christian; but I do wish to make this clear, that Christianity is not a matter of faith only, but of faith triumphing in the presence of doubt.

I love to recall the prayer of the early church for Peter's deliverance from the hands of wicked men. When Peter came back from the prison and knocked at the door where the church was at prayer, the believers exclaimed, 'It is his angel'. Do you see? There was faith there, true faith, the kind of faith that could bring an answer from God; and yet the weakness of man was still present, and doubt lurked just around the corner, as it were. But to-day the faith many of God's people claim to exercise is greater than that exercised by the believers gathered in the house of Mary the mother of John Mark. And they are so positive about it! They are certain God will send an angel, and that every door in the prison will swing open before him. If a gust of wind blows: 'There's Peter knocking at the door!' If the rain begins to patter: 'There's Peter knocking again!'

These people are too credulous, too cock-sure. Their faith is not necessarily the genuine article. Even in the most devoted Christian, the earthen vessel is always there, and, at least to himself, it is always in evidence, though the determining factor is never the vessel but the treasure within. In the life of a normal Christian, just when faith rises positively to lay hold of God, a question may simultaneously arise as to whether perhaps he might be mistaken. When he is strongest in the Lord he is often most conscious of inability; when he is most courageous he may be most aware of fear within; and where he is most joyful a sense of distress readily enough breaks upon him again. Only the exceeding greatness of the power lifts him on high. But this paradox is itself evidence, both that there is a treasure, and that it is where God would have it be.

It must ever be a cause for great gratitude to God that no merely human weakness need limit divine power. We are apt to think that where sadness exists joy cannot exist; that where there are tears there cannot be praise; that where weakness is apparent power must be lacking; that when we are surrounded by foes we must be hemmed in; that where there is doubt there can be no faith. But let me proclaim strongly and with confidence that God is seeking to bring us to the point where everything human is only intended to provide an earthen vessel to

contain the divine treasure. Henceforth, when we are conscious of depression, let us not give way to that depression but
give way to the Lord; when doubt or fear arises in our hearts,
let us not yield to these but to the Lord, and the treasure will
shine forth all the more gloriously because of the earthen
vessel.

JOY AMID PAIN

In the last of his letters, Paul writes to Timothy of the perils
of the 'last days'. He warns them that grievous times will
come, when men will be (among other things) *without natural
affection* (2 Tim. 3. 1-3). This is something of which we ought
to take note. Here is a danger of the last days of this age—that
men will have no feelings, no natural sensitivity, no human
affections. This is of course a non-Christian state of affairs. An
extreme example of it is that of a modern society of which I
have heard, which, it is said, made one of the qualifications of
its active agents that they should have killed one of their near-
est and dearest. Yet these verses to Timothy are written for
Christians, not for unbelievers. Are we to conclude, then, that
this state of affairs will have invaded Christianity and be found
among believers in the end times? It may be so, and that men
will come to the place where they disclaim responsibility for
parents, wives or children, and *think that in so doing they are
being good Christians.*

Of course, it is true that the Lord Jesus said: 'If any man
cometh unto me, and hateth not his own father, and mother,
and wife, and children, and brethren, and sisters, yea, and his
own life also, he cannot be my disciple' (Luke 14. 25, 26). Yes,
He said that, but He certainly did *not* say, as some even in our
day have seemed to think, that only those who *rejoiced* to leave
father and mother and wife and children could be disciples of
His. In the name of service to the Lord, people have deserted
their own kindred and dependents out of sheer heartlessness,
and not out of love for Him. 'I am so spiritual', they say, 'that
I don't want anything to do with my family'. I knew a
Chinese brother who claimed to be very devoted to the Lord
because he did not mind leaving his family and going off to

serve Him in the Gospel, when all of us knew that, as a matter
of fact, he had never truly cared for them. This kind of thing
is all too common, and God has no place for it.

True spirituality is to *care*, but yet to let the Cross of Christ
deal with the things that stand in the way of the will of God.
That is to say, we go forth because the Lord calls us, and not
because we are glad of an easy escape from our home responsibilities. It is a fairly safe rule that if there is *no cost* in going
forth for Him, something is wrong and the move is not a spiritual move. There is a place for the family life to be sanctified
and held in honour *and yet* for the natural strength in us of the
carnal life and affections to be touched and dealt with by God.

For remember again, God looks for the treasure *in the vessel*.
Here is Christianity, not that we camouflage the vessel by
steeling ourselves to suppress all feeling, but that we let the
earthen vessel be seen with the treasure inside. It is not a case
of getting through painful situations because one has become
insensible to pain, but of retaining full consciousness and being
carried through by Another, despite the feeling of pain. The
earthen vessel is there, but the treasure is also there. What is
the treasure? It is the life of the Lord Jesus—the triumphant life
of Him who 'wept' and 'groaned within himself', and who
'sighed deeply in his spirit' and was 'exceeding sorrowful, even
unto death' (See: John 11. 33, 35, 38; 12. 27; 13. 21; Mark 8.
12; Matt. 26. 37, 38).

Yes, our humanity is an earthen vessel. Wherein, then, do
we differ as Christians from other vessels? Not by any difference in the material of the vessel, but by the difference of its
content. The only thing that distinguishes us in the miracle of
the treasure enshrined within.

I knew a brother who was very attached to his wife. On
one occasion it had been arranged that he should go on a
preaching tour that would keep him away from home for
some months, and it happened that, at the time he was due to
leave, his wife was in poor health, having been confined only
six days before. A friend sent me with a letter to him, and as
I turned into his street and drew near his house, he came out
with a man carrying his luggage. I saw him, but he did not see

me. I watched him come out and walk a little distance, then stop and look back at his house, and then after a little hesitation begin to return slowly. I did not wait longer, but sensing some conflict in his spirit I went ahead to the river-boat by another route, as I did not wish to intrude by going down with him. When he arrived at the boat I said to him, 'Brother, may the Lord bless you'. He seemed quite happy, and replied: 'Yes, may the Lord indeed bless us.'

When after some months he came back from the tour, I asked him if he remembered the incident, explaining what I had seen without his noticing me. He said: 'Of course I remember. It was just six days after the birth of the baby; my wife had no servant, and there were the two other little children to look after. Added to that, I had not been able to leave much money with her. As I stood there I felt I *could* not leave her like that; it was cruel to do so. But as I was retracing my steps that verse came to me: "No man, having put his hand to the plough, and looking back, is fit for the kingdom of God." So I turned again, and went down to the boat.'

I like to tell that story, because it illustrates so clearly what is the earthen vessel and what is the treasure within. 'Your body is a temple of the Holy Ghost which is in you' (1 Cor. 6. 19). That is the Christian life. Some people do not seem to have any earthen vessel; they are disembodied spirits, not human beings—or at least that is what they try to be! But to hold on to the plough whilst wiping our tears—this is Christianity. It is the transcending of the earthen vessel by the treasure within.

ANGER WITHOUT SIN

Finally, I want to apply this principle practically along a rather different line. For Scripture occasionally indicates a positive sense in which this duality of our existence on earth— the human vessel and the spiritual life planted within it by new birth—should operate. In Ephesians 4. 26, 27 the apostle Paul says: 'Be ye angry, and sin not'. What do we know of this? Of course, to get angry and sin is always wrong; but how many of us think that the only way to avoid sinning is not to get angry! We simply do not know *how* to get angry and yet not sin.

Here again it is most helpful to look at the humanity of the Lord Jesus. When He crossed the sea with the disciples in the storm, we read that they were afraid and cried out. What did the Lord do? He did not just help them in their need; we read that He also rebuked them, saying: 'Why are ye fearful, O ye of little faith?' (Matt. 8. 26). I am glad the Lord could feel things strongly and could speak such plain words. How many saints throughout the centuries have been helped by that challenge! Again, when the disciples brought to Jesus the lunatic boy, He said: 'O faithless and perverse generation, how long shall I be with you? How long shall I bear with you?' (Matt. 17. 17). How many of us have been stirred too by these words to seek to learn the lesson of that incident!

To the Pharisees, when the occasion demanded, He could speak with tremendous force: 'Woe unto you, ye blind guides!' 'Ye have made void the word of God because of your tradition. Ye hypocrites!' (Matt. 15. 6; 23. 16 ff). And when He went into the temple and cast out those that sold and bought, and overthrew the tables of the money-changers, it was said of Him: 'The zeal of thy house hath eaten me up' (John 2. 17). He was stirred with indignation. But alas, how few Christians know that Spirit-controlled stirring within that the Lord knew, and consequently, how few know anything of the spiritual authority that accompanied it! Yet there was no contradiction in Him. He could declaim: 'Woe unto thee, Chorazin! woe unto thee, Bethsaida!' and yet we read that, at that very season (and without inconsistency), 'He rejoiced in the Holy Spirit, and said, I thank thee, O Father, Lord of heaven and earth' (Luke 10. 13. 21; cf. Matt. 11. 20–25).

The point is this, that there exists for Christians an anger which is apart from sin, and yet even sincere Christians often do not understand how to distinguish sin from anger and so they cast both away. There are many things in the world which ought to be rebuked, but how many really know how to administer that rebuke? Alas, very few. We have lost that power. To clap a man on the shoulder when he is wrong, while turning a blind eye to his deeds for the sake of his friendship, is a cheap way out. To rebuke him may be costly, but the Lord may require it of us.

Why cannot we rebuke? Because almost always, in doing so, we expose ourselves in turn to rebuke, for we do not know how to get angry without yielding to sin. We are not truly under the Holy Spirit's constraint in this as we should be. Indeed many of us have not gone the way that makes that constraint possible. For anger that is without sin is always costly, presupposing as it does God's initial dealing with us by the Cross. In our own thoughts and emotions (as we are by nature, and apart from the Spirit of God), sin and anger are indeed inseparable, for unlike that of the Lord Jesus, our humanity is a fallen humanity, our flesh a sinful flesh. In us there is a basic contradiction where in Him there was none, and if we yield to anger we shall surely sin.

Yet to be angry without committing sin is not only a possibility; it is a command. 'Be ye angry, and sin not; let not the sun go down upon your wrath: neither give place to the devil' (Eph. 4. 26, 27). Implied in these words is one secret of being angry and yet not sinning, namely, to see that we do not sustain our anger until the evening. In other words we are not to enter into it. If we harbour wrath after the event, it is evidence that the thing has touched us; and when we are touched by it, then be sure there is sin. So here God has set for us a helpful time-limit: we may be stirred to wrath, but we are not to allow the sun to go down upon it. Anger can be free from sin when, being full of anger, we are yet under divine control, so that when the time comes for the anger to stop, it stops. It is when we enter in and take hold that anger cannot be stopped.

Most of the Lord's children know that anger is a human emotion, and when justifiably angry they know that it is wrong to give way to it by letting it be prolonged. In spite of this there are, sadly enough, all too many who repeatedly give it rein and let their emotions get quite out of control. But at the other extreme are some who have sought escape from the problem by trying to suppress all natural emotion in themselves. Things can go past such people, and they contrive to remain aloof and quite untouched by them. Now of course, the first of these extremes we can justly see reason to blame, but we do not so easily see that the second also is a too easy escape from responsibility. We are not meant, by gripping tight on to ourselves, to suppress all human emotion until we end up frigid as ice. Indeed those who achieve that state are a constant drain on others around them, who must somehow make good from their side the deficiency in 'natural affection' if relationships are to remain even reasonably comfortable. No, we must rather allow God's Holy Spirit to make His own use of our emotions and powers of expression. Of course it is true that *He* must be in command. Of course we must *have* the divine treasure—yes, but not in cold storage! We need, along with it, the simple earthen vessel that should contain it and through which it should express itself.

To be angry and sin, is sin; but I repeat, there *is* an anger that is without sin. We can be angry and yet have love in our hearts. It is perfectly possible to be aroused to anger and yet to weep for those towards whom that anger is stirred. Paul could weep, but he could still be firm. 'I made you sorry with my epistle', he writes. 'Who is made to stumble, and I burn not?' And again: 'If I come again, I will not spare'. (2 Cor. 7. 8; 11. 29; 13. 2). God wants that earthen vessel, not covered or camouflaged, but *controlled by the treasure*.

Herein lies the glory of Christianity, that God's treasure can be manifest in every humblest vessel of clay. Christianity is a paradox, and it is as we Christians live this paradoxical life that we get to know God. Indeed, the further we go on in the Christian life the more paradoxical it becomes. The treasure becomes increasingly manifest, but the earthen vessel is the earthen vessel still. This is very beautiful. See the divine patience in a man who by nature was impatient, and compare the sight of that with a man whom nothing could ever move. See the divine humility in one who was by nature haughty, and compare that with one who was always of a retiring disposition. See the strength of God in a person of weak temperament, and compare that with a naturally strong character. The difference is immeasurable.

People who are naturally weak are apt to underrate their value to the Lord, just because of the very evident earthenness of their vessel. But where is the ground for dejection, when the treasure within is of such a nature as to acquire added splendour from the very fact that it shines forth from such a vessel? Brothers and sisters, let me say once again, the whole question is one of the quality of the treasure, not of the deficiencies of the vessel that contains it. It is folly to stress the negative side; our concern is with the positive. There are some Christians of whom we can readily see that they are quick or slow, fearful or impulsive, credulous or impatient, by nature. Yet—and this is the miracle—there is at the same time present in them a precious treasure which, because the mark of the Cross is upon their human frailty, shines triumphantly through it all. The exceeding greatness of the power is not of ourselves—but of God.

CHAPTER FIVE

GOD'S SURE FOUNDATION

THE autobiographical sections in 2 Corinthians have brought to our attention an aspect of the Christian's personal walk with his Lord that is there thrown into relief by the apostle's account of his experiences as a minister of the Gospel. Coming now to what we regard as the peculiar and characteristic element in Paul's ministry, we will begin by turning back to his letter to the Romans, and especially to its later sections. Chapter 12 of that letter opens with an appeal to us to present ourselves as servants to the will of God. Such a consecration is the 'reasonable' outcome of all that he has said up to that point, both as to personal faith and divine election. Immediately upon that, we find him alluding to 'the Body of Christ', and this term best covers the topic of study immediately before us. 'We are one body in Christ', he says, 'and severally members one of another.' What does he mean?

From eternity there has been, he explains, something held in the very heart of God, which the incarnate Son of God was anointed to bring to realization. He speaks of it as a 'mystery' —that is to say, a divine secret, held in reserve through the ages and only now made known by God to His servants through 'the preaching of Jesus Christ' in this new day of the Spirit (Rom. 16. 25, 26). Its unfolding presents us with a fundamental difference between our idea of salvation and God's—between our conception of the redemptive work of the Cross and the full divine conception.

As we said above in speaking of chapters 1–8 of Romans, we all of us believe that the Cross of Christ is central to the whole work of God, and we praise God for making this fact clear to our hearts. But we must remember that the Cross was and is a means to an end, never an end in itself. The divine end to which it is intended to lead is this that Paul terms 'the Body of Christ'. If we know the Cross in the way in which God means it to be known, we shall inevitably find ourselves within the Body. It cannot be otherwise. If we are not there in spirit, we shall have to confess that in us the Cross has as yet done only a part of its transforming work.

Salvation, forgiveness, justification, deliverance, personal holiness, victorious living, walking after the Spirit: all these most precious fruits of redemption are ours to enjoy, but they are not meant to apply to us merely as so many myriads of separate units, scattered over this earth for God. Their values are intended to go further than that. Salvation is in terms of the Body, deliverance is in terms of the Body, personal holiness is in terms of the Body. It may be true that the children of Abraham are as the sand on the sea-shore in multitude. Nevertheless, as Christians, God would have us see ourselves not as men but as a Man. The goal of the divine thought is in fact one heavenly Man, not a host of little men.

One day, I confess, I could not resist saying this in answer to a questioner when I was preaching the Gospel in a Chinese village. A scholar had been listening attentively, and after a while remarked, 'Mr. Nee, you preach your religion to bring us poor sinners to heaven; but I do not think *I* will get in there at all. It will be far too crowded!' In the circumstances, my reply to this was hardly a fair one, and looking back I fear that, apart from the Spirit's help, its point must have been largely lost on him. 'You are wrong,' I said. 'Heaven will never be crowded. Throughout heaven there will only be one Man, not two, and certainly not a crowd! The only Man in heaven is God's one new Man—God's Son Himself and those who by faith are in Him. *That* is where He wants you!' And of course that is true. God views His people not as unrelated units but as that one heavenly Man: Christ the Head, and we the members. This was the discovery the apostle Paul had made.

He does not tell us how this new revelation of Christ came to him. Indeed, though he was a man of deep experience and of much secret history with God, it is remarkable that he keeps

very quiet about the nature and means of his 'visions and revelations of the Lord'. It would not be profitable, he said, for
him to boast of them, and only against his desires and under
strong compulsion of circumstances did he speak of the visions
of 'a man in Christ, fourteen years ago' (2 Cor. 12. 1, 2). Fourteen years! And yet with many of us, directly we have something from God, the whole of Shanghai knows it! To suppress it even for two years would be a feat. But Paul, even
after fourteen years, does not tell us *what* that vision was, save
that it was a further revelation of Jesus Christ. What is clear,
however, is that it made a deep impression on him, and there is
no doubt that what he saw came out in practical terms in his
ministry.

THE CROSS AND THE BODY

'Now in Christ Jesus ye . . . are made nigh by the blood of
Christ. For he is our peace, who made both [Jew and Gentile]
one . . . that he might create in himself of the twain one new
man . . . and might reconcile them both in one body unto God
through the cross' (See Eph. 2. 11–22). What, we must ask
ourselves, is this 'one body', this 'one new man'? What is this
mystery of Christ that Paul has come to see?

In Romans 6. 6 he has spoken of 'our old man', by which he
means everything that comes to us from 'the first man, Adam';
and he sees this 'old man' as having been nailed to the cross
with Christ. In Colossians 3. 11, 12 he speaks of 'the new man'
as the sphere where now 'there cannot be Greek and Jew . . .
but Christ is all and in all'. For our old man there was only
crucifixion with Christ; in the new Man we are found in
union with Him, risen and ascended. Between the one and the
other towers the Cross as the only gateway into this fellowship
with one another in Jesus Christ.

You ask me, what do I mean when I use the term 'the Cross'
in this way? I think it is best summed up in the words the
crowd used of its Victim: 'Away with him!' Crucifixion
humanly speaking, is an end. The Cross of Christ is intended
by God to be, first of all, the end of everything in man that has
come under His sentence of death, for there it was that He

took our place, and the judgment of God was fulfilled upon Him.

But the Cross has a further value for us, for it is there also that the Christian believer's self-sufficient and individualistic natural life is broken, as Jacob's strength and independence of nature were broken at Jabbok. There comes a day in God's dealings with each of us when we suffer in our souls that incapacitating wound, and ever afterwards 'go halting'. God never allows this to remain for us a mere theory. Alas, I must confess that for many years it *was* no more than theory to me. I myself had 'preached the Cross' in this very sense, yet without knowing anything of it in my own experience—until one day I *saw* that it had been I, Nee To-sheng, who died there with Christ. 'Away with him!' they had said, and in saying it they unwittingly echoed God's verdict upon *my* old man. And that sentence upon me was carried out *in Him*. This tremendous discovery affected me almost as greatly as did my first discovery of salvation. I tell you, it left me for seven whole months so humbled as to be quite unable to preach at all, whereas for long, I have to confess, preaching had been my consuming passion.

But if to see this somewhat negative aspect of the Cross can be so drastic an experience, it is not surprising that its positive aspect—the revelation to our hearts of the heavenly Body of Christ—has proved for many to be no less revolutionary. For it is like suddenly finding yourself in a place which you have hitherto known only by hearsay. And how different the reality proves! Reading a guide to London is no substitute for visiting that city. Nor can a book of recipes take the place of a spell of work in the kitchen. To know anything experimentally, we must sooner or later find ourselves personally involved in it.

Yes, there are certain fundamental experiences we must have, and this 'seeing' of the Body of Christ, the heavenly Man is one such. What is it? It is simply a discovery of values that, as I have said, lie on the resurrection side of the Cross. There, what has been for us already a way of release *from* our old selfish 'natural life' in Adam becomes the gateway *into* the

new, shared 'everlasting life' in Christ. For unlike other
Roman crucifixions, the Cross of Christ is not just an end; it is
also a beginning. In His death and resurrection, our disunion
gives way to oneness of life in Him.

God is not satisfied with single, separate Christians. When
we believed on the Lord and partook of Him we became
members of His Body. Oh that God would cause this fact to
break upon us! Do I seek spiritual experiences for myself? Do
I make converts for my denomination? Or have I caught the
wisdom of the one heavenly Man, and realized that God is
seeking to bring men into that? When I do, salvation, deliverance, enduement with the Spirit, yes, everything in Christian
experience will be seen from a new viewpoint, everything for
me will be transformed.

We shall now seek to develop some aspects of this subject
further. In the New Testament we find the Church variously
described, as a spiritual house or temple ('a habitation of God
through the Spirit'), as a body or a man ('the Body of Christ',
'one new man'), and as a wife ('a bride adorned for her husband'), and we must keep these analogies in mind in what
follows. In the remainder of this chapter we shall speak of the
Church's foundation, and then, in four subsequent chapters,
we shall touch in turn upon her eternal character, her fellowship, her ministries, and her present high calling and task. We
shall not, even then, have finished with this matter of the
Church, for so great is its significance to God that, when we
come to the ministry of the apostle John, we cannot fail to see
the large place it takes at the end.

UPON THIS ROCK

'According to the grace of God which was given unto me,
as a wise masterbuilder I laid a foundation', writes Paul to the
Corinthians. What was this foundation of which he speaks?
It was certainly nothing peculiar to Paul, nor did it originate
with him. It was something which the apostles had in common, and we must turn back briefly to the Gospels and to the
words of the Lord Jesus Himself for a first definition of it.

Hear Him at Cæsarea Philippi, as He addresses Simon Peter in these remarkable terms; 'Thou art Peter, and upon this rock I will build my church' (Matt. 16. 18).

It is important to understand this passage, for as we shall see, it really defines the point from which, later, Paul in his turn begins. What did Jesus imply? Thou art *Petros*, a stone—one who is to be builded with others into the basic structure of My Church (see Eph. 2. 20; Rev. 21. 19)—and on this Rock I will build. What then is the Church? It is a structure of living stones founded upon a rock. And what is the rock? Here it is that we need to be very clear. It is a *confession* based upon a *revelation* of a *Person*.

Jesus, who never seemed to care what men said or thought about Him, suddenly put the question to His disciples: 'Who do men say that I, the Son of Man, am?' Then, turning from the views and speculations of others, He went a step further: 'Who say ye that I am?' His challenge drew forth spontaneously from Peter the historic confession: '*Thou art the Christ, the Son of the living God*'. Thus it is true to say that the Church is built upon a confession, for to 'say' is to confess, not merely to hazard an opinion. Moreover it was no empty confession such as might to-day be based on study or deduction or 'point of view'. As Jesus made clear, Peter's confession was called forth by a God-given revelation. 'Flesh and blood hath not revealed it unto thee, but my Father which is in heaven.' And further, it was a revelation of the true character and meaning of Jesus, and not merely of facts about Him—not merely, that is, of what the Gospels tell us He did, but of what and who He is. As to His person, He is the Son of the living God; as to His office and ministry, He is the Christ. All this was contained in Peter's words.

This dual discovery was later, as we have said, to become Paul's starting-point. Read again, for example, his opening words to the Romans. The Jesus whom he had persecuted is now, he affirms, 'declared the Son of God with power, according to the spirit of holiness, by the resurrection of the dead; even Jesus Christ our Lord' (Rom. 1. 4). All he writes to the churches is founded upon this revelation concerning Jesus.

From everlasting to everlasting He is the Son of God: that is the first thing. But there came a day when, taking upon Himself the form of a servant, He became also the Christ, the Anointed One, God's Minister. All God's purpose, all God's hopes are bound up with that risen Christ. It is He who has been separated and anointed as God's sure foundation.

But if He is the foundation, we are the living stones. To recognize Christ is to recognize also the Christians, and God's plan through them for the universe. For we shall be of little use to God if we know only our salvation, and have caught no glimpse of the purpose for which He has brought us into relation to His Son. How many claim to have the anointing of the Spirit, and yet seem quite unaware that the object for which the Spirit is given to Christ and to His members is one and the same! It is directed to one and the same divine end. To see this is suddenly to see the extreme smallness of all our work that in the past has been unrelated to that end.

Let us be clear about this fact, that the Church is not merely a company of people whose sins are forgiven and who are going to heaven; it is a company of those whose eyes have been opened by God to recognize the person and work of the Son. This is something far more than man can see or know or handle—far more, even, than the outward experiences of those disciples who for three years, as His constant companions, ate and slept, walked and lived with Him. Truly theirs was a great happiness, and how many of us would not gladly exchange places with Peter for a few days? But even their experience did not unite them with Him as a part of the Church. Only revelation from God as to who Christ is can do that to you and me. The Rock is Christ—yes, but a revealed Christ not a theoretical or doctrinal Christ. Twenty years among Christians and a lifetime of exercise in theology will not build us into His Church. It is inner, not outer knowledge that brings that about. 'This is life eternal, that they should know thee the only true God, and him whom thou didst send, even Jesus Christ' (John 17. 3).

'No man knoweth who the Son is save the Father' (Luke 10. 22). Flesh and blood cannot know the man God has estab-

lished. Yet He must be known, for the Church's foundation
is not only Christ but the knowledge of Christ. And the
tragedy to-day is that many in the churches—indeed many so-
called churches—lack such foundation. But theory will not
prevail against hell, which is what Jesus declares His Church
must do. Have we perhaps forgotten what we are for? Visiting Western homes I have sometimes seen a beautiful porcelain plate, not put to use on the table but wired and hung up to
the wall as an ornament. It seems to me that many think of
the Church rather like that, as something to be admired for the
perfection of its form and pattern. But no, God's Church is
for use, not decoration. Head-knowledge, instruction, order,
may produce an appearance of life when conditions are favourable, but when the gates of hell come out against us they all
too soon disclose to us our true state. Very many saw,
followed, pressed upon, were touched and healed by Jesus, but
did not know Him. Yet to one who followed, these words
were said: 'On this Rock I will build'. We may think we are
just as good as—even possibly a little better than—Peter. He
was tempted and fell. Yes, but was he not better in his fall
than many who never do so? He denied—but he could weep.
For he *knew*. Many do not fall, but neither do they know.

It is first-hand knowledge that counts in the hour of testing.
I do not mean that members of the Church should not help
each other; but what is merely passed on from man to man is
of little use if there be, with it, no revelation from heaven. It
will not stand the fire. That is why in our word for a martyr,
hsuin taochoe, 'one slain for a doctrine', I think *tao* is wrong, for
who ever dies for a doctrine? At one time I used to fear lest
a modernist should come along and prove to me that the Bible
was unreliable, and with it therefore the historic facts in which
my faith was founded. If he did, I thought, that would finish
everything; and I *wanted* to believe. But now everything is
peaceful. If men were to bring as many arguments as there are
shells in the armouries of Europe, it would make not the least
difference to me—for I know! The knowledge we get from
men may deceive us. At best it is imperfect, and however
good it be, we may forget it. But the Father revealed the Son

He knew to Peter. This revelation is Christianity. There is no Church without it. I, from within, recognize Jesus as Son of God, and as Christ—that is the heart of everything. The response of Jesus to Peter was not 'You have answered correctly' but 'God has shown that to you!'

Thus the Rock defines the limits of the Church. They extend wherever such a confession goes up to God from the heart —there and no further. For remember, this was not a general confession; it sprang from revelation. And not from a general revelation either, but one that concerned a Man, the Son of man. Nothing gives God greater satisfaction than confession of Himself. Jesus often said 'I am'. He loves to hear us say 'Thou art'. We do it far too little. 'Thou art Lord!' When everything goes wrong and all is confusion, don't pray, but confess that Jesus is Lord. Today, when the world is in turmoil, stand and proclaim that Jesus is King of kings and Lord of lords. He loves to hear us say what we *know*. The Church is not only founded on revelation but on confession—on our speaking out what we know of God. The Church to-day is Christ's voice set down here upon the earth.

If God has not opened our eyes to see that death is the power, the weapon, of the gates of hell, we shall scarcely know the value of speaking out. But when suddenly, in some hitherto unforeseen circumstance, we find to our alarm that apparently faith does not work, prayer does not work, we shall learn the need to proclaim Christ, and in doing so shall discover what it was God was waiting for. 'Thou art Lord. Thou art Victor. Thou art King.' The best prayer of all is not 'I want' but 'Thou art'. By the revelation given to us, let us speak. In prayer meetings, at the Breaking of Bread, alone before the Lord, in the midst of the thronging world, or in the dark hour of need, learn to proclaim 'Thou art'. This is the Church's voice, God's voice in the earth, the voice that, above all else, hell fears.

HEAVENLY WISDOM

The apostle Paul stands in the main stream of a long line of men to whom God was pleased to make known something of

His purpose. 'Shall I hide from Abraham that which I do?' 'Joseph dreamed a dream, and he told it to his brethren: and they hated him . . .' 'Gather yourselves together, that I [Jacob] may tell you that which shall befall you in the latter days.' 'According to all that I show thee [Moses] . . . even so shall ye make it.' 'All this, said David, have I been made to understand in writing from the hand of the Lord, even all the works of this pattern.' 'Blessed art thou, Simon Bar-Jonah: for flesh and blood hath not revealed it unto thee, but my Father which is in heaven.' 'By revelation was made known unto me [Paul] . . . the mystery of Christ, which . . . hath now been revealed unto his holy apostles and prophets in the Spirit.' 'I shrank not from declaring unto you the whole counsel of God.' (Gen. 18. 17; 37. 5; 49. 1; Ex. 25. 9; 1 Chr. 28. 19; Matt. 16. 17; Eph. 3. 3; Acts 20. 27.) None of these men came into the work of God by the exercise of their wits, for all God's work is related to His eternal purpose in Christ, and that purpose can only be known by divine unveiling. What a difficulty this presents for clever people!

Of the many typical servants of God in the Old Testament, Joseph is perhaps the most perfect. Yet, while Scripture reveals no apparent flaw in his character, we know well that his was no easy pathway. When did his troubles begin? Surely with his dreams. In them he saw what God was going to do, and recognized his own place in God's plan. It was his dreams that started things off. They represent spiritual vision. By them he saw what his brothers could not see. 'This dreamer cometh', they said, and hated him. But because he saw, Joseph could stand fast through all those grim experiences, and by him God was able to fulfil His plan for His earthly people.

By the time Moses appeared the nation was formed, but still of course in Egypt. God raised him up to bring them out, and he was shown what God would do to relate them as a people to Himself as the centre of their life. Moses saw the pattern in the Mount. In due course Israel's whole life would come to revolve around that Tabernacle and the divine Presence in their midst. Thus Moses dedicated himself to build, not according to his own ideas—he dare not do that—but, as with Joseph, according to what he *saw*. For vision is not our opinion as to what God should do; it is *seeing* what He is going to do.

Where does the work of God begin? On His side its starting-point is in eternity past; on ours it is the point at which we receive revelation of Christ. The start of a true work of God with us is not when we consecrate ourselves to Him, but when we *see*. Consecration should result *from* spiritual vision; it can never take its place. That is where God's work begins. Our work may begin at any time; God's work through us can spring only from divinely given vision.

We must see His goal in Christ. Without that vision our service for God follows the impulse of our own ideas but cannot accord with God's plan. When we come to Paul, we see that for him this revelation was two-fold. 'It pleased God . . . to reveal His Son in me': that was inner revelation, subjective, if you like the term (Gal. 1. 15f). 'I was not disobedient unto the heavenly vision': that was outer vision, objective, concrete, practical (Acts 26. 19). The inner and the outer together make perfect completeness, whereas either is insufficient without the other. And this is the need of the Church, of the people of God, to-day. Inward revelation must go along with outward vision: not only knowing the Lord within, but knowing also God's eternal purpose; not stopping at the foundation, but understanding too how to build upon it. God is not satisfied with our just doing odds and ends of work; that is what servants do. We are His friends, and His friends should know His plans.

What called forth Paul's consecration of himself was that flash of light from heaven. The obedience sprang from the vision. For while it remains true that all self-committal to God is precious to Him, blind self-committal does not serve Him very far. There is I think a difference between the initial, pure but uninstructed consecration that follows conversion and the further consecration of ourselves that may follow a seeing of the plan of God. The one is individual, based on our salvation, and God may not at once make severe demands upon it. But when God reveals His need and shows us what He wants done, and when having done so He asks for our willingness and receives our response, then it is that His demands upon that consecration become intensified. We have given our word on the basis of a new understanding, and He takes us anew at our word. Praise God that, to the ever-increasing vision given to him, Paul was not disobedient. All he had went into it.

Vision of God's purpose to-day brings into view all the people of God, but it is also *for* all the people of God. That was not always so. What the Old Testament saints saw, great as it was, concerned only an earthly people, however typical they might be of the heavenly Church. And only chosen men such as Joseph and Moses were entrusted with that vision. It was not common property, but was only given to the few. To-day, however, it is different. Heavenly vision now is for the whole Church. Though it is true that Paul and others in the New Testament period were chosen of God in a special way, His purpose is not that the vision should be confined to the ones and twos, but that all should see (Eph. 1. 18). This is the special character of this age.

In an important passage in Ephesians 3, Paul writes to 'you Gentiles' of the 'dispensation of that grace of God which was given me to you-ward'. He tells them of the 'mystery of Christ' made known to him and to others by revelation (verses 2–5). This 'manifold wisdom of God', he goes on to explain, has God planned even now to make known through His Church to all spiritual observers (verses 10, 11). To this end it must therefore first of all become her possession, and Paul's own part in this, he says, is governed by a single object, namely, *'to make all men see'* (verse 9).

Put in a sentence, the grace of God was given to the apostle that through his labours *the Church might see the vision*. For though Paul's 'all men' embraces each member, the full revelation of God does not belong to the individual as such. What is to be made known through the Church can only be seen by the Church. It is 'with all saints' that we apprehend the measure of the love of Christ. Only so can we be filled unto all the fulness of God (Eph. 3. 18, 19).

THE PRECIOUSNESS OF LIGHT

So while nothing can take the place of vision, the problem is still to get men to see. It was the subject of the apostle's most earnest prayer (Eph. 1. 15–18). There is no difficulty about hearing, or even memorising and repeating to others the plan of God; the difficulty is always to see. And all spiritual work is based on seeing. However much God in His grace may bless what originates otherwise—and He does do so—it is but odds and ends. It is vulnerable. That is why Satan does not much mind men hearing about the purpose of God and understanding it mentally. His great fear is lest they should have inward illumination concerning that purpose. He knows that if they do they will have a new access of strength and power, and that the Church, the work, the warfare—everything will be seen by them in a fresh light.

What is vision? It is the breaking in of divine light. The veiling of that light means perdition. 'If our gospel is veiled, it is veiled in them that are perishing' (2 Cor. 4. 3). But 'God hath shined in our hearts'—and merely to *see* is salvation. As soon as we see the glory in the Saviour's face, in that instant we are saved. If we merely understand the doctrine and assent to it, nothing happens, for we have not *seen* the Truth. But the moment we really see *Him*, in that moment we have the experience.

This is true both negatively and positively, as to sin and as to the Saviour. Before conversion men talk about the doctrine of the wrong of lying. They see it in the Word, they know the Word says it is wrong, and they may even make an effort to conform to that Word. And yet they lie, and lie well! Then one day they are converted. There is no immediate advance in their *doctrine* about lying, but at once they see that lying is wrong without being told. With a new instinct, they shrink with horror from the habit that till now had gripped them. What has happened? Light has made manifest its true nature, and the light that makes manifest is the light that slays. The light that reveals the lie slays the lie. What was till now merely an ethic has become an inward experience. And the experience like that of salvation itself, follows the shedding of light within as instantaneously as the impression of a photograph in a camera follows the exposure of the film. The instant you open the shutter you get a portrait. And the vision of God's purpose, of what He wants to do in the Church, is of a like character, and no less revolutionary in its effect. But because it concerns not merely the individual but the whole plan of God in Christ, its implications are so much the greater. It is capable, as we have said, of transforming our whole conception of the service of God.

I am not suggesting that we shall start to upheave and overthrow the work that till now we have been doing for Him. God forbid! Simply to change outward things is no use. We cannot deal with and improve things which God does not approve, nor dare we risk overthrowing that of which He does. No, the light kills *in us* all that is not of God, without any need of our doing violence to outward things. It is not a question of our grasping things mentally and getting to grips with them. There are some things we cannot grasp. It is all a question of seeing or not seeing. The whole issue is one of alternatives: light or darkness, life or death. Were it merely a matter of doctrine we might dismiss it from our mind and soon forget it. But objective, heavenly vision becomes also 'His Son revealed in me'—the two are one—and there is no need to remember, or possibility of forgetting, that which lives. There is no need to hold on to or try to grasp spiritual vision. *It* lays hold of *us*. To see the plan of God from within is to have no alternative in work or way. Henceforth it is His way, or it is death.

If we want light, we can have it. In order not to have it we must shut it out. Of course this can be done, for someone has truly said that the smallest leaf can hide a star. We may let a trivial obstacle veil from us eternal glories. But given the slightest chance, light will find its way in through the tiniest chink. 'If therefore thine eye be single, thy whole body shall be full of light' (Matt. 6. 22).

The secret of spiritual vision is a readiness for the cost of it, which means a humble openness of spirit to the searching light of God. 'The meek will he guide in judgment; and the meek will he teach his way. The secret of the Lord is with them that fear him; and he will show them his covenant' (Psalm 25. 9, 14). 'Lord, I am willing to pay any price to receive light. I do not fear light. I am willing for Thee to search every cranny of my work and to shed upon it the light of Thine own purpose.'

As we go further with these studies, I hope some of the vast-ness of God's purpose in the Church will become apparent to us. But that is not enough. My prayer, my longing, is that we may see Christ in fulness. It is not sufficient that we seek here-after to build up, according to Scriptural doctrines, a good, earnest church as men reckon it. No, *light* is our cry. We dare to face the light. 'Lord, give me, like Stephen, to see the Son of man in heaven, and in His light to see what Thy Church is, Thy work is. And then grant me grace, not only to live and walk, but also to work, in the light!' The outstanding feature of God's work is not a doctrine but a life; and life comes by revelation in the light of God. Behind doctrine there may be nothing but words. Behind revelation is God Himself.

CHAPTER SIX

A GLORIOUS CHURCH

Introducing the subject of His Church, Jesus brings us straight to the Rock. He Himself is the 'precious corner stone of sure foundation' (Isa. 28. 16). Each child of God who has life and is redeemed by His blood stands upon this foundation, and upon it he builds. Unbelievers have no part here at all. Whether it be the Church universal or its local expression, the principle is one and the same: Christ is the 'tried stone' to whom we are brought and fashioned and fitted.

Paul too takes this as his point of departure, for certainly it is the only possible one. 'We are ... God's building', he writes to the Corinthians in one of his letters, and then goes on: 'As a wise masterbuilder I laid a foundation ... But let each man take heed how he buildeth thereon. For other foundation can no man lay than that which is laid, which is Jesus Christ' (1 Cor. 3. 9-11). In other words the choice of a foundation is no longer our responsibility. God Himself has laid it, and no man can lay any other; no man can begin anywhere else. The apostles witness to this, and God does not ask our approval! He has done it, and He knows what He is doing. Whenever a soul comes to Christ, and Christ enters into the life, that foundation is laid. On it the child of God stands, on it he builds. What does matter, however, is what he puts on it.

God looks for quality. He is not concerned so much with whether we do the work as with what we use to do it. Many argue, 'If my work is well done, surely that is enough!' But God asks not merely whether we have served Him, given ourselves to His work, and built on the foundation, important though these things are. His question goes deeper. What, He inquires, have we used to do these things? He looks, not only at the things done, but at the materials used. Among those who preach the Gospel He is aware of a difference of quality, and readily distinguishes the solid from the superficial worker. Among those who see spiritual truth He recognizes a like difference in their seeing. Among those who pray He discerns what lies behind each one's 'Amen'. This is what Paul means when he warns us: 'If any man buildeth on the foundation gold, silver, costly stones, wood, hay, stubble; each man's work shall be made manifest: for the day shall declare it, because it is revealed in fire' (verses 12, 13).

MATERIAL FOR BUILDING

It is weight that counts. Wood, hay, stubble are cheap, light, temporary; gold, silver, precious stones are costly, weighty, eternal. Here is the key to value. The heavy metals, the gold of the divine character and glory, the silver of His redemptive work: these are the materials He prizes. Not merely what we preach, but what we are, weighs with God; not doctrine, but the character of Christ wrought out in us by God's orderings, by God's testings, by the Spirit's patient workings. Work that is of God is work that has been to the Cross. When our work has been that way, we can rest assured that it will in the end survive the fire. Not, 'Where is the need most evident? What ideas and resources have I got? How much can I do? How soon can I put that doctrine into practice?' but, 'Where is God moving? What is there of Him here? How far is it His will for me to go? What is the mind of the Spirit on this?'—these are the questions of the truly crucified servant. He recognizes God's 'Go' and His 'Speak', but also His 'Wait', and His 'Go, but say only so much'. Aware of his own weakness and emptiness, his greatest lesson is to commit his way to God and learn to see Him move.

The problem lies in our failure to understand that, in God's work, man in himself is of no use. Wood, hay, stubble, these suggest what is essentially of man and of the flesh. They imply what is common, ordinary, easily and cheaply acquired—and of course perishable. Grass to-day may clothe the earth with beauty, but where is it to-morrow? Human intellect may give us a grasp of Scripture; natural eloquence may have the power to attract; emotion may carry us along; feelings may seem to supply a guiding sense—but to what? God looks for more solid values than these. Many of us can preach well enough, but *we* are wrong. We talk of the flesh but don't know its perils; we talk of the Spirit but would we recognize Him were He really to move us? Too much of our work for God depends not on His will and purpose but on our feelings —or even, God forgive us! on the weather. Like chaff and stubble, it is carried away by the wind. Given the right mood we may accomplish a lot, but just as easily, in adverse conditions, we may down tools entirely. No, as the fire will one day prove, work that is dependent on feelings or on the wind of revival is of little use to God. When God commands, feelings or no feelings, we must learn to do.

Such values are costly. Those unwilling to pay the price will never come by them. Grace is free, but this isn't. Only a high price buys costly stones. Many a time we shall want to cry out 'This is costing too much!' Yet the things wrought by God through the lessons we learn under His hand, though we be long in learning them—these are the really worth-while things. Time is an element in this. In the light of God, some things perish of themselves; there is no need to wait for the fire. It is in what remains, in what has stood God's test of time, that true worth lies. Here are found the precious stones, formed in what God graciously gives us of sorrow and trouble, as He puts us 'through fire and water' to bring us to His wealthy place. Man sees the outward appearance; God sees the inward cost. Do not wonder that you experience all sorts of trials. Accepted from His hand they are the sure way to a life that is precious to Him.

May God have mercy on the clever people, who give with one hand what they take with the other! Not even speaking for God can be done without cost. It is all a question whether the vessel is light or weighty, for weight shows the quality of the material. Two men may use the same words, but in the one you meet something you cannot get past; in the other— nothing. The difference is in the man. You always know

when you are in the presence of spiritual worth. No amount
of theorizing about the Lord's return, for example, will take
the place of a life that has been daily lived looking for Him.
There is no escaping this difference, and no substitute for the
real thing. Alas, some of us are so unlike our words that it
might be better if we said less about spiritual things.

Do not wonder, then, at God's concern for the materials of
His house. Imitation jewellery may have a certain beauty, but
what woman that has once possessed the real thing would give
it another thought? The apostle Paul leaves us in no doubt of
his own valuation. Ten coolie-loads of stubble can never approach the price of one single gem-stone. All flesh, all mere
feelings, all that is essentially of man, is grass and must vanish
away. What is of Christ, the gold, the silver, the costly stones,
these alone are eternal, incorruptible, imperishable.

It is this lasting character of God's Church that must now
claim our attention.

ETERNAL IN THE HEAVENS

It is in the later writings of the apostle Paul, and more especially in his Epistle to the Ephesians, that the eternal nature
of the Church of Christ is given the greatest prominence. As
the House, as the Body, as the Bride of Christ, as the people of
God, the Church is a special theme of Ephesians. We have the
Lord of the Body (Ch. 1), the material of the House (Ch. 2),
the eternal mystery of the Church (Ch. 3), the growth of the
Body (Ch. 4), the preciousness of the Bride (Ch. 5), and the
warfare of the people of God (Ch. 6); and every one of these is
seen in an eternal context. We have already touched on the
third of these, and we now have to speak a little about Chapters 1, 2 and 5.

What is God doing to-day? Ephesians helps us to answer
this question. First the apostle takes a backward look. 'He
chose us in him before the foundation of the world.' 'In him
. . . we were made a heritage, having been foreordained according to the purpose of him who worketh all things after the
counsel of his will' (1. 4, 11). Here he shows us God working,

not to a hoped-for end, but from a settled purpose. It is because God's eternal work first reaches back into the past that it then also reaches on into 'the ages to come' (2. 7).

Next the apostle looks forward. God has, he assures us, 'made known unto us the mystery of his will, according to his good pleasure which he purposed in him unto a dispensation of the fulness of the times, to sum up all things in Christ' (1. 9, 10). In this last clause he summarizes and defines God's work in time; it is 'to sum up all things in Christ'. To leave no loose ends of any kind, to have nothing out of harmony in His universe, to see realized in fulness in His own the oneness that now they only taste: that is His goal.

But instead, what is our common experience to-day? Perhaps a group of us are together in God's presence, and all that passes between us is so evidently of Christ, and therefore so good, that we feel we have touched the fulness. But then, at a point, one of us who should know better speaks or prays of himself—'after the flesh', as Paul would put it—and the life goes out of our fellowship. The spell is broken, and the thing we tasted has eluded us. Here on earth, how we long that such fellowship in Christ should be, in some measure at least, the normal experience in our churches and in our homes: 'all one in Christ Jesus', with nothing that is outside of Him! How we long and labour for this, and yet how hard it seems to realize it! We have to confess that to bring it to pass is impossible to us. Yet we praise God that He calls us to have a share in this 'impossible' work.

This is not a contradiction. God's fellow-labourer in this *is* the Church herself—every one of us, that is, and not merely preachers and special workers. And, praise God, Ephesians heartens us with the assurance that the oneness we but taste will indeed one day be true of the whole universe; there will be nothing outside of Him.

In this letter Paul points us both back to paradise and forward to paradise, back to what God did before the creation (1. 4) and on to what He is going to do to all generations (2. 7), both of them in respect of the Church. God's Son Himself is revealed in the Church, which is why she is here described as

'His Body' (1. 23). As a man's personality is expressed through his body, so is Christ displayed through the Church. She is in this age the vessel which, in a spiritual sense, contains and reveals Christ.

To be found 'working together with God' does not mean that many men are called to 'help' God. It means that what God has determined to do, the Church must make way for Him to do in her. And if it is indeed God's purpose for ever to reveal His wisdom and power through her, then surely to miss this is to miss everything. Paul himself held that whatever else he did counted for nothing if he failed to apprehend that for which he was apprehended by Christ Jesus (Phil. 3. 12). Ask yourself, 'The work I have done, that for which I have lived and poured out my strength, what is it?' May God give us grace once again, if need be, to weigh out work in the balance of the sanctuary. We dare not live for a small thing. When, in the light of His Word, we see God's purpose in His Son, everything is transformed. We still preach, but we see differently. Nothing we do thereafter stands alone. All is for one thing—the eternal self-revelation of Christ through His Body.

A second wonderful thing that Ephesians discloses to us is this, that not only is the Church's work eternal; in the sight of God, it is also in heaven. The place of blessing where she is seated, her standing, life, ministry, warfare—everything is in 'the heavens' and from 'the heavens' (1. 3, 20; 2. 6; 3. 10; 4. 8-12; 6. 12). This helps us to define further what it should mean to work for God. To create an earthly thing is easy for us. If we are content with an outward, technical Christianity —a 'movement' based on an earthly foundation, with an earthly structure and organization—then it is quite possible to do the thing ourselves. But we have been apprehended for something utterly different from this. The Church is spiritual, and her work is heavenly. It must never become earth-bound.

David 'served his own generation', and slept (Acts 13. 36). He could not serve two! Where to-day we seek to perpetuate our work by setting up an organization or society or system, the Old Testament saints served their own day and passed on.

This is an important principle of life. Wheat is sown, grows, ears, is reaped, and then the whole plant, even to the root, is ploughed out. That is the Church, never rooted permanently in the earth. God's work is the spiritual to the point of having no earthly roots, no smell of earth on it at all. Men pass on, but the Lord remains. The spiritual testimony of believers is to be heavenly, not earthly. Everything to do with the Church must be up-to-date and living, meeting the present—one could even say the passing—needs of the hour. Never must it become fixed, static. God Himself takes away His workers, but He gives others. Our work suffers, but His never does. Nothing touches Him. He is still God.

ONE NEW MAN

One very interesting consequence of this heavenly character of the Church appears in the second chapter, and in a parallel passage in Colossians. In Ephesians 2 Paul sets out to show how two mutually hostile elements in the world of his day, the Jews and the non-Jews, have been brought together by Him to become one 'holy temple in the Lord'. What he has to say concerning this 'habitation of God in the Spirit' is surprisingly different from what most Christians say to-day. To-day it is widely held that, if the people of God of different race or background or Christian denomination are gathered on the agreed ground of a creed or 'basis of faith', that is of the essence of the Church. To them, all sorts of Christians, of no matter what language or tradition or viewpoint or connection, *together* form the Church, and this is not affected by what various things they may carry in with them from outside.

The correction for this kind of thinking is the word 'new' in verse 15: '. . . that he might create in himself of the twain one new man'. We think Jewish believers plus Gentile believers (or whatever other groupings are in our minds at the moment) are the Church. But to leave us in no doubt as to what the Holy Spirit means, Paul expresses the same thing even more explicitly in Colossians 3. 11. Writing once again of the new man, he says that within its sphere: 'there cannot be Greek and

Jew, circumcision and uncircumcision, barbarian, Scythian, bondman, freeman: but Christ is all, and in all.' If we understand him aright this means that, if we want to be Christians, we cannot be anything else *but* Christians!

The trouble is that much of our thinking about these things starts from a false premise. Let me try to illustrate. Imagine yourself standing outside the door of the Church, symbolically giving away bread to the hungry. Any who care to do so are free to come and take a little, regardless of what they may be engaged in or encumbered with. All sorts and conditions of men come, and they eat. Are they not qualified to enter? And will they live together peaceably if they do? Your first reaction may be to answer yes, regarding the rabble that have gathered as partaking of a fellowship that unifies them on the basis of what they have received. But wait a minute! What about the bulky articles in their hands, and the burdens on their shoulders? What about the animals they drive before them, and the cartloads of furniture and merchandise they drag behind? You are overlooking what comes in with them when they come in. They have with them all the makings of a busy market, or worse!

Look again. The door is narrow. A Cross overshadows it, and beyond it lies a tomb. If the bread you distribute spoke of a shared life these symbolize something else. They tell us that in entering, not only is there something to be received; there is something also to be relinquished. 'Having abolished in his flesh the enmity' He made both one (Eph. 2. 15). There was in fallen man something to be broken down that constituted a positive barrier to fellowship, and that had to go.

We cannot evade this other symbol. We cannot escape this second condition of fellowship in life. Whatever our nationality or colour or Christian denomination, we must die, for only those who have been crucified with Christ, only those who have let go of something, find themselves at home there. Natural traits, national rivalries, class traditions, personal preferences, all the things that we would instinctively clutch to ourselves and seek to carry over, as it were, from the old life and order—all are by the Cross excluded. God's 'new man' is altogether and only new. Inside those limits, what is of Christ alone is found, and He must be 'all and in all'.

From what we have already said it will be evident that Ephesians sets out to give us the highest New Testament revelation of the Church. This appears again in the order in which the Church's history is treated in this letter. Here, as we have suggested, we not only see her as from sin redeemed; we are shown too her course from the beginning of creation. Whereas Romans introduces sin in Chapter 1, and only approaches the subject of the Body of Christ in Chapter 12 after dealing at length with the justification and sanctification of the individual sinner, Ephesians begins differently, going back further into history to do so. It is striking that, as early as Ephesians 1, the Church comes into view as already 'chosen in Christ', and that even though the question of sin follows hard after this statement, it is not treated at any length until Chapter 2. The letter as a whole sets out, in fact to give us the Church's complete history, comprising both her place in the fulness of God's purpose in Christ and the work of God's grace by which He redeemed her to bring her there.

This view of the Church goes back to the very start of things. It sees her there in the mind of God much as Eve appears in the second chapter of Genesis, before the irruption of sin into the creation.[1] This comparison makes Eve unusual, even unique, among the women of the Old Testament who may be felt to be types of the Church. In each of them some aspect of the Church is depicted. We see her presented to the bridegroom (Rebekah), chosen from among the Gentiles (Asenath), passing through the wilderness (Zipporah) receiving her inheritance in the land (Achsah), altogether dependent upon her kinsman-redeemer (Ruth), and militant for her Lord (Abigail). Yet, interesting as is this sequence of types, none is so instructive as that presented by Eve. For they all

[1] While the Church was no doubt revealed to man only long after the Fall, we must, I think, allow that she was planned by God before it.

succeed the Fall, and therefore directly or indirectly have moral issues and responsibilities associated with them. But Eve, viewed as in that blessed period before sin entered, remains uniquely typical of the Church as the one who fulfils all God's desire for her in union with His Son.

For Eve was one and alone; and she was absolutely for Adam. 'Have ye not read', said Jesus, 'that he which made them from the beginning made them male and female, and said, For this cause shall a man leave his father and mother, and shall cleave to his wife; and the twain shall become one flesh?' (Matt. 19. 4, 5). At this point the spiritual type, preceding the entry of sin and for the present untouched by it, expresses most perfectly God's original and eternal intention to have a Bride for His Son.

Moreover the figure of the Church that Eve presents is a double figure, and this may help us to understand Paul's language in Ephesians. First, as a part of Adam, taken from him in sleep, she was his body. Then, created, perfected and brought again to him, she became his bride. Other created things were brought to him, but not being *of* him they could not be his help-meet. This distinguishes Eve from the rest of the creation. It also typically distinguishes the Church of Christ from the entire old creation to-day.

For sin *has* entered. The Fall is a fact of history. 'Through one man's disobedience the many were made sinners'. 'The whole creation groaneth and travaileth in pain together until now'. The work of redemption thus became a divine necessity. The Cross had to become history, not merely now to fulfil the figure of sleep and waking and new creation foreshadowed by the sleep of Adam. It must deal as well with the new situation the Fall has created.[2] Sin and death must by it be met and done away. Christ Jesus must humble Himself for our sakes, becoming obedient even to the death of the cross. The price must be paid and Satan's power broken. Every individual sinner must come to the Saviour and find remission of sins through the atoning blood. So it is that we see ourselves—

---

[2] This is perhaps the reason why, unlike that of believers, the death of Jesus is never described in the New Testament merely in terms of 'sleep'.

and rightly—as in the valley of sin, the trophies of redemption. That, as I said, is Romans. Yet even after all this history, Ephesians finds God choosing, rather, to view us as within His eternal purpose, altogether *from* Christ and altogether *for* Christ.

Here is the miracle of divine hope, that even the disaster of the Fall could not frustrate but could only hinder. Adam has sinned; and apart from the grace of God, man in the flesh—yes, even redeemed man—can, and would repeatedly, sin. But by new birth there is planted in him that of Christ which sin cannot touch, and he is commanded to live by that. The very life of Christ Himself, released by the Cross and distributed to His members, supplies them with the power to do so. By it, sin's dominion over them is broken; in its resurrection newness, they walk (Rom. 6. 4, 6). There is no substitute. It alone can meet God's demands.

And it is to be shared, for in the sphere of divine purpose there are not many individual vessels, but one Vessel. God created one Eve, not many men. Without Christ, I personally do not possess life; without the Church His Body, I have not the means to live the life I possess as it should be lived.

But now, not only do I have the life; I have also with me the Giver of life Himself. Let us return for a moment to the latter part of Ephesians 5. In the passage from verses 25–30 I think we can distinguish these two things, the Bride and the Body. In verses 25–27 we have the first law of love, 'Husbands, love your wives', and it is based upon two things: the past tense of Christ's love for His Bride, expressed in His death on her behalf, and the future tense of His purpose for her. This is the *eternal* view. Again in verses 28–30 we have a second law of love, 'Husbands ought also to love their own wives as their own bodies', and this is based upon one thing: the present tense of Christ's love for that which is, in essence, Himself, His Body. This latter is the view *to-day*. The first passage sees Christ and His Church apart, having separate existence, and is concerned with her union, as Bride, with Him, the Giver of life. The second sees Christ and His Church spiritually identified, without separate existence, and concerns her identification and present unity of life with Him as His Body. From One there have become two; from being two they will again be one. This is the mystery of the Church, that all that is from Christ returns to Him.

The work of Christ now is to love and cherish her, to protect and preserve her from disease and blemish, caring thus for her because He loves her as His own self—because, speaking reverently, the Church *is* Christ! How does He nourish and preserve her? 'By the washing of water with the word' (verse 26). In this verse 'the word' is not *Logos*, the great, objective, eternal Word of God; it is *rhema*, the smaller, more personal and subjective spoken word. 'The words (*rhemata*) that I have spoken unto you are spirit, and are life' (John 6. 63). *Rhema* always suggests to us something very personal and intimate: 'Mary said, Behold the handmaid of the Lord; be it unto me according to thy word.' 'Now lettest thou thy servant depart, O Lord, according to thy word, in peace.' 'The word of God came unto John the son of Zacharias in the wilderness.' 'We toiled all night, and took nothing: but at thy word I will let down the nets.' 'He is not here, but is risen: remember how he spake unto you when he was yet in Galilee. . . . And they remembered his words.' 'The Holy Ghost fell on them. . . . And I remembered the word of the Lord, how that he said, . . . Ye shall be baptized with the Holy Ghost.' (Luke 1. 38; 2. 29; 3. 2; 5. 5; 24. 6–8; Acts 11. 15, 16.)

How is the Church's return to the plan of God effected? '*By* water *with* the word': the water of His risen life, checking us and exposing, by contrast with itself, all that needs to be eliminated; and His word, dealing with what has been revealed, and renewing us by cleansing away the blemishes. Sometimes maybe the word comes first and then the life, but the effect is the same. 'The second time the cock crew. And Peter called to mind the word . . . And when he thought thereon, he wept.' (Mark 14. 72). The Church to which God's word has no power to appeal is no Church. But the word is His instrument of cleansing and renewal. If only we realize this, and allow it to do its work, though we may fail, we shall not long remain unaware that we have done so.

And blessed be God, the day will come when the Body, taking its character wholly from Him who is its life, will have been made ready to become the Bride, His help-meet. Because, as His Body, she has attained to the measure of the stature of His fulness (4. 13) she will be presented to Him at the last, 'a glorious Church, not having spot or wrinkle or any such thing' (5. 27). Wholly like Him because wholly of Him, she will be wholly for Him. She has expressed His glory; she will be presented to Him clothed in that glory, with no scar of sin, no wrinkle of age, no time wasted, no flaw of any kind, but holy and without blemish. Christ, by His word, has left in her no ground for Satan or demons, men or angels—no, nor yet even for God Himself—to lay any charge against her. For in her, now, all is new, and all is of God. Should we not, then, if this is to be its blessed effect, greatly treasure the word that God speaks to us to-day?

CHAPTER SEVEN

BUILDING IN LOVE

From the heavenly mystery we turn now to the earthly expression. Having seen the Church, the Body, in her relation to her Lord, we must now consider her human relationships. The time has come to ask ourselves, How do the members function one towards another?

It seems likely that, of all the apostles, it was to Paul first that there came the concept of Jesus and His people as a body and its members. Certainly it is a view of the Church that is peculiarly his. It was, after all, bound up with his very conversion and calling, being contained in the Lord's first words to him: 'I am Jesus whom thou persecutest' (Acts 9. 5). To persecute those who believe is to persecute Jesus. To touch His disciples is to touch Him. Thus these words heralded the great revelation that was to be given to Paul of the mystery of the Church. They told him something new about the Lord, something till then no more than implicit in His statements while on earth.

But the Lord did not leave the matter there with Paul. He did not allow him to stay with the heavenly mystery. The command that immediately followed came right down to the practical consequences of such a revelation. 'Rise, and enter into the city, and it shall be told thee what thou must do.' *It shall be told thee.* Apart from those very disciples against whom he had set himself, Paul would be helpless; he would never know. The Lord Himself would not tell him what to do, save on the basis of the living Church. He would not lend His support to a merely individual calling and mission. For individualism is sin; it does injury to the Body of Christ.

So Paul reached Damascus, and there followed for him long hours of waiting. At first no man came. Only after three days of darkness did someone at length arrive—and even then, he

was but 'a disciple'. From Luke's use of this simple title we are
to conclude that Ananias, though devout and of honourable
character, was just an ordinary brother, with nothing special
about him to qualify him as the helper of the destined 'great
apostle of the Church'. But it is just here that the mystery of
the Church must become practical for Paul.

And for his part too, Ananias, who knew Saul of Tarsus by
repute and had every reason to fear him, must now give practical expression to a miracle of divine grace in his own heart.
His cautious 'this man' (Acts 9. 13) becomes 'Brother Saul'
(verse 17). Jesus has slain the enmity and all his fears are dispelled. Ananias' simple words of greeting express, in brother-
to-brother terms, the recognition by the universal Church of
another member of Christ, while his simple act demonstrated
the new-found oneness of these two men under a single anointing. In one Spirit they gave and received instructions that were
designed by God to have a worldwide outcome (Acts 22. 14–
16).

In his writings Paul gives us two somewhat different views
of the Body, one in Ephesians and the other in 1 Corinthians.
Whereas the one sees the Church in the heavenlies, the other
sees her planted firmly on the earth. In Ephesians the Church
—all of it—is the Body. To the Corinthian believers Paul can
nevertheless write: 'Ye are the body of Christ, and severally
members thereof' (1 Cor. 12. 27). If, as many do, we regard
Ephesians as a circular letter, this may help to explain why
Paul, thinking in large, universal terms, occupies himself there
with *the* Body of Christ, whereas in 1 Corinthians, writing
this time to the church in a particular Greek city, he shows us
that Body functioning in a given situation on the earth, and
doing so in the way *a* body functions.

That, I take it, is the explanation of a significant little clause
in 1 Corinthians 12. 21: 'The eye cannot say to the hand, I
have no need of thee: or again the head to the feet, I have no
need of you'. We should be careful not to misunderstand Paul
here. The Body of Christ, whether universally in heaven or
locally on earth, has only one Head, Christ Himself (Eph. 4.
15). There cannot be many local 'heads' of churches, or there

would at once be schism in the Body, and Paul is not suggesting that there can. Rather is he using in 1 Corinthians the *meta-
phor* of a human body to illustrate practical principles of re-
latedness and function, by which the heavenly and eternal
Body of Christ operates *down here*. Just as the Head, Christ,
cannot dispense with the least of His members, so, he affirms,
can no single member get along without any other member.

Thus in first Corinthians we see the whole matter treated in
relation not so much to divine purpose as to human responsibility. The former is essential, for none could function
without it, but the question is, are we bringing it down and
applying it where we are to-day?

The problem seems to be to have the two. It is easy to accept the Ephesian side—the heavenly view of what God will
have. Our troubles begin with 1 Corinthians. For the spiritually minded that letter is altogether too practical, and because
it is so, they are always in danger of evading the difficulties of
its application. They seek (and rightly) to avoid the extreme
of deducing, from the available evidence of New Testament
practices, a foolproof pattern or system of church life and then
following that slavishly. They know only too well this will
produce but a lifeless copy of that historic beginning. So instead they fix their eyes almost exclusively upon the glorious
heavenly Church set forth in Ephesians, only to fall into the
opposite error—that of keeping the vision so 'spiritual' that it
becomes almost, if not quite, imaginary!

Yet 1 Corinthians 12 is a very simple passage, and perhaps it
is just because it is so simple that its meaning is missed by
many. What is here is not heavenly, nor is it earthly, *but
heavenly and yet expressed on earth*. The revelation of the Body
in the heavenlies is intended spontaneously to issue in very
practical results, and it is these results that are there defined.

God's principle is the principle of incarnation.[1] God desires
—indeed for Him it is more than a desire; it is a divine necessity—to shew the heavenly life in an earthly expression, not in
angels or spirits but in men, not as something vague and

---

[1] We use the term with caution. It is unwise to carry too far the parallel between the Church and her incarnate Lord.

imaginary but in a form that is real and practical. It is blessed to be living in the heavenlies in Ephesians, but remember, the same apostle who wrote Ephesians also wrote Corinthians. God's character demands that His Church, universal, spiritual, heavenly, should have its earthly expression in local churches, set in places no less dark than the pagan city of Corinth. And because there is this earthly expression, men will always be ready enough to step in with their opinions, and have a hand in the arrangements. 'We must be earthly *sometimes*!' they say in extenuation. But 1 Corinthians 12 shows us that, even in such an earthly environment, the church is still to operate on the principles of the heavenly Body. For the local church is not merely an outward type, it is a real manifestation of Christ in the earth to-day. 'Ye are the Body of Christ'. Here in Corinth you Corinthian believers are called to be the whole Body in essence.

TAKING RESPONSIBILITY

So we turn to 1 Corinthians 12 and its treatment of the functional life of the Body. If we look closely at the section of this chapter from verse 12 onwards, I think we can discern four simple laws governing the Body's life.

The first is in verses 15 and 16: 'If the foot shall say, Because I am not the hand, I am not of the body; it is not therefore not of the body. And if the ear shall say, Because I am not the eye, I am not of the body; it is not therefore not of the body'. In other words, you must function as you are, and not as you would prefer to be. Because you are not someone else, that is no ground for declining to be yourself! It is as though the foot said, 'I had made up my mind to be a hand, and because I can't, I'll refuse to walk!' Such refusal springs from a comparing heart, and only individualism compares.

This habit of making comparisons reveals one thing, that we have not yet seen the Body of Christ. For tell me, which *is* the better member, the foot or the hand? There is, when you come to think of it, no way of comparing them. Their function in the human body is different, and each is equally needed there. And yet many thus minimize God's gift. Because they cannot be the special member they admire, they decline to take their place at all. Or they think all ministry begins and ends with public ministry, and because they have not the gift to function in a public way, they do nothing.

That is exactly the situation described in Jesus' parable of the men with the talents (Matthew 25. 14–30). There was a servant with five talents and another with two, but the whole emphasis in the parable is on the one-talent man. The danger is of the one-talent brother burying his talent. 'Since I have not got five talents, or two, what can I possibly do with one? Since I cannot minister in a conspicuous way, am I really any use at all? Since others are so well able to lead in prayer and set the tone of the prayer-meeting, is it not all right for me to keep silent? I cannot occupy a place of prominence; does it matter therefore whether I occupy any place at all?'

But the parable teaches that if two can grow into four, and five into ten, one can grow into two. It is by functioning that we discover life. The Church is suffering not as much from the prominence of the five-talent members as from the holding back of the one-talent members. The life of the whole Body is hampered and impoverished by the burial of those single talents.

If we have once recognized the heavenly Body, we shall be very glad to have the tiniest part in it. Of course, refusal to function because we have only one talent may reveal in us desires and ambitions outside the will of God, or worse, a dissatisfaction with that will. But no, if it pleases Him to make me the greatest member, praise the Lord! If He chooses instead to make me the least, praise Him no less! Am I a hand, or a foot? I will gladly be just that. I am perfectly satisfied with His choice, and willing to function in His appointed sphere, and if I accept His gift and use it, the one can grow to two, and very quickly there will be five or even ten.

Paul wrote: 'Encourage the faint-hearted' (1 Thess. 5. 14), and the word is literally 'small-souled'. We should encourage the one-talent man, not because of the magnitude of his gift— it isn't so very big after all—but because the Holy Spirit indwells him. His ground of expectation is to be God Himself. One of my own closest colleagues, before he was born again, was regarded by his friends as incredibly dull, indeed almost stupid. Yet when God took hold of his life and the Holy Spirit began to work in him, within two years he already showed signs of becoming, as he now is, one of the most gifted Bible teachers in China.

So the first law of function is that we use what we have been given. We cannot excuse ourselves and say, 'I am not needed here.' Nor shall we find spiritual refreshment by taking our Bibles and notebooks and retiring to a quiet spot to prepare for some imagined future ministry, if in so doing we are evading a present responsibility. Our physical body may be refreshed thereby, but not our spirit. No, the rule is always to serve others with what we have in hand, and as we do so, to discover that we ourselves are fed. Recall the story of Jesus at the well. He was hungry, for He had sent His disciples to buy food, and thirsty, for He asked the Samaritan woman for a drink. But when the disciples came back He could claim to have eaten. He had been strengthened by doing the will of God in ministering to one soul in need.

The fellowship of the Body is always two-way; receiving and giving. Wanting only to receive is not fellowship. We may not be preachers, but when we come to worship we nevertheless bring what we have. There must be help of the pulpit from the pew. Sitting and looking on will not do. We must give others to drink, not necessarily by speaking, but maybe by quiet prayer. And if we do just sit and listen, we must *be there* in spirit, not somewhere else!

'Occupy till I come': what a great range of ministry we have got *where we are*! The bit of work entrusted to us is for the Body, so there is no room for jealousy of others. We cannot draw comparisons, and complain to our brother, 'God uses you and he doesn't use me'. Would some of us prefer to be like Peter and win souls? Let us remember, the eleven stood up with Peter. Peter was the mouthpiece, but he could never dare to say, 'I won those souls'.

So every member of the Body has a ministry, and every

member is called to function in the place appointed by the
Lord. It makes no difference who does the work if the glory is
His. We must turn to God's account the position given us by
Him, and not run off hoping to grow in retirement. 'I was
afraid, and went away and hid thy talent in the earth.' There
can be no glory in that direction.

ACCEPTING LIMITATION

The second law of function is found in verses 17 and 18: 'If
the whole body were an eye, where were the hearing? If the
whole were hearing, where were the smelling? But now hath
God set the members each one of them in the body, even as it
pleased him'. The principle here set forth is that, in our life
together, we are always to leave room for the function of
others.

Putting it bluntly, do not try to do everything and be everything yourself! No one in his senses would desire to see the
whole Body function merely in a single way. It is not reasonable for the whole to be an eye, nor for the eye to attempt the
work of the whole. The Lord has ordered variety in the Body,
an ear and a nose as well as an eye and a hand; not conformity,
and certainly not single-organ monopoly. Thus, if the previous principle was for those lagging behind, this one is for those
who are too forward, wanting to *be* the whole Body. The
word to them, is I repeat, Don't try to do or be everything;
you are *not* everything!

There are those who, when they come to a prayer meeting,
can only pray themselves; they cannot listen to others. They are
willing to lead but not to be led in prayer. They want others
to listen and say 'Amen', but they are too impatient to listen
and say 'Amen' to what another prays. They want their own
contribution to be the high light of the meeting. They are
individualists, even when in prayer with others.

In conversation too they are individualists. They can only
talk about themselves and their work. They cannot listen
while the work of others is spoken of without breaking in with
something about themselves. They lack the ability to receive.

Individualism is a distressing feature of Christian work. It means that *our* work, *our* ministry, becomes so important that we have no interest in what others are doing.

There is much frustration and loss among the members of Christ to-day because some of us who are experienced servants of God are not willing to let others function. *We* have been given a ministry by the Lord, and for this reason we think we must bear the whole responsibility ourselves if others are to develop and grow. We have not understood that by doing so we are in fact hindering the development of those others. This mistake is a fruitful source of discouragement and even division, and its ill effects do not end there.

For let us suppose that I encounter a doctrinal point of which I cannot see the answer, and find myself in a fog about it. What do I do? Do I try to decide it myself, or do I go to the member whose special gift from God is the capacity to teach and clarify, and to lead people out of doctrinal fogs? If I do the former, I have opened the way for a new doctrinal difference, for it is at this very point that doctrinal differences have their birth. Instead of trusting the Lord to solve my problem through His teaching member, and so letting another member function for me in this matter, I have made it all too possible for the two of us to be found teaching different and even conflicting things. If, for example, as an evangelist, I take on also the teaching of my converts, this kind of confusion is very liable to occur. Rather must I serve, and then when my function is fulfilled, stand aside and make room for another. For a first principle of the Body is that 'he that planteth and he that watereth are one' (I Cor. 3. 8).

As a member, I must be prepared to receive what another member has to give. For myself I must be willing for limitation. Is the church at prayer? I must be ready to remain silent and to give room for the 'weaker' prayers. Have I a gift of preaching? I must learn to sit and listen to others. Be my measure small or large, I dare not, as a member, go beyond it, for the mark of the Cross is upon all that is over-size, all that is extraneous to the Body. I must be willing to be limited entirely to my sphere, and to let others serve in theirs. I must be

happy for others to function towards me, and to accept the
help ministered to me by them.

ESTEEMING OTHERS

Thirdly we come to verses 21 and 22: 'The eye cannot say
to the hand, I have no need of thee: or again the head to the
feet, I have no need of you. Nay, much rather, those members of the body which seem to be more feeble are necessary'.
Put quite simply, we must never seek to cut off another member. We must not think we can act in the capacity of the Head
and dispense with the members. Weakness or uncouthness in
a member is no warrant for our cutting him off.[2] We dare not
say to another: 'I have no need of thee'. Rather do we discover how much we can learn from members we would not
naturally esteem. We may often have to call for prayer-help
from those we might even be inclined to despise. Alas, how
readily do we feel we should demean ourselves and lose our
spiritual status by so doing! Yet the Lord affirms that He has
a place for, and can use, even the feeblest of His members.

Once, years ago, I was facing a very big problem in my life.
It concerned the whole question of personal enduement with
the Holy Spirit for service. I was both under a deep sense of
the need for this, and also in some confusion of mind about
the doctrine. Yet somehow, pray as I might, the Lord seemed
unwilling either to answer my questions or to show me the
way through into the experience. I knew He had something
more for me, but it remained out of my reach, and I felt I
must somehow get clear on this or I could not go on. It is
no exaggeration to say that my whole ministry hung in the
balance.

I was engaged at the time in preaching the Gospel in a remote part of the country, far removed from other servants of
God with anything approaching the knowledge of the Lord
that I felt I had. I had been sent there by Him, and there was
no doubt of the need or of the readiness of people to hear. But

---

[2] Of course there is such a thing as discipline in the Church where sin is concerned. Of this we shall speak later, but this is not what is in view here.

something was lacking. My preaching was void of power, and
there was very little fruit from it. Yet what God was seeking
to give me I seemed unable to receive. I could not get
through alone; what I needed above all just then was fellowship.

But where was I to find it? True there was a handful of
simple believers, country folk, among whom I had been staying, but I felt they knew so little of the Lord that they certainly
could not help *me* in the great problem facing me. They
would scarcely even have a sufficient foundation from which
to pray intelligently for me in it, and certainly not enough to
bring me through. I was forgetting the Body!

At last I reached an impasse. There was nothing left but to
call them in, if I was not to give up and go out altogether. So
at my request those simple brethren came to me in my need.
I told them what I could of my difficulty, and they prayed—
and as they prayed, light dawned! The thing did not *need*
explaining. It was done, and done in such a way that it has
never needed to be repeated. From that day on the tide of
blessing flowed.

Yes, God will bring us often to places where we cannot get
through alone. For the life that asserts that 'God and I are
enough' is only in fact hindering Him. The Lord taught me
that day how those members of the Body which seem to be
more feeble are indeed to Him most precious.

KEEPING THE UNITY

And fourthly, verses 24 and 25 tell us: 'God tempered the
body together, giving more abundant honour to that part
which lacked; that there should be no schism in the body; but
that the members should have the same care one for another'.
What the apostle here says in conclusion is that we are resolutely to refuse schism. It is totally disallowed. The divine
will is that *there should be no schism in the Body*.

In previous chapters we have spoken of unity in general
terms. The Church, as seen in heaven, cannot be divided.
Praise God, it is one for ever. Yes, but there can be inroads

upon that unity in the church on earth. As to its heavenly life
the Body is untouchable; but in its functioning on earth it is all
too sadly true that it can be touched and even mutilated, as the
Corinthian situation abundantly shows. Paul condemns this
state of affairs in no uncertain terms.

What, then, is the secret of practical unity? Here are two
statements about it. 'For in one Spirit were we all baptized into
one body, whether Jews or Greeks, whether bond or free; and
were all made to drink of one Spirit' (1 Cor. 12. 13). 'There is
one body and one Spirit' (Eph. 4. 4). What they reveal is a
remarkable relation between the Body and the Spirit. The
hidden reality, the Spirit, has its counterpart in the manifestation, the Body. The Body is one because the Spirit is one. For
remember, the Holy Spirit is a Person and you cannot sub-
divide a person. 'God tempered the body together', because
the one Body is to be a manifestation of the one Spirit. There
is always unity in the Spirit. The divine fact is certain. The
only question is, do we always give diligence to *keep* the unity?
(Eph. 4. 3).

Before proceeding to a further word about the Holy Spirit
and the Body, let us remind ourselves that the starting-point
for spiritual unity is life. You may already have observed that
the four principles we have outlined above are not in fact expressed as command at all. They appear in 1 Corinthians 12 in
the form of statements of what the Body *is like*. They describe
it in terms of the spontaneous manifestations of life and growth
in a human body. This is significant, and it brings us to consider an important feature of life, namely, consciousness.

All animal life has its consciousness, but especially is this true
of life from God. Where there is life there is consciousness. A
biologist has no way of taking up life as a separate thing and
handing it to us to touch or look at, nor is there any way by
which we could see it if he did. Yet all will agree that, because
of our inward consciousness, we know we have life. We are
in no doubt at all that we live.

And the same is true of the new life. Though the life that
God gives cannot be handled or seen, it is certainly possible for
us to be conscious of it. We know new life because with it

there is awakened in us a new consciousness. When a man is born again, he receives new life from God. How does he *know* he has received it? How do any of us know we possess new life? We know by a new life-consciousness. If the life is there, the consciousness will be there and will very soon manifest itself, towards God, and towards sin. If we sin there is distress. We lose something of our peace and joy. It is this that proves the presence of life. Because the life of God hates sin, there has come to be in us a new consciousness towards sin. When a man constantly needs someone to point out his sins to him and is otherwise unaware of them himself, then, however willing to listen he may be, it is more than doubtful whether he possesses life.

To-day we place great emphasis on life, but that is not enough. We should emphasize also the consciousness of life. A being without consciousness has very little evidence of life. For it is a misunderstanding to think of life as abstract. It is concrete, real. In a human heart, either new life is present or it is absent, and life-consciousness is what confirms its presence. Nor is this consciousness merely negative, towards sin. It is also blessedly positive, towards God Himself. The Spirit witnesses with our spirit that we are the children of God—yes, but it is no use *telling* people that! Either they know it, or they don't. If they possess God's life they know it by the Spirit. Many, sad to say, pray prayers which have neither consciousness of sin nor love to God in them. One can only describe them as angels' prayers, for they bear none of the marks of the prayers of God's children.

But if what we have said is true of the life of the individual, it is no less true of the life of the Body. Those who possess life possess it in common with others, and they who know the Body are conscious of the corporate character of that life. For the Body is not only a principle or a doctrine; it too, implies a consciousness. As we are conscious of new life, so, if we are within the Body, we must necessarily be conscious also of that.

Some act towards the Body much as people do who determine to love their enemies because it is a Christian duty, or not to tell lies because it is wrong. But while it is very important whether we lie or not, what is far more important is whether, if we do, we are troubled inside. Inner consciousness of God and inner sensitiveness to sin are the basis of Christianity, these and not outward rules. So it is little use trying to live by the principle of the Body unless we are conscious that something is wrong when we do not. It is one thing to be told, and quite another to see. Consciousness is that inner sense that sees *without* being told. If the entrance of divine light can give in our hearts the consciousness of God, and of sin that is against God, it can give a like consciousness of the Body, and of conduct that is against Christ as Head of the Body. It was light from God that awakened in Paul a consciousness of the Body, and showed him that he was opposing himself to Jesus in the person of His members. Without the consciousness that comes from revelation and life, all is empty indeed.

'LOVE ONE ANOTHER'

Let me try now to illustrate the working of this faculty that I have called 'Body-consciousness'—this sensitiveness to the Body of Christ. It works first of all in the matter of love. 'We know that we have passed out of death into life, because we love the brethren' (1 John 3. 14). All, who are members of the Body, love. This is remarkable. It is not that any need to wait till they are told. Spontaneously, whether they think about it or not, they love. They may need exhortation, but that is in order to stir up what they have. I remember a friend telling me how, when his first child was put into his arms, his heart went out in love to him. No one needed to tell him it was a father's duty to love his child. He simply found love there. But is it not equally true that, no matter who or what a brother is, as soon as you know he is a Christian, your heart goes out in love to him? This is consciousness of the Body.

It works also in regard to division. Whereas in respect of love it is active and positive, in respect of division it is passive and negative. To those who have truly discovered the meaning of the Body, all division, and everything that makes for division is hateful in the extreme. To be found differentiating between Christians is, for them, to have stepped into a foreign world. Whether it is right or not to glory in denominationalism, those who recognize the Body of Christ know that to do so is an impossibility. A sectarian spirit, however hallowed by tradition and use, soon becomes intolerable to the man who possesses life.

Again, factions and cliques are becoming far too common among Christians to-day. There may be a company of twenty believers, all born of the Spirit, gathering around the Lord. In comes a brother, and immediately draws to himself a separate clique of a few. That is not the Body, and it cannot become the Body. But if, knowing our oneness in Him, we find ourselves drawn into doing such things, do we not at once become inwardly conscious of wrong? Something is surely lacking if we do not. If the Body means anything to us, all that divides, within and without, becomes abhorrent. Even to begin to create division is to forfeit our inward peace. We know we cannot go on. The consciousness of the one life will not allow it, and that is the sufficient answer.

This is not doctrine, but the living consciousness of our fellowship in Christ, and it is a very precious thing. The instant life comes to us, it awakens in us a growing and deepening sense of 'belonging'. We can no longer live a self-interested, self-sufficient Christian life. The nature of the butterfly, always 'going it alone', has given place in us to the nature of the bee, always operating from the hive, always working not for itself but for the whole. Body-consciousness means that we see our own standing before God, not as isolated units but as members one of another.

Units have no special use, exercise no ministry, can easily be overlooked or left out. Whether they are present or not is no one's concern. They scarcely affect even statistics. But members are otherwise. They cannot be passive in the Body; they dare not merely stand by looking on. For none are so hurtful as onlookers. Whether or not we take a public part in things is immaterial; we must always be giving life, so that our absence is felt. We cannot say 'I don't count'. We dare not attend meetings merely as passengers, while others do the work.

We are His Body, and members in particular, and it is when all the members fulfil their ministry that the life flows.

For all is bound up with life and the source of life. The head is the life-source of the human body; injure it, and all movement, all coordination ceases. A headless torso has neither life nor consciousness of life. As members of Christ, we receive new life from Him; but that life is 'in the Son' it is not something that we can carry away with us apart from Him. Detach us for one moment from Christ, and we should have no life. We well know how even a shadow between ourselves and Him may stem for a while its flow. For our life is *in Him*; we possess nothing in ourselves. They have the life who have the Son.

God does not therefore tell us to hold fast our fellow members, but to 'hold fast the Head'. This is the way of fellowship. For Christ is not divided; He is one. Lay hold of Him, and we shall find welling up in our heart a spontaneous love for all who do the same.

Oneness is Christ's, not ours. Because we are His, *therefore* we are one. For example, to say we have fellowship with a brother because we like him is to violate the oneness by centring it in ourselves. Though we may not naturally take to some so readily as to others, to let this affect our fellowship is simply to reveal its false basis. Or again, do we do something for a brother, and then complain of his ingratitude? That can only be because we did it seeking thanks, and not for Christ's sake—not because, in the first place, God so loved us. Our motive was wrong, because our relation to the Head was deficient.

It is 'holding fast' to our fellow members that leads to exclusive friendships. The Body has no room for these. If one Christian becomes infatuated with another, so that an unhealthy friendship develops, sure enough, before long their friendship will issue in faction. For fellowship that is 'after the flesh' is on a wrong foundation and can only lead eventually to sorrow. When two members cling exclusively to one another, we may justifiably fear that the love they express is not purely of God. 'Love one another' is either something in the sphere of the Body, and therefore Christ-centred, or it is wrong. May God save us from uncrucified natural choices, and help us in these things to follow the Spirit.

The anointing of the Spirit is God's gift to every babe in Christ (1 John 2. 18–20, 27). When we received Christ as Head we received the anointing—indeed the absence of it would be serious evidence that we were not yet united to him (Rom. 8. 9). John shows us this anointing as an inward thing, conveying even to those babes in Christ the teaching of the Spirit 'concerning all things'—that is, not just concerning the Scriptures. What do I mean? Let us take a practical illustration. Suppose I want to know whether or not to make a trip to Hong Kong. How do I decide? Do I seek a verse of Scripture? Or the advice of friends? Or do I set my mind to deciding the right or wrong of it? No, as we have often said, the basis of our life is not 'good or bad' but the anointing. 'Is the Holy Spirit in this thing? Is my heart empty or full as I approach it?' It is not a question of feeling or comparison, but of an enquiry Godward: 'Does the Spirit witness life? Does He assure me of the Father's good pleasure in this step?' That is the only safe test. For while the way we choose may be perfectly correct in itself, what really matters is that the Spirit is moving that way.

Herein lies the simplicity of the life of God's children. There is no need for so much questioning. Disobedience to the anointing will very soon give us a bad time with the Lord, whereas the mind of the Spirit is always life and peace (Rom. 8. 6).

Because the Spirit is one, when His children move thus, there will be no problems about fellowship. For the Body knows one law: that of the anointing. Rules are good in society, but not in the Body. The Pharisees were fundamentalists as far as the letter of the Old Testament was concerned. They lived by the letter; they knew all the rules—and so, perhaps we might feel, do we. But what if our knowledge of those rules permit us, as it did Saul of Tarsus, to stifle the Holy Spirit's voice? He knew the law, it is true, but he knew nothing of the Son of man in heaven (Acts 7. 55, 56). And to quench the Spirit is to stifle the very consciousness of our life together as the heavenly Man. It is to injure our relationship to the Head just as terribly as an affection of the nerves of a limb severs that limb from effective control by the higher centres. Do this, and soon, like Saul, we shall be found breathing out threatening and slaughter.

Saul's life of fellowship began when he said, 'What shall I do, Lord?' That is the secret. To 'hold fast the Head' is to *obey* Christ through the Spirit. To follow the Spirit is to be subject to the Lord Jesus in all things. The Spirit will never never impose that obedience on the members, but they who live by the anointing will always, instinctively and gladly, subject themselves to Christ; and in doing so, they will discover their oneness. Oh to see Him, then, as unquestioned Lord?

CHAPTER EIGHT

MINISTERING LIFE

THE highest purpose of God for the Church to-day is that she should build herself up in love by a ministry of life, and so grow up in all things into Christ. This is the goal set before her in Ephesians 4. Moreover in 1 Corinthians 13, a chapter that follows immediately on the passage about the Body we have just been considering, Paul shows us that it is love, not gifts, that God uses for the lasting edification of the Church. Gifts are expressed outwardly in works and speech, by miracles, healings, prophecy and so forth. Love is the fruit of the Holy Spirit's inward working through the Cross in the lives of the members. Gifts are the temporary method—God's method, to be sure—but it is in love that the Body builds itself up. (Eph. 4. 16). And when all else passes away, love remains.

Here we have an example of something we shall now take account of as we come to consider the ministry of the Church. I refer to the frequent emphasis in Paul's writings upon the better of two good things. Sometimes, within a given context, that emphasis is quite strong; at other times it is only implicit, but none the less to be taken account of. In this instance he is laying stress on permanency. Notwithstanding much that is said elsewhere about spiritual gifts, when in 1 Corinthians he contrasts them with love, he draws attention to their comparative impermanence (verses 8–11).

Spiritual gifts may not necessarily, in a given instance, be intended by God to be lasting; for gifts need not be at all dependent on the spiritual stature of the one gifted. Theirs is an objective ministry, whereas God's ultimate purpose in man is a subjective one, through the formation of the Spirit within him, and not merely by His temporary abode upon him. So gifts are called 'spiritual', not because the recipient is spiritual but because they come from the Holy Spirit.

Why is it that so many who have been greatly used often seem later to be set aside? In reply to that question I would first of all ask: How do we know that God *wanted* always to use them in that kind of way? May He not have had other plans? For God signs no contracts! And after all, do we not ourselves often employ a servant for a few days on an urgent task, well aware that he is unproved or inexperienced, and with no guarantee of keeping him on for ever, untrained, in that particular service? We reserve the right to make changes. May it not be that God similarly uses men for a time, and then, in this wisdom, changes the nature of their employment?

God *lends* His strength, and it remains a divine loan, never to become our possession. Samson, for example, had the gift of strength. It seemed there was nothing he could not do. Yet in spiritual understanding or purity of life, he was of small account before God. Remaining foolish he yielded to compromise, and so compassed his own downfall. When we compare him with Samuel who followed him, we see that God could only use him to fulfil an immediate purpose; no more than that.

It is thus a mistake to measure spirituality merely by the presence of gifts. By themselves they are an inadequate basis for a man's lasting usefulness to God. They may be present and they may be valuable, but the Spirit's object is something far greater—to form Christ in us through the working of the Cross. His goal is to see Christ inwrought in believers. So it is not merely that a man does certain things or speaks certain words, but that he is a certain kind of man. He himself *is* what he preaches. Too many want to preach without being the thing themselves, but in the long run it is what we are, and not simply what we do or say, that matters to God; and the difference lies in the formation of Christ within.

GOD'S GIFT OF MEN

In 1 Corinthians 12 Paul defines three subjects with which he sets out to deal, namely, gifts and the Spirit (verse 4), ministrations and the Lord (verse 5), workings and God (verse

6). These three correspond, I think, in a general way to the subjects treated in the following sections of the chapter: gifts with verses 7-11, ministries with verses 12-27 (the passage we have already considered in some detail), and workings with verses 28 and 29, and it will be noted that in the third instance priority is given to the *men* concerned—apostles, prophets, teachers.

The Spirit gives gifts; God gives men. Here is a distinction that I think we do well to notice. It is of course the special emphasis of Ephesians 4 (see verses 11 and 12), but the whole tenor of Paul's writings, and not least here in 1 Corinthians, is upon the character of the men whom God can use.

If we are content to emphasize only gifts and the teaching of truth, and to stop short there, we can be sure of blessing and fruit—on that level. But is that enough? Do we want merely to be used? Samson was used. So were Balaam and Saul—for a time. But tell me, does what they represent satisfy us? Saul was but a temporary king; Balaam a temporary prophet. For it is not just a question of their words or acts, but of the men themselves. It is worth noting that when Jesus quoted the Old Testament He did not say 'the prophecy of Isaiah' but 'the prophet Isaiah'. It is not 'Ye have rejected the prophecies' but 'Ye have rejected the prophets'. The Lord lays great emphasis on the men. Not to receive the prophets or the apostles is not to receive the God who sent them.

This, I believe, should be the basis of our training. Some people have expressed surprise that young men and women desiring to serve the Lord come to us in Shanghai, when we offer no courses of lectures in Bible knowledge and homiletics, or similar subjects. But our hope is that those who come may become better men; not merely that they may learn more doctrine or acquire greater skill as preachers. The need is not for greater gifts, but for men whom God can use. Too often others are helped by our gifts, but hindered by what we are. The living water has had to content itself with unclean vessels. There is shame in that.

It is of course true that God does take up those who are not worthy and permit them to speak His words years before they fully understand their import; but He does not wish any of us to stop there. We may go on in that way for a while, but is it not true that, from the time when He begins in us His work of formation through discipline and chastening, it growingly dawns on us how little in fact we knew of the true meaning of what we had been saying? He intends that we should reach the place where we can speak, with or without manifest gifts, because we *are* the thing we say. For in Christian experience the spiritual things of God are less and less outward, that is, of gift, and more and more inward, of life. In the long run it is the depth and inwardness of a work that counts. As the Lord Himself becomes more and more to us, other things—yes, and this must include even His gifts—matter less and less. Then, though we teach the same doctrine, speak the same words, the impact on others is very different, manifesting itself in an increasing depth of the Spirit's work within them also.

To His servants God gives the gift of prophecy; to the Church He gives prophets. And a prophet is one who has a history, one who has been dealt with by God, one who has experienced the formative work of the Spirit. We are sometimes asked by would-be preachers how many days should be spent in preparation of a sermon. The answer is: At least ten years, and probably nearer twenty! In this matter the proverb is true: 'The old is better'. For the preacher matters to God at least as much as the thing preached. God chooses as His prophets those in whom He has already worked what He intends to use as His message for to-day.

For to understand doctrine, and to know God, are two very different things. Spiritual things are never carried in the head. We lay weight upon good words, but God seeks good men. Some speak, and we are helped; others say the same words, and we are empty. The difference lies in the men themselves. We cannot deceive the Church with intellectual instead of spiritual values. The Church knows! Nothing can be a substitute for what a man is before God.

So the question is: Are we like the words we say? 'Lord, if I do not know Thee, and the meaning of Thy Cross, and the formative hand of Thy Spirit upon me, save me from presumption in speaking, and begin in me to-day whatever work is needed to remedy the deficiency. Break, mould, test, try me, so that I may speak that which I know.' This must be our cry; for to speak in His Name what we do not know will serve God, if at all, only a very little way.

GIFTS AND LIFE

'There are diversities of gifts, but the same Spirit. And there are diversities of ministrations, and the same Lord' (1 Cor. 12. 4, 5). We have suggested already that the latter statement finds its parallel in the passage from verses 12 to 27 which deals with Christ and the mutual life of His Body. But in the two statements I think we can recognize another useful distinction, namely, that between gifts and life, between the means used for ministering and the thing ministered.

Gifts are the means received from the Holy Spirit by which I give of Christ to the Body; the ministry (or 'ministration') is *what I give* of Christ to the Body. Each ministry contributes something more of Christ; and it is ministry rather than gifts that is compared here by Paul to the human body's functions of sight and hearing and movement. Thus, whereas different men may have the same gift, the same is not true of the different 'ministries' of life suggested by the language of this passage. Each is peculiar—the unique life-contribution of each member to the whole. It is that which you or I have received specially from the Lord to share with His people, and it may even be something the Body has never before received. For the fulfilling of this ministry of 'giving Christ', spiritual gifts are but the tools. I make use of them to give to the Body the Christ I know.

This is important, for it shows much so-called spiritual revival to have been on a wrong basis. Gifts are displayed, but without Christ, and that is like having many utensils but nothing to use them for. But it is worse, for without Christ, gifts are not only empty; they may also be deceptive. Some of them at least can be simulated in a way that a ministry of Christ can never be, whereas what matters to the Body is not our gifts, but the personal knowledge of Christ that we convey by them. In a hospital two nurses may use exactly similar spoons, but what they give in those spoons is the important thing; one may give costly and curative medicine, the other a mere palliative. It is *what* we minister that counts. The health and growth of the Body come from a ministry of Christ alone; they can never come merely from gifts as such. While gifts are needed (for 'to each one is given the manifestation of the Spirit to profit withal') they are never a substitute for Christ. Our first duty is to ask ourselves 'Have I anything to give?' and to learn by the Spirit how to give Christ to the Body.

How can I have a specific ministry? Not first by doctrine, but by life. Abraham learned faith in the place where only faith in God remained possible to him, not by being taught a doctrine. Abel learned in experience the value of forgiveness by blood. First come trouble, desperation, experience—*and life;* then afterwards doctrine. It is not in searching, studying, comparing, but at the place of desperation that God gives life. We should take every opportunity to study and learn, but therein we shall not find our ministry. Preachers are in special danger here, always looking for new light on the Scriptures, new themes for sermons. But the way to ministry does not lie there. Our special experience of Christ is what constitutes our ministry, and it is the trial of our faith that works in us experience.

At this point I would like to draw your attention to a significant change of emphasis that takes place in the writings of Paul himself, between his two letters to the Corinthians. 1 Corinthians, it seems, is occupied in the main with the ministry of gifts; 2 Corinthians with the ministry of life. In 1 Corinthians 12 and 14 many gifts are mentioned: wisdom, knowledge, healings, miracles, prophecy, discernment, tongues, interpretation and so on; and since these gifts are given for the good of the whole Church, the question mainly discussed there is: What is their special value? In 2 Corinthians 3 and 4 on the other hand, when Paul comes to speak of his own ministry, he does not emphasize gifts at all. He is clearly much more concerned about the formation of Christ within. Christ, the treasure in the vessel, is both the source and the theme of the ministry of the Church (2 Cor. 4. 7). 'Pressed, yet not straitened', 'pursued, yet not forsaken', 'smitten down, yet not destroyed', or as we might put it, 'done for—and yet not done for!': it is the triumphant survival in Paul of *this treasure* that is the secret. The death of Christ working in him becomes the source of a life to be shared with the people of God.

We may paraphrase Paul's expression in verse 10, 'the dying of Jesus' that I 'bear about in the body', as: 'the putting to death of Jesus that works death in me'. This working of death is, as I have said elsewhere, something different from the once-for-all death of Romans 6, for it is a constant daily process in the child of God. And it leads first of all to life in me (verse 10). But—and here is our present point—it does not stop there, but goes on, praise God, to minister also '*life in you*' (verse 12).

Life, Paul tells us, is that with which he serves the Church, and in so saying he defines the thing upon which all true ministry in the Church is founded. Death, working in the servant of God, produces life; and because he has life, others too have life. The Church receives, because some are willing to bear the Cross. It is their reception of the death of Jesus that counts. This is Paul's new lesson for the Corinthians. By allowing God to work through their trials and testings, praising Him and submitting to His will, His children make it possible for Him to bring life to others. But only those who pay this price receive this costly ministry. For life is released through death, but only so. And whereas gifts by themselves are less costly, what gifts may enable us to do and say can never make good deficiencies in what we are as servants of God.

Thus we see two ministries by which the Body is built up—gifts and life; and we may ask ourselves: In which do we discern God's highest purpose? I reply: Not in gifts, but in the life from Christ which comes through death. Gifts are not to be dispensed with (1 Tim. 4. 14; 2 Tim. 1. 6; 1 Peter 4. 10) but to set the greatest store by them is still to 'think as a child' in spiritual things (1 Cor. 13. 11). For it is in 2 Corinthians 3 and 4 that Paul points us forward to the thing most to be prized, and it is this, that out of our knowledge of Christ, acquired through the way He has led us, we minister to our brethren the life that the Spirit has formed in us.

To-day, many minister by gifts; comparatively few by life. That may not be wrong where believers are young in the Lord, and where the measure of life through the working of the Cross in them is limited to the brief span of their spiritual history. Then, for the edification of young churches and the winning of souls, spiritual gifts may take on a special significance. But they are not in themselves a mark of maturity, and they are certainly never something of which to boast. Their display establishes faith, but with an increasing measure of spiritual life in the church, the need to depend upon them becomes less, and so does the danger of pride that accompanies them. Such progress does not mean that the things said or done are necessarily different, but that the meaning within God's servant grows. The words may not have altered, but they spring from a deeper inward consciousness. Not gifts, but the working of the Cross: this is the measure of a man's spiritual stature. Only the foolish are proud of the words God gives, for has He not shown that He will speak, if need be, through an ass!

In a sense, then, whether or not we use gifts is secondary. The important thing is that we minister life—the life we receive from the Lord. And whether or not God allows individuals to retain certain gifts, and to increase them, is His affair. But one thing is certain, that in the progress of *His Church*, God makes ever greater use of life and less of gifts. At least in their more conspicuous manifestations, gifts tend to diminish, life to increase. For effective ministry to the Church neither speech, eloquence, miracles nor tongues are of first importance. God uses men as His mouthpieces for a time, and then, as far as these things go, He may choose to set them aside. But the life of the Body goes on. To trust in gifts is therefore folly, unless they minister life from the Giver of life.

THE ATTACK ON THE CHURCH BY DEATH

While He was on earth Jesus was Himself the vessel of divine life. When men touched Him they touched God; when they saw Him they saw God. All the fulness of the Godhead dwelt in Him in bodily form (Col. 1. 19; 2. 9). To-day that divine life is entrusted to the Church, His Body. She is the vessel of that life, destined to be filled unto all the fulness of God (Eph. 1. 23; 3. 19). All that is of Christ is intended to be seen in the Church. This is the purpose for which she has been left here by God. She is to contain and to display the life of His Son.

He is the Light, the Way, the Truth; He is the Son, the King, the 'I AM'. But what is His most distinctive rôle? In John 11. 25 He tells us: 'I am the resurrection and the life'. Surely this is the feature most characteristic of Him; and, as the opening chapters of the Book of Revelation show us, the Church is to know Him thus, as the risen and living One, so that she too may bear this same character. Her task is to manifest the life and resurrection of Christ.

From Eden onwards, God's controversy with Satan has been on this issue of death and life. (See for example Gen. 3. 3, 4; Rom. 5. 12, 17, 21; 1 Cor. 15. 22.) All of God is characterized by life, all of Satan by death. It is not only a question of holiness. There is much false holiness in the world, and we can readily be deceived by it, but life is one thing that cannot be simulated. Is there life in me? Do I touch life in another? These are the questions. For life is something deeper than thought, more real than feeling and doctrine. Where there is life there is God. The great difference between Christ and all others is that, whereas others are dead, He lives. Death could not touch Him. And God who destroyed death through Christ, now uses the Church for the same purpose. To-day she is God's vessel of life, called to reveal the risen life of His Son, and to bring men to the knowledge of that life.

But if this is the Church's work and ministry, we can readily see what will be the nature of Satan's attack upon her. Death will be his weapon. Note the importance of this. If the attack came by way of sin, or the world, or by direct assault only, we should know how to guard against it. But even when the question of sin is settled, and even if the world has no attractions for us, yet Satan still has power. It is no use stopping one hole if the vessel has several others!

Sin is but the road; death is the goal. To deal with sin is still not to have touched death. If you have already arrived at a place, the destruction of the road thither does not get you away from that place. Satan's power lies not just in the love of the world, or sin, or in any kind of direct assault, whether on mind or body or anything else. We may overcome all these things and yet not be overcomers for he still has power through death.

Praise His Name, God has shown us right from the outset from what quarter the attack upon the Church will come. We are to expect it from 'the gates of Hades'—that is, of death. This expression occurs only once in the New Testament, but there in Matthew 16. 18 it is in its right place. Satan's greatest fear with regard to the Church is of her resistance, not to sinning, or to the love of the world, or to any of his direct attacks, but to his power of death.

For Satan's power was through death, and wherever he has dominion, it is death you touch. Neither demon-possession nor sin are his most characteristic works, but death. For this reason, the work of Christ could not stop short at redemption. The heart of His work was to bring to nought *through death* him who had the power of death (Heb. 2. 14). This fact is a very great one. In the death of Jesus Christ, Satan's power of death met its match once for all. That death out-dies all other deaths. Death in Adam does not finish a man, but death in Christ does; it is a mighty death. In Christ all those who deserve to die have died, with the result that he who had the power of death no longer has dominion over them; they are dead. And ashes are something of which you can never make a fire. If a house is once burned to ashes there is no way of repeating the performance, for if the first fire has done its work, there is nothing for the next to do.

So the controversy between life and death that began in

Eden ended in Gethsemane and at Calvary. There death was abolished, and life and immortality brought to light. Not only is Satan destroyed, but for us redeemed sinners, because we have already died a death in Christ, death too is gone, and we have become possessors of His incorruptible life.

Yet we should not regard the controversy as concluded even there. If 'the gates of Hades' suggest a force, 'shall not prevail' implies a continuing campaign. It is still in progress to-day. Satan's special object to-day is to spread death within the Church. In this little while, death is still his power. If he can bring death to the people of God now, he is satisfied; nor does he mind how much virtue there is so long as, with it, death is also present and active.

'The mind of the flesh is death; but the mind of the spirit is life and peace. . . . So then, brethren, we are debtors, not to the flesh, to live after the flesh: for if ye live after the flesh, ye must die; but if by the spirit ye mortify the deeds of the body, ye shall live' (Rom. 8. 6 ff.). Words such as these, addresses as they are to believers, warn us to keep ourselves in life. But leaving aside sin, whose reward is death anyway, how many of us realize that to be merely passive in respect of life is to be a spreader of death? For in so doing we are giving room to the flesh.

Take a familiar example. There is no such spreader of death as scandal and criticism, *no matter how true to facts it be*. God wants us silent, but our tongue must work! He wants us quiet with Him, but our legs keep going! To go when He wants us to stay, or to gossip when He wants us silent, these things spring from the lust of the flesh, just as truly as do its cruder manifestations. To bring the flesh—even 'neutral' flesh—into God's work is to invite attack from the gates of Hades, and if we speak when God does not require it, be sure there is death in our words.

Life cannot be explained. When we touch it, we know it is life. But how? Not by thought or feeling or a 'sixth sense'. Those who know, know. Those who don't, don't. Those who know can never explain to those who don't—until they themselves know. Those who know life recognize it in others.

Those who have death in themselves recognize neither life nor death. The natural man may discern between warmth and coldness, good doctrine and bad, but not between life and death. Many think that if nothing goes visibly wrong in the Church, then all is well. But to be thus unable to discern what is life and what is death is a fatal lack. We shall not know when we are being attacked. May God grant us this discernment!

Because it is the earthly expression of Christ and is so precious to Him, the Church is the scene in which, if he could, Satan would stage a come-back, and for us to scatter death there is to be found cooperating with him. Alas, all that some of us do is just that! All our boasted 'ability' in the work of God becomes a tool in his hands. Our natural genius and brilliance, unrestrained by the Cross, brings death to the Church. Even our sound doctrine, if seized upon by the natural mind—yes, and our spiritual 'gift' too, if held and misused by the carnal man—spreads only death there. Remember Samson! Nothing that is not truly of God, the Fount of Life, can minister aught but death. In short, wherever men touch *me* rather than *Christ* in me, there they touch death and not life.

In this matter pretence is of no avail. The truth will out. For other things can be simulated, but life never. And as our spirit is, so is the impression we make. If death is there, death is what men meet; if life, then life.

This spreading of life or death is a present fact, in the home, the church, the prayer-gathering—everywhere. It is easier to preach when some are present, harder when others are there. Why? It has nothing to do with the persons. It all depends upon the pouring in or the draining away of life. Since the Body is the expression of Christ, only by ministering Christ can we contribute to the Body; and Christ is life. Those with life minister Christ in meetings. Others—even their 'Amen' is dead! The spiritual power of the gatherings for Breaking of Bread and for prayer depends on whether those present are merely negative, or are bringing in life. For here in this age is still echoed the controversy fought out in Eden and at Calvary.

Is resurrection life present? That is the question everywhere. Every member has a responsibility before God to bring into His house a ministry of the risen Christ.

MINISTERING LIFE TO THE BODY

The fact to which we find ourselves repeatedly brought back is that the Body of Christ is one. We cannot escape that fact, and Paul throws it once again into relief when he says: 'And whether one member suffereth, all the members suffer with it; or one member is honoured, all the members rejoice with it' (1 Cor. 12. 26).

It is important to note carefully what is said here. If one member suffers, what we are told is not that all the members ought to suffer, but that they actually *do* suffer with it. Nor is it said that if one member is honoured all the others ought to, but that they actually *do*, share the honour. If the oneness of the Body is not a fact, then these are no more than just beautiful sentiments. But because the oneness of the Body is a divine fact, it is also a fact that all the other members suffer with the suffering member. It is not just that they try to, or ought to, but that they actually do. Verse 26 is to be read, not as guidance or exhortation to Christians how to act, but as a statement of what in fact takes place. Because the Body is eternally one, the whole suffers when the member suffers, and the whole is uplifted when the member is uplifted.

The children of God are sometimes made aware of this as a matter of experience. A dear friend of mine in South China told me of her sense of deep spiritual burden at the time of outbreak of the Boxer rising elsewhere in the country, the news of which had not yet filtered through to her district, and again of a sense of life and uplift of spirit during the Welsh revivals in Britain, of the occurrence of which she was otherwise quite uninformed. Another friend whom I visited in the West surprised me, when I spoke to him of a particularly severe time of testing in our work in China, by saying, 'Of course we felt the reaction here some time before your letters reached us'.

But whether we are informed of such things or not is not the point. The fact is that whenever there is a movement on the part of the Lord, there is a reaction on the part of the Body, and all the members are subject to that reaction. Our awareness of it depends not upon information but upon our knowledge of the Lord by the Spirit of life.

If a member of the Body commits some grievous sin, or is subject to some great suffering, the spiritual members will surely feel the pressure. Conversely, if a fresh influx of life comes to any member, other members who are vitally in the life of the Body will as surely know an uplift. At times you may go through great travail before you receive revelation from God; at other times light breaks in without your seeking it. In the first case, I suggest, you are breaking through to a fresh influx of life that is to be ministered to others; in the second you are reaping the benefit of the sufferings of others through which increase has come spontaneously to the Body as a whole.

But there is another side to this. If you are one who seeks increase for personal ends, you are cutting off the flow of life to yourself from the whole Body; and should you attain the increase you seek, not only will it not profit you, it will be actually detrimental both to yourself and to the rest of the Body besides. The counterpart in the physical body of such a condition is the disease we call cancer. Cancer results from the over-development of one cell. That one cell multiplies itself without restraint or control, and in doing so consumes all the nourishment that comes its way, instead of passing it on to the rest of the body. Functioning as a separate unit, it encroaches on the tissues around, imposing its own distorted character upon them. And whereas the spontaneous working of nature tends to correct other diseases, it is no correction for cancer, for the more life the body pours into the diseased area the more the cancer absorbs for its own advantage. Because the outflow is arrested, all inflow only increases the trouble. How true this is of spiritual things! In the normal course, a fresh influx of life coming to any member of the Body instantly ministers increase to the whole; but if one member becomes isolated through desire for personal gain, then the more the member grows, the greater the menace to the whole Church of Christ.

How precious therefore is the Cross of Christ! It lies within the scope of every single member to raise the tide of life in the whole Body, provided he will let the Cross deal drastically with the life of nature in him. For the Body's sake let us pray: 'Lord, shatter in me all that is selfishly individual and that will weaken Thy Body, and for the sake of Thine own increase, cause me to touch realms of life never touched before!'

We have seen already how, in 2 Corinthians 4, the death of Christ operating in one place ('in the body', verse 10; 'in us', verse 12) allows Him to manifest His resurrection in two places ('in our body', verse 10; and 'in you', verse 12). Here we have fruitfulness of life and fruitfulness of ministry, and of course they are ultimately one, the only difference being in the place of manifestation. In the first instance, the life is manifested in the place where death operates; in the second, somewhere else. When the manifestation is in me I call it life, when in others I call it ministry.

Where there is no Cross there is no life, and no ministry of life. The object of suffering is that there may be a full and abundant ministry. Theory is no substitute for this. Poverty of ministry results from the choice of an easy road. Those who have an easy time all too often have little to give. They do not understand men's needs. Of course I don't mean we are to invite trouble, or by austerity to ill-treat our bodies. The Spirit Himself takes responsibility for our experience, leading us in paths where we encounter, in body, heart, or spirit, that measure of 'the dying of Jesus' that will mean enrichment to our ministry. It is our part only to follow.

You ask me how you can be used to minister life to the Body. Not by setting out deliberately to do a lot, nor indeed by running away into retirement and doing nothing, but simply by letting the Cross operate in the normal course of your walk with the Lord. Those who only serve by words and works find they have no ministry if at any time they are reduced to inactivity or silence. But the measure of your ministry is not determined by the measure of your activity.

Only let 'the slaying of Jesus' work in you, and life *must* manifest itself in others. It cannot be otherwise, for it is an abiding principle of the Body that 'death worketh in us, but life in you'. So you need make no special effort to bring increase to the Body in this way, or anything God takes you through by way of the Cross will spontaneously bring increase there.

Nor need you talk a lot, for it is not necessary to testify to your death experience in order for it to become vital to others. Provided you are willing for death, others *will* know life. Reality communicates itself; it is not dependent upon human communications. We 'despise not prophesyings', but we affirm nevertheless that ministry in the Body is not only a question of preaching or testifying. What we go through in secret with the Lord is quite sufficient to minister life to His members. If we suffer for the Lord's sake, that suffering will bring increase to others, without our making known the story of our suffering. Talking about it is not only superfluous; in some circumstances it is an abomination.

If you forgive a brother, the reality of your forgiveness will minister life to the Body quite apart from any expression of it (though in this case the Lord may of course require of you that it be expressed). If you truly love a brother, that love will build up the Body though you may never tell that brother how you love him. I found myself once, at short notice, taking part on the platform in a large convention meeting in England where, unknown to me, a Japanese brother was to be one of the speakers. We had not met before—and our two countries were at war. I do not know what that brother felt, and we had opportunity for only a brief conversation. I only know that while he spoke I was aware of the love and fellowship of a brother in the Lord, a love that leaped over national barriers and that did not demand words for its expression.

The Body of Christ is ministered to, not first of all by preaching and working, but by inward reality. The Holy Spirit is concerned with what is real and true, and will never witness to what is not real. What you communicate by words is what you are already bringing of Christ to the Church, for as we have said, the Body is ministered to by a communication of life. And life is communicated to others, quite simply and spontaneously, as death operates in us. So the question is not, How much are you doing or saying? but, How much are you going through under the hand of God?

Ministry on any basis other than the oneness of the Body is unreal. Until you have seen that fact, you constantly wonder how you can function; but when you see it, you know that as soon as you yourself have received something, the Body *has* received it. What is yours *is* the Body's, and there is no need to struggle to pass it on. Do you want to build up the church? Then let it be built up in you. What you receive from the Head, the Church, His Body, spontaneously receives; and what you have not received, it can never receive through you. The question of ministry is settled when the question of receiving is settled; and the question of receiving is settled by 'the dying of Jesus'.

WORDS THAT ARE SPIRIT AND LIFE

Of course there is a place—and a great need—for the ministry of the Word. We can, if we like, classify spiritual gifts into gifts of *work* or action (such as healings, miracles) and of *word* (such as prophecy, teaching, tongues, and so forth), and if we do so I think we shall discover that Paul tends to lay his main stress on the latter. Whatever they may possess of other gifts, all the three classes of men—apostles, prophets, teachers—that head his list in 1 Corinthians 12. 28 are surely, first of all, ministers of the Word of God. We are told for example that this, together with prayer, was the main concern of the Twelve when they sought release from administrative tasks to 'continue . . . in the ministry of the word' (Acts 6. 4). So Paul concludes his comments on this list with the exhortation to 'desire earnestly the greater gifts', and then, returning to the subject after his intervening discourse on love, adds: 'but rather that ye may prophesy' (12. 31; 14. 1). Indeed Chapter 14 that follows is quite taken up with gifts of speech, and passes over miracles or gifts of action altogether.

So for the building up of His Church, God emphasizes the ministry of the Word above the ministry of works. The Church is not to trust in miracles, for they may only lead to outward things. Israel in the wilderness continually touched God's works, but missed His life. So did the multitudes in the Gospels, who witnessed the Lord's gracious acts but knew nothing of the life He came to give. Even the disciples fell short here, for having performed miracles themselves, they fell at last to arguing who of them should be the greatest. Here was no building in love!

But 'the seed is the word'. Apart from God's Word of life, nothing counts for much. Miraculous works may support the Word; they cannot by themselves minister life. It is by the eternal Word of the Lord that the Church must grow.

Many ills of the Church to-day spring from the fact that Christians are content with a merely objective acceptance of doctrine. They seek an outward, mental light on the Scriptures, but stop short of a subjective application of the Word of God to experience. They find many mental difficulties in the Bible, and light, to them, is the solving of these. For many, general truth has taken the place of specific truth. They feel that all is well if they are 'conservative' or 'orthodox' in their doctrine, and give mental assent to this and mental dissent from that. By this reasoning, fundamentalists consider themselves on a far higher plane than modernists; yet they measure up spiritually in God's eyes only in so far as they possess a true inward revelation of Christ, and no further. They may be perfectly *right*, but unless they possess life, they lack the one supreme essential.

To-day the Church has the letter of the Word, and we praise God that she does! We have our Bibles and our translations, and we thank Him for them all. But the letter—even the fundamental letter—kills; it is only the Spirit that gives life (2 Cor. 3. 6). If we are to bring life to others, we must not only preach the Word according to God's thought of centuries ago; we must know also how the Spirit applies that Word to men to-day.

For a 'prophet' in the New Testament is one who, like Elijah or John the Baptist, proclaims God's present purpose for His people. His preaching is of the utmost importance, because it brings to light through the Word the mind of God for his own day. Three things characterize a prophet: a history before God, an inward burden, and divinely-given words that express and interpret that burden, so that having ministered the Word he returns home with his burden gone.

For such a ministry to-day the study of the Scriptures is essential. Of course, any reasonably intelligent person can learn a lot of the Bible in a year, but if we are serious with Him, God will not let that pass without taking steps to ensure that what we are tallies with what we say. For understanding of the Scriptures comes in two ways, one merely from study, the other from knowing and following the Lord Himself, and there is a vast difference between the two. On the mere level of the understanding of doctrine, a graduate in theology may be able to systematize perfectly for you all that the Scriptures contain. Yet he will not be proclaiming the Word until that Word has come to him directly from God, and he has responded. Another man, with no knowledge of theology as a science, may yet minister out of a deep knowledge of God, because God speaks to him through the Word, and because whenever God does so, he unquestioningly obeys.

When a brother stands up and speaks, you know at once whether he stresses doctrine or life. If it is the former, he never runs risks. He keeps carefully within the limits of his doctrinal system, in order to be absolutely safe and to avoid all possible chance of misunderstanding. He presents his many reasons in logical order, and at length, by a process of induction, arrives at his incontrovertible conclusion. But one who stresses life will be far less concerned with technical correctness, or with the exhaustive treatment of his subject. His approach will be a quite different one, for he has himself known conditions through which doctrine alone could never carry him. If only, therefore, he can fulfil his one object, which is to present Christ to his hearers, he will not feel the absolute need to produce for this purpose a fully logical and fool-proof case.

For the Bible itself is not like that. In His Word God has never given us a completely systematic setting forth of any doctrine—never, that is, as we understand system. The Bible does not reach its conclusions by induction, and there are in it many passages capable of being misunderstood. Sometimes, I am afraid, we may almost dare to feel that, had we been writing it, we would have put things far more plainly! The great spiritual facts, the mighty eternal truths of God, seem often half obscured in His Word, so that the natural man cannot easily discover them. Nevertheless, through the Spirit, things hidden from the wise and prudent have been revealed to babes. Blessed be God, that has been His way! Salvation, righteousness by faith, sanctification, life—do we know these things merely as doctrinal themes, or as actualities? God's thought is not that we should only grasp them with our minds, but that we should experience them in life.

A vast knowledge of the Bible will not make up for a little knowledge of the Lord. We must know *Him*, and the Bible as *His* Word, the expression of His present mind in regard to His people. You ask, *Can* we know the mind of God? Yes indeed, for God has not withdrawn Himself. He still speaks through the Scriptures as He always did, even to-day when the Church is so sadly defeated. He still chooses those with a history before Him, to be His spokesman in their generation. In an hour when men are so largely unconcerned about divine things, the Church's desperate need is of men with such knowledge.

God seeks true ministry in His saints. That is why we have such bad times! We must not question it if He leads us into the unexpected, for when He does so, we can be sure it is with some definite goal in view. For the ministry to the Body of a personal knowledge of Christ can lift every member onto a new spiritual plane. Perhaps our greatest service to the Lord would be to make way for Him to do the unprecedented with us, and so make possible a new enrichment of life for the entire Body of Christ.

Should we not, therefore, gladly place ourselves in His hands, that we may be found with some definite discovery of Christ to contribute? 'Lord may I receive from Thee some measure of life that the Body has never before received, that Thy people may be enriched and Thy heart satisfied!'

CHAPTER NINE

GATHERED IN THE NAME

IN earlier chapters we have placed strong emphasis upon the unity of the Church. Always and only have we seen her as one and undivided. Now we have to ask ourselves a question: Is there any point at which this view of her has to be qualified? For does not Scripture speak not alone of 'the Church' but also of 'the churches'. Where and at what point does the Church of God become the churches of God?

If we look carefully into this, we shall discover that the basis of division (if we can use that word at all) is a single one—that of locality alone. If the New Testament is to be our guide, the *only* ground of division contemplated is geographical. There is in the Word of God no room for the grouping of Christians together into things called 'churches' on such grounds, for example, as history or doctrine, mission-connection or personal allegiance, or even a special message or ministry. The names given to churches in Scripture are invariably those of cities, that is, of local centres of community life. We read of 'the church of God which is in Corinth', 'the church of the Thessalonians', 'the seven churches that are in Asia' (each, of course, named after a single city), and so forth. It is such expressions alone that designate the Church of God distributed on earth, and Scripture knows no exceptions.

But this brings us to another thing, and it is this, that the very same word 'church' is used locally as is used universally (for of course in Greek there is no distinction by capitals and lower case). We read of 'the Church which is His Body' but we read also 'the church of God which is at Corinth' and 'the church in thy house' (Eph. 1. 23; 1 Cor. 1. 2; Philemon 2). Surely this means that the church in a locality *is* the Church which is His Body (with all the profound wealth of meaning that goes into that term) finding her local expression in that place at that time.

But if this last statement is true, it places an altogether new emphasis upon one thing of which we may till now have missed the significance, namely, the importance to God of the present local expression of the Body comprising all the members of Christ in any one place. In Corinth or Laodicea, Rome or Lystra, all the members of Christ by new birth were called upon to function against the secular background as an expression of the one Body. Every dividing of them up on other principles would only touch their life and testimony adversely.

Leaving aside, of course, the more limited grouping together of brothers and sisters for special tasks in the work of the Lord, I affirm again that the Church embraces all the believers; it has no room for sectarian alliances. It was one of the reproaches held against the church in Corinth that parties had begun to appear there claiming personal allegiances. To-day that kind of thing has become perpetuated in various ways, but to this Paul's challenge is as strong and clear now as it was then: 'Is Christ divided? Was Paul crucified for you? or were ye baptized in the name of Paul?'

In a passage at the end of Romans touching on the subject of church life, the apostle begins his discussion with the words 'God hath received him', and ends it with 'Christ also received us' (14. 3; 15. 7). Here is the simple basis of all our life and fellowship with others. It is that they belong to the Lord, and so do we. That is sufficient. We do not join with them because they and we belong to the same denomination or owe our Christianity to the same mission, nor because both share a liking for a certain preacher or his message, nor yet because they hold particular doctrinal views and we hold the same views, nor even because they have had a certain Christian experience and we have had a like experience. No, we join with them solely and sufficiently because they belong to the Lord and we too belong to the same Lord. It is in Him that we are one.

It is not my desire here to attack denominational Christianity as wrong. I only say again that, for the Body of Christ to find effective local expression, the basis of fellowship must be a true one. And that basis is the life-relation of the members to their Lord and their willing submission to Him as Head. Nor am I pleading for those who will make a fresh sect of something called 'localism'—that is, the strict demarcation of churches by localities. For such a thing could easily happen. If what we are doing to-day in life becomes to-morrow a mere method, so that by its very character some of His own are excluded from it, may God have mercy upon us and break it up! For all those in whom the Lord, the Spirit, has liberty are ours and we are theirs. No, I am pleading only for those who will see the heavenly Man, and who in their life and fellowship will follow after that! Christ is the Head of the Body—not of other 'bodies' or units of religion. Involvement in the spiritual Body of Christ is what secures the committal of the Head to us, His members—that, and that alone.

'CONCLUDING THAT GOD HAD CALLED US'

We must now consider this matter of divine committal to the Church along three lines—those of guidance, discipline, and prayer. God has made a three-fold provision for our guidance in the Christian pathway: we have the Holy Spirit, we have the Word of God, and we have the Body of Christ. The Word of God shows me the will of God for me; the Holy Spirit reveals the will of God in me; the Body, by putting that will into the larger perspective of the divine purpose, shows me how it is to affect my relationships as a member. (This will, no doubt, recall what we said earlier about the two-fold will of God, 'A and B'.) Unhappily, because of our reaction against the tyranny of Rome which has made so much of the political world-Church, we are inclined to discard altogether the third of these divine gifts. But every error arises out of a distortion of truth. The truth here is that the Body *is* one, and that fellowship in the Body remains an essential factor in my spiritual illumination. I must know the mind of God, not only by the Word of God to me, nor yet alone by the Spirit of God in me, but together with both of these, by taking also my place among God's people in His house.

We would all agree that there is such a thing as individual prayer and there is also such a thing as Church prayer. But equally there is such a thing as light given to the individual and there is also such a thing as light given to the Church. Is it not true that, without the nature of our problem being known to anyone, we often receive light in a church meeting that we cannot discover at home with the Word? Why is this? Surely because the Church is the House of God, the place of manifestation of divine light. Outside we may have the light of nature, but in the sanctuary there is no light, natural or artificial, save the Shekinah of God Himself.

This principle of fellowship in guidance was one of the foundations of Paul's life and ministry. We see it in Acts 13, where, as with several others he is found waiting on the Lord, the Holy Spirit says to them 'Separate me Barnabas and Saul for the work whereunto I have called them'. We said earlier that the anointing of the Spirit is given for the personal guidance of every individual believer, and in keeping with this, we know that on at least two occasions Saul had earlier received a personal call of God to go to the Gentiles (Acts 26. 16–18; 22. 21). But now the time and way of that leading forth is revealed to several together. Luke says 'they sent them away', but he also describes them as 'sent forth by the Holy Ghost' (13. 3, 4). Here we have the Church and the Spirit acting in conjunction, the initiative of the one Spirit being expressed in the one Body.

Again, at the end of chapter 15 we find Paul and Silas being 'commended by the brethren to the grace of the Lord' as they set out for Syria and Cilicia. Though it is never safe to argue from silence, it may be significant that the going forth of Barnabas to Cyprus, which is not covered by a similar statement of commissioning by the Church but seems to have been a more personal move, takes him also at that point out of the Scripture record (verses 36–41).

A little later, in Troas, a vision appeared to Paul: 'Come over into Macedonia and help us', and after describing it Luke goes on: 'We sought to go forth . . . concluding that God had called us to preach the gospel unto them' (16. 9, 10). The Lord often gives a vision to an individual, but the movement is not based on that individual alone. It is based on a corporate seeking of God. And in this passage too it is the Holy Spirit who takes the initiative (verses 6, 7). It is because we move with the Holy Spirit that we are found moving with the Body. The real test of the vision will always be that the Spirit of truth witnesses to it.

'RESTORE SUCH A ONE'

In Matthew chapter 18 the Lord tells me how I may need to be rebuked by a brother, and how when he comes, if I decline to heed what he says, the point may be reached where the witness of the church as a whole needs to be called in to bring me to see my error. (Or of course the situation may be reversed, and my brother be the offender.) The thought immediately presents itself: How totally out of place it is for one sinner to discipline another! If we are to have any part or lot in such a ministry of correction, it can never be on the ground of our superiority to those with whom we seek to deal. They and we have alike sinned, and our hope in dealing with them is that there may be shown to them by God the same grace that has been shown to us.

Now suppose, in the example given, you are the offended party, then you are also the one appointed to deal with the offender. How are you going to do it? To flare up and vent your wrath on him will be to treat him as an enemy, remote from you. But just to forgive him and ignore the whole affair will be no better. You are treating him instead as a stranger and an inferior, for thereafter, whenever he sees you he remembers that he has wronged you, and whenever you see him you remember that you have behaved magnanimously in forgiving him.

No, he is your brother, and your attitude towards him is to be that of a brother dealing with a brother. You should treat the matter exactly as you would had the offence been committed against someone else and not against yourself. Deal with the case as if you were a third party (like the brother who may be called in later to help *you* if the need arises). And the Lord states very clearly what is to be your object in doing so. It is not the winning of your case, but to be told, 'Thou hast gained thy brother'.

We are to take this clause, surely, as covering the whole incident. That is to say, if your brother does not respond, and you are compelled to take two or three others with you as witnesses and seek him out again, your attitude is to be no different. It is still one, not of bringing a charge, but of seeking to win a brother. And in the extreme case where the whole church has to be called in, there is even then to be no change of purpose. The goal of the discipline remains that brother's restoration. Even one in spiritual advance of another dare not take a 'better-than-thou' position, standing as one on a superior level to correct an inferior.

'Ye which are spiritual', says Paul, 'restore such a one in a spirit of meekness; looking to thyself, lest thou also be tempted' (Gal. 6. 1).

This brings us a step further, for our passage in Matthew 18 proceeds with these significant words about the authority of the members together: 'What things soever ye shall bind on earth shall be bound in heaven: and what things soever ye shall loose on earth shall be loosed in heaven' (verses 15–18). 'What is this? It is not the tyranny of the church's overseers, nor is it the verdict of the majority over the minority. It is the church arising to purge the church.

The discipline of a member should never be a mere matter of business; rather should it be one of heart concern for the whole church. It is an abominable thing to see the disciplining of any child of God carried through in a trifling manner, as though it were a light thing; but it is no less abominable to see it carried through as a serious matter, if the seriousness is only that of a law-court. No discipline should be without grief and tears on the part of those who exercise it, nor can it ever be if they have recognized what the Church is. Paul wrote: 'There is fornication *among you*'. He did not, in the first place, locate that sin in any individual believer; he located it in the church. And he wrote: 'Ye are puffed up, and did not rather mourn' (1 Cor. 5. 1, 2). The sin was the sin of the whole Body, and the shame and the sorrow should not be just of one member but of the whole.

In Church discipline we need to see the oneness of the Body of Christ, but we need also to see not just the fact but also the potentiality of sin. I must first locate *in myself* the sin that is manifest in my brother, and not till I have judged it in myself dare I judge it in him. By the grace of God I may not have committed the same act, but I have within me the sin that provoked that act.

Discipline is always a remedial measure, and has as its object the recovery of the sinning brother. Even in the most extreme case the end in view is 'that the spirit may be saved in the day of the Lord Jesus' (1 Cor. 5. 3–5). Where God's children are concerned, there is mercy in all His judgment; and when we judge any of His children on His behalf, whether we do so as the whole church or as individual members, we should be full of mercy. Even though our outward act may have to be one of discipline, our inner attitude should be one of love.

After His resurrection, our Lord said to His disciples, 'Receive ye the Holy Spirit', and added immediately. 'Whose soever sins ye forgive, they are forgiven unto them; whose soever sins ye retain, they are retained' (John 20. 22, 23). Rome appropriated this falsely, and reacting against Rome, we repudiate it. But in doing so how much have we Protestants lost! And how much is God losing! For what belongs to the Church of God cannot be lightly thrown away. Though 'the church' be but a handful of simple village believers gathering in a home, if they see themselves in Christ as an expression of His Body, and if, confessing before Him their weakness, they claim His wisdom and power, the Lord stands by that. 'For where two or three are gathered together in my name, *there am I.*'

THE LIMITATIONS OF GOD

We have seen guidance and discipline in the Church; we will turn now to the Church's prayer. As we have said, funda-

mentally there are two kinds of prayer. The first is individual
and devotional. We find it repeatedly alluded to in John's
Gospel in such promises as the following: 'Whatsoever ye shall
ask in my name, that will I do, that the Father may be glorified
in the Son' (14. 13; compare verse 14 and chapters 15. 7, 16;
23, 24). There are no conditions here. It is a promise for every
individual member of Christ, and it makes prayer a very great
thing. If, in the light of such statements, God does not hear
and answer our individual prayers, we may feel there is surely
something wrong with them.

But the second kind of prayer both includes the first and
goes beyond it. It is that described in our passage in Matthew
18: 'Again I say unto you, that if two of you shall agree on
earth as touching anything that they shall ask, it shall be done
for them of my Father which is in heaven' (verse 19). This is
the Church's task, her God-given ministry of prayer. For the
promise here is conditional; there must be at least two, and
they in agreement.

And why is their prayer answered? The next verse explains:
'For where two or three are gathered together in my name,
there am I in the midst of them'. They 'are gathered' (passive
voice); they do not just meet. We see the difference, for to be
gathered is not merely to go of ourselves; it is to be moved by
the Spirit, as they were moved who gathered at Hebron to
make David king. And they come, not on their own affairs,
but having a single common concern for His. It is this that
unites them 'into' His Name. And when this is so, then 'I am
in the midst', leading, revealing, enlightening. And, praise
God, that is not a promise, it is a statement of fact! We *know*
when He is present, and that presence explains why two on
earth have such power.

God waits for the prayers of His children to bring in His
Kingdom. For if this age is important, the age that follows is
infinitely more so. All the privileges and power we enjoy now
are only a foretaste of the powers of the age to come. The
fulness of God that is hidden now will be manifest then. In the
light of this, we see the importance of what we call 'The Lord's
Prayer'. For thousands of years God commanded His people

to pray, but through the centuries He gave them no instruction as to what they should pray about, apart from this one prayer.

'Thy kingdom come!' We are to pray for this. If His Kingdom would come of itself, we should not have been given that command. But God's people are to pray, for His work is always done in response to His people's cry. The Lord's prayer is not just a model prayer for me; it is a revelation of God's heart. 'True prayer begins at the heart of God, is made known to the hearts of men, is prayed back to God again, and God answers.' That is more than a definition; it is, I believe, the principle of God's working in the universe.

'Thy will be done!' Yes, but where? 'On earth', for this is the only place where to-day God's will is not done. Then how can God's Kingdom be brought in down here? By the created will, in union with the Uncreated Will, seeking the displacement of the rebellious will of the devil. For prayer is always three-sided. It involves someone prayed to, someone prayed for, and someone prayed against; and on earth there *is* someone to pray against—a will that is opposed to God's. Against that rebellious will, God will not act alone. He awaits our prayers.

There are many passages in the Gospels which affirm that God has subjected Himself to limitations. We find Jesus prevented from entering a Galilean city, or refused passage through a Samaritan village, or again, powerless to do any mighty work in Nazareth (Mark 1. 45; Luke 9. 53; Mark 6. 5). 'How am I straitened!' He could cry; 'How often would I have gathered thy children . . . and ye would not.' 'Ye will not come to me, that ye may have life'. (Luke 12. 50; Matt. 23; 37; John 5. 40.) So the grain of wheat has no other course than to 'fall into the earth and die'; and still to-day the word of God must be sown 'among thorns' (John 12. 24; Matt. 13. 22). The same thing continues on into the later New Testament history, as well as being found, of course, everywhere in the Old. The water of divine deliverance depends upon the provision of human ditches. The oil of the Spirit flows until 'there is not a vessel more'. 'Behold, the Lord's hand is not shortened, that it cannot save; neither his ear heavy, that it cannot hear: but your iniquities . . .' (2 Kings, 3. 16, 18; 4. 6; Isaiah 59. 1, 2).

How did it come about that Omnipotence became limitable by man? And will it continue throughout eternity? For surely, God is El Shaddai, 'God Almighty'; eternity past and eternity to come hold nothing able to limit Him, nothing to arrest or hinder or delay.

But God has a will. He seeks communion with a people who will share His life and manifest His Son. To that end He created heaven and earth—and man; and then the trouble started. For, in keeping with His purpose, God had created man a being with free-will, and He has determined not to accomplish that purpose without the free co-operation of man's will. This is a solemn principle; none more so. It means that, whereas in the eternities God was absolute, here in time He has chosen, instead of compelling His creatures, to limit His own omnipotence to their free choice. Man has been given power to make way for, or to obstruct, the power of God.

To such limitation God was prepared to subject Himself, knowing the triumph of divine love that would as a result be manifest in the future of eternity. He works towards that goal. His glory is that, in the ages to come, man's free-will will be one with the will of God. The omnipotence then will be morally greater even than in eternity past, because there will be a *possible* limitation. Man will still be *able* to disobey, but he will never choose to do so. The separate, created will of man will be wholly set for God; and that is glory.

We know the risk God was willing to run in order to gain this end, and that when man's first choice led him in a wrong direction, the Father sent the beloved Son to redeem the loss. Here was One whose will was absolutely identified with God's, and, praise God! through His death and resurrection and by the power of the Spirit, a Body was formed whose members will be no less committed to that Uncreated Will. In them the divine limitations will be for ever done away. The Church is to secure for God the release of His power into the world, by bringing it to bear on evil situations in the realm of the spirit, for their overthrow. The Church is—I speak reverently—to restore to God His own omnipotence.

Prayer is the present exercising of my will in God's favour; declaring that His will shall be done. For this is true prayer, that what God makes known, we express. Man wills something that God has already willed, and gives it utterance. We do not ask ourselves 'Is my prayer *according to* God's will?' but '*Is* it God's will?' The will of God is the starting-point; we voice it; God does it. And if we do not voice it, it will not be done. Our prayers thus lay the track down which God's power can come. Like some mighty locomotive, His power is irresistible; but it cannot reach us without rails. When men cease to pray, God ceases to work, for without their prayer He will do nothing. It is they who direct heaven's power to the place of need.

Read again Matthew 18. 18–20 and see the tremendous range of the Church's responsibility in prayer. The measure of the Church is the measure of God in the earth to-day. As once He was revealed through Jesus Himself in Jerusalem and Galilee, so now He is revealed through His Church wherever it is found world-wide. He cannot go beyond the extent of the Church, for the Church alone represents the coming race. She stands for God on the earth, and what she looses and binds, heaven looses and binds. On earth to-day God's power is as great as her prayers; no greater. All that He does in relation to his eternal purpose, He does through her, and where she falls behind in her work, to that extent He is limited.

The Church cannot increase God's power, but she can limit it. She cannot make Him do what He does not will to do, but she can hinder that which He does will. There are many things that He would bind and loose in heaven—things which hinder to be bound, things of spiritual value to be loosed—but movement on earth must precede movement in heaven, and God always waits for His Church to move.

'What things soever': these are precious words. Here heaven is measured by earth, for there is always more power in heaven than the measure of our asking; there is always more to be loosed or bound in heaven than we ask down here. Why do we want deliverance from sin? Why do we cry to God for enduement? To pray 'Thy will be done in me' is a good beginning, but we must go on to 'Thy will be done *on earth*'. The children of God to-day are taken up with far too small things, whereas their prayer is intended for the release of heaven's mighty acts. Prayer for myself or my own immediate concerns must lead on to prayer for the Kingdom. Here is the answer to the question: What is the ministry of the Church? She is to be heaven's outlet, the channel of release for heaven's power, the medium of accomplishment of God's purpose. Many things have accumulated in heaven because God has not yet found His outlet on earth; the Church has not yet prayed.

How is God to get this? How is He going to have His Church on His side? Only by every one of us remembering, in the solemn conditions of to-day, that this ministry of being God's outlet is our greatest possible work. God shows what He wants, we stand and ask, and God acts from heaven: this is true prayer, and this is what we must see fully expressed in our prayer meetings. If the Church here in Shanghai, not to speak of other places, does not know this ministry of prayer, may God forgive us! Without it, all else is empty; God has no vessel here. 'Not every one that saith unto me, Lord, Lord, shall enter into the kingdom of heaven; but he that doeth the will of my Father which is in heaven' (Matt. 7. 21). With the Kingdom in view, all we have and all we are must be set for the will of God. God needs this. He must have a few throughout the nations who hold on in prayer, and who, by driving a wedge into the power of the enemy, bring in the next age. That is overcoming. Whether the members be many or few, may God maintain our strength to work for Him in deep, strong, prevailing prayer.

SPOILING THE STRONG MAN'S GOODS

'And ye shall chase your enemies, and they shall fall before you by the sword. And five of you shall chase an hundred, and an hundred of you shall chase ten thousand: and your enemies shall fall before you' (Lev. 26. 7, 8). This was the promise of God to Israel as a people; but in the event, the reckoning seems to have been even more astounding, for one is said to have chased a thousand, and two to have put ten thousand to flight (Deut. 32. 30). Here surely is a picture of prayer, individual or corporate, alone or with two together. For where two agree on earth, heaven binds ten thousand foes. How often have the people of God, in an hour of crisis, taken these words of Jesus at their face value and proved them! So on the night when Peter lay in prison, the church throughout Jerusalem got to its knees and prayed earnestly, and all Herod's authority was as nothing before the response of heaven to that prayer. Another Kingdom had invaded his territory, and even the great prison door yielded and gave way of itself.

Another Kingdom had invaded his territory. To elaborate this statement, let me take an illustration from modern history. As most Westerners are aware, a century ago the great foreign powers trading with China used their force of arms to impose on the Chinese people a principle against which they have ever since harboured a deep resentment. I refer to what is usually termed 'extraterritoriality'. By this principle, areas of Chinese territory were ceded to the foreign powers, and the citizens of those powers were made immune from legal action by the Chinese authorities for any personal infringement of the laws of China. They could be tried only by a consul or other public functionary of their own country, and according to that country's foreign laws. It was a high-handed way of doing business, and to-day all recognize the imposition as having been unjust. Yet perhaps, without fear of misunderstanding, we may use it to illustrate something quite different and in no sense unjust, namely, the present invasion of this earth by heaven's gracious rule.

How does this illustration apply to us? It does so in two ways. First as to ourselves, God has 'made us to be a kingdom' (Rev. 1. 5, 6). As far as this world is concerned, we are citizens of a 'foreign' power. Delivered from the kingdom of darkness we are no longer subject to the prince of this world, under whose sway it lies. Instead we own allegiance to another King and are subject to another law. As to our persons, we have 'extraterritorial rights'.

But secondly, as to this world itself, here too we have claims to make. For over it man was created to have dominion, and what he lost, the Son of man has recovered. To-day, spiritual world-rulers have usurped that dominion, and the Church's vocation is to reclaim it from them. Though he is its 'prince', Satan is in fact a usurper—an illegal squatter on God's inheritance.

Suppose a man somehow gets into your house and occupies it without your authority. What do you do? You go to the magistrate, and, appealing to the law of the land, you get a verdict against him. You return armed with a court order, and you turn him out. He may be fortunate not to go out in chains! But the situation in this world is no different. God's 'statute book' has already ruled against this world's illegal occupant. He is to go! What matters it that in Satan's eyes the law of the Kingdom of heaven is a 'foreign' law? Calvary has established the superiority of that Kingdom. At the Cross, Christ overthrew Satan's whole legal standing. Now it is the Church's task to see that other law is put into effect. Crying to God like the widow in the parable, 'Avenge me of my adversary!' she is to obtain the order for his eviction, and throw him out. God waits for that cry. In a given situation, and at His word, we are to put down our foot on a piece of spiritual territory occupied by evil powers, and to lay claim to it for God.

What kind of men are needed for this task? I say again: just simple believers, it may be only two or three together, but with the Lord in the midst. For we do not ourselves have to bind the strong man—that is already done—but only to remind him that he has no real escape from his bonds! Let me illustrate by telling you a story.

In a certain city in China there were two sisters. They were unlearned, and, humanly speaking, not 'bright', but they had known the Lord for some while. One day they were confronted with a woman possessed with a demon, violent and dangerous, and in great distress. Having sought the Lord together, they approached her, and in the Name of Jesus commanded the demon to go out. To their dismay, nothing happened, and their inclination was to go away and seek the help and advice of someone more experienced. But as they hesitated and lifted their hearts to the Lord, asking Him what they should do, a sudden thought came to them. Going back and again addressing the evil spirit, they preached to it Jesus. At once, through the woman but in its own peculiar voice, the spirit replied, 'Oh yes, I know Jesus! I have worshipped him all my life!' And with that the possessed woman arose, and crossing the room pointed them to an idol shrine in the courtyard.

Then they understood! The demon was, as we say, 'trying it on' with them. Now they knew what to do. Beginning again from the beginning: 'Do you remember two thousand years ago', they said, 'Jesus of Nazareth cast out many of your fellow-demons, until at length they all turned on Him and slew Him? Nevertheless He rose again, stripping off principalities and powers, and is now exalted far above all rule and authority. And there was a proclamation made: In that Name every knee in heaven and on earth and under the earth shall bow! Do you remember? Now, in *that* Name we command you to go!' And the demon obeyed.

When I asked them afterwards from where they got this light, they could not explain. They could only say that the Lord Himself had come to their aid and exposed the subtlety of the enemy. But this incident surely disposes of our question: What sort of people are needed for this task? The answer is that no sort of people can stand up to Satan. Demons only recognize Christ. 'If I by the Spirit of God cast out devils, then is the kingdom of God come upon you' (Matt. 12. 28). Our enemy is too subtle and dangerous for us, but the Body of Christ not only provides for us; it covers us. We can all put on Christ as our armour. Against Him Satan's shafts are of no avail!

It is the Church that overcomes. Spiritual warfare is the task of the Church, not of the individual. We take Ephesians 6 for ourselves individually—and I do not say there is *no* individual application of the armour—but the individual by himself cannot 'put on *the whole* armour of God' any more than he can comprehend alone the measure of the love of Christ. Seen in the light of the rest of Ephesians, it is, I feel sure, armour for *the Body*—a special piece for each member. For to try and fight this warfare alone is to invite trouble from an enemy who has no fear of the individual, but who dreads the one Body. Without the protection of the whole armour, he will single us out. Under its shadow he cannot touch us.

This explains why, faced with a true spiritual issue in the realm of the heavenly warfare, we shall always find ourselves driven *together* to pray it through, even if it be with only one other member. The Lord cannot use heroes, but praise God, He can make great use of weak members of the Body!

THE FULNESS OF HIM

As we close these chapters on the Church, I want us to pause and put to ourselves a question. Some of us are serving the Lord in mission fields, others at home, and we praise Him for His calling wherever it may be. But let us ask ourselves now, Is our ministry purely that of evangelism as a thing sufficient in itself, or is it bound up with something altogether larger? Having glimpsed the full thought of God as it is revealed especially through Paul, is it possible that we could be content to stop short at the business of bringing souls to the Lord, and not be deeply concerned also for the greater purpose into which those souls are being brought?

Dear brothers and sisters, this is a great challenge. I know many feel that to be evangelical and to win souls is all that God requires of us in these last days; but is it so? We bless God for Peter's primary ministry, without which the House of God will have no 'living stones'. We long to see men saved from perishing and won for His glory. What is more, God has not only given to His Church 'some evangelists' for this task, but surely too He says to every one of us, 'Do the work of an evangelist' (Eph. 4. 11; 2 Tim. 4. 5).

But, do we stop there? When we see three or four thousand

converts, all saved and all going on fairly well spiritually, do we feel a task has been accomplished? Should we not regard it rather as a task just begun? Ought we not to ask ourselves how many of those three or four thousand have yet caught a glimpse of the one heavenly Man into which God has brought them? Are they still just units, fishes in the net, figures in a list of 'campaign results', or does that supreme vision possess them? It will certainly not do so unless it first possesses us. So I ask again, Are we burdened, as were the apostles, to see them grow up in all things into the Head, even Christ?

I am well aware that this question has implications that are far from easy. To face them may well bring some of us into collision with ideas and traditions from which such high thoughts have long been left out of account. A great deal of own work may have to be re-evaluated. Many 'heads' may have to be chopped off, many minds readjusted, many human authorities—our own included—made to give way to the Headship of the One.

I confess I would like nevertheless to plead with you—yea, if I could, to persuade you—to press on at any cost into the full thought of God. But persuasion and entreaty are useless if we do not *see* what God has in mind—and by that I do not mean see the reasonableness of it. If we only see its reasonableness, we shall have very often to remind ourselves how it was we arrived at that conclusion, or we shall very soon be as easily swayed back again. But if once we have seen God's new Man in Christ, a heavenly reality is opened to us, and things will never be quite the same again. Many a time reason would say, 'It may be well enough in some parts of the world, but in my situation here, things are difficult, nay, impossible. I see no hope of realizing what I see in the Word, so let me be content with simpler things.' But oh, my friends, while we may never underrate the blessed ministry of the net that brings men in, let us seek grace to follow on with Paul to the vision of the Body, the earthly tabernacle where God would dwell amid His own and manifest His fulness to-day.

For the Church, he tells us, is 'the fulness of Him that filleth all in all.' She is the vessel to contain and express His wisdom, life and power. Such fulness cannot be known individually. The apostle is emphatic about this. It is together that we become a habitation of God through the Spirit. It is through the Church that the wisdom of God is manifested to spiritual powers. It is with all saints that we receive the full knowledge of divine love. It is as the Body of Christ that we attain to the full grown Man. It is clad in the whole armour that we withstand in the evil day. (Eph. 1. 23; 2. 22; 3. 10, 18, 19; 4. 13; 6. 11.) Every analogy he uses in Ephesians reinforces his argument that the Church, not the individual, is the vessel of fulness.

Because God's children to-day do not function together as the Body, they have become as a leaking vessel. Shatter a glass tumbler and what happens? Each piece may perhaps hold a little water, but it is as nothing compared to what the unbroken tumbler held. So is it in spiritual things. The individual receives in but two dimensions, as it were; the Church in three. Ten thousand Christians are one thing; ten thousand members of the Body are quite another.

Revelation is perfect only when it is revelation to the whole Church. To-day the Head has much more to give, but the Body is a leaky vessel, unable to contain it. It is quite true that individuals do make some progress in many points of the faith —but merely as individuals; they do not, as such, advance one inch in the stature of the fulness of Christ. There must be a return to the one vessel. Not to believing the same doctrine, nor to using the same methods, nor even to having fellowship with all: none of these is enough. We must see ourselves in the same Body, one in Christ Jesus. Let us ask the Lord to illumine our hearts.

CHAPTER TEN

JOHN—AND THE TRUTH

As he approached the end of his life, Paul wrote a letter to his young fellow-worker Timothy. Tragically, we may feel, this last-preserved of the apostle's writings has as its burden the sad fact of spiritual declension and departure. Yet it is just because that spiritual departure had set in even before the death of the apostles that there is found within the pages of the New Testament guidance for the saints under like circumstances to-day.

In an hour when many are losing their faith and hope, and are lowering their Christian standards, it is easy to become confused. We are tempted to say, If the faith of God's children can so change, is there anything that cannot? True, the Lord Himself never changes; but while we can look up and praise Him, nevertheless we look around and are troubled. So the Spirit through Paul shows us something else that is unchanging. 'The firm foundation of God standeth, having this seal, The Lord knoweth them that are his: and, Let every one that nameth the name of the Lord depart from unrighteousness' (2 Tim. 2. 19).

Men may go; Phygelus and Hermogenes, Hymenaeus and Philetus, yes, all Asia too, may prove unfaithful to the Lord; and when one by one they do, we begin to look around and wonder who at all is to be counted upon. But *the Lord knows* them that are His: that is the first seal inscribed upon this sure foundation. We may be mistaken; God never is. We need to confess before Him that we may estimate wrongly, but that He sees into all hearts. We over-rate men because God in mercy uses them; but He has used us too, and yet, God knows, we need His mercy! Let us beware of thinking we know human nature. Only God has that knowledge. Men may disappoint, but have we not all of us at some time failed the Lord?

So there is a second element in this seal or inscription, a command laid upon all who would 'call upon the Lord out of a pure heart'. They who name His Name are to *depart from unrighteousness*. The unshakeable foundation of God tells us this. When we see spiritual breakdown around us, we are to look to ourselves. For they who are the Lord's are to be sanctified men. The verses immediately following elaborate this. They speak of a great house with its furnishings, vessels of gold and silver, wood and earth, suitable to various tasks. Men are likened to such vessels, but are urged to qualify themselves for places of honour there.

What is this 'great house' with its vessels destined to honour or dishonour, and the implication of moral qualities behind those words? In 1 Timothy the Church of God *is* the house of God (3. 15); but here I believe Paul has in view not that, but the outward profession of Christianity. The 'Church of the living God' could never itself be a ruin; it could never degenerate into this 'great house' with its element of mixture. But the Church's outward testimony may, alas, at any particular time be in ruins.

What now distinguishes between these vessels? We note at once that only their materials are specified, not their function. Clearly, in keeping with the construction of the house which we considered earlier, here again it is not relative usefulness but quality of materials that counts. Gold and silver vessels are less practically useful than wooden furniture or earthenware pots, but God is not here discussing with us what they will be used for; He is judging their lasting value to Himself. In a day of declension God looks beyond mere usefulness to intrinsic worth, and a few ounces of gold may equal in value a whole hall full of wooden benches! In spiritual terms, two different men may utter almost identical words, but the power lies not merely in what they say but in who they are. Balaam and Isaiah both spoke of the Kingdom, but we know well to which of the two we would turn in personal need.

What do we prize in a day when values are slipping: the

wood and the earth of human cleverness and wordly resources, or the gold and the silver of divine origin and redemption through the Cross? Many things in Christianity have become too cheap today, but there is no easy short-cut to spiritual worth. Preaching, prayer, witness, these may not seem difficult, but to be of value they will be costly in years and blood and the discipline of God's dealings. The 'vessel unto honour' is the man who has waited for the Spirit to teach him, and who has not been ashamed meanwhile to admit he does not know. For there comes a day when the true character of things is tested. Preaching, in an hour of departure and confusion, is of little value unless men see God in it. At such a time they can tell whether the speaker has really been taken by God through the things of which he speaks. What has not already touched him deeply will have little power to touch others in that day.

Though the very idea of a 'vessel' suggests formation for something, 2 Timothy hints at circumstances in which we should do well to leave to God the destiny of the vessels, and to concern ourselves above all with their quality. 'If a man therefore purge himself from these, he shall be a vessel unto honour.'

HIS SERVANT JOHN

This brings us at length to the beloved disciple. In point of time his writings fall, in general, after those of Paul, and in keeping with this, his most distinctive contribution to the New Testament revelation is, as we have said, just this very emphasis upon recovery. At a time when the Church was taken up with outward things at the expense of the inward life, John came on the scene to remind men of the true divine qualities. This, we suggested earlier, is illustrated for us at the outset by the account of Jesus discovering him and his brother James 'in the boat mending their nets'—making good, that is, damage occasioned by the previous night's toil.

John of course was no less a 'fisherman' in the full sense than was Peter, and equally it would seem that, within his sphere, he was no less a 'builder' than was Paul. We find him at the beginning of the Acts sharing fully in the preaching and fellowship of the early phases; and like Paul he too can write authoritatively 'to the church' (3 John 9). But seen in the context of the New Testament as a whole, the feature of John's writings that stands out most prominently is surely this particular ministry of recalling things to their original or divinely-intended state.

As we all know, John's is the last of the four Gospels. His Epistles too are the last epistles; and his Revelation is placed last in the whole Book of God. All his writings are in some sense 'the last'. In John's Gospel you find everywhere the reflection of this fact. John touches on very little of the work of the Lord as it is set forth, for example, in Mark. Neither does He concern himself with the commandments of the Lord as they are dealt with by Matthew in the Sermon on the Mount. He is not so troubled about what you should do if someone takes away your coat, or whether, when pressed by your neighbour, you should go with him one mile or two. That is not his first concern now. His burden relates to the life of the eternities and to your right relation thereto. If you go back to that, he implies, everything else will follow. In this he is quite different, too, from Luke. He is not occupied with outward and temporal things—with dates and genealogies, even though they take you right back to Adam. His whole burden is this, that we must get right behind these various things to *the Life*. Everything here now is in disrepair. Go back to the Life that 'came down from heaven', and when you get back there, Peter and all that he stands for will be preserved, and so will Paul. In a sense, John has nothing new to offer. He does not take us further, for the furthest point has already been touched by God. The purpose of the revelation entrusted to John is to bring back people again to that original purpose, by bringing them into a fresh touch with the risen Lord of life Himself.

Reading through the Gospel of John you cannot but be impressed with the fact that the first chapter is the key to all that follows. In that first chapter you find grace and truth, the two streams flowing from Christ. 'The law was given by Moses; grace and truth came by Jesus Christ' (1. 17). Throughout the

Gospel you find the same double emphasis, upon truth on the one hand and upon grace on the other. Truth will always make demands, and grace will always be there to meet them. In the incident recorded in Chapter 8 of the woman taken in adultery, truth shines forth. Jesus did not say to her, 'It is all right; you have not sinned'. He did not tell the Jews that what she had done was nothing serious, and that He was not deeply concerned about it. No, the Lord said: 'He that is without sin among you, let him first cast a stone at her' (8. 7). The truth was there: 'She has sinned, and according to the law she ought to be stoned'; but so also was the grace, for when all had gone out, He turned and said to her: 'Neither do I condemn thee'. Throughout the Gospel of John you will find truth is always matched by grace in this way.

When however you turn to the Epistles of John, you find something more. You hear less of grace and truth as such, for these letters are written at a later date, and an even more fundamental recovery is necessary. You therefore find John pointing you further back still. 'God is light' (1 John 1. 5). 'God is love' (1 John 4. 8). Whereas, in the Gospel, Christ coming from the Father was revealed among men as grace and truth, here in the Epistles, Christ in existence with the Father is revealed to men as light and love. What has been truth in the Gospel becomes light in the Epistles. What has been grace in the Gospel becomes love in the Epistles. Why is this? Because that which is light in God, when transmitted to men, becomes truth; that which is love in God, when brought to men, becomes grace. Love goes back to God, but grace stays here. Everything that is in God is light and love, but coming out to men it becomes truth and grace. And it is always possible for grace to be misused, truth to be mishandled; men have mis-appropriated these things to themselves. But God is light and God is love, and you cannot climb up there and touch that; that is beyond mishandling. So John's method is to take us right back there to the Throne, not to offer us something novel, but to confront us again with the original. It is by going back again to the Source that we shall recover and preserve what has been lost.

But it is when we come to the last, and in some ways the most important, book in the whole Bible, the Book of the Revelation, that we see this principle of the apostle's brought fully into play, and I think we shall find that his emphasis here is especially upon the Lord Jesus as 'He that is true' (Rev. 3. 7). I think none of us could read that book without realizing that it represents the supreme restoration. It marks the complete reversal of Genesis. Everything of failure and breakdown that entered in at the beginning is now undone; everything that was lost is recovered; every question raised there is answered here.

In Genesis I see a serpent. What is going to be the end of this? I see a curse. What is going to be the end of that? I see death and sin. Where will that end? I see man barred from the Tree of life. What will be the issue of these things? I see their beginnings, but what is their end? And what is going to be the end of me? God in grace has made a beginning with me, but what if salvation were to end with the present? The purpose of the Book of Revelation is to answer these questions by introducing me to Jesus as alive for evermore, the Beginning *and* the End.

For the Revelation is the unveiling, the *apokalypsis*, of Jesus Christ. It draws aside the curtain and reveals His Person. Its object is not primarily to enlighten us regarding coming events—the antichrist, the supposed revival of the Roman empire, the rapture, the millennium, or the ultimate destiny of Satan. John's remedy for our ills is not a matter of so many seals and so many trumpets, nor is it an answer to the question whether the rapture is 'partial' or 'complete'. It is not in fact designed to satisfy our intellectual speculations at all, but to meet our spiritual need by revealing Christ Himself in fulness, that we may know *Him*.

True, the Revelation does answer our questions as to ourselves, and in ways surpassing even our dreams. For what John presents to us at the end is in fact more than we lost at the beginning. God began with a garden and He ends with a city. In Genesis He visited the man whom He had made; in Revelation His dwelling-place, nay, His very throne, is in the midst of men. For what had been the Church in Paul has become the Holy City in John. Yet in the divine intention this was always so. For what God had set Himself to do at the first, He will indeed do; and Revelation assures us that, in His own mind, He has already done it. So in essence John presents us, as before, with nothing new; he only shows us that what God intended He will carry into effect.

All this John does, I repeat, by bringing us back to the divine Original. What is the destiny of this world? What is to be the outcome of the Church's conflict? What will be the end of me? Everything, John affirms, has its answer and its fulfilment in the Lord Jesus Christ. Is Christ my Beginning? He is also my End. Is He my Alpha? He is also my Omega. Christ is the answer to all my questions. If I am clear first about Him, I shall know all I need to know about coming events—the reason for them and the rightness of them. But that is the inescapable divine order. No one is qualified to study the subsequent visions recorded by John who has not seen that first vision of the Lord Himself. For that tells us who He is, even the risen and victorious King of kings, and the events that follow are the outcome of His being that.

This was true for John personally. Even the beloved disciple who had lain on Jesus' bosom must have a revelation of his eternal Lord that shattered him in the dust. Only after that might he be shown 'things to come'. The first seeing is fundamental to all other seeing. For what is in view is a kingdom; and it is the King and His subjects, not the experts in prophecy, who proclaim war on all that is contrary to His kingdom. Coming events are not revealed to provide food for idle speculation; their goal is the overthrow of the enemy and the universal reign of the Christ.

So in the Revelation, God shows us an aspect of His Son not shown to us in the Gospels. In the Gospels we see Him as Saviour, in Revelation as King; in John's Gospel as Alpha, in Revelation as Omega. The one displays His love, the other His majesty. In the upper room Jesus girds Himself about the waist, for service; at Patmos He is discovered girt about the breasts, for war. In the Gospels His mild eyes melted Peter;

in Revelation they are as a flame of fire. There His voice was gentle, calling His own sheep by name, and gracious words proceeded out of His mouth; here His voice is terrible as the sound of many waters, and from His mouth there proceeds a sharp two-edged sword, striking death to His foes.

It is not enough that we know Jesus as Lamb of God and as Saviour of the world; we must know Him also as God's Christ, God's King, God's Judge. When we see Him as Saviour, we say 'How lovable!' and lean on His bosom. When we see Him as Monarch we say 'How terrible!' and fall prostrate at His feet. The one issues in thanksgiving, the other in worship. To see Him now as King is, one might almost say, to see 'another' Christ, to experience 'another' salvation. We behold Him now as the faithful and true Witness, the divine Guarantor that, though the purposes of God may perhaps be hindered, they can never be finally thwarted.

HE THAT IS TRUE

In studying the Apocalypse, we need to be careful to avoid over-spiritualizing what we read. John's new heaven and new earth are real, not imaginary, and his new Jerusalem is real, just as truly as the risen Lord is real. The spiritualizing away of divine things is the desperate expedient of people who do not possess the reality. Many dear folk amass spiritual and prophetic truth only, I fear, to build for themselves with it an unreal world. To do this is to escape from reality, just as truly as do those who, as we saw earlier, are ready enough to-day to live in the spiritual atmosphere of Ephesians but want to avoid facing the practical challenge of 1 Corinthians. But remember, this was the very delusion that overtook Laodicea, making it possible for them to believe a lie.

The mark of spiritual maturity will always be that divine things become real to us because Christ is real to us. We see Him as real life, real holiness—as 'the truth', in fact; and I use 'truth' here in a sense very different from my use of it above when speaking of 'prophetic truth'. Many confuse truth and doctrine, but the two are not the same. Doctrine is what is said on earth about the eternal truth. I know well that our word truth in Chinese is *chen-li* (roughly, 'reality-doctrine') but the Greek meaning is in fact *chen* without the *li*, 'reality' without the 'doctrine'. The Jesus who said, 'Ye shall know the truth' (John 8. 32) Himself embodies all that is true (Rev. 3. 7; cf, 1. John 5. 20), and it is thus that we should know Him.

Truth 'is in Jesus' (Eph. 4. 21), and, like grace, it 'came through Jesus Christ' (John 1. 17). We welcome His grace; but do we know His truth? Grace came to us in an historical act when He gave Himself upon the Cross; but no less certainly is truth intimately bound up with His Person and work, and not merely something expressed through His preaching. Thus if grace extends to us now, truth should just as surely extend to and embrace us who, through faith in that finished work, are now found united with Him.

Yet while many know Him as the Way and the Life, too few in fact know Him to-day as the Truth. This is a serious deficiency, for truth, we said, is reality. Before Him and apart from Him there is no reality. And we can enter into the truth, if we will, because His finished work remains for us to-day the truest thing in the world. What we are before God, we are *in reality* because of what He has done.

This has an important bearing on our practical experience. My theoretical difficulty is always this, that what I am before God, when compared with what I am here, reveals all too frequently that much is wrong. What Christ's work has made me is one thing, but what I experience on earth far too often appears to contradict the truth of that. How do I make good the discrepancy? How do I live so that my conduct here expresses consistently what I know to be true there?

What I have to see is that what, through the work of Christ, God has made me to be in Him *is the real thing*. And it is the foundation of all my true Christian experience. Nothing else is. What I have become by virtue of being in Christ is the eternal truth. My one fault will be to dwell in my feelings and experiences, my strivings and failures, my misgivings and hopes, and not to fix my faith upon 'Him that is true'.

Everything centres in Him. At the very heart of Scripture

we see Christ on the Cross. In His death we were included, and when He arose we arose with Him, members of His Body. John reveals Him to us as He is to-day, and, praise God, His ascension and glory are ours! But whence do we derive our certainty of these things? Not from our feelings, but from the reality of His Person and His work. What Christ has done is the resting-place of our faith. It is not our feelings, nor even our knowledge, that 'makes us free'. It is the truth. What John 8. 32 shows us is that, until we see these things, we remain enslaved, but that because Christ's work is real, and because what we have become in Him is the truth, the mere discovery of these realities opens the way for them, by their very nature, to bring to an end our bondage.

This is the great value to us of John's new unveiling of Jesus. Viewed from a merely human level—from the standpoint, for example, of a Roman prisoner in the isle called Patmos— Christ's victory is more unlike reality than almost anything we can think of. That was so then, and it is so to-day. We look at governments, society, outward Christianity, and see bondage, oppression, frustration—anything but liberty. So we pray and ask for victory, and in doing so give the lie to the victory of Calvary. The truth, the glorious reality, is that Christ has already conquered, not that He is going to. What God does to-day is something already *done* in Christ. Our supreme need is to see that fact.

'O send out thy light and thy truth' (Psalm 43. 3). The two are connected. The truth is complete in Christ, but the need of our hearts is to have God's light shed on it. All spiritual experience comes from divine light on eternal truth. Truth preached without light becomes doctrine; with divine light it becomes revelation. It always comes to us as one or the other. But the Truth, the eternal reality, is Christ Himself, and then, what God by His grace has made us to be in Him.

CHRIST AND TIME

Spiritual reality has this outstanding characteristic, that it bears no mark of time. The time-factor vanishes the instant you touch that reality. Take, for example, prophecy. From the human point of view there is such a thing as prophecy, but from the divine point of view no such thing exists. True, we read, 'Thou art my Son, this day have I begotten thee', but with God 'this day' is always. Our Lord says He is the First and the Last, the Alpha and the Omega; but remember, He is both together, both at once. It is not that at one time He is First and at another time He is Last; He is First and Last simultaneously. Nor is it that having for a while been Alpha He later on becomes Omega; He is Alpha and Omega from eternity to eternity. He is always First *and* Last; He is always Alpha *and* Omega. Of course, in the sight of men He is not Omega until He is manifested as Omega, but in the sight of God He is Omega now. With man, past and future are separate and distinct; with God they synchronize. With me the 'I' of yesterday differs from the 'I' of to-day, and the 'I' of tomorrow differs still further; but Jesus Christ is the same yesterday and to-day and for ever. He is the eternal 'I AM'.

It is here that the knowledge of God becomes so precious to us. Our Lord said to Nicodemus, 'No man hath ascended into heaven, but he that descended out of heaven, even the Son of man, which is in heaven' (John 3. 13). You note how these two positions synchronize in Christ. There is no change of time or place with Him. He is at once there and here. So of God it is written that He is 'the Father of lights, with whom can be no variation, neither shadow that is cast by turning' (James 1. 17). He is that in Himself; He is that in His Christ; and praise His Name, He is that, too, in His Church!

Have you ever come across the Church that Paul describes in Ephesians 1. 18 in terms of 'the riches of the glory of his inheritance in the saints'? Or that depicted in 1 Corinthians 6. 11 as 'washed ... sanctified ... justified in the name of the Lord Jesus, and in the Spirit of our God'? Oh, you say, that describes the *position* of the Church. No, it describes the *reality* of the Church. In writing to the Romans, Paul was more daring than were some of his translators. He wrote 'called saints', or 'saints by calling', but they felt it was running too great a risk to translate literally, so they safeguarded their conception of spiritual things by writing 'called *to be* saints' (1. 7). If we are only called 'to be' saints, how long shall we have to be 'being' before we can actually *be*? Praise God, we *are* saints!

The expression translated 'We are his workmanship' (Eph. 2. 10) could as well be rendered: 'We are his masterpiece'. The Church is the very best God can produce. It can never be improved upon. We look around and see breakdown everywhere, and we wonder, 'What is the Church coming to?' I tell you, she is not 'coming to' anything; she has arrived. We do not look forward to discover her goal; we look back. God reached His end in Christ before the foundation of the world, and we move forward with Him on the basis of what already is. As we move in the light of that eternal fact, we witness its progressive manifestation.

Christian progress is not a question of attaining to some abstract standard, or of pressing through to some far-off goal. It is wholly a question of seeing God's standard. You advance spiritually by finding out what you really are, not by trying to become what you hope to be. That goal you will never reach, however earnestly you strive. It is when you *see* you are dead that you die; it is when you *see* you are risen that you arise; it is when you *see* you are holy that you become holy. Seeing the accomplished fact determines the pathway to the realizing of that fact. The end is reached by seeing, not by desiring or working. The only possibility of spiritual progress lies in our discovering the truth as God sees it; the truth concerning Christ, the truth concerning ourselves in Christ, and the truth concerning the Church, the Body of Christ.

In Romans 8. 30 Paul tells us that those whom God has foreordained He has called, that those whom He has called He has justified, and that those whom He has justified He has glorified. Thus, according to God's Word, all who are called have already been glorified. The goal is attained. The Church has already come to glory!

'Oh, but this is too difficult!' you exclaim. 'Surely the

Church must need cleansing! Please come back to Ephesians 5, and tell me again how you explain the statement that the Church is cleansed by the washing of water with the word?' Very well, but kindly first observe the context. It tells us how a husband and wife should act. Love is required of the husband, and submission of the wife. The question is not how to be a husband or how to be a wife, but how, being a husband or a wife, you should live. It is not that you must love in order to be a husband or that you must obey in order to be a wife, but that, being a husband you should love, being a wife you should obey. The whole point at issue is not of doing in order to be at all, but of doing because of being.

Now does not the same principle apply in regard to the Church? The called-out ones are not washed in order to be the Church; they are washed because they are the Church. That is why I suggested earlier that Paul here is looking beyond the question of sin. The object of washing may be refreshment by removal of the tarnish and dust of the world, in the sense implied in the Lord's words in John 13. 10. And that is, I think, what is intended here. The Church *has been washed* (1 Cor. 6, 11), so by washing she is now kept fresh. The husband acts as a husband because he is a husband; the wife acts as a wife because she is a wife; the Church is washed because she has been washed. The Church has reached the standard, so she is helped to live in accord with the standard, whereas that which is not the Church could never become the Church by any amount of washing.

As we stated in an earlier chapter, whereas Romans arrives at the statement 'them he also glorified' (8. 30) by working through the whole story of redemption. Ephesians deliberately goes outside of time into eternity past and future, and takes the eternal fulness as its starting-point. For the ultimate reality is always before God, and God speaks of His Church in the light of that reality. The time-factor in the Bible is one of the greatest problems to the human mind, but it vanishes from the horizon when once our hearts have been enlightened to know the glory of His inheritance in the saints. God sees the Church utterly pure, utterly perfect. To know to-day the ultimate glory in heaven is the one sure way of living in the power of that glory on earth.

CITIZENS OF HEAVEN

It remains a sad fact, but a true one, that many Christians have only seen the outward form of Christianity. They have never seen the inward reality, and so as yet have no knowledge of its essential nature. And no wonder, for to-day so much that is merely external has become attached to Christianity that it is difficult to discern what is truly of God. Yet Christianity is not, after all, merely a system of externals. It is 'the Truth'.

The Gospel of John comes to our help here by presenting to us the Holy Spirit as the Spirit of truth, and assures us that He will lead us into all the Truth. We shall have something more to say of this in our concluding chapter. But surely we may deduce from this statement that what comes to us apart from the Holy Spirit's instruction and enlightenment is something less than the Truth. What we can arrive at by thought and study, by the seeing of the eye and the hearing of the ear, is all outside the realm of eternal verity; it is not spiritually real.

The human mind has adopted some wide extremes of view on divine things. The Church of Rome, for example, has sought to give them a sacramental or materialistic explanation. Men have fixed their gaze on the material water of baptism and credited it with regenerative power. The material elements of the Lord's supper are likewise said to be miraculously transformed into the physical body and blood of Christ, providing us with the well-known doctrine of transubstantiation. And in keeping with these ideas, the outward form of the Church, as Rome understands that outward form, is held by her to be the one true Church. At the opposite extreme the intellectual man, puzzled by the evident inconsistencies resulting from such a view, has sought to remove them or explain them away by developing what we may call the Reformed view of things. He distinguishes between the outward ceremony of baptism and the inward reality. He sees the elements of the Supper as symbols that are merely representative and typical. And he solves the problem of the Church by arguing for a true and a false, a heavenly and an earthly, and a so-called 'Church within the Church'.

I ask you, does either of these extremes do real justice to the plain statements of Scripture? The Word says nothing of true and false, or of representation or symbolism, but makes only firm statements of fact. 'We are buried therefore with him through baptism into death', says Paul (Rom. 6. 4; Col. 2. 12). To him there is no such thing as a baptism not involving a dying and rising with Christ. He had no thought that a Christian could experience baptism on a certain date, and at a later date enter into the experience of death and resurrection with Christ. Similarly our Lord's words concerning the cup. 'This is my blood', go far beyond mere symbolism on the one hand, while on the other, His allusion to it almost in the same breath as 'the fruit of the vine' equally disposes of the idea of transubstantiation. It is His blood, but it is also still a cup of wine. There is not here the 'representative' and the 'real', the type and the anti-type, but only one divine reality.

We need anointed eyes to see. We can only be brought to the truth of baptism and the Lord's supper by the Spirit of truth. When we have been, there will cease to be a 'doctrine' of these things; there will be reality alone. We may speak words that to extreme Reformists sound alarmingly like the words Rome speaks, but we shall be seeing what Rome never saw. For to those who have seen the Ultimate, the doctrine and type both give way to that vision of Him. There is only the Truth.

But what we have just said about the reality of Baptism and the Lord's table is no less true when we come to speak of the reality of the Church. Nowadays, at the very mention of the word 'Church', many evangelical Christians become quite apprehensive. Whenever the subject is brought up, great precautions are taken to clear the ground lest any confusion arise in the minds of the hearers. Care is exercised to differentiate between the true Church and the false. But in the Lord's Word, and in the thought of God, there is no such distinction.

The Lord put no footnote in Scripture when He spoke of the Church. He did not seek to safeguard the spiritual reality by differentiating between an inward and an outward, a real and an unreal. He did not even draw a clear line of demarcation between the local and the universal. In the Word of God there is only 'the Church'.

Notwithstanding this, the subject of the Church continues to be widely regarded as a controversial one, to be studiously avoided for the sake of evangelical unity. At a great Convention in England I asked a worker, 'Why at this Convention does one hear no mention of the Church?' 'Oh,' he replied, 'because this Convention is for the deepening of the spiritual life.' So, if his view was a representative one, the Church and the spiritual life of the Christian are thought by many to be unrelated, whereas nothing is more intimately related to the spiritual life of the children of God than is the Church.

'Oh to be like Thee!' is a hymn which the individual may sing, but not the Church, for the Church *is* the heavenly Body of Christ. To discover this is to have one's Christian life revolutionized. For though most Christians admit that to struggle and strive after heavenliness is wrong, yet still they struggle and strive. They have been taught to regard heavenliness as something to be attained, and so, for them, Christianity is an endeavour to be what they are not and to do what they cannot do. They struggle not to love the world because in fact, at heart, they really love it; they strive to be humble because, at heart, they are so self-assured. This is the experience of so-called Christianity, but, I repeat, it is not the experience of the Church. For though we may work our way across the Atlantic or the Pacific, we can never work our way from earth to heaven. Heaven is not a place that the Church will reach at some future date. The Church *is* there, and never was anywhere else.

Heaven is both the origin and the abode of the Church, but not her destination. And since the Church has never known any other sphere but heaven, the question of striving to reach heaven can never arise for her. This may seem a drastic statement, but it is a fact. Like everything else in the Word of God, it is something to be seen by the Holy Spirit's revelation to our hearts; and not till we see it do we know our heavenly calling. That calling does not call us into heaven, but makes known to us that we are of heaven and in heaven. So the Church is not a company of Christians working their way heavenward, but a company who are actually now citizens of heaven. Remember again: 'No man hath ascended into heaven, but . . . the Son of man, which is in heaven.' The Church need not pray that she may become like Christ. She needs only to see her place there in union with her Lord.

We need to revise our thinking about the Church. It is not an organization to be planned, nor is it just a company of people to be completed. It is not a concept to be grasped, nor an ideal to be attained. Like so much else that is ours in Christ, the Church is a reality to be seen with the help of the Holy Spirit through the Word. When we recognize the real heavenly character of the Church, then the heavenliness of our own renewed nature dawns upon us, and we *know* that our starting-point as Christians is not earth but heaven. The Church is perfect, perfect beyond any possibility of improvement. Theologians say: 'Oh, but that is the standing of the Church; her state is not so.' But in the sight of God there is no imperfection in the Church eternally. Why be bothered with the endless questions that relate to the old creation? They simply vanish when, by divine grace, we see the eternal reality. The Church is the sphere in which God exercises His authority in the earth, and to-day, in the midst of a polluted universe, He has a sphere of unsullied purity for His own abode.

GOLDEN LAMPSTANDS

How nervous we are about the Church! How reluctant to trust ourselves to her! We say: What if the Church should make a mistake? What if she should come to the wrong conclusion? But the Lord made no provision for failure of any kind there. It is as though, in His thought, no such contingency could arise. We think of the Church in Corinth as a church far below standard, but it was to that church that Paul wrote: 'Ye were washed ... ye were sanctified ... ye were justified'. Even in Rome at the end, he does not see Demas and Alexander the coppersmith and a host of false brethren constituting some kind of false church, to be carefully distinguished from the real. Whenever in his epistles Paul mentions the Church, he speaks of her as altogether perfect, and he inserts no modifying clauses for the sake of avoiding misapprehension.

With John it is no different. In Revelation 2 and 3 we are shown the Son of man moving among the lampstands, and affirming the individual responsibility of each to Himself. Our eyes, following His, readily detect the many failures in the churches; but has it occurred to us that John nowhere distinguishes between the churches that are right and the churches that are wrong? For all their faultiness, he writes of them as the Lord Himself still sees them, namely, as 'seven golden lampstands', seven candlesticks *all of gold*.

To those upon whom divine reality has once begun to dawn there is only that reality. We say: From God's point of view the Church ought to be this or that. No, the Church *is* this or that! The Church is what from God's point of view it ought to be, because Christ is that. To see eternal reality in Christ is to cease to differentiate between what the Church is potentially and actually. And once the Lord has begun to open our eyes, we no longer despise small things. We no longer say, when we meet only a handful of believers in some place, 'Of what use is this to God? There are so few here!' We do not complain, 'There is only one other brother with me in this pagan city!' We look at the Acts, and we cease to be distressed at the fewness of the believers who in Chapter 13 took such far-reaching decisions (for that is what they indeed proved to be). We cease to think: There was an inadequate representation of the Church there; such important steps as these ought to have awaited a general council of the Church's leaders.

No, we are satisfied that those believers saw the heavenly reality, and hence were not unduly bothered about niceties of technique. And when we see the reality of the Church as they saw it, then we shall recognize the Church in operation when we encounter it anywhere, be it even in a small group of believers with, as men would say, no special standing as its 'duly appointed representatives'. If they themselves are truly subject to the Head in all things, and if they are making much, not of themselves or the Church, but of Christ, then the Spirit of God will always bear witness to them.

Take an extreme case. When in Damascus Ananias went to Saul, he went alone, and alone he laid hands on Saul. 'Out of order!' you exclaim. 'Quite contrary to the principles of the Body! Surely that was independent action!' Not at all! Ananias was just a disciple, it is true, but one moving (as a member of the Body should) under the direction of the Head. And in that hour the Lord's eyes were not on Ananias alone, but also on the other man. It was the very action of Ananias towards this new brother that expressed so clearly his own subjection to Christ; and under these conditions, when he moved, the whole Body moved.

If you have been brought into the eternal reality of the Church, the day may well come when you yourself are called to speak and act for the whole Church. Will you refuse to do so then? A movement on the part of any one member of the Body who is truly subject to the Spirit of Christ is a movement of the whole. The life of such a one in that hour transcends all externalities, for men recognize that God is moving through that member.

The implications of all this are very great. We have no business to view things materialistically or intellectually—that is, through the eyes of Rome or of the Reformation—but only from the standpoint of God. God sees 'seven golden lampstands'. He knows only 'the Church', and when we permit the Spirit of truth to lead us into the spiritual truth of the Church, we shall see only the Church that God sees.

As I speak of these things to Christians in various countries, I find that they all, leaders included, have the same questions. 'Do you mean to tell me,' they exclaim, 'that it is possible to have something according to God *down here*? You are an idealist. You are following a mirage. But even supposing you are right, and it is possible to see these things come to pass in some measure in your lifetime, what about the next generation? What you are experiencing now will go the way of everything else. Its character will change, and within a few years it will survive only as a caricature of your vision.'[1]

Yes, I suppose if you look at things only from the standpoint of the ministry of Paul in the New Testament, such an attitude may appear a right one; but thank God, there is still the ministry of John. What God was doing through these men is eternal—not just something for ten or twenty years. There is no 'first generation' and 'second generation' about God's spiritual house.[2] It is 'from generation to generation'. What God has in view He will never abandon, for the very good reason that He Himself never changes. Dare we then accept another standard? A person who cannot afford to wear pearls buys a string of paste beads and thinks of them as imitation pearls. But the one who can afford to wear pearls does not think of the paste beads even as imitation pearls. To her there are not real pearls and false pearls; there are only pearls. The paste beads have for her no more connection with pearls than have any other beads; the only pearls she recognizes as pearls at all are real pearls.

'And having turned I saw seven golden candlesticks.' 'And he carried me away in the Spirit to a mountain great and high, and showed me the holy city Jerusalem, coming down out of heaven from God, having the glory of God: her light was like unto a stone most precious. . . .' Keeping our eyes there, we can praise God for the ministry of John!

[1] It may be well at this point to remind readers that, for the past thirty-five years, the author has witnessed the growth, through the preaching of the Word, of a most fruitful work of the Spirit of God in China, and one that, through the power of Christ indwelling His own, has weathered the severest storms.—Ed.

[2] The allusion, of course, is to the difference between first and second generation Christians—between those delivered to Christ from paganism on the first wave of an evangelical missionary movement, and those who so often grow up after them as Christians only in name.—Ed.

CHAPTER ELEVEN

HE THAT OVERCOMETH

JOHN the apostle reaffirms that God's end is certain, and that His ways now are consistent with that end. Just as, in the heavenly City at the last, the principles of the Body find their fullest development and expression, so is the reverse also true. Whenever the life of the eternities has a free course in us to-day, we shall find every feature of the heavenly City, every true character of the Lord Jesus, manifesting itself through His Body here on the earth. And who that has once caught a glimpse of God's heavenly Man can ever be satisfied with any-thing less than this?

But now we must be practical, and take a look at conditions around us. Most of us will agree that outward Christianity to-day is in a sorry state. It manifests all the ailments and weak-nesses of the world. Its work is reduced to a little preaching and a little social service. Its impact on men is negligible. This is a fact; but what should cause us even greater personal dis-tress is the tragedy that, as God's people, our conscience has been so little exercised about this fact. We take things as a matter of course, and many seem indeed to accept them almost as though they ought to be as they are. Christians to-day do not believe that what Paul has set before us is possible. Such unbelief should have the effect of driving us back to the ministry of John, and compelling us to look again at its special character.

What the Lord revealed through Paul concerning the Body of Christ was intended, as we saw earlier, to be realized in local churches each expressing that Body. In different localities there would be a true practical expression, not of a host of different bodies, but of one Body. This was the divine inten-tion, and this was how things began. But we know how sadly they failed, and how the Lord Himself had to speak again from heaven. In doing so He touched a new note concerning the Church and the churches, and this is why the second and third chapters of Revelation are so helpful. In those chapters, the Lord Jesus uses John to bring to light a further divine provision for His Church. I refer to the seven promises at the ends of those seven letters. In them we have John's special message for a time of general departure. It is that, amid conditions of decay and general ruin, God looks for those of His people who will be His overcomers within the churches.

What is the meaning of an 'overcomer'? To avoid misunderstanding, let it first be clear that these people are not Christians who are abnormally good. It is not that they are individually better than others, and that therefore they are destined to receive greater glory. Please remember, overcomers are simply *normal* Christians. All others have become, for the moment, sub-normal.

In past eternity God had a definite plan, a design which He has never abandoned. Overcomers are those who, having seen that design, have set themselves by God's grace to stand by it. They are *not* certain imaginary people who have gone further than Paul, or who take a different line from that revealed through Paul. They are, I repeat, no more than normal in God's eyes; they can claim no special credit.

Overcoming, in John's writings, does not mean simply the question of personal overcoming. It is not a matter of overcoming sin, which is better termed 'deliverance', nor of personal holiness—the so-called 'victorious life'. The overcoming spoken of by John is the kind of overcoming that, in a given situation, lays claim to and holds that situation for God. In an hour when the Pauline message is rejected by so many, the Christian is tempted to say, 'That is how things are. What can we do about it? We must just try to keep ourselves straight on certain lines, but we shall have to let some things pass as hopeless. They are beyond recovery. There is nothing we can do to improve them.' Beset by circumstances, real and hypothetical, which we simply do not know how to contend with, it is easy to resign ourselves to the view that our particular situation is beyond recovery. There are too many things in it to be adjusted, too many painful steps to be taken in the out-working. The thing is impossible.

It is in such an hour that overcomers reassert, by their life and testimony, that God is not a man that He should change. His standards, they affirm, have not altered, and He has still set Himself to have a heavenly City at the end, a heavenly Man to-day. What the whole Church, *as* the Church, ought to be doing but has left undone, they, representatively and *for* the Church, are raised up by God to do. Standing true to the victorious heavenly Man, they hold their ground. That is the 'overcoming' spoken of here in the Word.

John in Revelation shows the sphere of the overcomers. It is within the defeated church to-day. Those of importance to God are those who now, each in his own situation, lay claim to those situations for God. There is a part of God's plan which concerns each of us, just where we are, and for it He needs overcomers. I say again, there is no special goodness about them; their only distinction is that they are not abnorm-ally bad! They abide by God's standard, that is all. But know-ing the Christian life, the heavenly calling of the Body, the warfare of the Church, they are like a lever in God's hands to dislodge Satan from his throne. They prepare themselves on the Church's behalf, and they fight for the Church. They put out all their effort, not for their own sakes but for the sake of the Body; and because they are ready, God sees the Church prepared as a bride. They set the torch as it were to the fire, and what the overcomers inherit the whole Church inherits.

YOU YOUNG MEN

Exodus, Leviticus, Numbers—these three books of the Old Testament offer an interesting parallel to Christian experience. I have likened them to the 'sit', 'walk', 'stand' of Ephesians. (See Eph. 1. 20; 4. 1; 6. 13). Exodus sees Israel delivered from Egypt by a mighty hand, and established as the people of God through an irreversible work. Leviticus lays down the basis of their communion with Him by blood, and their walk of holiness by the Cross. Numbers orders and arrays them for warfare, with a view to the enjoyment of their God-given inheritance. This last is stated clearly at the commencement of the book of Numbers, where, in Chapter 1. 3, Aaron is told to number 'all that are able to go forth to war in Israel.'

Just prior to this statement, in the final chapter of Leviticus, it seems that the Lord sets out to assess which of His children are going to be of the greatest value to Him. I refer to the instructions given there about voluntary vows (Lev. 27. 1–8). We must distinguish carefully between this and the passage in Exodus 30 which speaks of the redemption money for their souls. That was commanded of every Israelite, and in every case it was exactly the same, namely, half a silver shekel. It speaks, I think, of what God is going to be *for us*; but here in Leviticus 27 it is a question of what we may be *for Him*, and so this is expressed not as something commanded, but as a voluntary act. 'When a man shall make a special vow, according to the estimation of persons unto the Lord, then thy estimation shall be . . .' and there follows a scale of values in shekels, according to age and sex, which we may tabulate thus:

Age	For men	For women
Below 5 years	5 shekels	3 shekels
5–20 years	20 ,,	10 ,,
20–60 years	50 ,,	30 ,,
Over 60 years	15 ,,	10 ,,

God does not discount anybody, not even the children and babes, but we may ask ourselves: Why is there this high valuation on the over-twenty age-group? Surely it is because, as we have just seen, the next book, Numbers, opens by defining those able to go forth to war as 'from twenty years old and upward'. This means, surely, that the value of our giving of ourselves, heart, mind, will and life to God is measured by Him in terms of our fitness for war. On our part it is merely a vow—and God forbid that any of us should be vow-less Christians!—but on God's part it has definite values. Yes, it is good to save souls, good to have personal holiness, good to do a hundred-and-one useful things for God, but above all it is supremely precious to Him that we be fit to take part in the age-long battle of the Lord, to dislodge His foes and to bring His people into the enjoyment of their inheritance in Him. Jehovah is a man of war, and energy for war is what He prizes most highly.

The great Old Testament tragedy, of course, was that of the old men, when, in normal circumstances, their physical strength for war began to fail. But this is where we must at once come over in thought to the New Testament, for there, 'though our outward man is decaying, yet our inward man is renewed day by day' (2 Cor. 4. 16). The tree by the waterside does not wither. In a real Christian life there is no afternoon, no falling off of strength. Like that of Caleb, who was the true overcomer in the book of Numbers, our strength for war at eighty years can be as it was at forty, if we will wholly follow the Lord.

This is what I believe John is taking up and developing in his first Epistle, when he says: 'I write unto you young men, because ye have overcome the evil one.' Young men are naturally full of vigour, and this statement suggests once again the divine approval of their spiritual energy and of its fruits. But let us remember, John's classification of his readers into little children, young men, fathers, is not to be identified with that in Leviticus. He is talking to spiritual babes who already have assurance of forgiveness of sins, to spiritual warriors in whom God's Word abides, to spiritual fathers who carry along with them all they have gathered up as babes, children, men of war, into the full-ranged knowledge of Him who is the very Origin of all things. To-day no spiritual age-group is excluded from a part in war. True, there should be no delayed maturity in the Christian life, just as there should be no retiring age in spiritual things. (And the term 'young men' includes the young women, too, in the spiritual scale of military values, though in a sense this was already true in Leviticus.)

Whatever, then, be the length of our spiritual history, the question each of us must ask ourselves is: What will be my up-to-date value in the sanctuary? God has a definite estimate of how each of us counts for Him. He knows us individually, and His sanctuary-value for every one is measured on the scale of spiritual strength. There is no need for any of us, whatever our years, to be written off at fifteen shekels when we can be priced as high as thirty or fifty. Oh to drink to-day, every one of us, of Caleb's militant spirit!

THE ACCUSER OF THE BRETHREN

John wrote to his 'little children' of the assurance of the forgiveness of sins. In one sense we are always, in John's term, little children, for in this life we never advance to a point where we have left behind our need for the precious Blood. It is indeed the very first weapon of the overcomer. Writing in Revelation 12 of the Accuser of the brethren 'which accuseth them before our God day and night', John tells us that 'they overcame him because of the blood of the Lamb, and because of the word of their testimony, and they loved not their life even unto death' (verses 10, 11).

The basis of overcoming in the spiritual warfare is always the precious Blood. No one can ever get to the place where the Blood is not necessary. Satan is a murderer and a deceiver, he entices and he attacks, but to-day he specializes in accusing. In a very real sense he is the Accuser of the brethren, and it is here that our Lord meets him as Priest and Mediator. Heaven recognizes Satan's work and so must every Christian. Night and day he accuses us, and his accusation is directed at our conscience, which is the point where we most feel we lack the strength to fight him. His object is to drive us to think in despair. 'Of what possible use am I to God?' Why are some Christians found from morning to night reproaching themselves and crying, 'I am a hopeless failure. God can do nothing with me!'? It is because they have allowed themselves to accept the charges of the enemy as unanswerable. And if he can get us to this state, he is indeed the victor, for we have given the battle away. If, instead of looking at the glory of God, we only accept his accusations, and stop there, we are certainly left with no power to fight him.

Conscience is a very precious thing, but to repeat endlessly, 'I am no good! I am no good!'—*that* is not Christian humility. It is healthy to confess our sins, but let us never carry confession to the point where, for us, our sinfulness looms larger than the work of Christ. The Devil knows there is no weapon more effective against the Christian than the creation of this illusion. What is the remedy? It is to say to the Lord, 'Lord, I *am* no good!' but then to look away to His precious Blood, and to add: 'But Lord I am abiding in Thee!'

Satan does not accuse without reason. There are, no doubt, plenty of sins to which he can point us; but the Blood of Jesus Christ cleanses us from all sin. Do we believe that? Then it is the answer to his charge. Sin calls for the Blood, but the Bible does not tell us that sin calls for accusation—not, that is to say, if we plead guilty. Of course, if we say we have no sin, John warns us that the door is then wide open to the Accuser. But if, standing in the light of God, we confess to him our guilt, then the Blood is powerful to cleanse, and all Satan's charges are rendered ineffective. Praise God for such an Advocate! Praise Him for such a Priest! Let us never, never answer Satan either by boasting our good conduct or by bemoaning our sins, but always and only by the Blood. It is our wholly sufficient defence.

The precious Blood of Christ is our defence; the word of our testimony is our weapon of attack. By this is meant our testimony to man, but not to man alone. The victory of Christ, the fact that He reigns, that His kingdom is near, that we have been translated from Satan's kingdom into His; all these are facts to be declared, not to men only, but to the powers of darkness. Affirm that God is King, that His Son is Victor, that Satan is defeated, that the kingdoms of this world are shortly to become the Kingdom of our God and of His Christ. These are positive divine facts, and they are our shafts of offence. Satan fears such declarations of spiritual fact. For the word of our testimony can move back the gates of hell. Declare that Jesus is Lord; that His Name is above every name. Declare it! *Say* it to the enemy. Many a time such testimony brings more results than does prayer.

Prayer has two sides: to God, and to the mountain. 'Thou shalt say unto this mountain, be thou removed.' We can say to Satan, 'Leave this place!' Peter and John said to the paralytic man, 'In the name of Jesus Christ of Nazareth, walk.' They dealt directly with the case, where to-day we would probably have called a prayer-meeting. Don't neglect prayer, but counting upon the efficacy of the precious Blood, speak also a word of testimony. Often times when we come to God, the atmosphere is oppressive and we cannot pray. What should we do? Don't give in, but taking God's Word, turn and speak to Satan. Declare the victory of the Lord. Declare that He has given us authority to tread on serpents and scorpions and over all the power of the enemy. And *then* pray!

Alas, we pay far too much attention to-day to the doctrine of the Gospel, and far too little to the fact. And without the fact, we have no testimony. But Calvary is history. The Gospel—the good news of this fact—is with us. For nearly two thousand years the fact of the Gospel has been in the earth. The Lord has given us the precious Blood, and a sure word of testimony. Let us face the enemy with these.

And finally these overcomers are men and women who know what it means to be nailed to the Cross—that is to say, to be 'ruled out' altogether as men, so that whatever they accomplish, the glory is only His. We need not enlarge on this again here; but remember, it was Satan who challenged God concerning Job: 'Skin for skin, yea, all that a man hath will he give for his life' (Job. 2. 4). But now, as if in answer to this, a great voice in heaven affirms concerning these who overcame: 'They loved not their life even unto the death' (Rev. 12. 11). Well could that same voice proclaim: 'Now is come the salvation, and the power, and the kingdom of our God, and the authority of his Christ'!

'AND WHAT SHALL THIS MAN DO?'

We have spoken of some high matters, and lest we overreach ourselves I think it wise now to come briefly to something very practical, and to talk quite simply to my young brothers who desire to serve the Lord. In the last chapter of John's Gospel our Lord made a series of very personal challenges to his disciple Peter. Peter responded with some hesitation, and then we are told that at a point, as if to divert attention away from himself, he began to show a sudden interest in his fellow-fisherman, John. Looking round and seeing this 'disciple whom Jesus loved' following, he said to Jesus: 'Lord, and what shall this man do?'[1] But Jesus would not allow this switch of attention to someone else, and returned once more to the personal challenge to Peter himself: 'What is that to thee? Follow thou me.' What this incident says, it seems to me, is that no single one of us may evade the obligation to ask the same personal question of himself: 'Lord, and what shall *this* man do?'—or in Paul's words: '*What shall I do, Lord?*' (Acts 22. 10).

Some time ago, in England,[2] I was invited to meet a group of young men and women, most of whom were at that time preparing themselves to serve the Lord as missionaries in the East. They asked me if I would tell them what I regarded as the essential qualifications of a missionary. I replied that I indeed felt the days of missionaries are not over, and that God has called his servants of all nations to work alongside, one another in the field. The notes that follow contain the essence of what I said to them then. They will be found to echo several of the matters we have treated at greater length already in these studies.

The Assurance of Salvation. This is the starting-point, and experience warns us that it is never safe to take it for granted in making such a list of qualifications as this, or when addressing any group of men or women. The foundation of all service for the Lord is that we should have met Him and come to know Him for ourselves, and have received the absolute assurance that, in Him, we are eternally saved.

Christ our Life. We have to remind Christians to-day that many ancient religions of the East have a high ethical and moral code. In Chinese society, as in some others, while there may be less exacting standards on some matters, such things as

---

[1] Literally, 'Lord, and what of this man?'
[2] The time was 1938.

anger and impatience in a man or woman are regarded as serious signs of lack of self-control. Yet missionaries who do not themselves know the victorious life of a Christian often display these things, and do not realize how much their testimony suffers as a consequence. Those to whom they are seeking to witness are, by this fact, given ground to regard themselves as religiously and morally superior. If we are to witness to Christ effectively among a people who already worship 'self-mastery', and who even despise those who need recreation and comfort, it is necessary that in a real and convincing way we give proof by our lives of the true answer to 'self'. We must know the Cross as our deliverance from sin and the flesh, and find in Christ risen the sufficient power to walk in newness of life.

Entire Dependence on the Lord. It is easy to exercise a 'group faith'; it is much harder to trust God alone, and to do so without letting our eyes wander from Him to the channel of supply. Westerners talk of 'rice-Christians', but can we not recognize in all of us a sneaking tendency towards what, in more modern terms, we may call the 'life of faith and hints', or as someone has shrewdly put it, 'faith and postage-stamps'? It is quite wrong for God's servants to speak or write 'on behalf of the work', and they must be very true with Him about this. The less our hands touch the miracles of God in this way, the better. We should not be afraid to make things hard for God —so hard in fact that no one dare 'join' unless he is called. Perhaps our surest safeguard is to concern ourselves with the needs of others. Care for them, and God will care for us.

A Specific Ministry. As His children, we all of us have the general obligation of witnessing for the Lord, but the servant of God should go further than that. He should be marked by some special Spirit-wrought knowledge of God that is distinctively his own. Out of this should his ministry spring. We shall be of little use to the Church in China, or anywhere else for that matter, if all we can do is preach the Gospel and edify in a general way. This is expected of every Christian, but Chinese believers will look in us for something more, something specific. Nor shall we satisfy their need with a special teaching or doctrine, however excellent, but only, I repeat, with a knowledge of the Lord that characterizes us because it is peculiarly our own. We complain sometimes that people are not hungry for the Word, but believe me, if we had something distinctive to give them, they would be. Are we, by our presence, creating in people a hunger for God? Food itself can create hunger if it is sufficiently appetizing, and people become hungry when they see men and women filled with the Spirit, full of love, not just preaching, or dispensing a general knowledge, but ministering spiritual riches that bear the marks of personal dealings with Him. Yes, there is something wrong with us if we are not hunger-creators.

The Attitude of a Learner. Always travel with a large 'L' on your back![3] Those who set out to be 'teachers' of others put themselves in a dangerous position. Many over-stretch themselves, and by talking about things they have not put to the test of experience, create problems in the minds of simple saints. If we are over-sure, and ready enough to say something hastily, we put ourselves under the necessity of remembering next time what answer we gave, or we may discover we have now given a different one! The more we profess to know, the more room there will be for our hearers to criticize, because they will be led to expect more of us. It is such superiority, born of the over-confidence that we *know*, that imperceptibly but surely closes the door to what we may indeed have been given to share with others. Rather do we need grace to admit our ignorance, and to ask the Lord about it. We must be willing to say, 'I do not know'. People will not be hard on the worker who adopts the attitude: 'If you have something to say, I am willing to listen, because I too am a disciple of the Lord'. My counsel to you therefore is to remain for very long a learner. Keep that 'L' on your back for at least ten years!

A History of the Acts of God. I believe, further, that every servant of God should have some things in his history which are

---

[3] At the time when this talk was given, the 'L' plate on the cars of those driving with a Learner's Licence had not long been introduced in Britain, and the idea of thus publicly proclaiming oneself to be a 'learner' appealed strongly to the author.—Ed.

an abiding proof of the presence and power of God with him. I have given an account elsewhere of an incident where God answered the prayer of faith for rain in a quite miraculous way that none of us who were present ever forgot.[4] But Western missionaries have a background. There are certain things for which they have worked out an explanation, and Christian teachers are ready enough to-day to excuse doctrinally the comparative infrequency of miracles in our time. Such excuses will never be accepted by simple believers, for often enough they have seen the hand of God at work themselves.

I remember one such, Chen the tailor. He was indeed very simple. Moreover he had never met another Christian. All he had was a copy of Mark's Gospel, but through reading it he had met the Saviour, and he had believed. Then he came to Chapter 16—the so-called 'doubtful passage'!—and after reading it carefully he said to the Lord, 'Lord, I am so small that one small gift will suffice me. Give me the gift of healing!' At once he went out, and going from house to house, prayed for the sick in his village. When later we met him and questioned him closely, it became quite evident that his humility, together with his absolute trust in God quite regardless of the gravity of the diseases he tackled or of any immediate evidence of an answer, had in fact led to some wonderful happenings in that village. Idolators had been convinced of the Lord's superiority to heathen gods, and some had believed. Yet we found him still just a humble brother, making no extravagant claims, and quietly continuing to witness to the Lord Jesus as he pursued his employment as a simple village tailor.

I confess that, on one occasion in the West, when I was attending a conference of very sincere brethren and heard them become more and more deeply involved in discussion of some difficult doctrinal question, I was at length impelled to break in. 'My dear brothers!' I exclaimed, 'In my country, all your knowledge of these nice Scriptural details would avail you nothing if, when the need arose, you did not know how to cast out demons!' To-day we have become civilized, and as a result, we often close the door to God. It sometimes seems to

[4] *Sit, Walk, Stand*, Chapter 3.

me that God brings us up to a certain point of opportunity, and then, because our natural caution forbids us to step out in faith on Him, instead of a miracle of life, all we get is a new teaching. But surely, we must *expect* God to seal His Word with signs and wonders, If we truly know God, His wondrous acts cannot be far away. And to-day Satan's seat is to be challenged by our faith in a living God.

THE CALLING OF GOD

No master has so many servants as our Master; and for each He has a suitable employment. For Joseph He had a particular task, to save Israel from famine. Samuel came at the hour chosen, for the very special work of setting aside the priest in favour of the king, even as later Elijah came to set aside the king for the prophet. The little maid was at hand to testify to Naaman in his need. Even an ass was ready for Jesus to ride into Jerusalem.

Many murmur against the position God has given them, or against the task He has entrusted to them in the Body. They want to do this, but God puts them into that. They have an ambition to serve Him here, but His plan for them lies somewhere else. When faced by such apparent reverses, it is well to remember that the purpose of God for us in His Church goes back before our conversion, for His foreknowledge has prepared our circumstances and determined our way even before we were born. Isaiah was chosen from birth, Saul of Tarsus 'from the womb', Jeremiah still earlier, before he was formed in the womb. True the case of Saul puzzled Ananias, in view of what he had heard from others of this 'chosen vessel'! But the whole road is wonderfully prepared for His servants by God. He determines whose child we shall be, though sometimes we may think we have been born into the wrong family! Some of us approve of our parents, but would like perhaps to change our brothers and sisters, or our other relatives! But Joseph said: 'God sent me before you to preserve life'. If we have not seen God's hand in His choices, we have lost a great opportunity to bring Him praise.

David's work began with Goliath, but already he had learned the lesson in his shepherd days. 'Jehovah delivered me out of the paw of the lion,' he could say. Peter was a fisherman, familiar with the drag-net. Perhaps for this reason he could better understand the 'great sheet' at Joppa. Paul found Aquila and Priscilla through his ability to make tents. There was no need for someone without that trade to acquire it in order to help these two to become, as they did, careful exponents of the way of God. And in a time of declension in Ephesus, a Timothy was at hand who from a babe had known the sacred writings.

God never does a thing suddenly; he has always prepared long, long before. So there is nothing to murmur about, nothing to be proud of, in the calling of God. There is also no one of whom to be jealous, for other people's advantages have nothing to do with us. 'It is not of him that willeth, nor of him that runneth, but of God that hath mercy' (Rom. 9. 16). Our heritage, our birth, our natural equipment: these are things already determined by God. We may pick up other things on the way, for we are always learning; but the way is His way. When we look back over our life, we bow and acknowledge that all was prepared by God. There is no need to fear we have missed something. To have such an attitude of heart, *that* is true rest.

God is a God who works, and He started many years ago. When He wants a special kind of servant, or when the Church needs a special kind of help, God is not unprepared. He never encounters an emergency. In the history of His children, His hand is everywhere. Each of us would say, if we pondered a minute, 'All my life His grace has followed me'. The words of Paul, though used, it is true, in another connection, effectively summarize such an attitude to the providence of God: 'Let each man abide in that calling wherein he was called' (1 Cor. 7. 20). When we see the purpose of God, such words as these can take on a large meaning. God has called each of us, and is preparing us, for tasks foreknown to Him. 'I press on', Paul says elsewhere, 'if so be that I may apprehend *that for which also I was apprehended* by Christ Jesus'.

THE SPIRIT OF TRUTH

Finally, I would say a little more about the work of the Holy Spirit. In earlier chapters, especially when discussing the ministry of Paul, we have spoken frequently of the need for a revelation of divine things. More than once have we said that it is essential to *see* the purpose of God, to *see* the Person and work of Christ, to *see* the Church, the Body of Christ. To this some reader may be goaded to reply, concerning one or other of these things: 'I *don't* see that. What do you suggest that I do?'

For answer I could point once more to the Spirit of truth, recalling again that He is a Person, close at hand—nay, dwelling now within our hearts—ready to help each one of us in our need. It is the apostle John who tells us how, at a time of great mystification for the disciples, Jesus assured them of the Holy Spirit's coming, to bear witness of Himself, and to guide them into all the truth.

Whether it be for the initial revelation to our hearts of divine things, or amid the discipline that must follow ere those divine things become truly a part of us, we shall find it necessary to turn again and again to this gracious Helper of our infirmities. It is by His revelation alone that we behold spiritual realities; it is by His loving discipline that we enter into those realities. By the former, He opens the gateway to progress; by the latter, He leads us on in the pathway of progress. The former is the foundation, the latter the superstructure. Without revelation by the Spirit we cannot commence the course, but without the discipline of the Spirit we cannot complete it. Both these aspects of the Spirit's work are equally essential, but for both we can assuredly count upon Him.

The Father has conceived a plan; the Son has carried it out; now it is the Spirit who communicates to us what the Son has accomplished for us. We readily acknowledge the completeness of the work of the Son, when he said 'It is finished', and sat down at the right hand of the Majesty on high. But if we do not doubt that the Son has perfected the work committed to Him by the Father, why then do we doubt that the Spirit will perfect the work committed to Him by the Son?

The work of the Son is as comprehensive as the work of the Father. It does not go one whit beyond it, but nor does it fall one whit short of it. As great as is the work of the Father, so great is the work of the Son; and as great as is the work of the Son, so great is the work of the Spirit. There is not one particle of the work completed by the Son for us that will not be completed by the Spirit in us. All the fulness of spiritual reality that is in Christ will be imparted to us by the Spirit of Christ. Of Himself, Jesus said 'I am the Reality', and of the Spirit, 'He shall guide you into all Reality.' The question of coming into all the fulness of spiritual reality rests, therefore, not with us but with the Spirit. It is not a question of our capacity, or of our ability, but of the absolute faithfulness of the Holy Spirit of God. Can He be depended on to do all the work committed to Him by the Son? We must learn to trust him. We must learn to count upon His twofold work, first of revealing to us the nature and the dimensions of divine reality, and secondly of bringing us into every whit of the reality He has revealed.

As we look around us, we cannot fail to observe a tragic lack in the experience of so many Christians. There is nothing about their lives to indicate fulness. They have not sufficient for their own needs, much less have they anything to spare for others. Why are they so poor? Is it not because they do not know the discipline of the Spirit? The Psalmist says, 'In pressure thou hast enlarged me' (Psalm 4. 1[5]). The object of all pressure is enlargement. James says something similar in his Epistle: 'Did not God choose them that are poor as to the world to be rich in faith?' (James 2. 5). The object of temporal poverty is eternal enrichment. God never intended that pressure and poverty should issue in nothing. His purpose is that all pressure should lead to enlargement, all poverty to enrichment. God's goal for His people is neither continuous straitness nor continuous poverty. For straitness and poverty are never the end; they are only the means to God's end. Straitness is the pathway to expansion, poverty the pathway to wealth.

[5] J. N. Darby, *New Translation*.

Read again Revelation chapter 21. What a picture you get there of fulness! You may spend much time on the book of Revelation and still understand little of its meaning, but you surely cannot fail to understand this, that Chapter 21 speaks of a wealth, an abundance, a glory, that this earth has never yet known, no, not even in the fabulous days of Solomon. When were the streets of earth ever paved with gold? When had this world no need of the sun to light it? What riches! What splendour! Never was earthly empire so wealthy or so radiant as New Jerusalem. And what breadth! Never was city seen on earth one hundredth part of the scale of this. And he that overcometh, we are told, shall inherit these things!

Some have asked why, in the new heavens and the new earth, we read of God and of the Lamb, but find there no mention of the Holy Spirit. Surely the answer is that just as, to-day, Christ has finished His work, and the outcome of that work of Christ is seen in the Church, so, in that day, the Holy Spirit will have finished *His* work, and the outcome of that work of the Spirit will be seen in the New Jerusalem. For all that is there is real—the full realization by the Spirit of what He came to do. When you touch the Church to-day, you touch Christ; but it will be no less true that, when you touch the City then, you touch the Spirit of Christ. There the Church will be filled with the Spirit of God in His sevenfold fulness; there, as the City, she will manifest in herself the Spirit's work in completeness, for she will be holy, as her Lord.

But how does the Church reach that goal? Only by travelling the pathway from pressure to enlargement, from poverty to enrichment. You ask: What do we mean by enlargement through pressure? When three are shut into a furnace and the three become four, that is enlargement through pressure. Some find a furnace rather close quarters for three, so they seek a way of escape; others accept the limitation, and in accepting it, make room for a Fourth. Not to let difficulties shut us out from God, but to let them shut us in to Him, that is enlargement through pressure. For Paul and Silas, the prison gates could only shut the world out and shut God in; so their prison, instead of cramping them, released them into greater fulness. God let trial upon trial press upon Job, but his trials only pressed him to God's goal. To John, in the island for the testimony, the risen Lord Himself opened the door and showed him the glorious consummation of all things. Some, through pressure, reach God's end; others come to an end in the pressure. Some die in straitness; others, through straitness, find fulness of life. Some murmur when trials befall them, and find in them only limitation, restriction and death; others praise God in the trials, and find in them the pathway to enlargement, liberation and abundance of life.

Many Christians are so poor that they have not even sufficient to meet their own needs. Alas for any who go to them for help! Other Christians are so rich you can never assess their wealth. You can never meet a difficulty they have not met; you can never find yourself in a situation where they are unable to help. They have abundant resources to meet the demands of all who go to them in need. Many Christians do not go utterly bankrupt simply because they are being ministered to by others, who continually pour their wealth into the Body. Such Christians little know how much they owe to other believers, some of whom they might even be tempted to despise. It may be that, when a friend comes from a journey and expects bread from us, the Lord will permit us to turn to a neighbour for something to give him; but it may be that He will say to us, 'Give ye them to eat.'

Spiritual poverty and spiritual straitness are two of the greatest problems in the Church, but poverty is effect, not cause, and straitness is effect, not cause. The cause of poverty and the cause of straitness is lack of the Spirit's discipline. Those who are wealthy and those who are enlarged are they, and they only, who have experienced such discipline. They have been through deep waters, and have a spiritual history with God, because they have suffered for the Body's sake. Their sicknesses, their domestic problems, their adversities— all were for the increase of Christ in His people. Those, on the other hand, who by-pass such disciplines, choosing instead a life of ease and comfort in a pathway of prosperity—they are the straitened and the poverty-stricken. The poor and needy come to them in vain for help. They have no overflow.

Do you think preaching is just preaching? Do you think ministry is just ministry? Believe me, they are not. Serving God is not just a matter of words or works, but of how much you have been through. If the Spirit is never allowed to trouble you, you will be condemned to poverty all your life. You will never learn how blessed it is to draw fulness from the Lord, not for yourself, but for others. And *that* is ministry.

Revelation waits upon discipline. It is our acceptance of the discipline of the Spirit that opens the way for Him to reveal to us the realities that are in Christ, and to bring us into these. Avoidance of that discipline denies Him the opportunity of doing so. Every day God is looking for opportunities to enlarge us, but when difficulties arise we avoid them, when trials come we circumvent them. Oh, but at what loss to ourselves! And at what loss to God's people! Of course there is no way of dodging divine chastening that comes to us when we have deliberately moved out of the will of the Lord; that is something different, designed for our correction and cure. We cannot escape that; but we can, if we will, dodge the creative disciplines of the Spirit. If however we are willing to commit ourselves to His dealings, He will take us in hand and bring us to God's goal. Are we willing to say, 'Lord, I will drink the cup Thou givest to its last dregs; I will bear the cross, and seek no relief in gall or vinegar.'? Oh for an utter consecration in His people, that will enable God to do all that in His heart He has planned for them! That will lead to fulness, the fulness of the New Jerusalem. There is not one nugget of gold in that City but has been tried in the furnace; not a precious stone but has been passed through the fires; not a pearl but has been produced through suffering.

When Peter put to Jesus his question about John, what was our Lord's reply? 'If I will that he tarry till I come, what is that to thee?' *Till I come!* The ministry of the Spirit of truth set forth by John will go on until the story is completed; nothing can stop it. The purpose of God in His Church is going to be accomplished; it can never be thwarted. The vision of the

Holy City, made ready as a bride adorned for her husband, will unfailingly come to pass, and we shall see it. No one can touch that 'till I come'; it is settled in heaven.

Shall we not, therefore, put ourselves into our Father's safe hands, that He may order our lives as He wills? It will be His care to see that the transforming work of the Holy Spirit within us is no less perfect, no less sure, than was the redemption first accomplished on our behalf by His beloved Son.

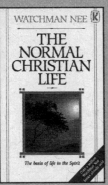

WATCHMAN NEE **K**

THE NORMAL CHRISTIAN LIFE

The basis of life in the Spirit

WATCHMAN NEE **K**

SIT, WALK, STAND

Our relationship to God, the world, and the devil

WATCHMAN NEE **K**

CHANGED INTO HIS LIKENESS

The work of God in the life of the believer

3 Books in One

Classics from

WATCHMAN NEE

Other titles in the Kingsway Classics Series

3

Books
in One

Classics
_on_

PRAYER

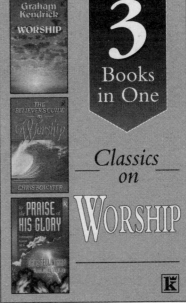

3

Books
in One

Classics
_on_

WORSHIP